MICHAEL MAKOVSKY

Churchill's Promised Land

ZIONISM AND STATECRAFT

A NEW REPUBLIC BOOK

YALE UNIVERSITY PRESS   NEW HAVEN & LONDON

Copyright © 2007 by Yale University.
All rights reserved.
This book may not be reproduced, in whole or in part, including illustrations, in any form (beyond that copying permitted by Sections 107 and 108 of the U.S. Copyright Law and except by reviewers for the public press), without written permission from the publishers.

Set in E & F Scala by Binghamton Valley Composition.
Printed in the United States of America.

Library of Congress Cataloging-in-Publication Data

Makovsky, Michael, 1963–
Churchill's promised land : Zionism and statecraft / Michael Makovsky.
p. cm. — (A New Republic book)
Includes bibliographical references and index.
ISBN 978-0-300-11609-0 (cloth : alk. paper)

1. Churchill, Winston, Sir, 1874–1965. 2. Churchill, Winston, Sir, 1874–1965—Views on Zionism. 3. Zionism—Great Britain—History—20th century. 4. Great Britain—Foreign relations—Middle East. 5. Middle East—Foreign relations—Great Britain. I. Title.
DA566.9.C5M24 2007
320.54095694—dc22
                                                2007001336

A catalogue record for this book is available from the British Library.

The paper in this book meets the guidelines for permanence and durability of the Committee on Production Guidelines for Book Longevity of the Council on Library Resources.

10 9 8 7 6 5 4 3 2 1

In loving memory of my mother, Nancy Elbaum Makovsky, *who instilled in me a love of life, and in loving admiration of my father,* Donald Makovsky, *who inspired my passion for history and world affairs*

CONTENTS

Preface   ix

Acknowledgments   xiii

Introduction   1

1. Churchill's Worlds   9

2. "The Lord Deals with the Nations as the Nations Dealt with the Jews," 1874–1914   38

3. "Zionism versus Bolshevism," 1914–1921   69

4. "Smiling Orchards," 1921–1929   98

5. Together in the Wilderness, 1929–1939   140

6. Champion in War, 1939–1945   171

7. Zionist at the End, 1945–1955   227

Conclusion   259

Notes   267

Bibliography   299

Index   323

Illustrations follow page 110

PREFACE

WHEN VIRGINIA COWLES told Winston Churchill in 1950 of her plans to write a biography of him, he growled good-naturedly, "There's nothing much in *that* field left unploughed" (quoted in Cowles, *Winston Churchill*, vii). This is not another biography of Churchill or even a study of his diplomatic decision-making. Instead, it is an examination of how he thought, viewed, and approached a diplomatic subject that engaged him for much of his career, and what that signified about his worldview. The subject in question was not just any normal world issue but Zionism, a movement that emerged as a political cause in the late 1890s, just as Churchill began his political career.

Churchill is perhaps most famous nowadays, at least in the United States, for warning against the rise of Nazi Germany in the 1930s and the Soviet Union in the 1940s, and for leading Britain to victory in the Second World War. He is well known as a practitioner of realpolitik, and many leading theorists and practitioners of the realist foreign policy school, such as Hans Morgenthau and Henry Kissinger, have looked to Churchill as a model. Indeed, Churchill was fundamentally concerned with British power and security, and he advocated and pursued policies that enhanced them, based on his own historical study of earlier British and European statesmen. But he was a very complex person with varied interests, who also had a romantic approach to foreign affairs. His view of the British Empire, and of Britain's role in the world, was rather sentimental. Sentiment also played a part—positively and negatively—in his opinion of other Great Powers, such as Russia, Germany, France, and especially the United States, where his mother was born and grew up, although his attitude toward these nations was ultimately shaped by British power and strategic interests. But sentiment was the *predominant* factor in his long-standing interest in Zionism, with considerations of power at times important but generally secondary. Thus, in studying Churchill's view of Zionism, we get a different angle on, and a fuller, more nuanced, multidimensional grasp of, his worldview than if we just analyzed his approach toward a Great Power such as Germany, as so many have done before from varying perspectives.

Fundamental to Churchill's worldview was the belief that priorities had to be rigidly ranked. He inflexibly maintained perspective and prioritized his goals, especially when he was in government and was forced to make decisions. He fixated on his supreme interests and pursued them vigorously and single-mindedly, though he was flexible in the tactics used to achieve them. This is how he engaged British strategic and imperial matters and at times even his own political needs, which were among his chief concerns. For instance, he normally studied strategic issues very carefully, poring over intelligence reports, speaking with well-placed sources, reading obscure books and speeches, and assessing threats and possible allies, then produced prescient, analytical, lucid, often brilliant memos and speeches on these issues and, when in government, actively pursued appropriate policies. The objective was self-evident as was the need to subordinate other demands to it.

Churchill approached Zionism, and other lesser but still significant issues, differently. His mood and actions toward Zionism were usually shaped by his primary concerns, and he engaged it with less diligence, consistency, rigorous thought and analysis, and creativity. The objective here was not always apparent to all, and a myriad of complex considerations—racial, ideological, civilizational, humanitarian, paternal, personal, historical, romantic, mystical, and religious—went into his view of Zionism over time. Churchill liked to judge which events were historically significant and which were not, and both early in his career and near the end of it he declared the restoration of a Jewish state in the Promised Land to be of exceptional historical significance. Eventually,

Zionism became very dear to him and integral to his worldview, and he supported it at great political cost, contributing to his unpopularity among his colleagues and other members of the political and government establishment.

I approach this subject not as a scholar of Zionist or Jewish history, or even of Britain or the Middle East, but as a diplomatic historian focused on Churchill. With some exceptions, I have generally tried to focus on Churchill's mind and not on his policy-making. I am interested in policies only to the extent that they illuminate his thinking about Zionism. I am more interested in how his mind characterized Zionism and why, what the context of his thinking was, who or what influenced him, and how much effort and attention he devoted to the issue, and am less interested in the details of a particular policy or event that have been discussed ably in other works. Indeed, I am strictly interested in how he thought about Zionism, whether in policy form or not, whether in government or out. For that reason, I have tried to be as thematic as possible within a given narrative, providing just sufficient background, as opposed to following a strict chronology that can be gleaned elsewhere.

ACKNOWLEDGMENTS

THIS BOOK IS BASED ON SEVERAL CHAPTERS of my doctoral dissertation, *Power and Civilization: Winston Churchill's Worldview,* and I extend my deep appreciation to Professors Bernard Bailyn, Akira Iriye, and Ernest May, who composed my dissertation committee in the Department of History at Harvard University. I am most grateful for their insightful instruction, singular dedication, and encouragement, and I am extremely fortunate and honored to be their student. Each of my professors made a unique contribution to me and my work. Akira Iriye, a prominent diplomatic historian, guided me throughout my academic studies; he was my advisor in college at the University of Chicago, chaired my dissertation committee at Harvard, helped shape my dissertation, and reviewed a late draft of this book. Throughout all of these roles, he showed unusual dedication and offered penetrating insight. Ernest May, the leading U.S. diplomatic historian, always offered incisive and uncommon guidance, including the suggestion to expand the Zionist portions of my dissertation into a book. One of the highlights of my education was the yearlong private course on Colonial American history that Bernard Bailyn kindly agreed to teach me for no academic credit. Bailyn was also very engaging, encouraging, patient, and generous with his thoughts and advice during my doctoral studies and while I wrote this book. Bailyn's books and articles have served as model for me, as they have for several generations of historians.

I am indebted to Chili Lati, my lovely, curious, and ever-patient wife, whom I met and married early in the book-writing process and who put up with its constant and at times seemingly unending demands. She also reviewed several chapters and made many insightful comments. I am very thankful to Aaron Lobel for his comprehensive, thoughtful, and incisive critique of the manuscript, and to Michael Hurwitz for his deliberate and insightful review of the chapters, and steadfast and wise counsel on various aspects of the book's publication. David Bergman offered many penetrating and subtle comments about the content, and was a helpful sounding board. I am also grateful to David Makovsky for his beneficial comments on some of the chapters, and to Rochy Novoseller Duker for faithfully managing the maze of the Central Zionist Archives in Jerusalem to secure many documents on my behalf. I further benefited from Liz Evans's conscientious research in the National Archives in Kew, England, during the latter stages of this book. I am grateful to my fellow Lincoln Fellows at Claremont Institute, who contributed to the formulation of the book's title. I am obliged to Douglas Feith for his meticulous review of several relevant chapters of my dissertation and for the thought-provoking dialogue. Anyone who studies Churchill is heavily indebted to the monumental effort made by Martin Gilbert in making this very large subject more accessible through many books that he wrote and edited. Gilbert also offered helpful advice early in my doctoral studies.

I am very appreciative of Keith Condon, my editor at Yale University Press, who wisely and patiently guided the book and me through the whole publication process. Jessie Hunnicutt, my production editor, had a keen and meticulous eye. I am also obliged to Larisa Heimert, the editor who initiated consideration of my manuscript at Yale University Press before departing for another press.

I am indebted to Marty Peretz, editor-in-chief of the *New Republic*, for his confidence, encouragement, and deep interest in my book, and for the interest he has taken in me over the years. I am also thankful to Roger Hertog, chairman of the *New Republic*, for the interest that he took in me and the book.

I am grateful for the constant encouragement and astute advice of

Daniel Yergin and his wife, Angela Stent. I will always be indebted to Alan Makovsky for his wise and conscientious guidance and encouragement, and I am appreciative of Jay Freedman for being liberal with his sage counsel.

I am very grateful to Irwin Stelzer and his wife, Cita, for their very warm and generous guidance, assistance, and encouragement. For their moral support, I wish to thank Jeff Kahana, Lyn Lustig, Winthrop Burr, Larry Hartstein, Morris Hartstein, and Merrill Cohen. I will be forever thankful to Judy Katz, who encouraged and helped me in my early academic career. I am obliged to Paul Jacob, the CEO of an energy-trading company in Boston where I worked almost full-time while researching and writing my doctoral dissertation and some of this book; he offered uncommon understanding and support. I am very grateful to Jason Grumet, executive director of the Bipartisan Policy Center, where I began to work at the latter stage of the drafting process; he was very encouraging and supportive.

Many dedicated librarians and archivists were especially helpful. They include Walter Ross-O'Connor, Thomas Bahr, Paul Vermouth, and the late Dave Paul at Harvard University, where the libraries and librarians generally are in a class unto themselves; Margaret W. Ellingson at Emory University; Julie Ash of the National Archives in Kew, England; and Caroline Herbert of the Churchill Archives in Cambridge, England, who reliably and cheerfully answered my numerous inquiries.

I will always remain heavily indebted to the late Karl Weintraub, the inspirational and legendary intellectual historian at the University of Chicago, who spent many hours giving me extra private instruction in college and who ever since has served as a model intellectual, historian, and teacher. I am also grateful for the confidence and moral support of my late great-uncle, Walter Freedman, a standard-bearer of excellence in every way, who at the age of eighty-six offered many useful comments on my doctoral dissertation.

Introduction

WINSTON CHURCHILL CAME TO CONSIDER himself a Zionist, though he had trouble pinpointing the source of this development. In 1921, he traced it to contact with North-West Manchester Jews a dozen years earlier, while in the 1950s he connected it with the Balfour Declaration of 1917, which committed Britain to a Jewish homeland in Palestine. At other times in the 1950s, he claimed to have been a Zionist his entire life.[1] It was only natural for Churchill to be puzzled, because he frequently conveyed conflicting and confusing messages about Zionism. He advocated a Jewish homeland in 1906; extolled the virtues of a Jewish political entity or state based in Jerusalem in 1908; implemented the Balfour Declaration as colonial secretary in the early 1920s, which ensured continued Jewish immigration and Zionist development in Palestine; and publicly championed Zionism in the 1930s, earning a reputation as one of the leading Gentile Zionists in England. As prime minister during the Second World War, Churchill eagerly and confidently battled the overwhelming majority of officials in his Conservative Party and government bureaucracy who were unsympathetic to Jews and Zionism, and he worked diligently but ultimately unsuccessfully to fashion a postwar Middle Eastern settlement that included a Jewish state. He also pushed for closer relations with the State of Israel from shortly after its founding in 1948 through his second premiership in the 1950s. Yet, he avoided contemplating or raising Jewish claims to Palestine when the government—in which he held the senior post of first lord of the Admiralty—deliberated a postwar Middle East in 1915, neither said nor wrote anything about the Balfour Declaration when it was issued in 1917 by a government in which he was a mid-level minister of munitions, disparaged the Zionist movement in the late 1910s and early 1920s, committed 75 percent of Palestine to an Arabian prince in 1921 as colonial secretary without even consulting the Zionists, did little to help Jewish settlement in Palestine in the economically depressed late 1920s when he was chancellor of the exchequer, and virtually abandoned the Zionists following the Second World War as head of the political Opposition when they battled British troops and invading Arab armies in their arduous quest for an independent state.

Churchill's opinion of Zionism evolved, albeit in a nonlinear fashion. He was predisposed to support Zionism when he first confronted it while campaigning for office in 1905 in North-West Manchester, a commercial city with a sizable Jewish population. He was naturally philo-Semitic, personally comfortable with Jews, and sympathetic to their causes, following the instincts and practices of his father, Randolph. He respected the Jewish race, religion, role in history, fortitude, and alleged political power in Britain and the United States. He thought it important to be good to the Jews and took to heart an adage he periodically quoted and attributed to Benjamin Disraeli, the Jewish-born nineteenth-century British prime minister who influenced Randolph: "The Lord deals with the nations as the nations dealt with the Jews." Still, Churchill sometimes patronized Jews and, like his father, manipulated their causes on behalf of more important personal and strategic considerations and objectives.

Churchill did not share the common European view in the nineteenth and early twentieth century of a "Jewish problem," which held that the Jews, a rootless quasi-nation spread across the globe, were racially inferior, devoted to a noxious religion, socially estranged and a source of social and political turmoil. Even many Jews shared this view, or at least parts of it, while many other Jews adamantly rejected it. Zionists renounced Diaspora Jewry and believed that by establishing their own state in Palestine and joining the ranks of the other nations of the world, the Jews would "normalize" and thereby help stabilize European nations. Theodor Herzl, one of the early founders of political Zionism in the late nineteenth century and the person who put the issue on the international diplomatic map, was among those who employed this argument to enlist Gentile support for the Zionist dream. The closest Churchill came to perceiving a "Jewish problem" was in the highly charged anti-Semitic environment of the late 1910s and early 1920s, when he was vexed over the disproportionate number of Jews in Communist movements. He certainly was not concerned about Jews in England; he never saw them as troublemakers, competitors for jobs, or difficult to integrate into society, as even some other Gentile Zionists did. But neither did he regard Zionism, as Herzl did, as an existential necessity for the Jewish people; he had far too much faith in European civilization and mysterious Jewish fortitude. He also never saw Zionism as a normal nationalist movement, as Herzl somewhat did, but one that stood for particularly lofty ideals—a view shared by socialist, cultural, and religious Zionists.

Churchill considered Zionism to be not a corrective for current societal ills or an existential necessity for Jews but a rectification of a historical injury and a positive force for the present and future. He felt this way upon first engaging the issue in 1906–1908, when he also ascribed some possible British imperial value to it. But it remained a somewhat vague concept for him, as the new movement was even for many Jews. While serving as colonial secretary in 1921–1922, Churchill immersed himself in many of the relevant issues, visited Palestine, and met Palestinian Arabs and Jews, which led to a fuller and deeper understanding of the issue. He came to see Zionism as a cause that restored dispersed, persecuted Jews, a great ancient race whose heritage was integral to the foundation of Western civilization, to their historic homeland, where they could observe their traditions and civilize an area left barren by primitive, anti-British Arabs. He did not immediately come to this formulation, which largely matched the Zionist movement's, nor did he ever articulate it so cogently. During the 1930s and 1940s, with the rise of Nazism, the Second World War, the Holocaust, and his own political "wilderness years" and then ascension to prime minister, Churchill also attributed urgent humanitarian and strategic value to Zionism and came to identify personally and ideologically with the Zionists and Jews, sharing common friends and foes.

Although Churchill's notion of Zionism evolved, his perception of the Zionist political movement remained generally static. The liberal, moderate, dignified, upright, bourgeois, and even romantic image that Herzl fashioned at the First Zionist Conference in Basle in 1897, which was perpetuated and reinforced by subsequent Zionist leaders, was the picture Churchill almost always conjured in his mind when he thought of Zionism. His contact and friendship with Chaim Weizmann especially endeared him to the Zionist cause. Weizmann, a contemporary, was a magnetic, charming immigrant who shared Churchill's romantic image of England, nineteenth-century liberal English values, and burning desire to advance the cause of civilization, like many other Russian-born Jews of that generation did.[2] Rishon Lezion, a beautiful early pioneering settlement filled with dedicated Jewish laborers who successfully cultivated a barren wilderness, became the permanent face of Jewish Palestine/Israel following Churchill's sole extended visit there in 1921. Given Zionism's subordinate importance in his worldview, Churchill never became an expert on Zionism or Palestine, never met or mentioned Herzl, and never developed a deep understanding of the movement or the many practical difficulties it faced. With few exceptions Churchill did not originate ideas relating to Zionist policies; instead, he reacted to proposals made by others. He rarely if at all encountered or interacted with Arabs or Muslims in England growing up, but he took a very dim view of them in his youthful years as a soldier, which he generally maintained for the rest of his life. That view was reinforced after his extensive contact with them in 1921 as colonial secretary. He forever saw the Palestinian Arabs as intransigent, backward, and anti-British.

One of the most intriguing fixed images in Churchill's mind was that of the Zionists as civilizers. He shared the view of many nineteenth-century British writers and public figures that restoring the Jews to Palestine would benefit the world. Many of these thinkers were evangelical Christians who believed restoration would spur the Second Coming of Christ, but he perceived the global benefit in broadly secular terms: the physical and moral advance of civilization. This was not very different from Herzl's argument that Jewish restoration would benefit the world by bringing stability to Europe and creating a liberal bastion in the Middle East. Other Gentile Zionists shared this view as well. Initially

Churchill viewed the Zionists as potential colonists on behalf of the British Empire, but this idea did not linger long; even after Britain took on the League of Nations mandate he never viewed Palestine as part of the empire (and it technically was not). The interest the Zionists served was not that of the British Empire but of Western civilization as a whole. This was a fine but significant distinction. So powerful was the civilizational argument for Churchill that to him it overrode whatever historical claims a people might have. Any group that did not properly develop land; advance science, literature, or philosophy; or introduce liberal laws, culture, and institutions on their land—in other words, contribute to the progress of civilization—in effect mortgaged their right to that land. Perhaps this argument too had a loosely religious basis, a secular equivalent of the biblical injunction in Leviticus that God expelled nations from the Holy Land that did not live there morally. In the case of the Jews, Churchill believed they had in their favor both the civilizational and the historical arguments. He retained an abundant curiosity about the land of Palestine and its development, at times inquiring about the minutest agricultural matters. He saw the Zionists as kindred civilizers who, as he declared as late as 1949, managed to "bring back into economic usefulness lands which the world cannot afford to leave lying idle." Throughout his whole life he believed every land across the globe had to be properly developed in order to nourish people and advance the cause of civilization. As early as 1908 he pronounced in a travelogue about Africa that everyone—no matter his or her race—had an obligation to civilize the world and contribute to its progress: "No man has a right to be idle, whoever he be or wherever he lives. He is bound to go forward and take an honest share in the general work of the world."[3] Churchill believed the Zionists fulfilled this mission as the British and other allegedly advanced white races had.

To appreciate fully the romantic and prescient nature of Churchill's Zionism, it must be understood that there was nothing inevitable about the establishment of the State of Israel in 1948. A half century earlier the nascent Zionist movement appeared to most Jews and Gentiles to be absorbed in a fantasy. Who would have thought realistically that a people scattered for almost two thousand years around the globe, persecuted in virtually every single locale in which they lived, would return to the land from which they had originated and where they had lived as a nation before their defeat and exile by the ancient Romans? Churchill predicted such an eventuality with confidence in 1908 and felt it even more likely beginning in the 1920s. But few outside the Zionist leadership regarded Churchill's Zionism, when he expressed it, as being on the right side of history. This was especially true early on, but it remained true as late as the early 1940s, when millions of Jews were being murdered in Hitler's ovens. Who also would have believed that the Jews, who for centuries were denigrated and degraded in practically every European state for allegedly possessing negative racial and personality traits and nefarious social, economic, and political designs, would become one of the chief promoters of nineteenth-century liberalism in the darkened first half of the twentieth century, marked by Communism and Nazism? Churchill was one of the few who instinctively grasped that early on. And, finally, who would have imagined that the Jews, who for centuries were banned from various professions and virtually forced into financial and mercantile fields, would become expert agriculturalists and make the desert bloom? Churchill ascertained this when he visited Palestine in 1921. Churchill, with a nimble and nuanced mind, stood out for all these imaginative insights and others, not only amid the overwhelming majority of Gentiles but amid many Jews as well. As one Anglo-Jewish leader and well-known writer, Israel Zangwill, observed in 1905, "For Mr. Winston Churchill, unlike alas! So many of our own leaders has shown himself possessed of that quality of political imagination which does not call visions unreal because they are not yet solid, which understands the creative force of great ideas."[4]

A further improbability in this tale is that Britain was an essential agent in the founding of the Jewish state. The Britain in which Churchill was born in 1874 had a very mixed historical record in its treatment of Jews and Zionism. It was the scene of one of the most bloody anti-Semitic massacres in the Middle Ages, the first European country to charge Jews with ritual murder, and the first to expel them en masse. Yet, by the late nineteenth century, Britain had granted full political rights to the Jews, had a Jewish-born prime minister, and offered asylum to eastern European Jewish refugees fleeing persecution. Also, in the mid-nineteenth century an evangelical movement grew that supported a Jewish entity in the Holy Land. In the early twentieth century, Britain issued the Balfour Declaration, which helped lead to the founding of the State of Israel in 1948, although by that point Britain virulently opposed what it had helped instigate.

Despite Churchill's predisposition and overall support for Zionism, his trajectory on the issue was erratic. He was at various times moderately supportive, ardently supportive, opposed, and indifferent. This inconsistent attitude can be more fully comprehended through an understanding of his worldview. Ultimately, he was dedicated to the advancement of civilization, by which he meant what we would refer to today as the "Western" way of life—such as its values, customs, laws, and economic system. Since he considered Britain and its empire the chief champions of civilization, he fixated on British strategic and imperial interests. And as an ambitious politician who sought to be in Parliament and high government office to influence policy and events, he focused greatly on his political needs as well. These paramount issues, and sometimes others, mostly, though not always, determined Churchill's mood toward Zionism, even if they did not usually affect how he genuinely felt about it. This was because Zionism was for him a subordinate issue—a predominantly romantic and sentimental cause that had no direct impact on British survival or power and only intermittent bearing on British strategic or imperial interests.

The larger issues generally favored Zionism early in Churchill's career; he saw imperial benefits to Zionism and personal political advantage in pursuing it, but his attachment to the cause was weak. In the 1910s and 1920s, strategic, imperial, and political factors all led him to ignore Zionism and resent it. Still, in 1921, he began to understand the issue more fully and came to embrace it, particularly for civilizational reasons. From the late 1920s until the end of the Second World War, the preeminent issues—except politics—were aligned, as were ideological, humanitarian, and personal considerations. Churchill felt a deep identification with the Zionists during this time, and he championed their movement. In the 1930s, during his years in the political wilderness, his Zionism solidified and he became known as one of Britain's leading Gentile Zionists. From 1945 through 1948, the wider picture was hazy and conflicting, and for personal, political, and psychological reasons he ignored Zionism even though it tugged on his conscience. He reverted back to supporting Zionism from 1949 until the end of his political career.

With a few notable exceptions, such as the early days in Manchester, politics generally did not favor support for Zionism, and mostly Churchill's views toward Zionism were markedly out of sync with general public opinion. Often, therefore, his public remarks about Zionism, and even sometimes his private ones, were very much geared to his audience, with his intentions often hidden. This stood in contrast to his comments about Russia or other grave strategic matters about which he cared more deeply and on which he generally did not compromise for political expediency. As an ambitious politician, particularly in his early years, and a great rhetorician, Churchill excelled in fitting an argument to an objective, and never more so than he did regarding the politically controversial Zionist movement.

And yet, however often Churchill's primary concerns interfered with support for Zionism, especially early in his career, his other more sentimental interests—including religious, racial, historical, humanitarian, familial, personal, mystical, and civilizational—as well as his ideological interests drew him to it. The Zionist movement, which appeared so far-fetched early in his career and became so unpopular in England later in his career, captured his imagination and became integral to his worldview.

CHAPTER ONE

Churchill's Worlds

IT IS IMPOSSIBLE TO GAIN PROPER insight into a person's views on a subject without understanding that person's overall worldview. This is certainly true when examining Winston Churchill's approach toward any world issue, but especially Zionism, a relatively new issue that did not have much relevance to British imperial or strategic interests. More than most politicians and statesmen, Churchill often appeared erratic in his opinions, and yet in truth he developed a distinct perspective of the world.

Although he is perceived today by many, particularly in the United States, as a man of great principles and constancy, for much of his life and even after his death Churchill's convictions were often questioned and his positions considered functions of ill judgment and political opportunism. Shortly before the First World War, by which time Churchill had served in Parliament and government for more than a decade, the discerning journalist A. G. Gardiner reflected a widespread view of his fellow Liberal: "It is the ultimate Churchill that escapes us." Churchill was a "soldier" who "loves the fight more than the cause"; "whatever shrine he worships at, he will be the most fervid in his prayers." Indeed, during much of his career, especially early on, Churchill directed fierce rhetoric against whatever, whichever, or whomever was his enemy at the time. Contributing to the confusion over Churchill's core character was his shifting political allegiance, which switched from the Conservative Party to the Liberal Party in 1904, then to a center party in the early 1920s that never fully materialized, and then back again to the Conservative Party in 1924. All told, he was affiliated with the Conservative Party for thirty-five of his fifty-five years in active politics, but he was never completely accepted by it. His pedigree further muddled matters. His father, Randolph, came from a distinguished aristocratic family descended from the famous Duke of Marlborough, but Randolph was a distrusted maverick in the Conservative Party, and his audacious, meteoric political career ended abruptly. Churchill's mother, Jenny Jerome, was American, and many British observers considered that a significant flaw in Churchill's character. As late as 1940, Churchill, upon becoming prime minister at the age of sixty-five, was referred to by one Conservative politician as a "half-breed American." Many attributed to him American characteristics, such as overt ambitiousness, interest in money, hyperactivity, brashness, and capriciousness. These qualities, especially in a youth, were unacceptable to the stuffy, old-fashioned, inflexible, wealthy Conservative establishment. As the socialist dramatist George Bernard Shaw put it to Churchill in 1946: "You [are] a phenomenon that the Blimps and Philistines and Stick-in-the-muds have never understood and always dreaded." Churchill also did not fit in well in the period in which he lived. In 1898, the journalist G. W. Steevens described him at twenty-four years old to be the "youngest man in Europe" who had "the twentieth century in his marrow." Yet, decades later, it was widely believed that Churchill was stuck in the nineteenth century.[1]

Churchill did not belong only to one period, nor can his character be easily classified, especially not by the standards of the rigid, stratified British society of his lifetime. He had a complex world outlook that blended realism, sentimentalism, Victorianism, Edwardianism, Liberalism, Conservatism, and other credos. He essentially lived in three worlds, defined by the periods 1814–1913, 1914–1939, and 1940–1955. The first world, 1814–1913, was his favorite. It was this period that shaped his core principles, aspirations, strategic vision, and image of British power and prestige. The second world, 1914–1939, his least favorite, was a corruption of the first. The third world, 1940–1955, was a sort of hybrid, offering great promise before it too degenerated. Churchill worked to achieve the aspirations of the first world by applying the principles and values of that era to the realities of the second and third worlds. He sought guidance from history but shirked the stultified embrace of the past of some Conservatives. He avoided the love of newness for its own sake that characterized some Socialists, yet he often nimbly recognized and embraced new developments, such as scientific advancements, the rise of the United States, and Zionism. Steeped in the past, Churchill nevertheless always concentrated on the present and the future, which often put him at odds with public opinion. Churchill also remained fixated on his supreme priorities, such as British strategic and imperial interests and at certain times his own political goals. For someone with varied and complex world interests, this meant that his romantic and sentimental concerns frequently took a backseat to these primary objectives, except when they were aligned. Such certainly was the case with his approach toward Zionism, a sentimental cause that evolved into an important part of his worldview but always remained a subordinate issue for him. Thus, only with some fundamental understanding of how he looked at each of his three distinct worlds can we understand what he cared about and how Zionism fit in.

Throughout his life Churchill looked at the period dating roughly from the Congress of Vienna (1814–1815), which followed the end of the Napoleonic wars, to the start of the First World War (1914) as a golden age for Britain and the world. He embraced this era, which can be labeled the Victorian period since it was mostly marked by the reign of Queen Victoria (1837–1901). It became a "vanished age" to which he always compared subsequent eras. He regarded it as a period dominated by Great Britain and Europe, and marked by optimism, civility, grand statesmen, Great Powers, peace, stability, honor, romanticism, patriotism, and the relentless progress of civilization. In 1921, reflecting the national nostalgia for the Victorian period during the interwar years, he wrote shortly after his mother's death, "The old brilliant world in which she moved and in wh [which] you met her is a long way off now, & we do not see its like today." And in 1937 he claimed that future British generations would view the Victorian era "with the same wistful and wondering regard that the later Romans cast upon the Age of the Antonines." Even his nostalgia for the period was invoked in a Victorian manner, as the late Victorians often compared their age to the Roman era.[2]

The Victorian period was, Churchill wrote, one of "triumphant serenity," when the British Empire was unrivaled in global reach and power. He argued that the empire was a slowly built inheritance that should remain the size it was under Queen Victoria, no larger and no smaller, though its form might change. It was a fixed "monument" to Britain's historical and present grandeur. He deeply felt that this era was a time when civilization was continually on the march, a view widely shared among late Victorians, and considered the empire an essential instrument of that progress. Many Britons in the late nineteenth and early twentieth centuries justified their imperial rule with their civilizing mission. For Churchill, it was no mere rationalization. He firmly believed that Britain, within limits, had an obligation to "civilize" those peoples deemed backward. In 1897, weeks after Queen Victoria's Diamond Jubilee, he concluded his maiden public speech—at the Primrose League, founded by his father in honor of Benjamin Disraeli, the late-nineteenth-century Conservative leader whose romantic imperial view Churchill shared—by arguing against those "croakers" who thought the empire had peaked. Instead, he advocated continued vigor in maintaining the empire by which Britain carried out "our mission of bearing peace, civilisation and good government to the uttermost ends of the earth." In his 1899 book on the Sudan war, he relayed how Britain helped civilize alleged backward peoples: "What enterprise that an enlightened community may attempt is more noble and more profitable than the reclamation from barbarism of fertile regions and large populations? To give peace to warring tribes, to administer justice where all was violence, to strike the chains off the slave, to draw the richness from the soil, to plant the earliest seeds of commerce and learning, to increase in whole peoples their capacities for pleasure and diminish their chances of pain—what more beautiful ideal or more valuable reward can inspire human effort?" Exuding an almost limitless faith in Britain's role in the advance of civilization, he spoke in 1908 of pet plans for the development of British East Africa, which he had visited six months earlier as colonial under-secretary: "The work of civilization is going on." In that position, he took Britain's civilizing responsibility very seriously. His minute in 1906 on a seemingly petty issue in Ceylon was indicative: "Our duty is to insist that the principles of justice and the safeguards of judicial procedure are rigidly, punctiliously and pedantically followed."[3]

Race was integral to this world, though the focus on it was becoming increasingly disreputable in English society. Churchill conceived a hierarchy of races and civilizations, where the top-tier races had much to contribute to those on the bottom rungs. The British, their Teutonic cousins the Germans, their Anglo-Saxon brethren the Americans, and the Gaullist French were at the top of this racial totem pole. The Jews were in either this rung or the one below, and the Russians were much lower, along with other backward, despotic, and barbaric "Asiatics." Below the Russians were the Arabs, and below them the tribes of Africa and India. In the late 1890s and early 1900s, Churchill thought a good deal about race when he encountered Indians, Sudanese, and East Africans as a soldier and then as colonial under-secretary. He described these people as hardly superior to animals, using such terms as "barbarous" (Indian tribes), "simple-minded savages" (indigenous Sudanese), "debased and cruel breed" (Arab-Sudanese), "warlike" and "wild" (Arabs), and "filthy Oriental" (Turks). He felt that these races held back the advance of civilization. Many of these people followed Islam, and he wrote in 1899 that he considered the religion a retrogressive force: "How dreadful are the curses which Mohammedanism lays on its votaries! Besides the fanatical frenzy . . . there is this fearful fatalistic apathy . . . improvident habits, slovenly systems of agriculture, sluggish methods of commerce . . . wherever the followers of the Prophet rule or live. . . . Individual Moslems may show splendid qualities, but the influence of the religion paralyses the social development of those who follow it. No stronger retrograde force exists in the world." Even decades later he voiced such thoughts and used such language, and remained convinced of Anglo-Saxon superiority. This was common language at the time in England, which was historically a racially conscious country and was overwhelmingly white for much of Churchill's life. (Churchill in his youth also condescended to the lower socioeconomic rungs of white British society, although in less harsh terms, and as home secretary in 1910–1911 he became interested in the popular movement of eugenics, which favored sterilizing the "unfit" and maintaining "strength" in the English race.) No matter where a race stood on the totem pole, it had an obligation to advance civilization in whatever form or means possible. As he wrote in a 1908 book, "The Asiatic, and here I also include the African native, has immense services to render and energies to contribute to the happiness and material progress of the world." He insisted that everyone, from the superior Briton to the lowly African, shared this imperative, that "no man has a right to be idle, whoever he be or wherever he lives. He is bound to go forward and take an honest share in the general work of the world."[4]

Scientific advancement contributed to the progress of civilization in the Victorian period. Churchill was captivated by technological developments and participated in them. Although he grew up in the traditional arms of British imperial power—serving in the cavalry and becoming first lord of the Admiralty at a young age—he was so fascinated by the airplane and air power that he flew 140 times before the First World War and nearly received his pilot's license. He pushed development of the tank in the First World War and atomic power in the Second World War. He saw moral progress as underpinning scientific advances. Another factor in the progress of the age was the prevalence of grand statesmen such as Napoleon, Disraeli, and Liberal leader William E. Gladstone. Churchill remarked about the powerful men his father entertained that "it seemed a very great world in which these men lived," where they grappled with eminent matters.[5]

The man from this world whom Churchill revered the most was his father, Randolph, whose career he sought to vindicate. At a young age Churchill closely followed his father's speeches. He wrote later, "For years I had read every word he spoke and what the newspapers said about him." And the newspapers were very interested in Randolph's utterances. At sixty, Churchill wrote that after his father died (when Churchill was only twenty years old), "All my dreams of comradeship with him, of entering Parliament at his side or in his support, were ended. There remained for me only to pursue his aims, and vindicate his memory. This I have tried to do." He did so very deliberately, especially early in adulthood and his career. Churchill joined the Primrose League, which his father founded, and delivered his maiden political speech there at the age of twenty-two. When he crossed the aisle and left the Conservative Party in 1904 to join the Liberals, he notably sat down in the seat where his father had resided while in Opposition. Perhaps Churchill's grandest early act of fealty to his father was writing a fawning biography of him, though it also served some immediate political needs. Churchill sought his father's approbation throughout his life, even after the Second World War when he was old and had established himself as a legendary British and Western statesman. This was strikingly evident from a vision Churchill had in 1947 of an imaginary conversation with his father, who had been dead for more than fifty years and had apparently not had access to newspapers from the grave. The daydream was so vivid that he wrote it down. After explaining to Randolph how the world had changed since the late nineteenth century without mentioning his own role in global developments, Churchill envisioned his father replying, "As I listened to you unfolding these fearful facts you seemed to know a great deal about them. I never expected that you would develop so far and so fully. Of course you are too old now to think about such things, but when I hear you talk I really wonder you didn't go into politics. You might have done a lot to help. You might even have made a name for yourself." Randolph then showed a "benignant smile," lit a match for his cigarette, and vanished.[6] Churchill finally managed to impress his father, but he clearly was pained that his father never knew all that he had accomplished. That was one achievement that forever eluded him.

The Victorian period, Churchill maintained, was a time of grand and largely effective realpolitik diplomacy. It was subtle, civil, and conducted by grand statesmen of Great Powers who, from their enlightened and disinterested perches above the push and pull of petty party politics and popular passions, strove to maintain peace by establishing a balance of power. His model statesman was Robert Stewart Castlereagh, British foreign secretary in the early eighteenth century, who helped usher in the peaceful Victorian age at the Congress of Vienna following the Napoleonic wars. Castlereagh sought to establish a "just Balance of Power" by strengthening the areas around the aggressor, France, in order to contain it, while resisting attempts to impose severe territorial penalties lest it lead to French revanchism or weaken France as a potential ally against the emerging threat of Russia. He then strengthened central Europe, by reconciling Austria and Prussia, and formed an alliance with Austria and France to oppose Russia and Prussia over Poland and Saxony. Castlereagh also urged the European powers to form a Council of Europe, through which they could meet periodically to discuss their common interests and ways for maintaining the peace.[7] Churchill followed the methods and concepts of Castlereagh and other key members at Vienna to a remarkable degree: he always urged convening an immediate postwar peace conference to address looming crises, fashioning a moderate peace to prevent future revanchism and to contribute to a new balance of power, enlisting troops of a defeated power to fight a former ally and prospective enemy, strengthening countries around nations that required containment, keeping Russia out of central Europe, and erecting a superstructure upheld by the Great Powers overlaying a balance of power. Churchill did diverge from Castlereagh, however, by his willingness at times to interfere in the formation of other governments.

Churchill's awareness and shrewdness about the world grew over time. Early on he sometimes seemed overly flippant and eager to appear profound, such as when he wrote his mother in 1898 at the age of twenty-three that "loyalty promotes tyranny.... Patriotism shades into cant. Imperialism sinks to Jingoism." He possessed an especially youthful optimism in his early years, and for the first decade of his political career he was not unduly vexed about threats to British security and global peace, after a century of relative peace in Europe. In 1907, despite rising tension among the Great Powers and growing concern about Germany under Kaiser Wilhelm II, he declared the "whole trend and march of human affairs" was toward "one great human family." In 1908, he considered talk of an inevitable Anglo-German war to be "nonsense." Generally, his worldly thoughts, including those about the Great Powers, were limited to British imperial matters. The Great Power conflict often played out in imperial territories, and his own early military exploits took place on imperial battlegrounds—India, Cuba, Sudan, and South Africa. After entering Parliament, in 1901, he carried on the banner of his late father, who, as chancellor of the exchequer, had championed cutting the military budget and minimizing British involvement in continental conflicts. Churchill remained out of step with the emerging British strategy of looking beyond naval strength and building up the army for possible continental duty. He also was keen on collaborating with the anti-rearmament radical David Lloyd George, Liberal chancellor of the exchequer. Otherwise, Churchill's attention was focused on domestic economic and social issues, such as advocating free trade and opposing imperial preference, and on his rather tumultuous nascent political career. His early governmental positions—colonial under-secretary, president of the Board of Trade, and home secretary—reinforced, if not spurred, these priorities, as perhaps did the domestic orientation of the British public. Although Churchill hoped to avoid war, he saw it as a fascinating, romantic experience, even while he was repelled by its increasing violence.[8]

It was not until 1911, with the advent of the Agadir crisis, in which a German gunboat sailed to Morocco and demanded French Congo, and then shortly after when he became first lord of the Admiralty, that he began to fixate on the threat of war. Years later Churchill acknowledged that he had misread the flow of events leading up to the First World War, a mistake he did not repeat in the lead-up to the Second World War or the Cold War, when he was the prescient prophet of doom.[9] Indeed, from 1911 onward, the issues of war and peace were the overriding preoccupations of his career, even while he maintained a liberal belief in the ultimate progress of civilization.

Notably, in this world of great European Powers, Churchill grasped and welcomed the rising importance of the United States, which at the turn of the century was an established economic power but only just emerging as a military power. He visited New York in 1895 and had a wonderful time, coming away impressed by American youth, strength, energy, irreverence, freshness, utilitarianism, hospitality, as well as vulgarity. He wrote his American-born mother in 1898 that he was a "representative of both countries" and committed to promoting "good understanding between the English speaking communities." Churchill was one of the few leading British statesmen at the time who had visited the United States, though he was not alone in grasping the country's ascent. Some in the late 1890s even called for an alliance with the United States, which Churchill considered "foolish" and unrealistic based on what he considered insufficient common interests. He was generally skeptical of alliances at this time, particularly between democracies, but as a strong free-trade advocate he welcomed the United States as a trading partner. Unlike many others, he generally was not threatened by rising American might.[10]

The romance Churchill associated with this world and the optimism he possessed about the progress of civilization mirrored his feelings about his own life during this period. He had fought in several wars, was a famous war correspondent and renowned war hero who had escaped an enemy prison, had written several books, and had been elected to Parliament—all before the age of twenty-six. Then, after boldly switching from the Conservative to the Liberal Party in 1904, he held government portfolio after another, each more important than the one before, until eventually becoming, at the age of thirty-six, first lord of the Admiralty, one of the most powerful positions in the Cabinet. In Churchill's mind, the past was stupendous and the future brimmed with even greater possibilities—for himself, Britain, and civilization.

The First World War—its unprecedented horror and destruction, and the forces it unleashed—shattered Churchill's golden age. After the brief exhilaration of the war wore off, he realized that the unremitting advance of civilization, about which he had been so confident, had come to a thunderous halt. As he later wrote, "The old life of England suddenly ceased." After the war, the old order of Europe—the Russian tsar, the German kaiser, the Austro-Hungarian Empire, and many of the ideas that underpinned them—was largely gone. Churchill considered the new world that emerged, which spanned from 1914 to 1939, a corruption of the old world. Instead of stability, imperialism, liberalism, progress, optimism, great leaders, aristocratic democracy, romance, nationalism, patriotism, and balance of power, there now loomed anarchy, bloodshed, despair, self-determination, internationalism, pacifism, mass democracy, Communism, and Fascism. Some government leaders, such as U.S. President Woodrow Wilson and British Prime Minister David Lloyd George, regarded the unprecedented wartime carnage and the evils it spawned as natural products of the old world's inherent faults, which now had to be addressed. Churchill, however, maintained that the ills of the new world were only corruptions of the old world and needed to be purified. He did not easily give up on the old world. As he told Lloyd George over dinner in 1920, "You're not going to get your new world. The old world is a good enough place for me, & there's life in the old dog yet. It's going to sit up & wag its tail." Change now spelled trouble for Britain, which had much at stake in the status quo. Change often did not favor Churchill personally either. His career crashed from a great height and seemed finished in 1915 after the disaster with the Dardanelles (the strait that Britain sought to seize in order to take Turkey out of the war; also commonly referred to as Gallipoli). He managed to return to power from 1917 to 1929, when his career appeared over again, saved only by the outbreak of the Second World War in 1939 against which he had warned.[11]

The brutality of the First World War was shocking, and Churchill lamented that all aspects of society were directed toward creating more destruction. War had been shorn of romance and glory, and had "ceased to be a gentleman's game." Where once great generals such as Caesar or Napoleon commanded grand but brief battles on the fields, now impersonal bureaucrats waged prolonged, stagnant campaigns via telephone from their desks. Churchill feared that the next war, which he considered likely if not imminent, would be more bloody and all-encompassing, and would target civilian populations. France was fearful, Poland weak, and Germany bitter and becoming close with a Russia that was Communist and resentful. He wrote presciently in 1929, "Old antagonisms are sleeping, and the drum-beat of new antagonisms is already heard." He perceived the postwar period merely as an interlude before the next war: "Exhaustion which has been described as Peace."[12]

The development of a Russo-German friendship especially preoccupied Churchill's strategic thoughts. He correctly dreaded that Germany and Russia, under whatever forms of government, would team up as a powerful bloc against the victorious status-quo powers in revenge and revanchism. He conveyed his alarm in 1919 and 1920 in brilliant, prescient, but unsent memos. Churchill understood that Germany was the pivot upon which everything else turned, and that proper handling of the situation would minimize Britain's involvement in Russia's civil war. To steer Germany toward the West and prevent its succumbing to Communism, he called for a revision of the Versailles postwar peace treaty (signed in 1919 in Paris)—in part because he considered it unduly punitive against Germany, but also because he did not think Germany could be made to comply with tough peace terms—and advocated a treaty that committed the West to defend Germany against an attack by Russia. But there was no revision of Versailles until Adolf Hitler rose to power and accomplished it unilaterally in the 1930s. The West further bumbled by pushing Fascist Italy and Soviet Russia into the arms of Nazi Germany, making war more likely or, as Churchill wrote his wife Clementine in 1935, bringing on "the end of the world." He considered Nazi Germany early on to be a grave threat to civilization and a complete corruption of the Victorian world. He looked more favorably, however, upon the Fascist regime of Benito Mussolini, as did many in the United States in the 1920s. That sympathy deepened in the 1930s, as Churchill hoped Italy would serve as a counter to Germany.[13]

Just as with Germany, Churchill was determined that postwar Russia not adopt a government that was hostile to Britain and the West. He expected that Russia, whether Communist or not, would seek to recapture territories lost after the First World War, including the Baltic states and some of Poland. This did not concern him—he was not a fervent enthusiast of self-determination—as he suggested in a 1920 memo to the Cabinet: "After all, the reincorporation within the limits of the Russian Empire of these former Russian States that had not the wit to defend themselves in common, though a melancholy event, is not in itself a decisive event in European history." Rather, he obsessively feared that Bolshevism would spread and topple non-Communist governments in Europe and throughout the world, thus posing a direct and immediate strategic threat to Western civilization. He wrote of the Bolsheviks, "Theirs is a war against civilized society which can never end." Shortly after the war the Bolsheviks inaugurated the Comintern, or Communist Internationale, which propagated international Communist revolution, and Communist insurrections soon followed, including in Berlin. Bolshevism was ideologically anathema to all that Churchill held dear in civilization. This "scientific" political system rejected everything positive that the ages had produced, and in particular that which Britain had stood for in the nineteenth century. Churchill referred to Bolshevik leader Vladimir Lenin as the "Grand Repudiator," spurning religion, morality, capitalism, treaties, "the laws and customs of centuries," the "whole structure—such as it is—of human society." Churchill repeatedly and vividly insisted that Bolshevism was a morally repugnant political system that trampled on people's rights, butchered people on a mass scale, undermined Western civilization, and brought the world back to an earlier barbaric age. He was most concerned about this evil spreading outside of Russian borders, but he was not particularly alarmed over how it affected Russians, whom he considered generally "ignorant" and "primitive Asiatic people."[14]

As secretary of state for war and air (1919–1921), Churchill sought to destroy the Bolshevik regime in its infancy. He relentlessly tried to get the Cabinet to maintain active support of the White Russians and wage a victorious battle against the Bolsheviks during the Russian Civil War that followed the Bolshevik Revolution of 1917. Neither the public nor the Cabinet supported this effort very long, and it soon was dubbed "Churchill's Private War." This unpopular position cost him politically. It further alienated him from the political Left, the media, and Conservative Party leader Andrew Bonar Law; irreparably damaged his relationship with his Liberal patron Lloyd George; and reaffirmed his public image as a reckless, warmongering buccaneer who continually led the nation into disaster. These consequences did not overly concern Churchill since he was single-mindedly focused on destroying Bolshevik Russia, as he acknowledged in 1920: "I am accustomed at the present time rather to judge world events and world tendencies from the point of view of whether they are Bolshevist or anti-Bolshevist."[15] This was vintage Churchill and exemplified how he was always consumed by his top, rigidly prioritized objectives.

Churchill's perception of, and attitude toward, Russia evolved over the next two decades. An admirer of eighteenth-century British thinker and statesman Edmund Burke, he considered radical revolutions inherently destructive and ultimately reactionary, and he predicted early on that the same applied to the Bolshevik Revolution. He then carefully discerned this prediction coming to pass through a close, if not always accurate, reading of Russian domestic dynamics. An example of his probing tendency was his reading an obscure 1936 book, *Uncle Give Us Bread,* by a Danish poultry expert who worked on Soviet farms. He detected the transformation of Soviet Russia in the mid-1930s from a country that promoted international revolution to a more normal, dictatorial, nationalist state that was invested in maintaining the status quo and more strategically inclined toward the West. This development facilitated his interest, beginning in the mid-1930s, in having Britain form an anti-German mutual-defense pact with Soviet Russia and France (and, soon after, Italy). In 1938 he called in the House of Commons for such a pact and a "Grand Alliance." In a nod to the anti-Soviet Conservatives, he did not explicitly mention Russia, and in a nod to the anti-Fascist political Left, he argued that the alliance should rest on the Covenant of the League of Nations.[16]

Churchill's own transformation from anti-Bolshevik crusader in

1919–1920 to leading champion of an alliance with Soviet Russia in the late 1930s demonstrated a determined mental nimbleness and single-minded fixation on British national security, often at the expense of ideology and politics. In contrast, many of his Conservative colleagues were more ideological and less strategically discerning. Even after Germany conquered all of Czechoslovakia in March 1939, Prime Minister Neville Chamberlain adamantly opposed a pact with Russia. Foreign Secretary Lord Halifax (Edward Frederick Lindley Wood) had so lost strategic perspective as late as July 1939 that in order to prevent the Soviet ambassador's wife from becoming the ranking hostess of the diplomatic corps in London, he asked the Brazilian president not to rotate out the long-tenured Brazilian ambassador as planned. Churchill always insisted on keeping perspective in foreign policy, as he explained in a 1936 letter to a newspaper in response to his old friend Hugh Cecil's public opposition to an alliance with Russia, France, or Italy: "Some further refinement is needed in the catholicity of his condemnation. It might be a good thing, for instance, for him to put his censures down in order of priority, and then try to think a little less severely of the two least bad, or least likely to endanger our own safety. The problem would then simplify itself; and the picture would acquire the charm of light and shade." Despite Churchill's efforts, Soviet Russia, faced with Western indifference and weakness, made a pact with Germany in August 1939, triggering the Second World War.[17]

To Churchill's dismay, not only was civilization being undermined by the rise of Communism, Nazism, and Fascism, but even in democratic countries the old order was being corrupted by the rise of the masses and the trend toward universal suffrage. His fidelity to nineteenth-century values generally did not extend to those of the revolutionary movements. He lamented that no longer did great leaders calmly and paternalistically oversee the general welfare. Now, the masses pursued narrow interests, produced small leaders, and took the romance out of politics. As he wrote in 1929, "The leadership of the privileged has passed away, but it has not been succeeded by that of the eminent." Still, in Churchill's opinion, Britain remained better off than the United States, which was taken over by political machines that he felt had hurt him and destroyed his father.[18]

Whereas previously such great leaders as Marlborough and Napoleon waged war expertly and dispassionately, the masses now took the lead, and they were driven more by emotion than thought. The First World War was a "people's war," which Churchill believed could have been brought to a conclusion by the end of 1914 if not for the vengeful emotions of the masses and the media. Already in 1901 he had predicted, "Democracy is more vindictive than Cabinets. The wars of peoples will be more terrible than those of kings." Churchill's own terrible treatment by the press and the public over the Dardanelles debacle in 1915—which threatened his career, forever soiled his reputation, and brought him great personal heartache and melancholia—most viscerally intensified this feeling. He derided popular opposition to his war against the Bolsheviks in 1919 as the "unthinking opinion." He also contended that the people had no ability to judge matters of peace. A decade after the First World War he mocked Woodrow Wilson's trust in "plain people" who "knew nothing whatever about how to make a just and durable peace." The unthinking masses fervently and callously opposed helping the Germans and wanted instead to punish them, even though that undermined Britain's vital strategic interest. He felt that the newly enfranchised, particularly women, were most to blame for this sentiment, which was so strong that he felt compelled to appeal to it in the 1918 postwar election despite his contrary view. In such an atmosphere, the modern leaders of the world were incapable of calmly establishing a just peace, which, as Churchill noted, produced a striking contrast between the conferences of Vienna in 1814 and Paris in 1919: "In 1814 calm, deliberate conclaves of comfortable and firmly established personages: in 1919 a turbulent collision of embarrassed demagogues who were also great men of action, each of whom had to produce a triumph for himself and his Party and give satisfaction to national fears and passions well founded or not." The new diplomats consciously corrupted the nineteenth-century model of diplomacy. Wilson led the way among leaders in denouncing the old focus on power relationships, secret treaties, territories, imperialism, elitism, and status quo, which he blamed as the root causes of war and turmoil. Some in the British establishment agreed, including the British Foreign Office, which commissioned a critical study of the Congress of Vienna.[19] Paris reflected this rejection of the old and might thus be considered the "un-Vienna" in both form and substance.

Naturally, Churchill objected to this attack on the old international system, and he resented Wilson's self-righteous, high-handed, platitudinous, and naive attempts at the Paris conference to teach morality to the "wicked Old World statesmen" and "bend the world—no doubt for its own good—to his personal views." Churchill objected to much of the openness at Paris, the presence of journalists, and Wilson's attack on secret diplomacy and treaties. In particular, he opposed the excess of self-determination that Wilson and the Paris conferees championed. Before the war, Churchill had rhetorically sympathized with what he called "nationality," and one month after the war began he advocated "the setting free of those races which have been subjugated and conquered." Perhaps he thought such encouragement advanced the Allied war effort, but after the war he dropped even such ambiguous pretense. He saw self-determination as a corruption of the old international order. In 1919, he explained his opposition to tearing down historical developments in favor of impractical principles: "Instead of the higher organization of the European nations which has been slowly arrived at over centuries, and which no doubt presents many aspects of anxiety and forms of danger, we have Europe almost completely Balkanised, so far as it is not Bolshevised." The term "self-determination," in fact, had been popularized by the Bolsheviks in their advocacy of an uprising against the existing imperial order, and Churchill spoke often to this Bolshevik emphasis. He had moral objections to the fashionable concept that empires were inherently evil and small nations emerging from empires were morally superior. More important, he opposed excessive self-determination because, he argued, the new "patchwork" of small states would destabilize Europe and lead to war. These new states would unleash violent nationalist forces, Churchill cautioned; as he predicted in 1919, the "war of the giants is over; the wars of the pygmies have begun." A decade later he wrote about these new territorial adjustments: "Here we stir the embers of the past and light the beacons of the future. Old flags are raised anew; the passions of vanished generations awake; beneath the shell-torn soil of the twentieth century the bones of long dead warriors and victims are exposed, and the wail of lost causes sounds in the wind." He stood by Vienna's emphasis on stability and its principle that strong, larger nations were necessary to contain the expansion of potentially aggressive nations, in this case Russia and Germany. As he correctly warned in 1919, "All Europe is sheltering behind the frail defence of a chain of new and feeble Powers to prevent the union of the Bolshevist army with the discontent of the mighty German region."[20]

Churchill was particularly distressed about self-determination in the British Empire. Although he privately remarked once in early 1918 that nothing mattered outside Europe, he cared a great deal about maintaining the British Empire. In contrast to the first world, when he exuded limitless optimism about the empire and its mission, he now fought a rearguard action to protect and develop the Victorian imperial territories. He respected tradition and heritage for their own sake and because, in his eyes, they made sense. He pointedly objected to those who claimed the empire was an anachronism, especially following the disappearance of Europe's old autocratic and military empires, and he was very concerned that the empire was being corrupted by a lack of will, as well as by the Socialists, who came to power intermittently during this period. He worried about weakness in Egypt and, more important, about any loosening of control in India, which was always for him the premier imperial possession, as it was for many British imperialists. It was over Conservative-Socialist support of dominion status of India that Churchill resigned from the Conservative shadow government in 1931 and established himself as a political pariah for the rest of the 1930s. In 1929 he charged that the "same spirit of pusillanimity" and "lack of conviction in our mission" that is "liquidating the work of two generations in Egypt" would also "destroy the healing work of 10 generations in India." Similarly, in 1931, Churchill remarked that Britain was "suffering from a disease of the will. We are the victims of a nervous collapse, of a morbid state of mind." He made the same charge about the groveling reaction to the Nazi threat, and wrote his wife in 1935, "I endeavour to inculcate a more robust attitude." At the same time, Churchill was not an expansive imperialist; he simply wanted to maintain the Victorian empire in some form and develop it. He initially considered the addition of the Palestine and Mesopotamia mandates to the British Empire after the First World War to be corruptions that diverted scarce resources and undermined the old empire, despite the view of some officials that those additions augmented British defense of Egypt and India. In 1919 he argued against imperial jingoism and "new enlargements" that were "dissipating" existing imperial territories, the development of which many considered important to British economic health. The rise of Hitler and a more dangerous situation in Europe demanded an even greater economy of resources. The security of the British homeland became paramount and, as Churchill wrote in 1935, there was no room for "arrogant, blatant, voracious Imperialism."[21]

In this chaotic and dangerous world, Churchill was also dubious of another product of the Paris conference set forth to restore order and peace—the League of Nations. The explicit idea of a League had been developing in Britain and the United States since 1915, and by the 1919 conference it claimed many prominent supporters of various political stripes. Churchill was correctly seen at the time as an opponent of the League, which he considered an adornment to be admired but not a necessity of life, and certainly incapable of offering protection against the frightful forces swirling around the globe. He generally paid lip service to its ideal while dwelling on its practical shortcomings. At best, he thought the League similar to the post-Vienna Concert of Europe, which depended upon a consensus of the Great Powers and a sturdy global balance of power, including a strong British military. Britain was the guarantor of liberal Western civilization, not the legalistic and internationalist philosophy underlying the League. Churchill illustrated this starkly in a memo to the War Cabinet a few months into the Second World War, when he urged, in breach of League principles, the violation of Norwegian neutrality to interdict vital shipments of Swedish iron ore headed for Nazi Germany. "Humanity," he wrote, "rather than legality, must be our guide."[22]

Rather than putting his faith in the League, Churchill looked to his English-speaking brethren across the ocean to help Britain and Europe construct a secure international order. Unlike during the Victorian era, Europe no longer had the capacity and interest to erect such an order alone. The impact of the United States' (late) entrance in the First World War had disabused Churchill and others of any such notion. In 1919 he declared that when the "English-speaking nations" and France were united they were "safe and unassailable." An American alliance was also necessary to maintain order in Asia. Strong Anglo-American relations were fundamental to British strategy, more important than relations with France, Germany, Russia, or Japan—this too marked a radical change from twenty years earlier. For the rest of Churchill's life he essentially maintained this position, which put him at odds with many Socialists and Conservatives who either remained skeptical of the upstart North American nation or simply lacked proper strategic thinking. Still, Churchill's view of the United States was not simple, and he often expressed exasperation with his mother's native country. It represented much that he disliked about the new world: the relative decline of Britain, naive and platitudinous moralism, Hollywood superficiality, irritating anti-imperialism, and the championing of the masses and self-determination. He resented its initial wartime neutrality, well-meaning but destructive influence at Paris, irresponsible refusal to join the League of Nations, isolationism toward Europe, insistence on British payment of postwar debt, and naval competitiveness. Churchill's animosity toward the United States was apparently so well known that his wife warned him in 1928 that it could prevent him from becoming foreign secretary, a position to which he never was appointed. Still, he remained realistic and recognized that close relations with the United States were essential to British security, even though the United States remained an immature and irresponsible power—"unarmed, unready, and as yet uninstructed," he wrote in 1924.[23]

How distant the blissful first world appeared. This second world, which was bracketed by world war, began and ended with a vile totalitarian movement threatening to shatter much of known civilization and return the earth back to the barbaric Stone Age. The "new diplomacy" not only failed to achieve any semblance of a balance of power but managed to unite three powerful continental powers—Germany, Russia, and Italy—in enmity against Britain, with no existing buffers. The result was another world war, and a civilization on the brink of disintegration.

During the Second World War, Churchill tried to purify the second world's corruptions and fashion a third world in the mold of the first world while adapting to the new realities. It was in this third world, which spanned from 1940 to 1955, that he had the most impact. Initially, he was quite encouraged. Britain had again achieved eminent glory led by a great statesman (Churchill himself) who successfully championed liberty and saved civilization. Great men—so dearly missed and derided in the tumultuous and disheartening second world—had returned to play a decisive role by directing large global forces on a grand dramatic stage. Churchill, Joseph Stalin, and Franklin Roosevelt, known as the Big Three, defeated Hitler and met in grand conferences to chart victory and establish a stable postwar international order based on a Great Power settlement. Castlereagh would have felt at home in this world.

For one great man in particular, the war was an especially spectacular period. Churchill confided that 1940 was a "breathless moment," a year he would like to relive. In the summer and autumn of 1940, as the new prime minister, Churchill rallied the despondent British to wage the Battle of Britain and to withstand German bombings of the homeland as well as an expected invasion—all while Germany dominated Europe, Russia supported Germany, and the United States contented itself with neutrality. The war turned in Britain's favor only after Germany attacked Soviet Russia in June 1941 and Japan attacked the United States in December 1941. Churchill lamented that those closest to him—including his mother and father—had not been alive in 1940. Among the living, he was widely lionized for leading the British people to perhaps their greatest triumph and saving Western civilization. He indisputably refuted the charge that dogged him for years of having been unwise and irresponsible, and he replaced the Dardanelles and other allegedly failed foreign and domestic adventures as lasting legacies. After a long, turbulent, and always controversial political career, which had seemed prematurely dead several times, he could at last savor total and unmitigated vindication. He felt entitled to shape the new world.[24]

However, Churchill could not fully savor victory. For much of 1945 he suffered from some sort of melancholia; indeed, he seemingly suffered bouts of depression throughout much of his life. Beyond troubling immediate issues, such as German V-2 rocket attacks, deeper forces were at work. The psychological rush of five years of war leadership—and perhaps his whole career—was nearing an end, and he exuded mental fatigue and sullen aimlessness. After playing a role in all of Britain's wars of the prior fifty years, he now felt "very lonely without a war," as he confided to his physician. He also felt out of sync with the people and did a dreadful job campaigning for the postwar election, the loss of which only deepened his mood. He was bitter at his treatment by the people, as he was after the Dardanelles in 1915, and was incredulous that Destiny had denied him the chance to remain at the summit of power and settle the peace as only he could. He went away on vacation and even remarked about one of his greatest loves, "I don't mind if I never see England again." He mourned his life.[25]

Churchill also grieved for the world. At the Yalta conference in February 1945 with Stalin and Roosevelt, he discounted the impending good news of Nazi defeat and became anxious about the future. On his way there he wrote to Clementine, "The world is in a frightful state," and in another letter that same day he wrote, "The misery of the whole world appals me and I fear increasingly that new struggles may arise out of those we are successfully ending." At the conference he seemed to be experiencing "some sort of a menopause," according to one American participant. In May, only a few days before V-E (Victory in Europe) Day, Churchill lamented to his wife, "It is astonishing one is not in a more buoyant frame of mind in public matters," and he worried that "beneath these triumphs lie poisonous politics and deadly international rivalries." He became so agitated a few weeks later that he was uncharacteristically contentious with an envoy of the U.S. president.[26]

Churchill was always consumed with some struggle or battle, and the conflict he now saw looming was with a belligerent Soviet Union, which posed an emerging threat to world peace. Already by 1943 he knew that Russia would possess the most powerful postwar continental land army, but he remained unsure for the next several years about Russian intentions. Before Yalta he was hopeful, but he quickly became despondent over Stalin's aggression and his violations of their agreement. The strategic situation was dire: Russia controlled eastern Europe and had entrenched itself in the heart of Germany, which Churchill considered "the most melancholy [event] in history." Stalinist Russia was poised to dominate the continent in a way that neither Napoleonic France nor Hitlerian Germany had. U.S. and British troops, which checked Russia and Communism, were set to withdraw from the continent soon after the war. Perceiving Russia as an existential threat, Churchill privately wondered a few weeks after Yalta, "What will lie between the white snows of Russia and the white cliffs of Dover?" He wanted Anglo-American forces to contain Russian westward expansion (by grabbing key central European cities) and minimize Russian political consolidation of its eastern European domination. He even ordered the drafting of a contingency plan for defeated German troops to attack Russia, though after its rejection by the Chiefs of Staff he settled for a plan to defend the British Isles from Russian attack. Churchill might well have overestimated Russian strength and Stalin's preparedness to go to war, but he took no chances.[27]

Churchill thought it imperative to establish a lasting settlement before the balance of power changed—before Russia consolidated its control in the heart of Europe and became an even greater menace, and before the United States disentangled itself from Britain and Europe. Reaching some sort of settlement with Soviet Russia—whether through force or diplomacy—became his overarching objective during this era. He so desperately hoped for a settlement that, as he told the Commons after Yalta, he refused even to entertain the possibility that Russia's word could not be trusted. Very telling of his temperament was this undelivered portion of his speech: "There are some who fear it [the world] will tear itself to pieces and that an awful lapse in human history may occur. I do not believe it. There must be hope. The alternative is despair, which is madness." Perhaps the longing to hope derived from his own psychological wish not to succumb further to depression in the face of what he perceived to be an ominous global situation. And he might have imputed his own needs onto the people, whom he firmly believed could not psychologically endure a world riven between East and West without the West at least doing its utmost to prevent it. Churchill became overeager to find glimmers of hope, and at times he overreacted to friendly overtures by Stalin, though he never did anything rash or out of character, such as demonstrate weakness or offer unnecessary concessions. As the postwar Potsdam conference wore on in the summer of 1945, he gave up hope that Stalin wanted a settlement. Then came the electoral returns that forced him to leave and put Clement Attlee in charge. The conference ended with no Great Power settlement.[28]

Churchill saw the new global conflict in civilizational terms, as he often did. Less than a week after V-E Day, he wrote U.S. President Harry Truman of the "iron curtain" that had descended through Europe (repeating the phrase in public after V-J [Victory over Japan] Day and again more famously in 1946). In his mind, this curtain separated what he described in late 1947 as "Two Worlds" divided over ideology, ethics, religion, culture, and geography. This new conflict, in Churchill's mind, pitted liberal Christian civilization against the modern-day Mongols, who centuries earlier were primitive Asian heathens and vicious conquerors. The Russians were often compared to Mongols at the turn of the century, and Churchill remained disdainful of Russians, whom he never considered part of Western civilization. Beginning a few days after V-J

Day, when Stalin delivered a nationalist, unideological, and unthreatening speech, Churchill lambasted Soviet Russia in such harsh moral terms for the next half-dozen years.[29]

Churchill looked around him and saw a world "very ill." Unprecedented disorder and devastation followed Auschwitz, Dresden, and Hiroshima. Tens of millions of people were dispossessed and without shelter, while millions died of disease. So much was unsettled, and already new conflicts and wars raged around the globe. And in an interconnected, nuclearized world, Churchill warned in 1946, "war can find any nation." Also that year he said of Europe's plight, "Over wide areas a vast quivering mass of tormented, hungry, care-worn and bewildered human beings gape at the ruins of their cities and homes, and scan the dark horizons for the approach of some new peril, tyranny or terror. Among the victors there is a babel of jarring voices; among the vanquished the sullen silence of despair." The scale of murder both during and after the war had reached unprecedented levels. Churchill felt that the world had morally regressed; in 1944 he confided that people acted so revoltingly that they did not deserve to survive. More publicly, he noted in 1948 how people's sense of morality had become numbed; referring to four hundred thousand killed in Punjab, on the Indian subcontinent, he pointed out that it "is a horror at which, in any other but this stunned and bewildered age, the whole civilised world would have stood aghast." There was global "degeneration," and the world needed a "blessed convalescence." He now thought the period just after the First World War looked better by comparison.[30]

Contributing to Churchill's dismay was his keen recognition of the vast decline in British power and influence, which was hastened by the ascent of Clement Attlee, whom Churchill once described as a "decent, modest little man, who of course has a great deal to be modest about." Although Churchill now developed a more expansive conception of who was entitled to rule Britain, he remained adamant that a leader, from whatever background, be a grand statesman capable of directing global forces and without being consumed by them. Attlee was not that leader, and he went about tearing apart the glorious strategic and imperial inheritance that Churchill bequeathed. Heretically, Attlee described pre-1945 British history as the "mess of centuries." Churchill was still convinced of Anglo-Saxon superiority and the moral value of imperialism, though he recognized that its time had passed. He was baffled at other nations' indifference to British decline and their lack of gratitude for its (and his) heroic wartime efforts on behalf of civilization. The Americans imposed stiff terms for a postwar loan, and the Egyptians demanded millions of pounds from a Britain that expended a great deal of money (and manpower) defending them during the war. Britain was in worse shape than many of the countries it had saved. Churchill was haunted by British decline, privately bemoaning it many times over the postwar years. He relayed to his wife several times how it "depressed" him greatly. (Later, however, during his second premiership (1951–1955), he felt that he restored some modicum of British strength and respect.) However weak Britain was, Europe was weaker, and it mattered far less than in earlier eras. Still, Churchill remained Eurocentric, and he tried to dissuade undue U.S. involvement in Asia.[31]

Equally bewildering to Churchill was the persistent absence of what he called "a settled world order." There was no grand postwar conference as there had been in Paris, Vienna, or Utrecht (1714). There was only the fledgling United Nations, which lacked teeth and became meaningless in the face of global division. He regarded the muddled, drifting, dreadful state of East-West relations, later dubbed the Cold War, as a historical anomaly and corruption of the historical order of international relations. He related nostalgically that when he was young, "we lived through long years of dangerous tension between the great Powers in a very civilized fashion." He maintained that "this war of nerves and intimidation" and the breakdown in proper diplomatic discourse could not continue indefinitely. To restore peace and stability to the beleaguered earth, he sought to fashion a new world based on the Victorian era but allowing for new realities. He said as much at a dinner party in 1944: "The pomp and vanity must go; the old world will have had the honour of leading the way into the new." This meant a rejection not only of the ideology of Attlee and his naive cohorts but also of the equally rigid approach of the Americans, who were slow to realize the Soviet threat but then became so determined to oppose it that they forgot the purpose. Churchill insisted that the build-up of strength and Western unity to fight the Cold War was not an end unto itself but a means to negotiate a settlement with the Russians from a position of overwhelming strength at what he called a "parley at the summit" among the Big Three, what later became known as simply a "summit." He sought to restore the old world's regular, quiet, and courteous diplomatic contact among allies and antagonists away from the klieg lights and detached from the tumult of the masses. As he vividly and publicly opined in 1953, in a swipe at the Eisenhower administration's attitude, "Many people think that the best we can do is to get used to the cold war like eels are said to get used to skinning." In such a world, he confided, "life is not worth living." This was not just an old-world view but a recognition of the modern importance of public opinion; he thought people would sacrifice for the Cold War only if they knew every reasonable effort was made to end it.[32]

Churchill's approach toward a summit with the Soviet Union changed with the international situation. After several years of bafflement, he determined in 1947 that, based on his reading of internal Russian politics and ideology, which he considered the decisive factors in assessing Russian interests and intentions, Stalin and his colleagues had no interest in a settlement. He considered Russia threatening in the Berlin crisis of 1948–1949 and even thought an attack on Soviet Russia might be appropriate. He did publicly call for a Big Three parley in 1950–1951, but he had no hope that one would transpire and only advocated it to gain political advantage during two parliamentary elections (the second of which returned him and the Conservatives to power). But when Stalin died in 1953 and was replaced with a reformist leadership under Georgi Malenkov, Churchill determined that Soviet leaders had an incentive to reduce global tension and increase contact with the West, in order to buttress their own internal political position. He then dramatically renewed his call for a parley, though this time, with fewer negotiable issues left, he modestly lowered his sights. He now pursued a "piecemeal" approach that he hoped would lead to an "easement" (detente) in relations and the ultimate collapse of the Soviet regime. He wanted the West to recognize the Soviet Union's legitimate security needs, including a sphere of influence; sought more trade and contacts with it; and was prepared to accept a unified, neutral Germany, which he did not fear would drift eastward or attack westward. He was prepared to make it in the Soviet regime's political interest to accept this deal by threatening at least an intense propaganda battle behind the iron curtain, just as he previously was prepared to threaten it with conventional and perhaps nuclear attack. He also played rough with the United States by circumventing its leaders and going straight to the American people in his dramatic call for a parley. But he failed to bring even this summit about due to Soviet intransigence (the forces within the Politburo for a deal with the West weakened), American opposition, and his own physical infirmity.[33]

Fundamental to Churchill's quest for a settlement with Soviet Russia, whether through threats or talks, was an old-world belief in developing alliances to create a balance of power. The center of gravity in the West had shifted to the United States, and Churchill argued that British survival and global influence and leverage, along with the international order, depended upon close Anglo-American relations. It was initially very challenging to convince the United States to form an alliance; Churchill was careful to minimize unnecessary disputes, avoid whiffs of British imperialism, about which Americans were very wary, and emphasize the shared language and heritage of the two countries. He explained his perspective in 1951 when he opposed the Attlee government's unilateral recognition of China, a policy that offended the United States. "It is not a matter of whether there is a war with China or not," he declared, "but whether there is a rift between Britain and the United States or not. That is the thought that haunts me." He then emphasized, as always, the importance of prioritization in foreign affairs: "We should allow no minor matters—even if we feel keenly about them—to stand in the way of the fullest, closest intimacy, accord and association with the United States." Similarly, in 1954, he told his foreign secretary, Anthony Eden, who wanted the government to oppose American intervention in Guatemala on moral grounds, "A great principle only carries weight when it is associated with the movement of great forces." Churchill characteristically urged keeping perspective: "I'd never heard of this bloody place Guatemala until I was in my seventy-ninth year. . . . We ought not to allow Guatemala to jeopardize our relations with the United States, for on them the safety of the world might depend." When a senior Foreign Office official insisted that it was a moral issue, Churchill responded with a great snort. However, he frequently considered the United States clumsy and remained convinced, as he had been his whole life, that it needed to be properly guided by a wiser, more experienced, and steadier Britain (and Briton—himself), with an old-world approach toward international relations.[34]

Just as after the First World War, Churchill considered the restoration of Germany, preferably within the Western camp, integral to Western strength and leverage, as a means to balance Russia. Rebuilding and rearming Germany, even Western Germany, involved some moral if not emotional detachment, especially given the crimes of Nazi Germany, and a rejection of the sort of popular passions that dominated the second world. But Churchill remained focused on the present and future and avoided getting snagged in the past. As he said at a dinner party in New York in 1948, "You must obliterate all parts of the past which are not useful to the future."[35]

Still, Churchill looked to history for guidance. He explained in 1946, "Knowledge of the past is the only foundation we have from which to peer into and try to measure the future." An understanding of history—including when to dwell on it and when not to—was necessary to meet the significant challenges posed by science in the third world. The advent of the atomic bomb made him now more ambivalent about science, and he wondered whether "the human race have been gainers by the march of science beyond the steam engine." He was unsure whether humanity had progressed enough morally to manage this awesome power. Great leaders had to understand science and carefully shape policies based on that understanding, but they could not allow science to dominate them. Attlee, bereft of any respect for history, flunked this test and argued that the development of the atomic bomb—one of the major scientific advances of this world—rendered much of the postwar planning "out of date" and the bases in the Mediterranean and East Indies "obsolete," and generally insisted that the old power politics were anachronistic and the United Nations should be given supremacy over all strategic areas. Churchill considered this contempt of the past foolish. The development of nuclear weapons by the United States and then Soviet Russia influenced his perception of diplomatic leverage and at times enhanced his fears, but it did not fundamentally alter his thinking about foreign policy, including a settlement with Russia. Both before and after the bombing of Hiroshima his views about a settlement were driven by his perception of traditional strategic and internal Russian domestic realities. History was the foundation not only for a successful diplomatic and military strategy but also for an ideological one. History challenged scientific Communism at its philosophical core, and Churchill wanted to combat the spread of Communism in Europe by emphasizing the common heritage of Christianity and liberty shared by all European peoples. As he maintained in 1949, "Our inheritance of well-founded, slowly conceived codes of honour, morals and manners, the passionate convictions which so many hundreds of millions share together of the principles of freedom and justice, are far more precious to us than anything which scientific discoveries could bestow." He presciently predicted that this message would penetrate the minds and souls of those in Communist regimes who were subjected to ideological indoctrination through advanced technological means: "Tyrannies may restrain or regulate their worlds. The machinery of propaganda may pack their minds with falsehood and deny them truth for many generations of time. But the soul of man thus held in trance or frozen in a long night can be awakened by a spark coming from God knows where and in a moment the whole structure of lies and oppression is on trial for its life. Peoples in bondage need never despair."[36]

Churchill tried to create in this third world a new international order, modeled after the order of his youth. It was not a utopian vision but a flexible one that was directed by great leaders and that de-emphasized public passion and undue ideological and moralistic means. It involved reconciling with ex-Nazis as well as coexisting with Communists and Fascists, and it offered the hope of a more civil, peaceful, and stable age, leading ultimately to greater liberty and civilization. But neither Churchill nor Britain in their decline had the same Victorian leverage to shape the world. Faced with limited American imagination and Russian intransigence, the Cold War—that historical anomaly that Churchill so dearly sought to end—calcified and remained a fixture for another thirty years. This world, he lamented, was a far cry from the sublime world of his youth. But, he insisted, liberal civilization would ultimately maintain its march forward; time was on its side. As he declared in 1954, shortly before he resigned the premiership and active political life, "Nothing is final. Change is unceasing. . . . I am an optimist."[37]

In his three worlds Churchill focused on many vital matters that had little to do directly with Zionism and were, in his mind, far more important than it. And yet, over time, Zionism became integral to his worldview. It fed into his respect for history, admiration for his father and his father's friends and values, devotion to liberalism, fixation on British security, and obsession with the advancement of civilization. Zionism ultimately remained for him a sentimental cause, one that was subordinate to other more significant objectives and concerns, but it became part of his value system and of the worldview that he embraced.

CHAPTER TWO

"The Lord Deals with the Nations as the Nations Dealt with the Jews"

1874–1914

IN 1874, THE YEAR CHURCHILL WAS BORN, the Jews had been without a state of their own in Palestine for eighteen hundred years. They had lived a tenuous life as aliens in various countries, frequently persecuted, exiled, and killed. But now, Jews had achieved political emancipation in Britain and throughout much of Europe. Still, they experienced widespread, pernicious anti-Semitism, leading some Jews to consider a homeland in Palestine necessary for a normal life and even survival. This sentiment led to a movement in the late nineteenth century that became known as Zionism, a term that was coined in 1892 based on Mount Zion in Jerusalem and that came into common use with the 1897 First Zionist Congress.[1]

Churchill grew up during this period of Jewish and Zionist flux. During his formative years, he demonstrated an instinctive sympathy toward Jews and many of their causes. He imbibed and shared his father's personal comfort with Jews and devotion to Benjamin Disraeli's mystical portrayal of them as a great race that Providence protected, while also emulating his father's willingness to manipulate a Jewish cause for political ends. Churchill absorbed the views espoused by various English writers, theologians, and thinkers over the centuries, particularly those in the Victorian period, including Disraeli, who advocated the restoration of Jews to Zion. He was enamored by the romantic notion of Jewish restoration to their ancient homeland, ascribing to it immense historical importance. While Churchill was predisposed toward Jews and Zionism, the demands of his volatile nascent political career—which was his predominant immediate concern—served as the catalyst for his public declaration of views on Jews and their causes. He was sympathetic to appeals by important Jewish constituents and advocated a Jewish homeland in 1906, and he extolled the virtues of a Jewish political entity based in Jerusalem in 1908. The seeds of Churchill's interest and support of Zionism were planted at this time, but they did not take full root until many years later.

The British political philosopher Isaiah Berlin observed fifty years ago that the Jews had "enjoyed rather too much history and too little geography." The ancient Jews lived in and mostly governed the general area of modern Israel for about thirteen hundred years, from around 1200 BC until 135 AD. The Assyrians conquered the northern Jewish kingdom in 722 BC and deported thousands, then the Babylonians conquered the southern kingdom based in Jerusalem in 586 BC and exiled thousands more. The ancient Jews returned several decades later and restored their temple in Jerusalem and their sovereignty. Jewish rule ended when the Romans put down two revolts, the last one ending in 135 AD, by which time they had slaughtered hundreds of thousands of Jews and exiled, dispersed, and enslaved hundreds of thousands more. Rome changed the name of the area from Judaea to Syria Palaestina (hence the name Palestine). The Jewish community survived Byzantine rule and the Arab conquest of the seventh century to achieve a population of three hundred thousand in 1000 AD, until the European Christian Crusaders arrived and slaughtered most of them. The central Asian Tartars invaded and killed more Jews and devastated Jerusalem again. Jews began to trickle back into Palestine after the Ottomans' conquest in 1517, though increasingly harsh rule and a large earthquake in 1837 kept their numbers very small.[2]

Jews were also terrorized during the Diaspora, as they wandered from whichever country persecuted them to whichever country offered refuge. They were often demonized, depicted as having rejected and killed Christ by the Catholic Church and Protestant reformers, and portrayed as forces of destruction who caused mass plagues and individual deaths. They were expelled from England in the thirteenth century, France in the fourteenth century, Spain in the fifteenth century, and several Italian states in the sixteenth century. Jews did find refuge at times in various countries, but subsequent centuries witnessed huge massacres of Jews in eastern Europe. Political emancipation emerged in nineteenth-century Europe. Even assimilated Jews remained embarrassments and outcasts, however, insecure in their environs, lacking peace of mind, overanxious to fit in yet feeling shame for doing so, and generally clinging to a frail existence. The Jews remained an anomalous mixture of race, religion, and nation, and unlike other communities they had yet to reach statehood through some sort of national and cultural revival.[3]

The Jews arrived in England during the Norman Conquest of 1066, if not during the earlier Roman period, and endured the first recorded ritual murder charge in medieval Europe in 1144, the cruel York massacre in 1190, expulsion in 1290, a slow return under Puritan rule in the seventeenth century, and progress and virtual political emancipation by 1871—later than in other western European countries. Ironically, it was under Queen Victoria (1837–1901), who did not like Jews, that much of this progress occurred.[4]

Yet, in the Victorian era (in which Winston Churchill was born and which instilled in him so many values), Jews, no matter how assimilated or influential, were perceived as Jews first, and often not even considered to be English, no matter how long they or their families had resided in England. Jews were widely perceived as suspect, sinister, clever, rich, powerful, and—in the words of historian Elie Kedourie—"an agent of reaction or revolution, pursuing hidden aims of his own, divine or demonic as the case may be." There was considerable cultural and literary emphasis in nineteenth-century England on Jewish conversion to Christianity. Others, however, such as George Eliot, born Mary Ann Evans, a prominent writer and novelist, rejected that emphasis and instead profoundly sympathized with the Jews and promoted Jewish national identity. In Victorian England, deep and pervasive anti-Semitism coexisted with greater Jewish political rights and national self-identification as a leading state in tolerance. Victoria's son, Edward VII (1901–1910), during whose reign Churchill professionally arose, was known to be friendly with many wealthy English Jews. Indeed, when Edward ascended the throne, Churchill, then twenty-six, wrote to his mother, "Will it entirely revolutionise his way of life? Will he sell his horses and scatter his Jews or will Reuben Sassoon [Edward's wealthy Jewish friend] be enshrined among the crown jewels and other regalia?" The closeness to power of some wealthy Jews provoked anxiety among some and gave rise to conspiracy-mongering.[5]

The Victorian period's contradictions are manifested by the phenomenon of Benjamin Disraeli, a man whose views had a strong influence on Churchill. Disraeli was born into a bourgeois Jewish family in 1804, but because of a dispute with the synagogue his father had him baptized shortly before his bar mitzvah was to have taken place. From then on, Disraeli was a member of the Church of England. He entered Parliament in 1837, three decades before Jews were allowed to so. Yet in a society fixated on race, lineage, nationhood, status, and hierarchy, he was always considered a Jew, with the sincerity of his conversion sometimes questioned. Indeed, he likely thought himself a Jew despite his sincere devotion toward, and superior knowledge of, Christianity. He was often referred to as a Jew years later, even by Jews. Disraeli's Jewish heritage was thrown at him in ugly ways throughout his life, and his Christian political opponents, including the high-minded, moralistic Liberal Party leader William Gladstone, often ascribed Jewish (and not necessarily English) motives to some of his foreign policies, such as his pro-(Muslim) Ottoman and anti-(Christian) Russian policy. Many European Christians at the time lumped Jews and Muslims together as allied "Orientals," and indeed many Jews felt a kinship with Muslims and the last remaining great Muslim power, the Ottoman Empire, although that feeling of brotherhood was apparently not reciprocated.[6]

Unlike many other accomplished English Jews, Disraeli, also known as Dizzy, who became formally known as the Earl of Beaconsfield in 1876, embraced his Jewish origins and argued that the Jews were one of the world's great races, one of its aristocratic lines, and Tories by nature (supportive of property, religion, and monarchy), thus suggesting his own qualifications to head a party of aristocrats. Disraeli wrote in his novels that "all is race" and that Jews were an "unmixed race" that was the "aristocracy of Nature." This racial purity, Disraeli contended, allowed Jews to endure centuries of persecution and defy kings, emperors, and "Christian Inquisitors." (His reference to the Spanish Inquisition was poignant: he claimed descent from Spanish Jews, and the English at the time often contrasted their own alleged tolerance with that of Catholic Spain.) He considered this persecution unfair, because Christians were greatly indebted to Jews for founding Christianity—"the completion, not the change, of Judaism"—and for their extensive contribution to arts, philosophy, and politics. He detected mysterious Jewish influence everywhere, which was a common argument of those seeking Jewish emancipation and also, ironically, of many anti-Semites. Disraeli's argument, which he obsessively repeated, flew in the face of centuries of Christian anti-Semitism, which blamed Jews for rejecting and killing Jesus, an act for which Disraeli contended Christians should be grateful because it fulfilled God's will. His argument also defied and countered racial anti-Semitism that was well established in the increasingly secular early nineteenth century (the term "anti-Semitism" was coined in 1862). He contended that it was not only race that secured Jewish survival against all odds but divine guidance. He argued in Parliament in 1854 in defense of Jewish emancipation that God treated the nations as the nations themselves treated the Jews: "There is no country in which the Hebrew race has been persecuted which has not suffered, whose energies have not been withered, whose political power has not decayed, and where there have not been evident proofs that the Divine favour has been withdrawn from the land. The instances of Spain, and Portugal, and Italy are obvious." (This somewhat echoed a few notable mid-seventeenth-century English works that suggested English civil strife was due to its poor treatment of the Jews.) He concluded his speech by predicting that the Jews would get their emancipation since "so far as the Jews are concerned, I have faith in that Almighty Being who has never deserted them." Whereas many Christians throughout history saw Jewish dispersal and suffering as divine punishment for their rejection of Jesus, Disraeli saw Jewish survival as proof of their racial superiority and divine protection. Not only was England obligated to the Jews for their contribution to religion and the arts, but it was in the English self-interest to make good on that obligation. While perhaps self-serving, particularly in a religious society that venerated the past and the Bible, this argument jibed with Disraeli's romanticism and his belief in mysterious, irrational forces. Isaiah Berlin described the spectacle of the flamboyant, Jewish-born Disraeli heading the landed, aristocratic, Anglican Conservative Party, which he also helped found, as "one of the oddest and most fantastic phenomena of the entire nineteenth century."[7]

One Victorian Gentile British politician, and a Conservative no less, who seemed genuinely to like Jews at this time, and who was devoted to Disraeli in particular, was Randolph Churchill, Winston's father. Randolph grew up on the magnificent Blenheim estate in a great aristocratic family, the sort that often disliked Jews. Randolph's father opposed Jewish admission into Parliament, and Randolph's nephew, the ninth Duke of Marlborough, expressed crude anti-Semitic opinions. However, Randolph grew up in the company of many Jews, albeit very wealthy ones, and counted many of them as friends, including the Hirsches, (Lionel) Cohens, Wertheimers, and Bischoffsheims. As a boy, Randolph also befriended the Rothschilds, the very wealthy and prominent Jewish banking family, leading one reverend to report anxiously to Randolph's mother of "the allegiance he struck up with the Jews." He must have eaten a number of meals at Jewish homes since in 1873 he wrote his fiancée, Jenny Jerome, about staying at a wealthy Jew's estate, "Like all Jews' places it is a wonderful house for eating, every kind of food. I must confess I rather like it."

Randolph remained close with his childhood schoolmate Nathaniel, or Natty, Rothschild, who eventually became Lord Rothschild. After Disraeli's death, Randolph was one of two politicians who were closest to the Rothschilds, and he was especially seen as too close to Natty after becoming chancellor of the exchequer. However, his relations with the Rothschilds were not always smooth. He annoyed Alfred Rothschild by rashly resigning as chancellor after only a few months in late 1886. He then infuriated Natty by questioning the safety of investment in South African mining syndicates, when Natty had an interest in those syndicates and had paid for Randolph's investigative trip to South Africa. Randolph died at a young age owing £65,000 to Natty, most of which he borrowed after resigning from office. Still, Natty demonstrated his loyalty to Randolph after his death by taking an interest in Winston.[8]

Despite his affection for Jews, particularly wealthy Jewish financiers, Randolph's public declarations about both were unpredictable—a trait Winston inherited and evinced early in his career. Randolph publicly upheld Jewish causes and those of his Jewish friends. After he became a member of Parliament (MP), Randolph advanced the cause of some prominent Jews in the Conservative Party, ostentatiously resigned from St. Stephen's Club after it blackballed a Jew, urged the government in 1881 to explore (accurate) reports of a Russian pogrom against Jews, and spoke out in 1883 on behalf of Jewish political emancipation. In 1882, when nationalist Egyptian riots triggered the establishment of a British military force south of the Suez Canal to ensure the canal's security, he accused Liberal Prime Minister Gladstone of succumbing to political cowardice by sending a member of the Gentile Baring banking family to inspect Egyptian finances when he could have sent a Rothschild, whose financial house had an equal interest in Egyptian stability and British occupation. Yet, in 1883, Randolph invoked the specter of Jewish power to support a blistering partisan attack on the Liberal government's policy in Egypt. To convey sympathy for Arabi Pasha's revolt against the Gladstone-supported Khedive Tewfik regime in Egypt, Randolph labeled the conflict a bondholder's war and lambasted the "gang of Jewish userers in London and Paris seducing Ismail Pasha into their net" while Gladstone forced the wretched Egyptians "back into the toils of their Jewish taskmasters." (This statement, which was quoted in a newspaper at the time, was omitted from Randolph's collected speeches that he helped compile and was not mentioned in Winston's biography of his father.) The anti-Semitic charge apparently was Randolph's own contribution to the debate, since a book he cited that detailed British crimes against Egypt made no reference to the moneylenders being Jewish. Still, in the following year, he spoke movingly at a Jewish charity at the behest of Natty Rothschild.[9]

In addition to the Jewish financial titans, Randolph admired Disraeli. Randolph's mother's family was close to Disraeli, who visited Blenheim many times and took interest in Randolph's career. After Disraeli's death in 1881, Randolph consciously tried to claim his political mantle by embracing "Tory Democracy," founding the Primrose League (named after Disraeli's alleged favorite flower), and writing an article entitled "Elijah's Mantle." Winston, in his biography of his father, reaffirmed the Randolph-Disraeli political connection, although in reality it may not have been so strong.[10]

Randolph also publicly embraced Disraeli's depiction of the Jews. In early 1883, Randolph delivered a speech in the House of Commons asserting that admission to Parliament should be based on merit and not tolerance, and emphasizing that the Jews, who had been admitted only twenty-five years before, were so deserving. He borrowed heavily from Disraeli's ideas to make his argument. Randolph emphasized the similarities between Judaism and Christianity, such as their sharing the same God and Ten Commandments. He also extolled the Jewish character: "There was nothing in the Jewish creed or character which could in the slightest degree detract from any pledge which they might give, or unfit them for public confidence, or deprive them of general respect." Reflecting the culture's evangelist spirit, he hoped the Jews would see the light and accept the doctrine of the Trinity, and he looked forward to the time when "the scattered exiles from Palestine should be exalted far above all the other Gentile races of the earth." He perceived divine intervention in world affairs: "Surely the horrors of the French Revolution should give some idea of the effect on the masses of the State recognition of Atheism." This last line echoed a passage from Disraeli's 1851 political biography, *Lord George Bentinck,* on the very same subject: "Since the great revolt of the Celts against the first and second testaments at the close of the last century, France has been alternatively in a state of collapse or convulsion." Randolph, like Disraeli, espoused the belief that God specifically intervened concerning the Jews, making it in Britain's interest to treat them well. He referred to Disraeli's 1854 speech—in which Disraeli argued on behalf of Christian obligation to the Jews—as "one of the most powerful speeches he [Disraeli] ever made to the House of Commons." He also quoted Disraeli's statement that the Jews had outlasted various ancient states and pointedly cited Disraeli's dramatic conclusion: "I have faith in that Almighty Being who had never deserted them." Randolph championed the Jews in another speech in 1884 at a dinner on behalf of the Jews' Free School. He took issue with historic anti-Semitic canards by declaring about the Jews, "They are national and patriotic in everything but one thing; they are cosmopolitan in the greatest and noblest of all virtues, they are cosmopolitan in the munificence of their charities." British Chief Rabbi Hermann Adler cited these words and this speech eleven years later when Randolph died. Another prominent rabbi did the same and added that Randolph was devoid of religious prejudice.[11]

None of this was lost on Churchill, who at a young age carefully read every speech his father delivered and consciously appropriated many of his father's views. Among Randolph's attitudes that Churchill embraced was a devotion to Disraeli and his portrayal of Jews. Early on Churchill recognized the greatness of Disraeli. He recalled that when he was six years old and Disraeli died, "all the people I saw went about with very sad faces" over the loss of "as they said, a great and splendid Statesman, who loved our country." Sixty-six years later, Churchill still internalized his father's devotion to Disraeli. In the imaginary conversation with his father, Churchill visualized his father asking about Disraeli and asserting, "I always believed in Dizzy, that old Jew."[12]

Churchill also internalized his father's personal comfort level with Jews, which was more Edwardian than Victorian. At a young age, Churchill took his father's side when criticized by relatives for having too many Jewish friends, which likely led him, when he got older, to seek out those friends in order to feel closer to his father. Churchill came to count many of Randolph's wealthy Jewish friends as his own. He later wrote fondly of his father taking him "to important political parties at Lord Rothschild's house at Tring, where most of the leaders and a selection of the rising men of the Conservative Party were often assembled." Churchill toured Italy with Lionel Rothschild; often indulged the hospitality of Baron de Hirsch's adopted son, Baron Maurice de Forest (who never acknowledged his Jewish roots), whom he also helped politically; and was very close with Ernest Cassel, a phenomenally wealthy and philanthropic German-born Jew who was never fully accepted in British society even though he married a Roman Catholic (he also secretly converted to her faith). Cassel managed some of Churchill's money (as well as some of his mother's), hosted him at his house and Swiss villa, invited him to Germany for the kaiser's birthday, and gave him various gifts. Their relationship was well known, and one spurious journal in 1920 wrongly accused the two of conspiring to make a lot of money unlawfully during the First World War. Churchill wrote Cassel's granddaughter upon his death that Cassel was a "great man" who "was a valued friend of my father's and I have taken up that friendship and have held it all my grown-up life."[13]

Like Disraeli, Randolph, and most late Victorians, Churchill generally viewed Jews in racial terms. A Jew in Britain, Russia, or anywhere else was primarily defined by his Jewish blood and not his nationality. Churchill suggested that Disraeli was a Jew first and an Englishman second, portraying him as somewhat apart from English society. Years after Disraeli's death, Churchill wrote rather accurately that Disraeli "never became wholly assimilated to English ways of life, and preserved to his death the detachment which had led him as a young man to make his own analysis of English society." Yet, like his father and Disraeli and unlike many late Victorians, Churchill did not consider the Jews inferior Christ-killers but ranked them high in the hierarchy of races. He saw them in a grand historic and religious context, regarding them as a great ancient race whose heritage he respected and to which Christians were indebted. He recognized that the Jews originated monotheism and other fundamental morals and laws pivotal to Western thought. Later in his life he wrote, "No two cities have counted more with mankind than Athens and Jerusalem. Their messages in religion, philosophy, and art have been the main guiding lights of modern faith and culture."[14]

The Jews were a unique race, Churchill believed, that played a special role in world history. Like his father and Disraeli, Churchill discerned divine involvement in Jewish destiny, and it was appropriate and beneficial to treat them right both individually and communally. He made this clear on the occasion of a 1905 Manchester meeting protesting Russian anti-Semitic pogroms. Churchill strongly condemned this persecution (just as his father had in 1881) and pointedly warned Russia by citing an adage that he attributed to Disraeli: "The Lord deals with the nations as the nations dealt with the Jews." Although the quote captured what Disraeli conveyed in his 1854 parliamentary speech, as well as several of his literary works, Disraeli never put it exactly that way; the quote was apparently transmitted orally by Gladstone.[15] Churchill nonetheless took to heart this powerful precept and repeated it several times over the course of his life. It became one of the defining motifs of his approach to Jews and Zionism. For the rest of his life he believed he always adhered to Disraeli's dictum. It is a testimony to Churchill's sympathy for the Jews, and to his intellectual debt to his father, that he unquestionably sought guidance from someone born Jewish about how to treat Jews.

Churchill's early natural sympathy for the Jews—on both an individual and communal level—is evident from some of the private remarks he made about them to his mother. On one of the defining and divisive Jewish issues of the late nineteenth century, the Alfred Dreyfus case, in which the French Jewish captain was wrongly accused and convicted of treason, Churchill stood squarely with the Jews. In 1898, after the French military divulged that some of the evidence against Dreyfus was forged, Churchill, then twenty-three years old, wrote to his mother, referring to one of the writers investigating the case: "Bravo Zola! I am delighted to witness the complete debacle of that monstrous conspiracy." Churchill also chafed at anti-Semitic remarks, even if they were not especially malevolent. In 1906, at the age of thirty-one, he politely reprimanded his mother, whom he adored, for her derisive description of a Jew, Count de Bendern. He wrote to her, "When you say that Tuty was 'a bastard Jew' you *do* reveal a prejudice of a vy [very] strong character, for he could not help falling in either of those categories.... I know that I often say stupid and unwarrantable things that are not nice about people that I do not like."[16] Had his mother made a derogatory remark about an Indian or Arab, for instance, it is unlikely she would have received such a rebuke.

On top of his sincere concern for the Jews, Churchill faced a political incentive early in his career to say and do things publicly that were favorable to them. In 1904, a few years after he was elected to Parliament, he left the Conservative Party and became a prospective Liberal candidate and then, from 1906 to 1908, a representative of North-West Manchester, a middle-class commercial area that had voted Conservative since 1885. In this competitive race, an estimated 6.5–8.7 percent of the voters were Jewish, many of whom had fled anti-Semitic Russian pogroms. Perhaps another inducement for Churchill to court the Jews was that the Liberal Party professed compassion for religious refugees, and Jews in particular (though it too contained its share of anti-Semites, and many radical Liberals blamed the Boer War at the turn of the century on Jewish capitalists).[17]

As Churchill focused on winning and maintaining a parliamentary seat representing North-West Manchester as a Liberal, he publicly expressed his admiration for Jews and Judaism on several occasions. He consistently claimed that Jews, and their religious observance, posed no risk of dual loyalty. In 1906 at a Jewish school in Manchester he said, "The better Jews you become the better opportunity you will have to take your share in the service of the British Empire." That same day he told a Jewish men's club, "No Jew who is not a good Jew can ever really be a good Englishman." He attributed Jewish observance to the survival of the Jewish nation: "It is an inspiration and a source of great strength."

These remarks were evidently very flattering and inclusive to an audience likely made up heavily of immigrants, and stood out amid all the xenophobic and anti-Semitic sentiment in the country sparked by an influx of Jewish immigrants. Still, his comments also indicated a man somewhat conflicted about Jews, and thus someone who reflected the times. His words had an air of detached condescension, suggesting somewhat patronizingly that British Jews were an alien population living under British sufferance who must mind their ways. He did not even distinguish between immigrant Jews and those born in England. This attitude was common in Britain, though often expressed in far harsher terms.[18]

Churchill did not always offer clear-cut, unwavering public support for Jews and their causes. Sometimes, even when he argued on behalf of Jewish causes, he used language with anti-Semitic overtones, especially by today's standards. Occasionally his early political considerations clashed with his sympathy for the Jews, and when they did he made clear that Jews and their causes, including Zionism, ultimately were of subordinate importance to him, particularly during the tumultuous first quarter-century of his political career. Sometimes that meant he appeased Jews and their causes and sometimes it meant he manipulated them, a trait he shared with his father. Churchill took a similar approach to many other non-Jewish secondary issues as well.

Illustrative of the often-conflicting crosscurrents in Churchill's approach toward the Jews at this time was his response to controversial alien legislation, which was the most important Anglo-Jewish issue at the time. Pogroms in Russia beginning in 1881–1882 (with even more brutal attacks in 1903–1906) sparked the migration of 150,000 Jews from eastern Europe to Britain through 1914, causing the Anglo-Jewish population to quadruple from 60,000 to 250,000. The ruling Conservative Party sponsored legislation to curb this inflow. Churchill strongly opposed the legislation, which endeared him to the Jews but led him to be attacked in the press and elsewhere. He stated in the House of Commons in 1904, according to an account, that "he did not wish to close the door on the unfortunate Hebrews coming from the Continent" and certainly did not want to limit those en route to the United States. He also wrote a letter, published in the *Manchester Guardian* and *Jewish Chronicle,* to his strong supporter Nathan Laski, a Jewish leader in Manchester, declaring that this legislation violated the British tradition of "freedom and hospitality" and was politically inspired, intended to "gratify a small but noisy section" of Conservative supporters and "to purchase a little popularity in the constituencies by dealing harshly with a number of unfortunate aliens who have no votes." He argued that the legislation was anti-Semitic, xenophobic, and protectionist in intent. Many Conservatives certainly were the latter two, while Churchill shared none of these qualities. (Indeed, Conservative Prime Minister Arthur Balfour, who later championed Zionism, declared in 1905 that it may be disadvantageous to Britain's "civilisation" to have so many people, "however patriotic, able, and industrious," who "by their own action remained a people apart, and . . . only inter-married among themselves." This was not the first time Balfour complained about Jewish separateness, and he did not always seem comfortable in the presence of Jews at this time.). Churchill vigorously opposed much of the language of the Conservatives' proposed alien legislation in parliamentary committee, and the *Jewish Chronicle* credited Churchill with being largely responsible for scuttling the bill. Laski reflected Jewish opinion when he wrote to Churchill, "You have won the gratitude of the whole Jewish Community not alone of Manchester, but of the entire country." Still, Churchill's charge against the Conservatives of political maneuvering seemed itself part of his own scheme of political machinations. On the very day that his letter to Laski was published, he left the Conservative Party for the Liberals, intending to run for office in the heavily Jewish North-West Manchester.[19]

In 1904, Churchill heightened the irony of his assault on the alien legislation by proceeding to employ a rather anti-Semitic line of argument to attack a bill that was directed against Jews. Amid a sharp exchange with a Conservative MP in the Commons, he accused the Conservative government of withdrawing the bill in order to appease wealthy Jewish supporters, alluding to Lord Rothschild and others. (This prompted Harry Samuel, another Conservative MP, to exclaim, "Monstrous! Absolutely monstrous!" Samuel, who supported the restrictive alien legislation "as an Englishman . . . and a Jew," seemed more upset here as a politician than a Jew.) More deliberately, Churchill wrote in a letter later that year, part of which appeared in a newspaper, that it was "perfectly well known that the opposition of wealthy and influential Jews in their own [Conservative] party has always prevented, and probably always will prevent, their passing such a measure into law," one he noted was "vicious in principle." He then acknowledged that it was "an honourable fact in thorough accordance with the traditions of the Jewish people" for men such as Rothschild to try to gain asylum for Jews escaping persecution, and "perfectly legitimate" for the government to "yield to these gentlemen if they have a good case and are influential supporters of that government." After thus raising the specter of powerful Jewish influence on the government, somewhat as his father had in 1883 also at the Rothschilds' expense, Churchill hypocritically castigated the government for sponsoring doomed anti-Semitic legislation in order "to excite party cheers."[20]

However much Churchill's attacks were politically inspired, the thrust of his criticism of the alien legislation was genuine and fit into his worldview. There was no cant in his long speech in late 1905 vehemently protesting anti-Semitic pogroms, despite it occurring amid a political campaign in North-West Manchester. In a packed hall in Manchester, he condemned "the appalling massacres and detestable atrocities," "barbarities," and "unparalleled acts of brutality," for which "Russia has thereby placed herself outside the pale of humanity." To help Jewish refugees from these pogroms, he promised to moderate provisions of the Aliens Act of 1905, which the Conservative government had passed, "so that this country in the enlightened twentieth century should still remain, as ever, a refuge for those bowed down with affliction and in sore distress." A couple months earlier he called the act "a sham" that "contains absurdities which would make a deaf and blind mute roar with laughter." He later called the act "ridiculous and idiotic." After his election in 1906, he promised to work to reduce naturalization fees and introduced a Jewish delegation requesting support for such a policy to Liberal Prime Minister Henry Campbell-Bannerman. The Jews frequently reminded him of his promise, while he represented Manchester and after, and he once replied with some exasperation to a leading Jewish constituent, Dr. Joseph Dulberg, that he was doing his best but that he was "not omnipotent."[21] Churchill soon would also address Jewish yearning for a homeland, a world issue with which he would grapple for the next fifty years.

Although on the intellectual and geographic periphery of world Jewish life, England had long been receptive to the prospect of a revival of the historic connection between Jews and the Holy Land. Since at least the sixteenth century, various English writers, clergymen, thinkers, and politicians had thought about Jewish restoration to the Holy Land and their conversion to Christianity as part of a millennial vision. This intensified in the nineteenth century with the rise of millennial evangelism. One leading evangelical, Edward Ashley, the Earl of Shaftesbury, conceived of Britain as God's chosen instrument to restore Jews to the Holy Land and trigger the Second Coming. Meanwhile, there was growing Great Power involvement in the Middle East. This helped prompt British Foreign Secretary Lord Palmerston (Henry John Temple) to encourage the Ottoman sultan to allow Jews to return to Palestine, and he established a British consulate in Jerusalem in 1839. Shortly after, Colonel Charles Henry Churchill, Randolph's cousin who served in the Middle East, declared his support for Jewish restoration of sovereignty over Palestine: "May the hour of Israel's liberation draw nigh! . . . May the Jewish nation regain its rank and position among the nations of the world." It cannot be determined if Winston was aware of these statements. Jewish restoration also captured Disraeli's romantic imagination. Disraeli was much affected by his trip to Jerusalem in 1831, and he wrote his sister about his view of the holy city from the Mount of Olives: "I was thunderstuck. I saw before me apparently a gorgeous city." Two years later he wrote the novel *The Wondrous Tale of Alroy*, in which the protagonist, humiliated by the annual Jewish tribute to the caliph in Baghdad, dreams of leading the Jews back to Jerusalem. The protagonist says, "You ask me what I wish: my answer is, a national existence. . . . You ask me what I wish: my answer is, the Land of Promise." In practice, Disraeli did nothing to further this dream, though he thought it possible in 1851 that the cash-poor Ottomans would be receptive to the Rothschilds financing Jewish colonists in Palestine. Disraeli heavily influenced George Eliot, who promoted restoration of the Jewish nation-state not for religious or evangelical reasons but for the benefit of the Jews and the world. Her novel *Daniel Deronda* was highly sympathetic to Jews and admiring of their religion. In Palestine, she wrote, the Jews would have an "organic centre, a heart and brain to watch and guide and execute." Further, she wrote, "the world will gain as Israel gains. For there will be a community in the van of the East which carries the culture and the sympathies of every great nation in its bosom." However, the vast majority of those who thought about Jewish restoration at all considered the idea utterly absurd.[22]

Whether or not absurdly romantic, a surge of romantic nationalism across Europe in the mid-nineteenth century and a rise of racial anti-Semitism led some Jews—who for centuries prayed for messianic redemption and a return to Jerusalem—to begin thinking seriously about taking matters into their own hands and fulfilling their dreams of restoration. One such visionary was Moses Hess, a German Jew, who practically invented Zionism several decades before the word came into use. He was an unlikely Jewish nationalist, having rejected his religious upbringing and the continued need for Jewish existence, married a Catholic, fathered German Communism, converted Friedrich Engels to Hegelian Communism, and preached Communism to Karl Marx, whom he came to idolize and with whom he collaborated on a radical publication despite opposing Marx's violent "scientific" views. Hess was pained by the Damascus blood libel in 1840—when Jews were falsely accused of killing a monk and his Muslim servant to use their blood for Passover, leading to the arrest, torture, attack, and murder of a number of Jews—as were many Jews and Gentiles across the globe. But he repressed his feelings. It was only because of his ardent support for Giuseppe Mazzini's Italian nationalist movement that Hess revived his concern for his fellow Jews two decades later and wrote *Rome and Jerusalem* (1862), in which he advocated the eventual founding of a Jewish state in Palestine. Amid a period of emancipation and assimilation, Hess claimed that Germans hated Jews for racial, not religious, reasons and that Jews would remain despised until they respected their own "great national memories." He argued that a Jewish state, based on Jewish tradition (which he considered fundamentally socialist), would uplift the Jews from their parasitic position and heal their "ills," enrich the barren land of Palestine, bring European civilization to backward Asia, and raise up Europe by serving to destroy "the weed of materialism together with its roots." Hess correctly predicted that Jewish restoration would be facilitated by European powers and Jewish philanthropists, and that it would be built upon the immigration of more religiously traditional eastern European Jews. His book sold poorly, engendered great hostility—especially from German Jews active in the Jewish Reform movement—and was forgotten for the next few decades. Yet, virtually all of Hess's ideas were echoed by Zionist leaders forty years later and beyond, and embraced by Winston Churchill, even though neither he nor most early Zionists ever heard of Hess.[23]

It was not Hess's book but the government-inspired, widely supported pogroms of 1881–1882 in Russia, where half of the world's Jewish population lived, that concentrated Jewish minds on creating Zionist organizations and settling in Palestine, for reasons of socialism, spiritual renewal, and survival. By 1890, tens of thousands of Russian Jews had settled in Palestine, though many times that began to move to the United States. Although the Russian intelligentsia may have turned its back on them, the Jews of Russia subscribed to many of the same nineteenth-century values as the liberal intellectual elite who opposed tsarism: humanism, social democracy, scientific advancement, knowledge, equality, life on the land, and a spiritual bond with the soil. (Some Jews also shared the more violent beliefs of the Social Revolutionary Party.) All this was mixed with a respect for ancient religious tradition. Living a religious life in the Pale of Settlement—an area where the Russian tsar confined the Jews—amid overwhelming Russian anti-Semitic oppression, the Russian Jews developed their own institutions and a sense of nationalism that eluded the less secure, more ambivalent, and more outwardly tempted western European Jews.[24] Churchill grasped many of the secular and religious values that animated these Russian Zionists, and it spurred him to support them more ardently.

More than anyone else, it was Theodor Herzl, a distinctly assimilated Central European Jew, who astonishingly made Zionism a viable political movement and put it on the map of international politics. Herzl, born in Budapest in the Hapsburg Empire in 1860 to an affluent, secular Jewish banking family, became a worldly, well-educated, well-known journalist and writer with an aristocratic bearing. He came to focus on the Jewish predicament as a correspondent in Paris in the 1890s, and he once considered the solution to be a public mass conversion by Jews to Christianity. The Dreyfus affair, and the anti-Semitism it reflected and spawned in allegedly liberal France, galvanized him into fervently believing by 1895 in the dire need for a Jewish state for the sake of Jewish survival, just as the Damascus blood libel of 1840 did for Hess or the pogroms of the 1880s did for Russian Jews. In 1896, he published his trailblazing pamphlet, *Der Judenstaat* (commonly translated as *The*

Jewish State), which declared that the Jews required their own state—preferably in Palestine—to avoid extinction through assimilation or, more immediately, relentless persecution. Like Hess, of whom he became aware, Herzl anxiously insisted that the Gentiles "will not leave us in peace" and that anti-Semitism "increases day by day and hour by hour." In emancipated nations Gentiles resented both Jewish participation in revolutionary movements and their financial success after centuries of being considered "the most contemptible among the poverty-stricken." A state would be created, he predicted, because it was in the interest of the world's nations, especially those "scourged by Anti-Semitism." Herzl declared that the European nations should be heartened by his vision of an advanced liberal "model" state in Palestine that would "form a portion of a rampart of Europe against Asia, an outpost of civilization." He also argued that the nations should welcome the prospect of an abatement of anti-Semitism, which remained a destabilizing force for many regimes, as well as the employment gain to Gentiles from Jews departing for Palestine. He did not worry, as many Jews did, that Zionism would provoke a revocation of Jewish emancipation in the West since that act would drive Jews "into the ranks of revolutionary parties" and lead to an economic crisis. In effect, Herzl wielded anti-Semitism and anti-Semitic canards as clubs against anti-Semites and in favor of Zionism. He appealed not to Gentile hearts but to Gentile minds on the basis that their self-interest demanded support of a Jewish state. Unlike some eastern European Zionist thinkers (of whom he was mostly ignorant anyway), the cosmopolitan Herzl articulated his message in a way the broad European Gentile elite could understand. He wrote and acted not as some Jewish *shnorr*, or beggar, but as a Western visionary calling people to action.[25]

Herzl went about making his dream a reality. He organized a Zionist Congress in 1897 in Basle, Switzerland, with delegates (including some women) from fifteen countries, including the United States but not Britain, and including delegates from Palestine, representing the fifty thousand Jews there. The Zionist delegates agreed that "the aim of Zionism is to create for the Jewish people a home in Palestine secured by public law." They avoided the term "Jewish state," despite it being the title of Herzl's pamphlet, so as not to provoke the Ottomans or other Gentiles. The delegates also set up the organizational machinery of the movement. The conference was a huge success and commanded great press attention. Herzl later wrote in his diary, "In Basle I founded the Jewish State. If I said this out loud today I would be greeted by universal laughter. In five years perhaps, and certainly in fifty years, everyone will perceive it." Fifty-one years later the State of Israel was founded. Following the congress, Herzl conducted a whirlwind of diplomatic activity to secure the sponsorship of one or more Great Powers, appealing to their cold self-interest. He offered Russia and Germany a Jewish protectorate in Palestine that would siphon off undesirable Jews, including revolutionaries, in those countries, and he offered Jewish money to the debt-ridden Ottomans in return for a charter (which resembled proposals made by Disraeli and Palmerston). However, Herzl could not persuade many Jewish barons, such as the Rothschilds and Montefiores, to dedicate the funds, and the Ottoman option collapsed. At one point Lord Rothschild wrote Herzl that "the dream of Palestine is a myth.... Let one and all of us beware of the impossible." In a letter to a friend in 1901 about these unhelpful Jewish tycoons, Herzl wrote, "Fifty years from now people will spit on the graves of these men."[26]

Herzl then turned his attention to the British, whose prime minister was Conservative Arthur Balfour. Herzl, with eastern European pogroms in mind, told British Colonial Secretary Joseph Chamberlain, "Now I have time to negotiate, but my people has not." The anti-Semitic Chamberlain, with the Eastern European Jewish migration to Britain in mind, preferred that a Jewish refuge be somewhere else but England. Chamberlain suggested to Herzl in 1903 that it be in "Uganda," which was really British East Africa (later known as Kenya). Although this marked the first formal British recognition of the Zionists as a negotiating partner, it led to a deep chasm in the Zionist movement. By early 1904 Herzl backed off the proposal, but he remained convinced, correctly, that the British wanted to be a partner. However, on July 3, 1904, Herzl, forty-four years old and exhausted, died.[27]

Churchill apparently had no contact with or real knowledge of Herzl, whom he never cited in public or private conversations, writings, or speeches. In the month before Herzl died, the British Parliament debated Chamberlain's East African scheme for the Jews. David Lloyd George, a Liberal who had drawn up the initial draft charter for this plan, championed the Jews' position. Only few spoke in the debate, and Churchill was not one of them. Churchill first encountered and addressed Jewish interest in some sort of a homeland in late 1904, six months after he became a Liberal and decided to run in North-West Manchester. He wrote to a correspondent about the East African scheme, "The proposal to form a colony of refugees in some part of the British Empire not less healthy but less crowded than these islands, deserves fair and patient consideration." He was just getting his feet wet in the issue. He confronted the issue more directly in December 1905, when he was appointed under-secretary for the colonies in a new Liberal government, and when he also was campaigning to represent North-West Manchester.[28]

Although the Seventh Zionist Congress in 1905 rejected Territorialism, the movement in favor of Jewish settlement in British East Africa until Palestine became available, half of the British delegation supported it. Israel Zangwill, a well known Anglo-Jewish novelist, formed the Jewish Territorial Organization (ITO) in support of the movement and was backed by many prominent Anglo-Jews, such as Lord Rothschild. Many prominent Jews in North-West Manchester also supported Territorialism; they formed an ITO branch in October 1905 and by December claimed a membership of five hundred. The Territorialists considered their movement a practical response to the urgent need for a Jewish refuge in light of continued Russian persecution of Jews, and they believed it would attract the support of British imperialists seeking development of imperial lands by "one of the most potent white peoples on earth," as Zangwill put it. In Churchill's case, the movement also appealed to his political needs. In late 1905, Dr. Joseph Dulberg, the secretary of the Manchester ITO branch, promised Churchill volunteers and votes in return for supporting Territorialism; one week later, shortly before the election, Churchill obliged. Churchill wrote Dulberg about the obstacles to such a plan, including "the differences of opinion among the Jews themselves, . . . the doubtful suitability of the territories in question, . . . the rapidly extending settlements by British colonists in and about the area, & . . . the large issues of general state policy which the scheme affects." But he hoped these barriers would be "surmounted." He recognized that an important virtue of Territorialism was that it involved the development and civilization of imperial land: "From an Imperial point of view, it is in the varied excellence of its parts, that there is most surely to be founded the wealth, the happiness & the higher unity of the whole." However, he contended that Territorialism was no mere colonization scheme but contained a unique humanitarian benefit: "I recognise the supreme attraction to a scattered & persecuted people of a safe & settled home under the flag of tolerance & freedom. Such a plan contains a soul, & enlists in its support energies, enthusiasms, & a driving power which no scheme of individual colonization can ever command." (Churchill's father, Randolph, also described the Jews as a "scattered" people in an 1883 speech.) This was a strong statement that reflected his familiarity with the Jews' history and unique desperate plight, and that went beyond what was politically necessary even by Churchill's rhetorical standards. In fact, Zangwill seized on the term "soul" in a published letter to Dulberg, suggesting that Churchill captured Territorialism better than the Territorialists. Churchill demonstrated the same understanding and sympathy in his condemnation of Russian pogroms in late 1905 and his persistent opposition in 1904–1905 to the alien legislation. He clearly understood the humanitarian justification for a Jewish sanctuary, and explained to Dulberg that he sought not only humanitarian relief for the Jews and imperial development but some sort of Jewish territorial entity. He pointedly noted that he disagreed with Rothschild's focus on settling Jews in Canada and Argentina, and considered a Jewish homeland a "noble vision" that he would "do what I can to preserve it & fulfil."[29] This was a warm endorsement of a Jewish political entity, and it was Churchill's first on record. He had something larger in mind for the Jews, something still unspecified, that went beyond current demands of empire and refuge.

Churchill won over his prospective Territorialist constituents. Already, a fortnight before the election, Zangwill wrote Dulberg that he had no doubt about Churchill's sympathies. Churchill's "ringing words" at the antipogrom protest meeting had dispelled any such fears and demonstrated his "sympathy with all that is suffering and downtrodden." Jewish national aspirations had begun to capture Churchill's imagination, even if the idea did not yet become rooted in his being and he was spurred on by political purposes. Then again, as Zangwill himself hinted, few British Jews at the time supported a Jewish homeland of any kind.[30]

After the election Churchill's ardor for Territorialism subsided. In mid-1906, he was asked in Parliament about the Territorialist scheme in light of massacres of Jews in Russia. He responded curtly, "The [Territorialist] Society are in communication with the Secretary of State on the subject, but no practical scheme has yet been submitted." He thereby minimized his own involvement with the issue and placed the onus on his boss, Colonial Secretary Lord Elgin (Victor Alexander Bruce). A fortnight later, Zangwill wrote Churchill and appealed to Churchill's imperialist and humanitarian instincts, insisting that Territorialists, unlike Zionists, had provided a practical scheme to establish "an attractive centre." Churchill replied that the Colonial Office had rejected the scheme for Jewish settlement in East Africa, and pointed out the "serious" problems facing the proposal, including the increasing occupation of the land, the "apprehension at the violence of the local opposition which will certainly be offered by the existing settlers and by the whole official world," and the "undoubted division among the Jews themselves," which had undermined political support. Churchill again put the onus on Elgin, who he claimed required the commitment of significant money from wealthy Jews to the project. Churchill concluded reassuringly, "Believe me, your letter touches responsive chords."[31]

Churchill never much considered Territorialism again, and he remained skeptical—as many Liberals were—of any white settlement in East Africa. After visiting the region in the autumn of 1907, he wrote in his travelogue, published in 1908, that East Africa could never be "a white man's country" where the white race permanently settled, such as in Canada or Britain. The altitude, sun, insects, and other factors weighed against it. It was "a planter's land, where the labours of the native population may be organised and directed by superior intelligence and external capital." Despite impressive leadership and prominent support, Territorialism sunk into irrelevancy within a decade.[32]

Aware of divisions in the Jewish community in North-West Manchester, Churchill also pursued the political support of Zionists there and demonstrated far more enthusiasm for their movement. Unquestionably, the cause of returning Jews to their ancient biblical homeland of Zion captured his fertile imagination far more than the imperialist-humanist endeavor of settling Jews in some random African territory. In December 1905, at a gathering protesting fresh Russian pogroms, he was impressed listening to the brilliant and magnetic Russian-born chemist Chaim Weizmann, who had just immigrated to Manchester in 1904, address the crowd in Yiddish. Afterward, Churchill, at a dinner party in his honor hosted by the Jewish leader Nathan Laski, sought a private meeting to enlist Weizmann's support for the upcoming election in January 1906. Weizmann at first hesitated but then agreed to a meeting one day before the poll. The meeting was uneventful, except that Churchill promised that Elgin would be willing to meet a Zionist delegation.[33] Weizmann and Churchill, who were born the same year, eventually forged a friendship that lasted until Weizmann's death almost fifty years later.

Churchill had more success enlisting the support of another notable Zionist leader, Rabbi Dr. Moses Gaster, though that experience was less pleasant. A combative, arrogant, highly respected scholar who was expelled from his anti-Semitic native Romania, Gaster became the *Haham* (spiritual leader) of the Sephardic community (comprising Jews of Mediterranean and Central Asian descent) in England. Three days after Churchill's appointment as colonial under-secretary, Gaster wrote him criticizing the Territorialist scheme and arguing instead that the "heart of the Jew turns to Palestine and no other country in the world will be able to supplant that country." Churchill already seemed to grasp this concept. Gaster bluntly made clear that Jews would vote for those who supported their interests, referring not only to Zionism but also to alien legislation. Dulberg delivered a similarly blunt message in 1907 regarding the alien legislation and naturalization fees.[34]

Two months later, and one month after Churchill's successful election, Gaster wrote him claiming to have campaigned hard for various Liberal candidates (given Conservative support for the alien legislation), including Churchill. The combative Gaster went on to complain that Liberal Prime Minister Henry Campbell-Bannerman had issued a reception invitation to Chief Rabbi Dr. Hermann Adler, an anti-Zionist who Gaster bitterly contended "styles himself 'The Chief Rabbi'" and even campaigned for Conservative candidates. While he minimized the matter as "too paltry," Gaster claimed that his friends thought otherwise and asked Churchill to clarify matters with the prime minister in order to soothe his friends. Gaster added not too subtly, "You know my people have long memories." No wonder more than forty years later Churchill wrote about the Jews, "No matter how forlorn their circumstances or how grave the peril to their country, they are always divided into many parties, with many leaders who fight among themselves with desperate vigour. It has been well said that wherever there are three Jews it will be found that there are two Prime Ministers and one leader of the Opposition."[35]

Despite such heavy-handedness, Churchill remained in close touch with Gaster, and the rabbi offered Churchill plenty of opportunities to demonstrate his loyalty to the Jews. Most notably, Gaster invited Churchill to speak at the annual conference of the English Zionist Federation (founded in 1899), which was held in Manchester on February 2, 1908, and chaired by Gaster. Churchill declined to appear but was willing to have a statement read at the conference, leading Gaster, with characteristic bluntness, to reply that he was "exceedingly" disappointed and believed Churchill's attendance would have been "useful *all* round," alluding to the possible political benefit. However, Gaster was pleased with Churchill's draft statement, describing it as a "beautiful letter" with only some minor changes necessary. In his draft, Churchill dramatically recognized for the first time Jewish nationhood and the historical significance of a Jewish homeland. "I am in full sympathy with the historical traditional aspirations of the Jews," he wrote. "The restoration to them of a centre of true racial and political integrity would be a tremendous event in the history of the world." This was a powerful statement that went beyond anything he expressed to the Territorialists. His use of the word "sympathy" was meaningful; in eighteenth- and nineteenth-century literature the term suggested a keen sentiment-based identification with something or somebody that could be the basis for a deep moral commitment. His use of the word "centre" was also significant in that it suggested something less than a state. Churchill might have recalled Zangwill's use of "centre" in a 1906 letter, or perhaps he borrowed the word from *Daniel Deronda*, George Eliot's novel influenced by Churchill's icon Disraeli. Churchill's initial draft focused on the land and expressed support for Jewish "territorial" aspirations, which Gaster wanted changed to "historical" to emphasize the longstanding Jewish desire to return to their ancient homeland. Unwilling to alienate any Jewish constituents who advocated a Jewish homeland, Churchill avoided opining whether Palestine should be the immediate (Zionist) or ultimate (Territorialist) goal: "Whether the wide effort of the Jewish race should be concentrated upon Palestine to the exclusion of all other temporary solutions, or whether in the meanwhile some other outlet of relief and place of unification should be provided for the bitter need of those who suffer day to day, are questions on which I could scarcely presume to express any opinion."[36]

Then, in words that might have been added after he received Gaster's comments, Churchill indicated that he leaned toward supporting the Zionist objective of directing efforts to reclaim Palestine. He explained that his recent trip to East Africa confronted him with the many "difficulties" that lay before a Territorialist scheme, and that "this fact necessarily increases my sympathy with your efforts to reach what must be your ultimate goal." He concluded with a characteristic flourish: "Jerusalem must be the only ultimate goal. *When* it will be achieved it is vain to prophesy: but that it *will* some day be achieved is one of the few certainties of the future." The Jewish return to Zion clearly captured his romantic imagination, and it is surprising, despite the obvious political benefit, that he expressed such confidence in the realization of such a far-fetched idea. He also again saw imperial advantage to such a political entity and reiterated the historical value: "The establishment of a strong, free Jewish state astride of the bridge between Europe and Africa, flanking the land roads to the East, would not be only an immense advantage to the British Empire but a notable step towards the harmonious disposition of the world among its peoples." Churchill reconsidered and deleted these concluding remarks—which apparently were inspired by a conversation he held with Gaster—from his final draft, believing they went too far. As Edward Marsh, Churchill's secretary, explained in a note to Gaster, Churchill had to refrain from such expressions "until he returns to a position of greater freedom and less responsibility." As colonial under-secretary, Churchill could not take such a bold stand that was not endorsed by the government. It was not until 1917 that the British government officially supported a Jewish homeland, and even then it refrained from using the term "state." Gaster may have inadvertently helped convince Churchill to delete the conclusion by noting the political significance of the statement. Churchill's speech was reprinted in the major Anglo-Jewish and pro-Zionist publication, the *Jewish Chronicle*, but was noted prominently in other publications.[37]

It was the first of many instances in which Churchill tempered Zionist enthusiasm for political reasons. Still, the statement marked the height of Churchill's Zionism up to that point. It was a watershed event, one that put him on record as supporting Zionist goals, though he did not commit to do anything for the movement beyond his statement. Not only did he see some imperial and humanitarian advantage to Zionism, but he ascribed for the first time a momentous historical achievement to the reestablishment of a Jewish political entity in Palestine. He expressed the same sentiment after the State of Israel was founded. Still, his statements at this early stage of his career were triggered by his political interest in ingratiating himself with a significant constituency, and while Zionism resonated with him—certainly more than Territorialism—and fit into values he shared, he did not yet embrace it strongly. Zionism remained an abstract cause that he did not internalize or make integral to him. It was that way for most English Jews as well.

In April 1908, Campbell-Bannerman fell ill, Herbert Asquith became prime minister, and Churchill became president of the Board of Trade. The law required Churchill to resign his seat in the House of Commons and stand in a by-election. This time, he faced a Jewish electorate that was upset with the Liberal government for implementing the Aliens Act of 1905 and for concluding an entente with the despised, anti-Semitic tsarist Russian government in 1907. His challenge was compounded by a local socialist organization that put up a candidate and wooed Jews in English and Yiddish. Churchill met with a politically diverse group of Jews shortly before the election and expressed his own support for several of their causes, including weakening the Aliens Act, reducing naturalization fees, supporting Jewish schools, and permitting Jewish businesses to open on Sunday. (The government wanted to restrict Sunday commerce, while Orthodox Jews, who do not work on their Saturday Sabbath, wanted to continue doing business on Sunday.) The self-selected Jewish deputation, which included Laski and Dulberg, declared that they were satisfied with Churchill's comments and urged voters to support him. Then, on the eve of the election, Churchill made a strong public pitch for Jewish support in a couple of speeches. In one address, he drew upon the Jewish-born Conservative leader Disraeli: "Mr. Disraeli said a long time ago that all the great things of the world are done by the small peoples. Those who are Jews here to-day have behind them an immense tradition and a great world-wide reputation to sustain." In another campaign event, he painted his Conservative opponent, William Joyson-Hicks, as an anti-Semite, which apparently was accurate. He asserted matter-of-factly, "I do not think that in his anti-Semitic views Mr. Joynson-Hicks really represents the Conservative party, which, after all, once had as its great leader Mr. Disraeli, whose memory all honoured." Churchill then stated that Joynson-Hicks had put himself "altogether adrift from the interests and aspirations of the Jewish community" by claiming that the "Jews have no right to their own sectional and communal life." (Indeed, Joynson-Hicks said, "Those who put their Jewish and foreign nationality before their English nationality, let them vote for Mr. Churchill.") Churchill then argued in favor of special-interest politics, a practice that he had at least questioned if not opposed during the debate over alien legislation and that he emphatically denounced on many other occasions, particularly after the First World War. He welcomed to loud cheers Jewish input on "certain matters which affect their interests vitally" and proclaimed it a "foolish and an unwise thing for any candidate for Parliamentary suffrage to go about stigmatising that process as improper and illicit and describing any just concession made to a person of the Jewish faith as pandering to the Jews." (Churchill seemingly took a more favorable attitude toward Joynson-Hicks after serving in the Cabinet with him in the 1920s.) Laski, Dulberg, Gaster, and others publicly championed Churchill. The *Jewish Chronicle* reported on the eve of the election that Jews in the district were "obsessed" with the election, speaking about it everywhere, and strongly supported Churchill. (Some of the more recent immigrants called him "Tsetsill," others "Chochill.") He was aware of their fervor. At a speech to Jewish working men, who stood and cheered and waved their hats for several minutes, Churchill remarked in an aside, "The enthusiasm is magnificent." No wonder he told his then-fiancée, Clementine, "I have little fear of their [Jews] not voting solidly for me." The Jews apparently did vote solidly for him, though possibly not as overwhelmingly as in 1906 (reports differ). Still, he lost the election.[38]

Shortly thereafter, Churchill was elected in Dundee, but he said that he would "always cherish the warmest feelings of friendship and respect" extended to him by the Jewish community in North-West Manchester. The *Jewish Chronicle,* whose owner was a Liberal and a Zionist, reported that Jews were keenly disappointed by Churchill's loss; it was a "regret of a more personal and intimate kind," and they "firmly believed in the sincerity of his friendship." Dulberg, who twice in the prior year had asked Churchill for a political appointment, expressed his great disappointment and offered to help in any way, predicting that Churchill had a "brilliant" career ahead of him. Gaster sent his congratulations on the Dundee victory, and Churchill replied, "You may always count on me as a friend to your people." Six months after his defeat, Churchill returned to Manchester to open a new wing of the Victoria Jewish Hospital. It was his first public appearance since his marriage to Clementine. The Churchills received a rapturous welcome. The *Daily Mirror* reported that at the station they "were well-nigh mobbed by a delighted crowd, and had to struggle through a dense mass of enthusiasts to reach their hotel. At the hospital, the crowd gave Churchill an exuberant "three cheers" as he rose to speak. Soon after, Jewish ebullience for him began to wane.[39]

For the next fourteen years, Churchill represented Dundee, a Scottish industrial and predominantly working-class city with few Jewish voters or interests. And yet, by virtue of his experience in Manchester, his ties there, and his Cabinet portfolios, he still was forced to grapple with Jewish and Jewish-related issues, where his record became decidedly more mixed. He never managed to fulfill all the promises he had made to the Jews in the 1908 election, despite their repeated reminders, including by his early backer Laski. By the time he left as home secretary in 1911, no receiving houses had been established for aliens, the naturalization fee had not been cut, and no legislation for Sunday commerce had been enacted. He made some improvements on alien conditions and invited Jewish participation in some of the policy-making, and he tried to settle the Sabbath issue for commerce but did not succeed. Part of this was because he was only one minister, and Jewish discontent with the Liberal government grew, especially after Campbell-Bannerman resigned as prime minister (and died shortly thereafter) and was replaced by the less sympathetic Herbert Asquith. In the autumn of 1910, the *Jewish Chronicle* criticized Churchill for not fulfilling his 1908 campaign promises and considered his response "thoroughly unsatisfactory."[40]

Although Churchill might not have pushed Jewish issues to their satisfaction, he was careful not to hurt the Jews and even protected them.

In 1910, during Churchill's tenure as home secretary, an incident occurred known as the Sidney Street saga, in which some burglars shot three policemen, then were found to be immigrant anarchists who read Yiddish and Russian literature. This provoked a wave of anti-Semitic sentiment, including the portrayal of Jewish immigrants as un-English, and calls to clamp down on alien criminals, though no new laws resulted. Churchill drafted a bill in early 1911 that, he acknowledged in a memo to the Cabinet, contained "naughty principles" of differentiating the alien from the British citizen and allowing in certain circumstances the deportation of aliens before they had committed an offense. However, he never mentioned the Jewish angle in any context, and when writing about Sidney Street years later he referred to the criminals only as Russian anarchists and never mentioned their Jewishness. He was equally sensitive in the summer of 1911, when anti-Jewish riots erupted in Wales. He acted immediately to dispatch forces to guard the Jews and their property. Of course, this also fit into his law-and-order interest as home secretary. When Churchill ended his tenure at the Home Office in 1911 in order to move to the Admiralty, the *Jewish Chronicle* expressed in an editorial its gratitude for his consideration of Jewish interests.[41]

Churchill demonstrated less sensitivity to Jewish sensibilities in his handling of Shell Oil in 1914. Amid his attempt as first lord of the Admiralty in 1911 to run more of the navy on petroleum instead of coal, the Anglo-Persian Oil Company (APOC), which later became British Petroleum, convinced the government to take a 51 percent stake in the company and save it from a possible takeover by Royal Dutch Shell, a company whose largest shareholder, Marcus Samuel, was a British Jew, although the company was 60 percent owned by the Dutch and run by a Dutch Gentile, Henri Deterding. Oil prices at this time were skyrocketing, and there was much Anglo-American suspicion about nefarious practices by the big oil companies. Many Britons feared that in the event of a clash with Germany, Shell would side with Germany and stop selling oil to the Royal Navy, just as Germany sided with the Dutch settlers in the Boer War. Despite these misgivings, the Admiralty signed a major contract with Shell in late 1913. Earlier that year, Churchill stated to the Cabinet that prices were rising mostly for fundamental market reasons and that he did not buy into the hyped fear about Shell, yet when he made his case to Parliament in 1914 for the control of APOC he emphasized that fear and played the Jewish card. He attacked Shell and made a point of mentioning its leading Jewish figures: Marcus Samuel and "his spokesman, Dr. Dvorkovitz." He noted that Shell was willing to serve the Admiralty and British Navy "at a price," conjuring up alleged Jewish devotion to money. Targeting Samuel and the more obviously Jewish Dvorkovitz as bogeymen, even though the company was run by a non-Jew, was part of an easy and successful populist pitch by Churchill to ensure passage of the proposal in the Commons. Watson Rutherford, MP, accused Churchill in the debate of "Jew-baiting" and of blaming the oil price rise on "evilly-disposed gentlemen of the Hebraic persuasion." No other MP, including Marcus Samuel's brother, Samuel Samuel, repeated this charge.[42] (Marcus Samuel was honored after the First World War as Lord Bearsted and then Viscount.) Although Churchill's comments were more subtle here than during the alien debate, this episode demonstrated again his willingness to manipulate a Jewish issue, as he would other subordinate matters, for political gain.

During the first thirty-nine years of his life, Churchill's contact with Jews and their issues was unusually frequent and intimate for a British politician, especially one from the aristocratic class. He was naturally disposed to the Jews and their causes, and his initial experience with them was on balance positive. His favorable contact with the likes of Laski and Zangwill outweighed the more negative experiences with the pushy and difficult sorts like Gaster and Dulberg. Largely due to his respect and admiration for the Jewish race, and to his general openness (to certain races), he was not put off by personal contacts with all the recent Jewish immigrants who came from eastern Europe and were not immediately English in appearance, speech, or attitude. What might have put him off more were the continued demands—however legitimate—that Manchester Jews placed on him after he left the constituency he had represented a mere two years. He deemed Jewish issues of ultimate subordinate importance, except when it affected his political career.

However disposed he might have been to Jews, Churchill's personal contact with them triggered his interest in Zionism and educated him about it, but did not necessarily lead him to support it more. The Jews he knew best and felt closest to, such as Cassel and Rothschild and other enormously wealthy Jews, were generally anti-Zionist and sometimes intermarried with Gentiles. Also, their own success might have made him feel more sanguine about Jewish prospects. He recognized that Jews fleeing Russian pogroms needed a refuge, ideally in their own homeland, but he never conveyed a great urgency about it, whether in public or in private official discussions. His comments on that score were eloquent and meaningful but a bit detached. Many Jews were finding refuge in England, the United States, and elsewhere, and, unlike the many xenophobic and anti-Semitic Britons, he did not feel a dire need to be rid of these immigrants. He felt no urgency, therefore, for either England's sake or the Jews', to establish a Jewish homeland, whether in Palestine or elsewhere. He saw some imperial value for a Jewish homeland in Palestine, but he was not sufficiently vexed by the Jewish plight to urge any initiative with the Ottomans who controlled the land, and Gaster did not suggest he do so. That he was not overly enthused about Territorialism further demonstrated the little imperial value he attributed to a Jewish homeland somewhere. What most captured his imagination about Zionism at this juncture—when he was forced to confront it for political reasons—was the romantic notion of Jewish restoration to their ancient homeland. Here he was evidently influenced by Disraeli, Eliot, and other Victorian writers and leaders drawn to the cause for mystical, religious, strategic, and humanitarian reasons. Such restoration offered no real value to Britain, but it appealed to him for sentimental reasons and would signify a great historical achievement. Still, it remained an abstract idea for him, as it was for most Jews, and he did not feel deep, concrete attachment to it.

Such was Churchill's mixed but largely positive treatment of the Jews and Zionism heading into the First World War, an event that dramatically transformed the Zionist movement, as well as Britain's and Churchill's involvement in the Middle East.

CHAPTER THREE

"Zionism versus Bolshevism"

1914–1921

WHEN THE FIRST WORLD WAR broke out in August 1914, there was nothing to suggest that the fighting would much affect Zionism. The English Zionist Federation had been absorbed for years in internal squabbling, had made no progress in its efforts, and had not been the focal point of Anglo-Jewish attention.[1] However, official discussions, memos, and agreements emerged in response to events in Palestine, Turkey, Germany, Russia, and the United States that had a great impact on Zionism. On November 2, 1917, the British government issued the Balfour Declaration, which committed Britain to the establishment of a Jewish homeland in Palestine. The war had an unforeseen impact on Churchill's career as well. The outbreak of the war found Churchill as first lord of the Admiralty, one of the most prominent wartime positions. But within a year, he fell from grace, held an insignificant Cabinet post, left the government altogether, fought on the western front, returned to Britain, and remained out of power until becoming minister of munitions in the summer of 1917. He did not rejoin the War Cabinet, the principal decision-making body, until after the war, in January 1919, when he became secretary of state for war and air. Churchill paid no attention to Zionist interests during the war, ignored the Balfour Declaration, and disparaged British commitments to the Zionists after the war. Larger issues—war, politics, strategy, economy, institutional interests—

worked against Zionism in his mind, to the extent that he even considered the cause. His strategic interests, particularly his fixation with the Bolshevik threat, led him to be more wary of Jews and their international causes. His expressions of sympathy for Zionism in North-West Manchester seemed part of a bygone era that was shattered by the unprecedented horror and tumult of the war.

In November 1914, Liberal Prime Minister Herbert Asquith declared war on the Ottoman Turkish Empire, then announced that the British government sought to dissolve the empire. This pronouncement generated official discussions of how to divvy up its parts after the war. Herbert Samuel, a Liberal member of the government who hailed from an eminent Anglo-Jewish family, recognized an opportunity for the Zionist cause and championed it within the government. Samuel, known as intelligent, measured, and not especially romantic, had never met Chaim Weizmann nor evinced much interest in Zionism despite his friendship with Rabbi Gaster. But he proposed a Jewish state or entity in the autumn of 1914 to Foreign Secretary Edward Grey, whom Samuel claimed was supportive. Then in memos in January and March of 1915 Samuel insisted to his Cabinet colleagues that a Jewish "centre" in Palestine under Britain's protectorate would benefit the Jews, the British Empire, and the world. Due to Arab numerical superiority in Palestine, and expected local and regional Arab hostility, he suggested that a Jewish state might take a century to form but that it could eventually contain three to four million Jews. In the spirit of Moses Hess and Theodor Herzl, Samuel maintained that the Jews were a great race and that a Jewish center would transform the Jewish character and house "a brilliant civilisation," "enable England to fulfill in yet another sphere her historic part of the civiliser of the backward countries," add "lustre" to Britain given the "widespread and deep-rooted" Protestant sympathy for Jewish restoration to the Holy Land, offer imperial benefits, and engender the gratitude of Jews throughout the world for Britain, especially in the United States. Many of Samuel's ideas, expressed especially elegantly and enthusiastically in the January memo, were echoed in later comments by Churchill and other British officials. Yet, the memos did not persuade the anti-Semitic Asquith, who derisively considered them an updated version of Disraeli's 1847 philo-Semitic novel *Tancred,* and remained dubious that "the scattered Jews would in time swarm back from all the quarters of the globe, and in due course obtain Home Rule." Edwin Montagu, Samuel's first cousin, who like many established English Jews was terrified that Zionism undermined his position in society, penned a memo vehemently opposing a Jewish home in Palestine. Vehement anti-Zionism was not the only passion Montagu and Asquith shared; they both also loved Venetia Stanley, who soon married Montagu.[2]

These conflicting memos were part of a general discussion among senior government officials of postwar aims in the Middle East, on the eve of a naval attack at the Dardanelles to capture Constantinople (later called Istanbul) in order to relieve Ottoman pressure on tsarist Russia (Britain's ally) in the Caucasus and provide Russia with access to the sea. The debate mirrored and reacted to postwar demands by Britain's allies; Russia demanded Turkey and the Straits, and France demanded Syria, including its subprovinces that formed what was called Palestine. In March 1915, Churchill argued to the War Council against discussion of postwar distribution of Ottoman territories until the postwar peace conference. But at a Council meeting the following week, David Lloyd George advocated grabbing Palestine "owing to the prestige it would give us," while Field Marshal Horatio Herbert Kitchener, secretary of state for war, who had been to Palestine years earlier, saw no value in it. According to the meeting minutes, which can be selective and distorting, Churchill said nothing about Palestine but asserted that Britain should acquire something if Russia got Constantinople and France got Syria. A few days later, Asquith wrote in a letter to Venetia Stanley that only Samuel and Lloyd George supported a Jewish center in Palestine, the latter supposedly because he did not want the Christian holy places to be controlled by "Agnostic Atheistic France." Evidently, Churchill said nothing to make Asquith or others believe that Palestine should belong to the Jews. At another War Council meeting the following week, Asquith raised the issue of Palestine and noted French interest in it and Syria, among other areas, and Russian opposition to French possession of the "Christian Holy Places." Churchill asserted about the Ottomans, "Surely . . . we did not intend to leave this inefficient and out-of-date nation, which had long misruled one of the most fertile countries [in] the world, still in possession!" This belief that backwardness undermined a nation's claim to rule would later become a reason for his support of Zionism, though not here. He wanted a "clean sweep" made of the Ottoman Empire, like some of his Liberal colleagues, but wanted discussion postponed, particularly about the divisive issue of the Holy Land: "In this question of the partition of Turkey in Asia the main difficulty was likely to be between England and France, leaving out the question of the Christian Holy Places, in which Russia also was concerned." The War Council agreed the discussion was premature but supported creation of a Muslim entity that included Arabia. The minutes bear no record of Churchill mentioning the Jews, their claim to the land or "Holy Places," or the romantic hope in Jewish restoration to their ancient homeland. He thought that the Holy Land and surrounding territories should be divvied up by the main Allied powers. Of course, Lloyd George, despite his greater prior involvement in the movement for a Jewish homeland, did not say anything either (according to the minutes) and only demonstrated interest in Palestine for the prestige value and as a way to keep it out of French hands.[3]

On the same day as this meeting, Churchill made his most extensive direct comment (at least, of which there is a record) on Palestine since 1908. On a Foreign Office memo that discussed French demands for Palestine, Churchill scribbled to Foreign Secretary Edward Grey, "Palestine might be given to Christian, liberal & now noble Belgium." Two months earlier he had expressed sympathy for Belgium because of its occupation by Germany and thought it should be compensated; he now decided that its compensation should be Palestine. He saw Palestine in the context of the Great Power conflict, and thought that Belgium would be a good, safe compromise, nonthreatening to the regional and religious interests of Russia, France, or Britain. And yet Belgian control would still mean that a Christian country, and no longer the Muslim Ottomans, would control sites that were religiously dear to the Allied Great Powers. There was no consideration of any Jewish attachment to Palestine, religious or nationalist. Churchill's missive was a cursory, unexamined thought. Undoubtedly, he was too consumed with the Dardanelles expedition, which had begun only the day before, to focus on Palestine or any postwar issue at that moment, and he was in any case opposed to such considerations. Almost one week later Asquith recorded Churchill's views about the postwar division of Middle Eastern spoils

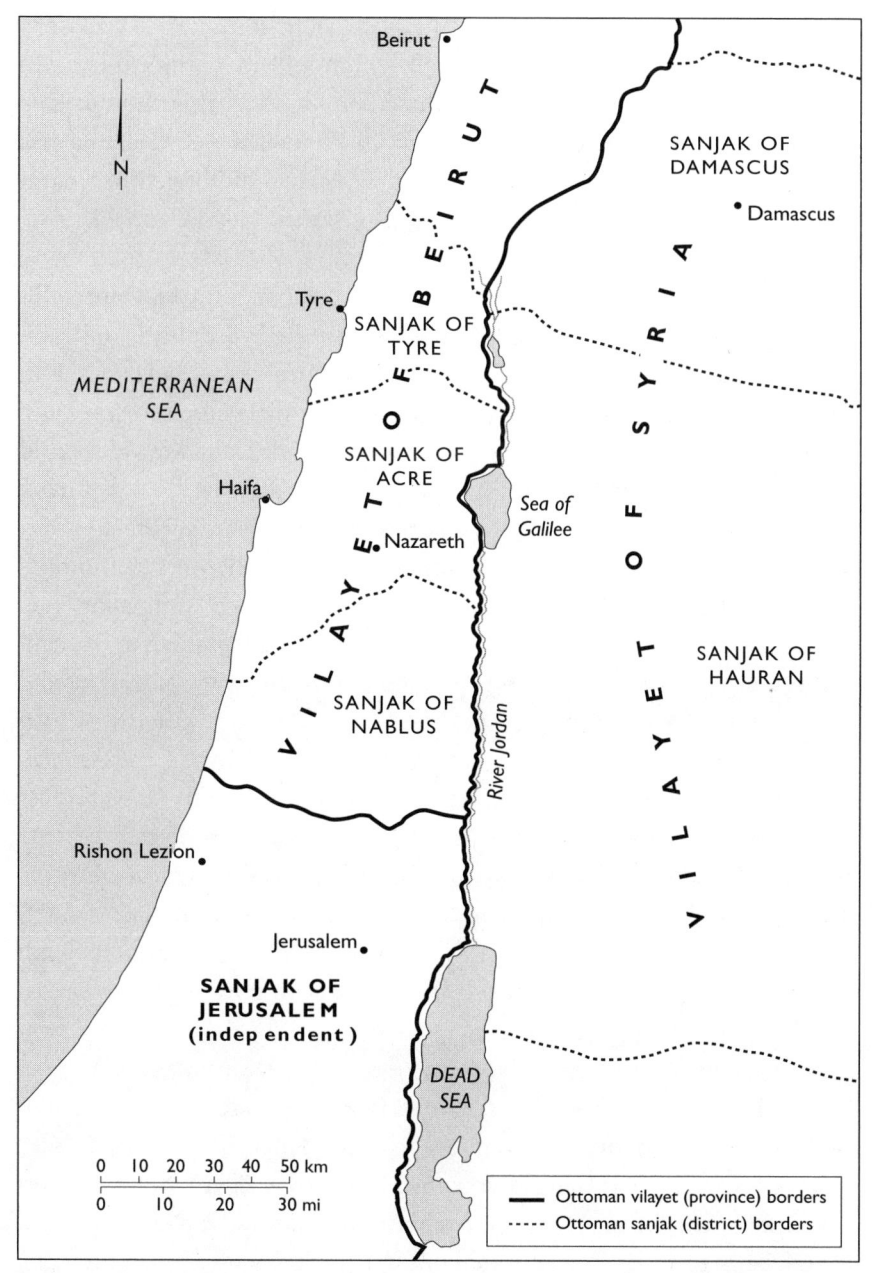

MAP 1 Holy Land and area, as divided by Ottoman administration on eve of First World War. Drawn by Bill Nelson.

without referring to Palestine, while accurately recording Kitchener's opinion on the subject. Coincidentally, Churchill met with Weizmann around this time to ask for Weizmann's help in alleviating the shortage of acetone, which was important for naval explosives, yet Palestine was not discussed. Neither person brought up Zionism, although Weizmann raised the issue with the longstanding pro-Zionist Lloyd George in 1915 or 1916.[4]

One would never know from reading or listening to Churchill's comments about the postwar Middle East that he had publicly and exuberantly extolled the virtues of Zionism only seven years before back in North-West Manchester. His mind was clearly focused elsewhere, and Zionism had not yet taken hold of him in a significant way. His mind drifted further away from Palestine after May 1915, when he was forced to resign from the Admiralty in disgrace over the Dardanelles debacle. Churchill was consumed with grief; all his ambitions for reaching the pinnacle of power, which he intensely felt he deserved, were shattered. He desperately sought vindication of his actions and a return to the center of affairs.[5] But the Turkish campaign continued without him, as did official discussions involving Palestine.

To help defeat the Ottomans, Britain sought out Jewish and Arab allies. Britain encouraged Arabs in the Ottoman Empire to rebel, and its overtures centered on Hussein ibn Ali. Hussein, head of the Hashemite clan, was appointed by the Ottoman Sultan in 1908 to be sherif of the holy Muslim city of Mecca, and aspired to replace the Ottoman sultan as "caliph," by which he meant political sovereign over all Muslims. He proclaimed himself in late 1916 king of the Arabs. (Hussein was defeated in Arabia in 1924 by Abdul Aziz al-Saud, more commonly known as Ibn Saud, who was emir of the central Arabian area Najd.) Hussein discussed possible territorial rewards for a rebellion against the Ottomans in a vague correspondence in 1915–1916 with Henry McMahon, Britain's high commissioner in Egypt. McMahon offered some sort of independent Arabia as well as an Arab entity that included some Syrian cities but that did not conflict with French interests (which it most certainly did). McMahon did not offer Palestine, which then was not a separate entity but consisted of Ottoman districts that were part of Damascus- and Beirut-based provinces. (Jerusalem, however, answered directly to Constantinople.) Meanwhile, the British held secret talks with the French, culminating in a 1916 understanding known as the Sykes-Picot agreement, which divvied up the Middle East between the two European powers with no provision for a Jewish or Arab state. Sykes-Picot soon unraveled. British officials also began to speak of Arab unity and restoration of the "Arab Nation" and conveyed to the Arabs in 1918 that they could keep whatever they took from the Ottomans. However, Arab forces, which often numbered no more than a few hundred and only occasionally a few thousand, did not take anything on their own other than the Arabian cities of Jedda and Mecca in 1916. Even Damascus, the great prize, was taken by Australian troops at the end of the war in late 1918. However, because the city was quickly handed over to the Northern Arab Army, the myth of an Arab Revolt was created—with the assistance of Thomas Edward (T. E.) Lawrence, later glorified as "Lawrence of Arabia." Generally, the Arabs fought alongside their fellow Muslim Ottomans, and not one Arab unit defected. This was especially true of the Palestinian Arabs, who were part of the Ottoman governing structure and firmly pro-Ottoman. Even Sherif Hussein was unreliable; as late as the spring of 1918 he offered the Turks peace in exchange for the caliphate.[6]

The British also looked to the Jews for assistance in the war effort. The Jews formed the Zion Mule Corps, which fought at Gallipoli, and a Jewish legion organized by Vladimir Jabotinsky participated in the battle for Palestine. In addition, a network of Palestinian Jewish spies, led by Aaron Aaronsohn and the Nili spy ring, provided intelligence about the Ottomans that contributed to the British victory in Palestine. The British also sought Jewish aid through less conventional means. Imbued with an exaggerated fear of Jewish power prevalent in Europe for centuries, which had been encouraged by Zionists since Herzl, many British officials were convinced that by issuing a declaration on behalf of Zionism, a movement they believed was supported by the majority of Jews worldwide (in fact, even Anglo-Jews were split, with many strongly opposed), they would gain greater support for the war effort in the newly allied United States (in which Jews despised the tsarist Russian ally) and Russia (whose pro-Allied government was tottering). They also hoped to preempt Germany from doing the same. (The Jews were perceived as ethnically German or at least pro-German and anti-tsarist.) This was reminiscent of the argument by some in Britain in the 1830s that granting

Jews emancipation would bring rewards from countries in which Jews were influential. Other broad humanitarian, cultural, and imperial factors, along with more immediate causes, came into play as well. A pro-Zionist declaration was opposed by Foreign Secretary George Nathaniel Curzon and Secretary of State for India Edwin Montagu—who, as the only Jew in the Cabinet (though not a member of the War Cabinet, which decided the matter), was petrified at being seen as Jewish and not English, as well as concerned about Indian Muslim reaction. However, several ministers, including Lloyd George, Arthur Balfour, and Jan Christian Smuts of South Africa, were already disposed toward Zionism for reasons of religion, humanitarianism, history, and gratitude.[7]

The British War Cabinet voted on October 31, 1917, in favor of a declaration committing Britain to the establishment of a Jewish national home in Palestine. The statement, which became known as the Balfour Declaration, took the form of a short letter sent on November 2 from Foreign Secretary Balfour to Lord Lionel Walter Rothschild, head of Britain's Zionist Federation:

> I have much pleasure in conveying to you, on behalf of His Majesty's Government, the following declaration of sympathy with Jewish Zionist aspirations which has been submitted to, and approved by, the Cabinet:
>
> "His Majesty's Government view with favour the establishment in Palestine of a national home for the Jewish people, and will use their best endeavours to facilitate the achievement of this object, it being clearly understood that nothing shall be done which may prejudice the civil and religious rights of non-Jewish communities or the rights and political status enjoyed by Jews in any other country."

The definition of "national home" was left intentionally ambiguous. The Zionists purposely used the term "home" in Basle in 1897, so as not to provoke the Gentiles, but had made conflicting statements since then about whether they intended a state or not. Weizmann considered development of a state a slow process, which certainly would have been necessary for the Jews to become a majority in Palestine. (At the time of the Declaration, there were estimated to be 50,000–65,000 Jews out of a total population of 700,000.) Balfour told the War Cabinet on October 31 that "national home" meant an entity under British or American protectorate which permitted the Jews to "build up . . . a real centre of national culture and focus of national life. It did not necessarily involve the early establishment of an independent Jewish State, which was a matter for gradual development in accordance with the ordinary laws of political evolution." With "centre," he borrowed the vague term Samuel employed in 1915. Balfour did not commit to a definition in public, but privately confided in 1918, "My personal hope is that the Jews will make good in Palestine and eventually found a Jewish State." The British press mostly understood the Declaration as promising a Jewish state. The ambiguity of the term "national home" and the dual promise to the Jews and to the non-Jewish inhabitants of Palestine caused a great deal of confusion and uncertainty, which successive British governments did little to ameliorate, and led to much agitation in the region for years to come. Still, the Jewish pro-Zionist press was ecstatic over the Declaration.[8]

The Balfour Declaration, which was not published in the press until November 9, prompted the Ottoman and German governments, who similarly feared Jewish power, to support efforts to facilitate Jewish settlement of Palestine. The British announcement was met with exhilaration by many Jews in the United States, Russia, and Britain, but German Jews remained faithful to their government. And despite efforts by Zionist leaders, the Declaration, which did not reach Russia until November 29, by which time Lenin had entered Petrograd and the new Bolshevik regime announced its exit from the war, made no impact on Russian policies. Prominent Jewish Bolsheviks were completely antagonistic to Jewish nationalism, and in early 1918 the commissar of Jewish affairs declared that his task was to combat Zionism, especially among Jewish soldiers. Although the Declaration did not have its intended effect, the British were soon in a position to make good on their promise to the Jews; on December 11, 1917, British General Edmund Allenby liberated Jerusalem from the Ottomans after a nine-month British campaign in Palestine.[9]

In 1920, at the postwar peace conference in San Remo, Italy, the Allies confirmed their wartime secret agreement to dismember the Ottoman Empire and establish Palestine and Mesopotamia (which became known as Iraq in 1921) as British mandates, Syria as a French mandate, and Arabia as independent under pro-British monarchs. Many of the borders for these areas were rather carelessly carved out of Ottoman provinces and districts, which contributed to subsequent conflicts. In 1922, the League of Nations approved these mandates, or trusts, with the Balfour Declaration explicitly part of the Palestine Mandate. The Palestine Mandate was essentially a trust for the Jewish people, officially intended to "secure the establishment of the Jewish national home, as laid down in the preamble, and the development of self-governing institutions, and also for safeguarding the civil and religious rights of all the inhabitants of Palestine." The three mandates became part of the Covenant of the League of Nations; the independence of each was to be recognized, subject to the "administrators advice and assistance" of the mandatory power until they could "stand alone."[10]

Through all of this, Churchill was utterly silent about Zionism. There is no record that Churchill commented at all on the Balfour Declaration while he was minister of munitions, whether in personal or official communication, even though other government officials and MPs did. In the *Zionist Review*, the official organ of the English Zionist Federation, almost 150 members of the government, House of Lords, House of Commons, and privy council were quoted expressing their support for the Balfour Declaration, but Churchill was not one of them. Even Joynson-Hicks, though probably not for philo-Semitic reasons, was quoted supporting the Jews "once more" taking "possession of their own land." On November 2, the day the Balfour Declaration was issued, Samuel, one of the leading Zionists in government circles, wrote Churchill a letter. Samuel, now chairman of the Select Committee on National Expenditure, penned, "Many thanks for your letter of Oct. 31st relating to the supply of machine tools and materials to the motor repair depots in France. The Director, who is very keen on the success of his Department, will be much relieved to know that he will soon get the things that he needs." Samuel did not even note the momentous Zionist event that occurred that day, apparently because he did not think that it meant anything to Churchill. Perhaps the closest Churchill came to commenting on the Balfour Declaration was when he praised British conquest of Jerusalem to a cheering crowd in Bedford in late 1917: "What Richard Coeur de Lion was not able to achieve, British troops have accomplished." He portrayed this as a triumph of Christians, or at least the British government, of which he was a member. Indeed, the purpose of the speech was to boost British morale after Bolshevik Russia cut a deal with Germany and withdrew from the war, freeing up German troops to fight on the western front. The bells of Westminster Abbey rang out for the first time during the war upon Jerusalem's capture to raise British spirits, which was exactly the War Cabinet's intent when it decided on the military campaign in the spring of 1917. As in the War Council discussions in 1915, Churchill gave no indication that the acquisition of Palestine had any relevance to the Jews or Zionism. Demonstrating little sensitivity to Jewish sensibilities, he compared Allenby's military campaign to the Crusades, which had slaughtered thousands of Jews (and Arabs). But this, evidently, was the perspective shared by many in the British public. The pro-Zionist Lloyd George depicted the event the same way in his memoirs in 1934. After noting that seizure of Palestine fulfilled the Balfour Declaration, Lloyd George placed it in historical British-Christian context, describing it as "the capture by British troops of the most famous city in the world which had for centuries baffled the efforts of Christendom to regain possession of its sacred shrines." Otherwise, Churchill virtually ignored Jerusalem's conquest. It did not capture his imagination at this time as a momentous historical event, whether for Britain, Christendom, or the Jews. As in 1915, he viewed Palestine merely in the immediate context of winning the war and increasing British postwar leverage and power.[11]

Nevertheless, there were institutional and political factors to Churchill's official silence. It was the War Cabinet, after all, and not the full Cabinet that considered and voted on the Balfour Declaration, and he had not been a member of the former since 1915. As minister of munitions, he participated in War Cabinet proceedings only when munitions were discussed, and that was rare in 1917 and 1918. His memos and correspondence during the crucial months before and after the Balfour Declaration mostly revolved around munitions issues. He did not much venture opinions about matters outside his ministry (besides wartime cheerleading) as he did frequently before and after his tenure at the munitions ministry, which so exasperated other ministers. Churchill tried to be more focused, disciplined, and circumspect, and for good reason. The Conservative Party, which never forgave his defection to the Liberal Party and which insisted on his head for joining a coalition with Asquith in 1915, was incensed over his new ministerial appointment. Their chief, Andrew Bonar Law, who detested Churchill, consented to

Churchill's appointment as munitions minister in 1917 only after Lloyd George, the Liberal prime minister, assured him that Churchill would not interfere in military affairs. Churchill had no political base, and he was politically vulnerable and dependent upon Lloyd George, who brought him back into the Cabinet only because he feared him more on the outside. Churchill certainly felt no political pressure from his constituency in Dundee to speak out in favor Zionism.[12]

Shortly after the war's end, in December 1918, a new unusual peacetime coalition government emerged, headed by Liberal Prime Minister Lloyd George, in which Conservatives outnumbered Liberals 339–136. The Liberal Party, of which Churchill was a member, split over whether to form this coalition and thus began its precipitous fall from power. Churchill was appointed secretary of state for war and air in January 1919 and entered the War Cabinet, but he remained politically weakened and more dependent on the now-dominant Conservatives, whose rank and file was now less sympathetic to Zionism than were the Liberals.[13]

However silent Churchill had been about Zionism, he was not indifferent to the Jews. On the contrary, this was a time when he devoted a fair amount of attention to Jewish power, both at home and abroad. During the war there was a rise in anti-Semitism in England, and that sentiment significantly intensified with the Bolshevik Revolution in November 1917. It was widely held among the political Right that Bolshevik leaders were mostly Jews of German extraction and sympathies—at a time when Britain was fighting Germany and after Germany had facilitated the ascent of the Bolsheviks, who then ended their alliance with Britain and France and signed a separate peace agreement with Germany. Such was the mood that one senior Foreign Office official wrote in a 1919 minute about anti-Jewish violence in Ukraine, "The Jews deserve all they get." What the Jews got, or suffered, in 1919 alone was one hundred thousand deaths in hundreds of pogroms in southern Russia, particularly in Ukraine, committed by mostly White (anti-Communist) Russians during the civil war. The raging anti-Semitic environment intensified in the autumn of 1919, when right-wing publications in England began to publish *The Protocols of the Elders of Zion*, a crude rant by alleged unnamed Zionist leaders planning to topple the current order and establish their own international government. The *Protocols* first appeared in a Russian newspaper in 1903 and in book form in 1905, but did not garner much attention until the conspiracy it allegedly documented appeared to manifest itself in the form of the Bolshevik Revolution. All this fit into the old anti-Semitic canard that Jews were powerful and unpatriotic. Jewish organizations challenged the validity of the *Protocols* and the charges about the prominence of Jews among Bolshevik leaders, seemingly to no avail. It was not until August 1921 that the London *Times* ran stories proving the *Protocols* a clumsy forgery, concocted by the tsarist secret police and paraphrasing an 1860s satire of Napoleon III. Also indicative of, and contributing to, rampant British anti-Semitism, was the Conservative Party's uproar over the harsh treatment meted out by Montagu, the secretary of state for India, to General Reginal Dyer for ordering troops in 1919 to fire on an unarmed Indian mob at Amritsar, resulting in more than three hundred dead and two thousand wounded. Churchill defended fellow Liberal colleague Montagu and condemned Dyer, but Conservatives, and even some Liberals, questioned Montagu's Englishness, confirming Montagu's worst fears. One leading Conservative, Austen Chamberlain, captured the parliamentary atmosphere in a letter to his sister: "A Jew, a foreigner, rounding on an Englishman & throwing him to the wolves—that was the feeling, & the event illustrates once again what I said of Dizzy [Disraeli]. A Jew may be a loyal Englishman & passionately patriotic, but he is intellectually apart from us & will never be purely & simply English."[14]

Keenly aware of the heated anti-Semitic political environment, Churchill warned Lloyd George in late 1918 against appointing too many Jews to the new postwar Cabinet: "There is a point about Jews wh [which] occurs to me—you must not have too many of them." Churchill felt that if three of the seven Liberal ministers were Jews it "might I fear give rise to comment." He was not overreacting, since the Liberals were already seen as overly sympathetic to Jews, if not Jewish themselves. His American-born mother, Jenny, had already written to him in 1916 when Montagu became the third Jew in the Cabinet, in the powerless position of Duchy of Lancaster, "We shall soon have a Jewish Govt! They are undoubtedly clever—but have really no nationality. Probably you won't agree." Jenny was right; Churchill did not agree and never wrote or said such a thing because, as she suggested, he was fundamentally philo-Semitic. Churchill's warning to Lloyd George was motivated by politics alone. Still, he believed, as he had in the early 1900s, that the Jews were very influential, and in 1919 amid the electric atmosphere he wrote to a British general, "The Jews are very powerful in England."[15]

Consideration of Jewish power played a role in Churchill's premier foreign policy fixation as secretary of state for war and air (1919–1921) and even as colonial secretary (1921–1922): confronting the Bolshevik threat to western civilization and European stability. In late 1919, he received a copy of the *Protocols;* it is unclear whether he read it, but he certainly advanced a number of its themes and the anti-Semitic conspiratorial ideas propagated by other sources. He genuinely considered the Bolsheviks an illegitimate minority consisting mostly of Jews ruling over the majority "real" Russians. In a 1920 speech he referred to the "international Soviet of the Russian and Polish Jew," and in an article that year he asserted, "With the notable exception of Lenin, the majority of the leading figures are Jews." He pointedly noted that while Commissioner of Foreign Affairs George Tchitcherin was a "pure Russian," he was eclipsed by Maxim Litvinov, his nominal subordinate and a Jew. In a 1921 speech he claimed the Bolshevik Revolution was "brought about by a comparatively small gang of professional revolutionaries, very few of whom are Russians." His original notes for the speech, which were given to the press, read, "A gang of professional revolutionaries[,] mostly Jews," and he stood by that version as well. Churchill privately responded to a complaint against his remarks by maintaining that while he was pro-Jewish, "Jews are undoubtedly playing a predominant part in the Bolshevik movement, and . . . the majority of the leaders are Jews." He then cited a number of Bolshevik leaders with their original Jewish names. He made other, more gratuitous public connections between Bolsheviks and Jews, such as his 1919 reference to the Hungarian Communist leader as "Bela Kun or Bela Cohen." He undoubtedly employed the specter of Jewish domination to ingratiate himself with audiences and garner support for his anti-Bolshevik crusade, especially among Conservatives, as he had done before during the alien and Shell Oil debates. He even highlighted the Bolshevik-Jewish link to convince the allegedly powerful British Jewry to "denounce the renegades in Russia and Poland who are dishonouring their race and religion" and encourage them to support the allegedly more democratic forces in those countries. Somewhat ominously, he privately suggested that English Jews would be "better advised" to do this than to challenge the validity of his argument. None of this made Jews' position in England or other European countries any easier. There were not always ulterior motives involved in his statements, since he also made similar comments in private to people to whom he had little to prove. For instance, he wrote the anti-Bolshevik Curzon in 1921 about "the tyrannic Government of these Jew Commissars," and in a 1922 unsent letter to his dear friend F. E. Smith, he wrote about "Semitic conspirators." Churchill genuinely believed, or at least came to believe, what he said and wrote in this matter.[16]

Churchill and right-wing Britons were evidently influenced by statements from their White Russian allies. In 1919, he wrote to Lloyd George, "There is a very bitter feeling throughout Russia against the Jews, who are regarded for being the main instigators of the ruin of the Empire, and who, certainly, have played a leading part in Bolshevik atrocities." It apparently escaped Churchill's notice that Russians had scapegoated Jews for a long time. Just during his own lifetime, for instance, many Russians, abetted by tsarists, had blamed the assassination of Tsar Alexander II in 1881 on the Jews and had attributed significant German military victories early in the First World War to betrayal by allegedly pro-German Russian Jewish spies. White Russians blamed the rise of the Bolsheviks on the Jews as well; many anti-Bolsheviks were even convinced (also incorrectly) that Lenin was Jewish. And yet Churchill obliquely signaled some level of understanding that any new White attacks on Jews were part of a larger continuum of tsarist persecution; he warned one British official to combat possible White attacks on Jews, what he termed "Jew pogroms," which might occur if the Whites defeated the Reds, though he attributed this danger to the "prominent part taken by Jews in Red terror and regime." He seemed at best to have a hazy recollection of his own criticism of anti-Jewish pogroms in 1905. Churchill did not recognize that the perceived prominence of Jews among Bolshevik leaders was partly due to the lack of Jewish prominence in tsarist governments. He certainly never credited the Bolsheviks for their initial ethnic inclusiveness, such as appointing Leon Trotsky foreign affairs commissar and Jacob Sverdlov official head of the Bolshevik state (though the Bolsheviks likely kept Jews, excepting Trotsky, off the Council of the People's Commissars in 1917 out of fear that it would alienate the anti-Semitic masses). He failed to appreciate that Jews, often more educated, were prominent in many of the movements opposing the old tsarist order that had intensely oppressed them over the years. For instance, since 1881 the tsarist government had prohibited Jews from acquiring property, settling in the countryside and some cities, and studying in universities, while encouraging and intensifying anti-Semitic scapegoating and pogroms. Russian Jews strongly welcomed the fall of the tsarist government in 1917, and like other Russians in this chaotic wartime revolutionary period, they groped for a political system to support in its place. They cheered the rise of the Kerensky reform government, which abolished tsarist anti-Jewish laws. And, indeed, a number of Jews were drawn to the Bolsheviks; centuries of anti-Semitism in Russia and elsewhere spurred many Jews to seek salvation, anonymity, and assimilation in a Communist movement promising equality and justice. Bolshevik absolutism also appealed to those seeking a complete break from the past. Churchill acknowledged this somewhat in a provocative 1920 article: "The adherents of this sinister confederacy are mostly men reared up among the unhappy populations of countries where Jews are persecuted on account of their race." To the extent there was consistency in his thought, he seemed to suggest that anti-Semitism led to Jewish Bolshevism which in turn led to anti-Semitism. In fact, many of these Jews saw themselves as Communists, and not Jews; they were creating a new man and had little use for old biblical texts. Churchill recognized that Jewish Bolsheviks had "forsaken the faith of their forefathers, and divorced from their minds all spiritual hopes of the next world."[17] Yet the thrust of his comments in the late 1910s and early 1920s about Bolsheviks was that their leaders were predominantly Jewish and that White Russians understandably were very resentful of this fact. Indeed, despite his many declarations on the importance of historical knowledge to statecraft, Churchill betrayed a lack of comprehension of Russian and Jewish history, or at least forgot what he did know—either intentionally or unintentionally—because of the influence of anti-Semites in England and Russia at that time and his absolute obsession with the Bolshevik threat.

Churchill's anti-Bolshevik fixation also affected his view of Zionism, or at least his public portrayal of it. In early 1920, he published a provocative and rather misunderstood article, "Zionism versus Bolshevism," that ultimately revealed more about his willingness to manipulate Jewish themes and issues for his own interests than his view of Zionism. He offered a strange, complex mixture of the popular conspiratorial perceptions of Jews as historic international evildoers, the idea of Zionism as a possible antidote to Bolshevism, and his own deep-seated sympathy toward Jews. He explicitly and implicitly borrowed heavily from Disraeli while perverting some of his ideas. Churchill began by intimating that the Jews held mysterious power and fortitude: "Some people like Jews and some do not; but no thoughtful man can doubt the fact that they are beyond all question the most formidable and the most remarkable race which has ever appeared in the world." He then invoked Disraeli—whom he referred to in Victorian racial terms as "the Jew Prime Minister of England" who "was always true to his race and proud of his origin"—with the quote, " 'The Lord deals with the nations as the nations deal with the Jews.' " He cited "the miserable state of Russia, where of all countries in the world the Jews were the most cruelly treated, and contrast it with the fortunes of our own country" as current proof of Disraeli's dictum. In fact, he argued, "nothing that has since happened in the history of the world has falsified the truth of Disraeli's confident assertion." He had last invoked Disraeli's adage in 1905 when he warned tsarist Russia against continuing anti-Semitic pogroms. This was an unusual statement, however, for Churchill to make in 1919–1920, when he usually downplayed tsarist anti-Semitism to buttress support for his anti-Bolshevik crusade. He also credited the Jewish contribution to Christian ethics. Also, whereas Disraeli saw the positive in what he alleged to be mysterious Jewish power, Churchill raised the nefarious flipside. Churchill insinuated a dark, conspiratorial nature to the influence of "this mystic and mysterious race" and postulated that Jewish dominance of the Bolshevik movement suggested they were the "chosen" people for "the supreme manifestations, both of the divine and the diabolical." Bolshevism was "as malevolent as Christianity was benevolent," and it "would almost seem as if the gospel of Christ and the gospel of Antichrist were destined to originate among the same people."[18]

Churchill commended those "National Jews" who "identify" with, and contribute to, the states that had "received them." He noted that many English Jews had distinguished themselves in the British army during the First World War and that many Jews had played an "honourable and useful part" in Russian national life "in spite of the disabilities under which they have suffered." He then criticized "the schemes of the International Jews," a "sinister confederacy" historically involved in subversive movements, which he empathetically attributed to their being persecuted for being Jewish. He also recognized that these Jews had betrayed their faith. He claimed that international Jews influenced the French Revolution, citing the recent work of the right-wing, anti-Semitic female conspiratorialist Nesta Webster, and added that they were "the mainspring of every subversive movement during the Nineteenth Century." He claimed that many in Russia associated Jews with Communism, exacerbated by the fact that "in many cases Jewish interests and Jewish places of worship are excepted by the Bolsheviks from their universal hostility." Churchill then turned his attention to the third type of Jew that was internationally oriented but in a positive way. He wanted to channel the energy of those internationally oriented Jews toward Zionism; he asserted that the majority of the "national" Jews did not want to go to Palestine. He issued his most supportive statement to date about this "inspiring movement": "But if, as may well happen, there should be created in our own lifetime by the banks of the Jordan a Jewish State under the protection of the British Crown, which might comprise three or four million Jews, an event would have occurred in the history of the world which would, from every point of view, be beneficial, and would be especially in harmony with the truest interests of the British Empire." This went beyond official policy, which only supported a "national home." The population range apparently was borrowed from Samuel's 1915 memo. The benefits Churchill envisioned for the British were not only imperial but strategic—namely, support in the struggle against Bolshevism. The Jewish-born Trotsky recognized the threat of Zionism and significantly attacked Zionists with a "fury." At stake was not only the survival of Bolshevism and a "Jewish national centre in Palestine" but a struggle "for the soul of the Jewish people." Churchill continued to argue that Jews must take a lead in denouncing Bolshevism and thereby "vindicate the honour of the Jewish name" and make "clear to all the world that the Bolshevik movement is not a Jewish movement." Moreover, he declared, "in building up with the utmost possible rapidity a Jewish national centre in Palestine which may become not only a refuge to the oppressed from the unhappy lands of Central Europe, but which will also be a symbol of Jewish unity and the temple of Jewish glory, a task is presented on which many blessings rest."[19]

The *Jewish Chronicle* condemned Churchill's article, calling it "reckless and scandalous." It charged Churchill with adopting "the hoary tactics of hooligan anti-Semites" and challenged his assertion that Bolshevik leaders were mostly Jewish, since Trotsky was the only Jew who held a ministerial portfolio in the Soviet government and even he had rejected Judaism. It also argued that Zionism was not an alternative to Bolshevism but preceded it and stood alone, and that Churchill was only seeking support for his anti-Bolshevik crusade and wanted the "limelight." The *Zionist Review* emphasized the positive, asserting that Churchill gave Zionism "his blessing," though it acknowledged that he "associated himself—though not in an extreme form—with the Jew-Bolshevist accusation."[20]

Certainly, the article was irresponsible in echoing the *Protocols* and right-wing conspiratorial propaganda and suggesting that some Jews sought world revolution and domination, especially given the charged anti-Semitic environment. Churchill's claim that Jews dominated the Bolsheviks was not only misleading but inflammatory as well. The same was true of his distinction between national and international Jews, suggesting that some Jews were not patriotic. In other ways, however, the article did not veer too far from what some philo-Semites and Zionist leaders said. In fact, Disraeli claimed the Jews' "fiery energy" helped sustain subversive and revolutionary movements. In *Lord George Bentinck*, Disraeli wrote of the revolutionary movements of 1848, "The people of God cooperate with atheists; the most skillful accumulators of property ally themselves with communists; the peculiar and chosen race touch the hand of all the scum and low castes of Europe!" Churchill likely thought that if the proud racial Jew Disraeli thought this, then it was all right for him to as well. And like Disraeli, Churchill ultimately blamed the Gentiles; as Disraeli wrote, "And all this because they wish to destroy the ungrateful Christendom which owes to them even its name, and whose tyranny they can no longer endure." It was also reasonable for Churchill to consider Zionism an antidote to Communism. After all, the Balfour Declaration was partly prompted by that proposition. Also, Herzl repeatedly argued that Zionism was a cure to Jewish seditious activity, and in

1919 Weizmann told peace conferees that the Zionist proposal "was the only one which would in the long run . . . transform Jewish energy into a constructive force instead of its being dissipated in destructive tendencies." Once these Zionist leaders advanced this argument, even if only to win over Gentiles to their cause, it became fair game for others. Still, these Zionists did not think Jews might be attracted to Zionism because some were naturally unpatriotic, as Churchill suggested, but because they believed that their only hope for freedom and survival was to live in a country of their own in their ancient homeland. That distinction seemed generally lost on Churchill during this frenzied period. Churchill's thesis about a struggle for the soul of the Jewish people was also not overly provocative. Weizmann on several occasions before the First World War debated various Communist leaders such as Lenin, Trotsky, and Karl Radek over Zionism versus Communism, in effect creating a proposition of conflict and rivalry between the two movements. Isaiah Berlin wrote that Weizmann regarded Russian socialist leaders "simply as so many rival fishers of souls, likely to detach from the movement of Jewish liberation and drive to their doom some of the ablest and most constructively minded sons of his people." Weizmann told one sympathetic British official in 1920 that Zionism was "constructive Bolshevism" but denied that Jews were pillars of Russian Bolshevism.[21] In fact, there was not an inherent conflict between Zionism and Communism. Unbeknownst to Churchill and most other people, the two movements coexisted comfortably in the person of Moses Hess, who remarkably was a leading intellectual father of each, though he would have deplored the violent, internationally subversive Leninist-Trotskyite form Communism took in Russia. And as Churchill himself came to observe in 1921, a number of Russian Communists moved to Palestine at this time.

In the crucible of the pressing conflict against Bolshevism, with which he was consumed, and amid a supercharged national and international anti-Semitic environment, Churchill had gotten carried away, as he often did—especially rhetorically and particularly early in his career—while fixated on an overriding objective. The *Jewish Chronicle* had correctly asserted that he intended the article to garner support for his anti-Bolshevik campaign. It was also meant to endear him to the Conservative majority in the coalition. As often before with other Jewish matters, Zionism was simply a vehicle for him to achieve more important goals, although here his rhetoric was far uglier and potentially more damaging to Jews. And yet it was only a small component of his anti-Bolshevik crusade. Despite the article's provocative claims, Churchill did not believe much of what he wrote—beyond the statements that Bolsheviks were Jews, Jews had a mysterious power, and Disraeli's dictum proved true. He never repeated in private or in any other public forum the proposition of Zionism as a constructive outlet for Jewish internationalism and a tool to fight Bolshevism. Nor was he as pro-Zionist at this time as the article suggested. Indeed, on the very day before this article was published, he privately derogated the value of Zionism to Britain. He wrote a memo to the Cabinet stating that the Palestine garrison cost £9 million per year, which was "far beyond anything which Palestine can ever yield in return."[22] He did not raise in this memo any practical imperial benefit nor mention that a Jewish homeland in Palestine would contribute to the war against Bolshevism. The fact was that Churchill was far less focused on combating Bolshevism in the realm of ideas, including far-fetched ones expressed in the article, than assailing it in more traditional, concrete ways on the battlefield (supporting the White Russians) and in diplomatic maneuvers (supporting the Turks/Ottoman Empire). And in these main venues of attack, Zionism was a distinct casualty.

During his tenure as secretary of state for war and air from 1919 to 1921, Churchill viewed the Middle East through the same anti-Bolshevik lens he used on Europe, and that lens barely had enough magnification to detect Zionism. His primary strategic concern for the region was maintaining Turkey as a counter to Russia, following the policy of Disraeli and other British leaders in the nineteenth century. In contrast, Lloyd George, like his Liberal predecessor William Gladstone in the 1870s, despised the Ottomans and wanted their empire destroyed. Churchill had been receptive to the idea of Russia possessing Constantinople as far back as 1897 and as recently as 1915, when Russia was an ally. But in 1920, he wrote, "We should thus recreate that Turkish barrier to Russian ambitions which has always been of the utmost importance to us." He feared a weak or antagonistic Turkey would facilitate Bolshevik Russia's continuing efforts to destabilize the Middle East, Central Asia, and even India, and threaten British interests. As with Germany, he wanted a moderate peace imposed on the Ottoman Empire so as not to drive it toward Bolshevism or Russia, or both. "We have always hitherto had either Turkey or Russia on our side," he argued in 1920, yet postwar British policy had driven these two countries into "an extraordinary unnatural union." In both Europe and the Middle East, Churchill regarded self-determination and the breakup of empires, fashionable principles that U.S. President Woodrow Wilson propounded, as destabilizing, threatening to the British Empire, and especially inviting to Communism. He sought a rough preservation of the Ottoman Empire, the withdrawal of European troops from Ottoman soil, and the renunciation of claims by various European nations on Ottoman lands. He opposed the secret wartime agreement to dismember the Ottoman Empire that was confirmed by the Allies in San Remo in 1920 and formalized later that year in the Treaty of Sèvres. The treaty was harsher than the one the Allies imposed on Germany at Versailles, but it was never implemented.[23]

Churchill also argued that a policy favorable to the Ottoman Empire, whose sultan was the caliph and thus ostensibly the master of the Muslim world, was smart imperial politics. With control over 87 million Muslims in India, Egypt, Mesopotamia, Palestine, and Transjordan, Britain was, as he wrote in 1919, "the greatest Mohammedan Power in the world." In particular, he worried—with encouragement from Indian Muslim leaders and the British General Staff—how Britain's harsh policy toward the Ottomans affected Muslim sentiment in India, which already was exercised by Bolshevik agitation. This affected Britain's position in the Middle East as well, since Britain relied on Indian troops stationed there. Overall, Churchill thought it important to get along with at least two of what he considered the four main powers in the Middle East—Greece, Russia, Turkey, and the Arabs. (Churchill borrowed the habit of other British officials of lumping all the Arabs together.) He wanted Britain to shift from a policy favoring the Greeks (which in 1920 had a pro-German king) and Russians to one favoring the Turks and Arabs.[24] In other words, he advocated an alliance with Muslims against eastern Christians. This alignment was not based on shared values but instead focused on the greater strategic, imperial, and civilizational imperative of countering the Bolsheviks.

Preserving some sort of integrity of the Ottoman Empire meant that Palestine would not be available for the Jews and that the Balfour

Declaration would be violated (though the Turkish nationalists, led by Mustafa Kemal, later called Ataturk, eventually eschewed retaining Syria, Palestine, or Mesopotamia). This troubled Churchill not at all, and he wished the pledge to the Jews had never been made. In a 1919 memo, he explained the negative implications of breaking up the Ottoman Empire and lamented that the United States was not willing to relieve Britain of its Palestine burden. He even expressed hostile exasperation with the Zionists: "Lastly there are the Jews, whom we are pledged to introduce into Palestine, and who take it for granted that the local population will be cleared out to suit their convenience." This was a shocking statement that misrepresented the Zionist position, ignored the existence of Jews already living in Palestine, and disregarded the Jews' historic claim to the land that he recognized years earlier. Moreover, it was devoid of any warmth, compassion, or even interest in the Jewish condition. Churchill often lumped the Palestine and Mesopotamia mandates together at this time, and considered retention of both to be an impractical imperial extravagance: "I know it will be found very hard to relinquish the satisfaction of those dreams of conquest and aggrandisement which are gratified by the retention of Palestine and Mesopotamia." Zionism, in his mind, was no longer a movement of great global significance, as he had suggested in Manchester years earlier. Rather, it was an obstacle to the maintenance of the Ottoman Empire and the global battle against Bolshevism, and therefore needed to be discouraged.[25]

But Churchill did not always belittle Zionism. Just after Easter 1920, a pro-Zionist political officer in Allenby's military administration in Palestine, Colonel Richard Meinertzhagen, complained to Curzon that the military administration, which did not publish the Balfour Declaration in Palestine, instigated Arab riots in Jerusalem to demonstrate the futility of the Zionism policy. Some MPs also were concerned about the severe sentence handed down to Jabotinsky for his alleged role in the violence. Beyond the parliamentary pressure, Churchill took these complaints seriously, including the suggestion that Allenby's administration tolerated anti-Zionist activities and propaganda by Sherif Hussein's family around the time of the riots. Churchill queried Allenby about them: "It looks as if the local administration was violently Anti-Zionist and thus at variance with the main policy." He asked Allenby to share his side of the story and suggested leniency for Jabotinsky.[26]

Significantly, it was an anti-Bolshevik strategic imperative that led to Churchill's indifference and even antagonism toward Zionism at this time, and not any concern for the Arabs or Muslims. In all his comments about Ottoman and Middle Eastern policy, Churchill demonstrated no interest, and apparently had no reason to be interested, in how Muslim Indians reacted to Britain's Zionist policy, nor did he discern a connection between British policy toward Arab Muslims outside of Palestine and British policy toward Palestine. He never intended that a pro-Arab policy should come at the Zionists' expense. He did not even seem that eager to appease the Arabs. He did argue in a 1919 memo against divvying up Ottoman territories among European countries because it would abet "a crime against freedom" and betray the "Arabs who fought so bravely with us in the war." But this was disingenuous and meant only to garner support for a pro-Ottoman policy; in fact, many Arabs would gain from the Ottoman Empire's dissolution. His lack of concern about the Arabs in Arabia was more evident; in 1918 he told the British ambassador to France that he was prepared if necessary to, in the ambassador's words, "desert the Arabs of Arabia and leave them to settle accounts with Turkey."[27]

Still, Churchill sought good relations with the Arabs and blamed Arab anger with Britain not on Britain's support for Zionism but on its support for France, its regional rival. France expelled Hussein's son Faisal from Syria in 1920 and declared its determination to keep forever all of Syria (Britain had installed Faisal in Syria in late 1918). As Churchill stated in 1920, "Mischief has been made between us and the Arabs by the French treatment of the Arabs." Churchill did recognize once in a 1920 memo that the "Zionist movement will cause continued friction with the Arabs," and here he intimated Palestinian Arabs. But he still considered the French, who opposed Zionism and sought "to cushion the Arabs off on to us," to be "the real enemy." He contended that the French sought to appease the Arabs after their conflict with Faisal and to gain a foothold in Palestine, which France coveted as part of Syria, by provoking the Arabs against the British. British tension with Sherif Hussein's family members, or "sherifians" as many British officials called them, was in any case unavoidable given the family's perceived need to distance itself from its Christian imperial patron that overthrew the only Muslim Great Power, the Ottoman Empire.[28]

Whatever tension they soon had with Britain, the sherifians initially gave Churchill and Britain no reason to think that Zionism mattered to them or conflicted with their interests. They did not let Zionism affect their relations with the British, which were necessary to the fulfillment of this Arabian family's substantial regional ambitions. Palestine represented only a sliver of Arab territories. Also, the sherifians even saw short-term advantages to Zionism, such as eroding the Sykes-Picot agreement, keeping France out of Syria and Palestine, and perhaps providing money and advisors for their conflict with France. Although Arab leaders were not consulted about the Balfour Declaration, Hussein did not protest it when it was issued, and in early 1918 he even welcomed the Jews to return to their "sacred and beloved homeland." Hussein indicated that Jewish immigrants would develop Palestine and benefit the Arabs there. Shortly thereafter Faisal warmly welcomed Weizmann in Aqaba, and later that year when they met again in London he declared, in an address drafted by T. E. Lawrence, "No true Arab can be suspicious or afraid of Jewish nationalism." Faisal and Weizmann signed an unpublished agreement in early 1919, apparently mediated by Lawrence, in which Faisal supported the Balfour Declaration and encouraged Jewish immigration into Palestine, provided that the Arabs achieved independence, namely in Syria (with him the leader). The following month, Faisal told the postwar peace conference that Palestine should be recognized as the enclave of the "Zionist Jews." Later that year, however, the sherifian-Zionist relationship broke down after their interests conflicted. Weizmann refused to support the sherifian anti-French line, and a weakened Faisal joined the anti-French, pro-Turkish Syrian nationalists who sought a Greater Syria that included what is today Jordan, Lebanon, and Israel. In 1920, Faisal claimed for the first time that Palestine was part of the territory promised to his father, and sherifian propaganda urged proclaiming Faisal king of Palestine. Thus early on, Churchill, like many British officials (including Lawrence), generally had some reason to believe Britain's pro-sherifian and pro-Zionist policies were perfectly compatible. In any case, the Ottoman Turks were his focus, not the Arabs, and it was his policy toward them, which was a function of his Bolshevik obsession, that more determined his view of Zionism.[29]

Financial constraints reinforced the strategic imperatives in arguing for a pro-Ottoman and anti-Zionist policy, and shaped Churchill's communication with other officials. In purely financial terms, a pro-Zionist policy was a dud. Of course, that could be said about many foreign policies, both valuable and misguided. Britain faced severe economic and social issues after the First World War; in the late 1910s and early 1920s, the British economy collapsed, exports slumped, unemployment reached unprecedented heights, and labor strikes erupted. Funds were scarce and politically dear, and a spotlight was shone on British expenses in the Middle East. Even with the postwar withdrawal of troops from Europe that Churchill engineered, Britain did not have the finances to meet all its troop commitments, especially in Persia, Palestine, Mesopotamia, and Turkey. Churchill and the military structure he headed begrudged the expenditure of precious funds on Mesopotamia and Palestine. In a letter to Lloyd George in 1920, he wrote, "Palestine is costing us 6 millions a year to hold. . . . The Palestine venture is the most difficult to withdraw from & and the one wh [which] certainly will never yield any profit of a material kind." Churchill went further in another note to Lloyd George later that year: "I deeply regret & *resent* being forced to ask Parlt [Parliament] for these appalling sums of money for new Provinces." Churchill certainly did not want to take the political heat for such a request. As secretary of state for war and air, he took great pride in having demobilized the armed forces sixteen months after the war's end, a move that was efficient, popular, and served to soften his image as a warmonger, and he wanted Lloyd George to explain to Parliament why Britain's "costly commitments in the Turkish Empire & in Persia" were to be maintained. Churchill also believed that the military simply could not meet the various challenges in so many theaters, as evidenced by an anti-British revolt in Mesopotamia inspired by the sherifians in Damascus and supported by the Shiites, who formed the majority of the population in Mesopotamia. The rebellion erupted in the summer of 1920 and was not quelled until early 1921, resulting in 2,000 British casualties, including 450 dead. In an unsent letter to Lloyd George in 1920, Churchill expressed his exasperation at the utter waste of valuable resources in this campaign: "It seems to me so gratuitous that after all the struggles of the war . . . we should be compelled to go on pouring armies and treasure into these thankless deserts."[30]

There were other, more important strategic and imperial priorities upon which dear resources should be expended. Explaining to Lloyd

George in 1920 why the government's anti-Turk policy was wrong, Churchill wrote, "You are up against a shocking bill for Mesopotamia, Palestine & Persia. More will have to be spent in these countries next year than the Navy is demanding to save our sea supremacy. The two cannot be compared from a National point of view." Spending on such new acquisitions did not rate in importance or value with developing existing territories either. He told the Commons in 1921, "Mesopotamia is not, like Egypt, a place which in a strategic sense is of cardinal importance to our interests." He repeatedly stated that he thought the same about Palestine. Since the end of the war, Churchill had focused on controlling and developing territories that had been British in the time of his childhood. It was a financial trade-off, and, as he explained in 1920 to the Cabinet, he did not want to shortchange "a province like Egypt, where we have been honourable [sic] established for so many years." Also, he maintained a long-standing interest in cultivating undeveloped British East Africa, which he had visited in 1907. (The territory had been acquired in the nineteenth century to secure Egypt and the approach to India.) As he insisted in 1919, "The need of national economy is such that we ought to endeavour to concentrate our resources on developing our existing Empire instead of dissipating them in new enlargements."[31] As much as Churchill believed in the financial argument against maintaining control of Palestine, he repeated it often to convince Lloyd George and others to support a pro-Ottoman, anti-Bolshevik policy. The financial argument also resonated with Conservatives.

After speaking in the House of Commons in 1920 about the burdens the government would shoulder in the Middle East until peace was reached with Turkey, Churchill was asked by an Opposition Liberal MP, "What about the pledges?" To which Churchill replied, "I am not aware that we have failed to discharge any of the obligations into which we have entered."[32] That might have been an accurate characterization of government policy but not of Churchill's. He pledged his support of Zionism to the Jews of North-West Manchester, but then in 1915, when he was a senior member of the War Council, he did and said nothing to advance Zionist claims during discussions of postwar control of Palestine. He concentrated his mental efforts on trying to engineer victory in the war and was only somewhat concerned with postwar strategic alignments among the Great Powers, let alone with sentimental causes. He also made no reference to the Balfour Declaration after it was issued. There were reasonable bureaucratic and political reasons for his official silence, though not for his personal silence. His detachment largely reflected the fact that Zionism did not yet mean enough to him, however much its values and goals resonated with him in 1908 and still might have had he given them more attention again. That certainly was true when he became secretary of state for war and air in 1919 and faced much greater priorities, such as Bolshevism, Germany, Turkey, demobilization, scarce finances, imperial development, and politics. Defeating Bolshevism emerged as his overriding obsession. His belief that Bolsheviks or their leaders were predominantly Jewish led him to be cautious of Jews and their causes. For the first time, and really the only time, Churchill considered the Jews dangerous actors in international relations. He did not seem to know what to make of Zionism in this context, and, despite what he wrote in the provocative 1920 article "Zionism versus Bolshevism," he considered Zionism an obstacle to his overwhelmingly vital war against the Bolsheviks. Zionism conflicted with his strategic interest to maintain some semblance of the Ottoman Empire as a counter to Bolshevik Russia, and it interfered with his need to conserve dear financial and military resources. Although Churchill depicted Zionists and Bolsheviks as struggling for the Jewish soul, it was he who insisted on making a choice between those two movements, and he clearly focused on (anti-) Bolshevism at Zionism's expense. In his mind, strategic imperatives always trumped sentimental and romantic causes. Thus, when he did focus on the Balfour Declaration in 1919–1920, he mostly resented it, derogated it, and wanted to violate it. The most that could be said of Churchill's Zionism at this time was that his thoughts and feelings had nothing to do with what Muslims and Arabs thought about it, although even they generally said—at least initially—positive things about Zionism.

Churchill was not the only one who had forgotten his early Manchester days. The Zionists themselves barely held him to his early comments. Perhaps the only leading Zionist who alluded to them was Weizmann, Churchill's old acquaintance from Manchester. In late 1920, Weizmann wrote Churchill requesting a meeting about Palestine, "in which you have, if I remember rightly, been good enough to take a sympathetic interest at an earlier stage." Virtually no one else associated him with his earlier pro-Zionist statements. For when Churchill became colonial secretary in early 1921 and had the responsibility for executing the Palestine Mandate, the *Zionist Review* did not recall his pronouncements in North-West Manchester but simply expressed the hope that he would facilitate Jewish development of Palestine.[33] By early 1921, Manchester was at best a distant memory and most likely completely forgotten, despite Gaster's warning to Churchill in 1906 of the Jews' long memories. To all concerned, including Churchill himself, it appeared that he was setting to work implementing the Balfour Declaration with a perfectly clean slate, with no special attachment to the Jews or their Zionist dreams.

CHAPTER FOUR

"Smiling Orchards"

1921–1929

IN 1920, AS SECRETARY OF WAR, Churchill offered Lloyd George his normally clear perspective on the top foreign policy issues: "Compared to Germany, Russia is minor: compared to Russia, Turkey is petty." What then was Palestine? Very trivial indeed, had he elaborated. Thus, when Churchill reluctantly became colonial secretary in February 1921—where he had official authority over mandatory Palestine but not relations with Germany, Russia, or Turkey—he acutely felt that he was in charge of subordinate matters that nevertheless carried supreme political risk at a time of his own political vulnerability. This required caution, at least by his own ambitious, hyperactive, and provocative standards. He shared his apprehension with Foreign Secretary George Nathaniel Curzon, writing in early January, "I look forward only to toil & abuse." Curzon wrote back the next day, "I do not know whether to congratulate or commiserate with you on taking over these ventures," to which Churchill replied, "Emphatically *commiserate*." When the more prestigious chancellor of the exchequer post opened up in March 1921, Churchill was disappointed it was given to another.[1]

As colonial secretary, Churchill faced a dilemma. On the one hand, the larger picture in his mind was unfavorable to Zionism. The government's pro-Zionist policy was a subordinate matter that complicated more important financial, imperial, and strategic objectives. It also was increasingly opposed by the Conservative Party, which generally did not like Churchill but was the rising party in the country and dominated the governing coalition. At one point he privately proposed abandoning the pro-Zionist policy. On the other hand, he now had prominent official responsibility for implementing the Balfour Declaration, which was supported by his Liberal patron, Prime Minister David Lloyd George. Churchill was willing to take politically risky stands if they involved significant issues, such as Germany, Russia, or even Ireland, but he was much less willing to gamble his career over a subordinate matter like Zionism. And political considerations framed much of Churchill's public and even private comments about Zionism at this time, occasionally obscuring his true thoughts. To British audiences he almost always focused on the need to implement the government's Zionist policy, crafting a politically appealing argument and rarely belaboring its merits. To Palestinian Arabs he repeatedly conveyed the government's firm commitment to the Balfour Declaration, while to Jews he often waxed poetic about Zionism. He played for time, hoping to emerge from his tenure at the Colonial Office with the Zionist experiment on firmer footing, Palestine relatively quiet, financial commitments substantially reduced, and his political standing among Conservatives enhanced or at least not diminished. In all this he succeeded.

Churchill came into office knowing little about Palestine or the Middle East. He never considered the region—other than its edges, Turkey and Egypt—to hold much strategic importance, and it generally did not much intrigue him. The Holy Land was more exciting as a romantic notion than as an administrative territory. He mostly displayed a short attention span with Palestine matters, dedicating sometimes deep but episodic interest to those subjects, and relied heavily on his Arabist staff for information, guidance, and policy implementation.[2] This was true during his relatively strong engagement with the issue throughout much of 1921 as well as during his general disengagement from the autumn of 1921 until his tenure ended one year later. He never acquired a true expertise or betrayed deep, complex thought about the region, and his memos lacked the sweep, crisp analysis, creativity, conviction, and brilliant prescience that he demonstrated with more vital subjects. These factors, coupled with a restless desire to establish some regional political framework early in his tenure, contributed to his transferring 75 percent of the Palestine Mandate to an Arabian prince without sufficient thought or even consultation with the Zionists.

Notwithstanding some of his words, actions, and priorities, Churchill's tenure at the Colonial Office transformed him more concretely into a Zionist. Zionism was no longer an abstract concept for him. Not only did he still support Zionism for historical, racial, and humanitarian reasons, but he came to recognize deeply that it contributed to the advance of civilization. He now saw the Zionists as kindred spirits who shared the Victorian values that were so under siege in the world. He came to this realization on his own, by seeing Zionist achievements in Palestine with his own eyes and actually meeting Palestinian Jews. Certainly, constituent politics had nothing to do with this understanding. He enacted policies that supported the Zionist movement (along with policies that did not) and now felt a personal stake in its progress. The Palestinian Arabs also became concrete entities, and the experience was very negative for him. To be anti-Zionist now effectively meant to support the Palestinian Arabs, and Churchill found that notion unappealing. He had yet to become an ardent Zionist, but he was on his way.

Upon becoming colonial secretary, Churchill felt compelled to address Conservative sentiment that was increasingly anti-Semitic, anti-Zionist, and fixated on cutting government costs. In mid-1921, George Younger, chairman of the Conservative Party, privately blamed two recent by-election defeats on "the strong anti-semitic feeling which is very prominent at the present time. Far too many Jews have been placed in prominent positions by the present Government." Younger was apparently referring to the controversial Edwin Montagu and Lord Reading (Rufus Daniel Isaacs), who was lord chief justice and then viceroy for India in 1921, both Jewish Liberals who apparently tainted the Conservatives in the coalition government. Many Conservatives openly expressed their negative views of the Jews; they begrudged what they understood to be British help to rich Zionist Jews, while considering all Russian Jews to be Bolsheviks. William Ormsby-Gore, a Conservative MP, summed up this sentiment in the Commons in 1922: "There is what I call quite frankly the anti-Semitic party, that is to say those who are convinced that the Jews are at the bottom of all the trouble all over the world. . . . It is the rich Jews who are all blood-suckers and the poor Jews all Bolshevists." In a speech that very day, Churchill recognized this hostility and pointed out that many in Parliament who supported the Balfour Declaration in 1917 opposed it in 1922. (Indeed, only one month later, the House of Lords voted 60–29 against the Declaration despite Balfour's powerful maiden speech in the chamber on its behalf.) He did not demonstrate sympathy with the anti-Semites but humorously acknowledged the environment when speaking in support of a Palestine electrification concession (for generating hydraulic power from the Jordan and other nearby rivers) championed by the Russian-born Jew Pinchas Rutenberg: "When you have Jews, Russians, Bolshevism, Zionism, electrical monopoly, Government concessions, all presented at the same moment, it must be admitted all those ingredients are present out of which our most inexperienced scribe or cartoonist or our most recently budding statesman might make a very nice case."[3]

Churchill was also conscious of, and sympathetic to, opposition to the expense of unnecessary new imperial commitments in the Middle East. Early on in 1921, he wanted ardent opponent Andrew Bonar Law to understand that he shared this view, writing in a note to the Conservative Party leader, "There are *millions* to be saved in the Middle East." On the morning of his first major speech in the Commons on the Middle East in mid-1921, he minuted to an aide, "You must remember that my audience, both those who will hear and those who will read, are almost entirely ignorant of the whole story and take hardly any interest in any part of it except how much money is to be taken out of their pockets." Even five months later, he told an aide, "Do please realise that everything else that happens in the Middle East is secondary to the reduction in expense." Thus, he often framed his arguments on Palestine in fiscal terms, which he decidedly did not do for more significant foreign policy issues. Churchill succeeded in addressing this financial concern; at the end of his tenure as colonial secretary, he had eliminated 75 percent of Britain's Middle Eastern expenditure. He further relayed that like many Conservatives he too thought it better to spend dear public funds on existing imperial territories, such as Africa, which would redound to England's economic benefit. This had been his opinion since he was undersecretary of colonies fifteen years earlier, and he felt it strongly during his time as secretary of war and after the economy had soured. He now made his view known so know one would miss it. In 1921, he expressed to a commercial association in trade-conscious Manchester—where he had first publicly expressed his support for Zionism, no less—his bitter resentment at the expenditure on the mandates, using the term "grudge" in two different speeches. He emphasized that there was greater value per shilling gained from the African territories than from the mandates because African lands were more fertile and the people more docile. Or as he colorfully related to an imperial conference of colonial prime ministers who wanted more funds shifted their way, "In the Middle East the population is of a most difficult and intractable kind; proud, impecunious chiefs, peppery politicians, bitter, hot-headed theologians, who are a large proportion of the ordinary members of the population, in fact, almost constitute the entire population, and all, unhappily, extremely well-armed." This was not mere rhetoric. As he wrote in a note in late 1921, there was "urgency of developing the Colonial Estate" in a poor economic environment with high unemployment.[4]

Generally, out of fear of and deference to the anti-Zionist sentiment, Churchill portrayed himself as a detached, impartial executor of the Balfour Declaration and not an initiator on its behalf. He wrote to the Cabinet in 1921, "I have done and am doing my best to give effect to the pledge given to the Zionists by Mr Balfour on behalf of the War Cabinet and by the Prime Minister at the San Remo Conference." He suggested the same about the Mesopotamia Mandate, writing Bonar Law early in his tenure, "I have not sought this odious Mesoptn [Mesopotamian] embarrassment; & have only undertaken it from a desire to give a hand where one is needed." He carried the same message to the public. On the eve of a monthlong trip to lead two pivotal Middle Eastern conferences in March 1921, which drew much domestic criticism, he wrote a letter to the president of the Liberal Association in Dundee that was published in a newspaper. In the letter, he claimed to have accepted the colonial post only with "very greatest reluctance" and insisted it was the Cabinet that determined he go to the Middle East. He even suggested that it was not the government's fault that Britain obtained the mandates but the fault of the Paris conferees: "We have accepted by the Treaty of Versailles Mandates for Palestine and Mesopotamia." In three major parliamentary speeches on the Middle East during his post as colonial secretary, Churchill defended the Zionist policy by emphasizing that Britain had "pledged" its support during the war and therefore had a "duty" to honor its commitments and a "reputation" to uphold. He further insisted, "I am bound by the pledges and promises [made]." In a few instances, he did acknowledge that the policy was "absolutely right in itself" and "of profound significance," and that "the merits are considerable." There was no discussion of the Jews' historic right to the land, no citation of Disraeli's injunction to be good to the Jews, and no expressed compassion toward a scattered and persecuted people; he simply asserted the correctness of an approach formulated by others. In fact, he hardly expressed any concern for the Zionists. He did not even mention telling Abdullah (the sherifian prince to whom Britain, at Churchill's instigation, gave eastern Palestine, later known as Jordan) not to interfere with Zionist activity in western Palestine, but only pointed out that he warned Abdullah not to interfere with the French, which was in truth his main concern. The one feature of Zionism that Churchill extolled in any depth and with any conviction was its civilizational value.[5]

Churchill tried to implement the government's Zionist policy without being tarnished by it, and to that end he sometimes flexibly employed specious arguments. For instance, he contended in the Commons in 1922 that the Palestine Mandate was necessary to secure the Suez Canal, which had appealed to many in 1917 and might still have, especially Conservatives, but it was not an argument to which he deeply subscribed. Similarly, he referred to the tsarist government as "despotic" in defending the electrification concession for Rutenberg, who was an anti-tsar, anti-Bolshevik, pro-Kerensky activist. Churchill did not usually criticize the former Allied tsarist government, which was overthrown by the despised Bolsheviks.[6]

Churchill's greatest feat of rhetorical acrobatics was his public emphasis on implementing the Balfour Declaration in June 1921 while privately urging the government to betray it that same month. He feared the implications of the impending battle between the Turks and the Greeks in western Turkey. Unless the Greeks defeated the Turkish nationalists, he believed, the Turks might grab northern Mesopotamia, deepen its ties with Bolshevik Russia, ally with the Palestinian Arabs, and foment regional uprisings against the British, all of which would challenge Britain and increase the financial costs to its regional presence. In a speech on the Middle East in the Commons that month,

Churchill declared that reaching a settlement with Turkey was the "paramount" regional objective, since it would reduce Britain's regional challenges and financial commitments. He wrote Lloyd George that if the Turkish issue was not settled, it would be best to take advantage of the League of Nations' postponement of approval of the mandates (partly due to American reservations) "and resign them both and quit" Palestine and Mesopotamia "at the earliest possible moment." The idea of giving up the Palestine Mandate was not in itself anti-Zionist; another nation might carry out the mission. Lloyd George, and particularly Balfour, wished early on to involve the United States in Palestine, even after the Balfour Declaration, though by the end of 1918 Lloyd George changed his mind, fearing the meddling of this "absolutely new and crude Power in the middle of all our complicated interests in Egypt, Arabia, and Mesopotamia." Churchill gave no thought, however, to the moral, legal, or humanitarian implications of breaking Britain's pledge to the Jews, or to whether the proposal was at all realistic. One week later, he wrote Lloyd George again that he was "vy [very] much taken with the suggestion you made today" that "we are willing to hand over to the charge of the US either or both of the Middle Eastern Mandates we now hold, if they shd [should] desire to assume them." Undoubtedly perceiving a means to promote himself with Conservatives, Churchill offered to announce the transfer proposal himself. Lloyd George immediately rejected the suggestion, arguing that the United States was unlikely to accept it and that it was inappropriate to make such a proposal in public. Only a few days later, Churchill delivered his first major address in the Commons on Palestine policy and stressed Britain's duty to its pledges, including the humanitarian implications of abandoning the Zionists, which escaped him in private communications: "We cannot, after what we have said and done, leave the Jews in Palestine to be maltreated by the Arabs who have been inflamed against them."[7] There is no record of Churchill privately disparaging the pro-Zionist policy again for the rest of his term as colonial secretary.

Evidently, Churchill's public comments and perhaps some of his private ones had their desired effect; he succeeded in convincing some diehard Conservatives that he was simply the caretaker of another's policy. Already in May 1921, a month before his first major speech in the Commons, the editor of the anti-Zionist, Conservative *Daily Mail* wrote to the paper's owner, "Churchill is not responsible for Mesopotamia or for Palestine either. So far as he is concerned they are inheritances. He did not initiate any of the liabilities there; the pledges were given and he is obliged to carry them out at the least possible cost. Mesopotamia and Palestine are twin babies in his care but he is not the father." Churchill could not have asked for better absolution. Overall, he managed to convince Conservatives of his allegiance to their views, as Max Beaverbrook, the maverick Conservative press baron and sometimes friend of Churchill, attested to Lloyd George in 1922: "His tendency is all to the Right and his principles becoming more Tory." This was a substantial accomplishment, especially considering that many of the party diehards opposed Churchill's Irish policy of 1921–1922. Austen Chamberlain went even further in a note to Lloyd George, claiming that Churchill "was more Tory than the Tory Ministers." Capping Churchill's effective maneuvering was his successful July 1922 speech defending the Palestine Mandate and the Rutenberg concession, which the Commons approved by a lopsided vote of 292–35.[8]

Upon taking over the Colonial Office, Churchill quickly went about getting up to speed on many issues. He asked his new staff penetrating questions about various Middle Eastern matters, though few dealt with Palestine. He readily acknowledged his ignorance; he admitted to one staffer, Hubert Young, that he had "a great deal to learn" about Mesopotamia but pointed out that he at least had "a completely virgin mind on the subject," to which Young replied, "I'm here to ravish it." Regarding Palestine and much of the Middle East, Zionist leader Chaim Weizmann correctly noted to colleagues in early 1921 that Churchill "was of a highly impressionable temperament." Churchill relied heavily on his staff not only for information but for their broad conception of the region, and he followed their recommendations on all the major decisions of his tenure that affected Palestine. And his staff, particularly the controversial T. E. Lawrence, whom Churchill recruited and admired, was generally sympathetic to Arab nationalism and especially to the sherifian clan, though not always at the exclusion of Zionism. Churchill also recruited Colonel Richard Meinertzhagen (whom Lawrence disliked) as his military advisor beginning in April, being well aware that Meinertzhagen, an ardent Zionist, had gone out of the chain of command to complain in 1920 that General Edmund Allenby's military administration was anti-Zionist and promoted attacks on the Jews. Meinertzhagen seemingly had limited influence, however, and resentfully recorded in his diary that Churchill's attitude toward Lawrence "almost amounted to hero-worship." Lawrence reciprocated that admiration. Churchill admitted to Lloyd George, MPs, and others, both in public and in private, that he was not an expert on the Middle East but relied on experts at his disposal. This was true, and the argument had the advantage of distancing himself from the government's policies. Churchill similarly depended on his staff as president of the Board of Trade in 1908–1910.[9] By contrast, he rarely emphasized the importance of his aides on such important issues as Germany or Russia, about which he was well versed and confident.

Guided by his staff, a sense that the issues involved were of subordinate importance, and a desire to achieve the urgent short-term objectives of regional stability and reduction in British troops and expenses, Churchill rashly made several major policy decisions that affected Zionism without sufficient information or thought. Foremost among these was a policy favoring the sherifians. Some British officials, including Lawrence, were intent on establishing a loose Arab regional federation based on the sherifian clan, with Faisal ruling Syria; his brothers, Abdullah and Zaid, dividing Mesopotamia; and their father, Hussein, as king of Hejaz in Arabia. (After Faisal was expelled from Syria by France in 1920, it was recommended that he get Mesopotamia.) This regional approach was broadly supported by Zionists and anti-Zionists alike. The anti-Zionist military administration in Palestine wanted Faisal's rule in Greater Syria extended to Palestine, while Herbert Samuel, the new British high commissioner of Palestine, proposed in 1920 that Palestine maintain an independent government as part of a loose, Damascus-based Arab federation headed by Faisal. Samuel thought this structure would reassure the Palestinian Arabs and undermine their extreme elements, thereby easing the burden of the British occupiers. Curzon, no Zionist, later deemed Samuel's idea dangerous since he was wary of the Arabs: "It is true that their [the Arabs'] present hostility is ascribed to our Zionist policy but I feel by no means confident that were that policy to be abandoned we could permanently count on Arab friendship. Our difficulties in Iraq, which no one can attribute to Zionism, should warn us against staking everything on friendly Arab collaboration." The historian

Elie Kedourie termed Samuel's conception "pan-Arabism" and deemed it illusory since the sherifians "had neither power nor following to control or influence events in Palestine. The illusion was widespread among both British and Zionists and took a very long time a-dying."[10]

While sharing Curzon's skepticism, Churchill still supported the regional approach. Already by early 1921, after meeting with Lawrence, Churchill became set on the regional approach and proposed to Lloyd George the establishment of a new Middle East department within the Colonial Office to address the "whole of the Arabian peninsula." Arabia was Foreign Office domain, however, and this was not the only instance of Churchill trampling on Foreign Office territory, much to Curzon's consternation. Yet more was involved here than a simple bureaucratic grab for turf. Reflecting the pan-Arabism of Lawrence, Churchill wrote, "The Arab problem is all one." He explained that Mesopotamia, Kuwait, Arabia, and Jerusalem were "all inextricably interwoven, and no conceivable policy can have any chance which does not pull all the strings affecting them.... All affairs in the triangle Jerusalem-Aden-Basra must be dealt with in their integrity by one single Minister and from one single point of view." Churchill generally conceived international relations in a comprehensive manner, and a regional solution must have particularly appealed to his core belief that empires and federations offered more stability than small individual entities or states.[11]

Based on briefings by his staff, Churchill understood that a sherifian Arab federation would contribute to stability of the region and permit the reduction of British troops and financial expenditures. Sherifian leaders would support each other and would not want to cause problems for the British lest it lead to less British support for the other sherifian leaders. (Of course, it could work the other way: the British might shy away from confrontation with one sherifian leader to avoid conflict with another sherifian leader.) That the sherifians were placed to rule foreign people (except Hussein, who ruled in native Hejaz), and that they were weak, made them further dependent upon British support. This would also reduce the chance of anti-Zionist and anti-French agitation in the region. British payment of subsidies to Hussein and Ibn Saud would keep those two from each other's throats and ensure some peace in Arabia. And while Churchill personally remained opposed to this expanded British presence in the Middle East, believing the possible benefit not worth the cost, the fact was that such a federation, if it worked, along with control of Egypt and Palestine, would compose a large sphere of British influence in the region that could contribute further to Indian security. Such at least was the theory.[12]

This plan proved costly to the Zionists because Churchill, in his haste to establish the sherifian structure, also decided to approve his staff's recommendation to give the sherifians 75 percent of Palestine. In 1920 British officials had struggled with where to delineate Palestine's eastern border. Late that year, General Walter Congreve, commander of the Egyptian Expeditionary Force whose jurisdiction included Palestine, proposed separating Transjordan (east of the Jordan River, now Jordan) from Palestine as a way to save money and disentangle from the conflict brewing there between the French, who coveted eastern and western Palestine, and sherifians and their supporters. In early 1921, several senior colonial officials, including Lawrence, recommended establishing a separate local government in Transjordan under the auspices of Abdullah, though it would be supported by Britain and would still report to the high commissioner in Jerusalem. They believed this would head off Abdullah, who was in Transjordan, from leading a party against the French, who evicted his brother Faisal. These colonial officials believed sherifian control fulfilled the promises made by Henry McMahon, Britain's high commissioner in Egypt, to Hussein in 1915–1916, and the mandate's instruction to respect the rights of non-Jewish inhabitants and to provide self-government (Transjordan was populated by Arabs). In 1922, McMahon objected to this interpretation of his correspondence, writing a senior colonial official that both he and Hussein understood that Palestine was to be "excluded from independent Arabia," while also insisting that the Jordan River was not to be a boundary. Churchill did not bother to immerse himself in such details and interpretations. In late February, he accepted his staff's recommendations without even consulting the Zionists—Weizmann's appeal came after the matter was decided. Churchill made this momentous decision within one month of his appointment to the Colonial Office. He devoted even less time than that to the problem, for he remained minister of air until April 1921 and must have spent a fair amount of precious time in early 1921 preparing the Air Force budget, which he discussed in the Commons in a lengthy speech on March 1. On the following day, March 2, he departed to the Middle

MAP 2 League of Nations' Middle Eastern mandates and region, 1923. Drawn by Bill Nelson.

East for two conferences in which he advanced these recommendations, prepared by his staff, which established a new Middle Eastern order.[13]

Churchill embraced the sherifian structure without properly considering whether the sherifians would be satisfied with the land they received. In fact, they desired all of Palestine and other lands in the region. Moreover, he gave little thought to what legitimacy these Arabian princes would have with the people they were to rule, and thus how truly effective they could be. It was not until several months later, in June 1921, on the morning of his first major address in the Commons on the Middle East, that he bothered to ask his staff about the religious affiliation and sympathies of the sherifians: "Let me have a note in about three lines as to Feisal's religious character. Is he a Sunni with Shaih [sic] sympathies, or a Shaih with Sunni sympathies, or how does he square it? What is Hussein? Which is the aristocratic high church and which is the low church? What are the religious people at Kerbela? I always get mixed up between these two." He asked these questions now even though he had been involved in Mesopotamian policy as secretary of war during that country's very bloody uprising in 1920, led by the Iraqi Shia and the sherifians. Churchill's staff replied that the sherifians were nominal Sunnis who favored Shiites, which, if true, might have addressed concerns about installing Faisal in Mesopotamia, with its majority Shia population, but should have at least raised some questions about Abdullah's suitability to rule Sunni-dominated Transjordan. In April 1921, the London *Times* questioned the wisdom of Sunni sherifians ruling Mesopotamia, but Churchill probably did not read that piece since it appeared while he was vacationing on the French Riviera on his way back from the Middle East. One week after his June speech in the Commons, Churchill regurgitated his staff's opinion to an imperial conference: "The Shereefs have a remarkable history in that they are neither obnoxious to the Shias nor to the Sunnis." In fact, the Shia and other major religious and ethnic groups in Mesopotamia opposed Faisal's installation as king there: the Shiites, who constituted the majority population, felt it was their time to rule after Sunni Ottoman reign; the Sunni official class, which supported the Ottomans, considered the sherifians as Arabian opportunists; the Kurds in the north opposed being ruled from Baghdad; and the Jews, who composed the largest religious group in Baghdad, also opposed sherifian rule.[14]

Churchill campaigning in Manchester, 1908. Corbis.

Churchill walking with T. E. Lawrence and Abdullah in the gardens of the Government House, Jerusalem, March 1921. Library of Congress.

High Commissioner's House, Jerusalem, March 1921. *Front, from left:* Hadassah Samuel, Abdullah, Herbert Samuel, Churchill, and Clementine Churchill. Central Zionist Archives.

Churchill walking to the Hebrew University site in Jerusalem, with Herbert Samuel, March 29, 1921. Central Zionist Archives.

Churchill speaking at the Hebrew University site in Jerusalem, March 29, 1921. On left, seated with long beards, are Palestine's two chief rabbis, Avraham Kook and Yaakov Meir. Further left, seated with short white beard, is Edmond de Rothschild. Central Zionist Archives.

Painting of Jerusalem, done by Churchill during his visit, March 1921. Churchill Heritage.

Churchill in Tel Aviv with Mayor Meir Dizengoff, March 30, 1921. Central Zionist Archives.

Churchill visiting a Jewish settlement, with Herbert Samuel, March 30, 1921. Central Zionist Archives.

Chaim Weizmann, Herbert Samuel, David Lloyd George, and his wife, Margaret, 1930. Central Zionist Archives.

Churchill convened two Middle Eastern conferences in March ostensibly to hash all these issues out, but these assemblies functioned more as a forum to implement and gain support for decisions already made by his staff. The Cairo conference was attended by forty leading British experts on the Middle East—dubbed by Churchill the "Forty Thieves," with perhaps unintentional irony. One of the attendees was Gertrude Bell, the well-known traveler, writer, and official, who strongly supported sherifian rule in Mesopotamia. Churchill successfully made the case before these officials for the sherifian solution. In Jerusalem, where Churchill held another conference, he told Abdullah, according to the meeting minutes, that he supported the sherifians "in a predominant position in the whole of the Arab countries so far as this was compatible" with Allied decisions (agreements with the French) and "promises made to third parties" (the Jews). This meant sherifians could not rule Syria or western Palestine. Abdullah tentatively agreed, according to meeting minutes, explaining that the sherifians did not regard themselves "in the light of spokesmen for the whole of the Arab nation. The first and most important point to them was the future of the peninsula of Arabia, the home of the Arab race." In other words, the sherifians were not intent on Palestine but accepted the Zionist home there. This was not in fact true, and Abdullah suggested a couple of times only moments later that he govern both western Palestine and Transjordan, but Churchill resisted. Churchill did concede that Britain would not promote Jewish immigration in Transjordan and that the local government would not have to promote Jewish immigration—in fact, the "Zionist clauses of the mandate would not apply" there. Upon returning to England, Churchill explained to Herbert Sidebotham, a pro-Zionist Gentile correspondent for the *Times*, what he implied to Abdullah but did not explicitly state: that Jews could settle in Transjordan but (in Sidebotham's words) "he hoped nothing would be said about it."[15]

To push this policy through, Churchill had to overcome the deep reservations of Samuel, who suspected Abdullah would agitate against the Zionists and French, and some in the government back in London. Prime Minister Lloyd George feared the price would be "high and the results doubtful" and suggested instead treating Transjordan as "an Arab province or adjunct of Palestine." Indeed, as Kedourie argued, "The settlement of 1921 . . . contained the seeds of its own destruction; for it gave power to men who were intent precisely on overthrowing such a settlement." Still, the arrangement was codified in the mandate, and subsequent Anglo-Abdullah agreements progressively separated Transjordan from Palestine until, in 1946, Britain recognized Transjordan as an independent state ruled by Abdullah. Notably, despite all Churchill's diplomatic activity at the conferences, his underlings complained that he delayed briefing himself and concentrated instead on writing his history/memoirs of the First World War, *The World Crisis*. They also criticized him for spending too much time painting Egyptian and Palestinian landscapes.[16]

In other, lesser ways, Churchill's detachment and reliance on subordinates led to a weakening of the government's Zionist policy. He opted not to get involved when Haj Amin al-Husseini, a rabid anti-Jewish, anti-Zionist, and anti-British Arab activist, was unofficially appointed in 1921, by the administration in Palestine, Jerusalem's grand mufti, a position created by Allenby's military administration, and then formally appointed in 1922 head of the Supreme Moslem Council, which carried a government salary and unsupervised control of various Arab positions and funds. Haj Amin went on to inspire violence against the Jews and Britain in Palestine, Iraq, and elsewhere. Churchill also did not interfere when, in the autumn of 1921, General Congreve disparaged the Zionists in a circular and expressed sympathy with the Arabs. On both issues, Meinertzhagen shared his objections with Churchill to no avail. However, it is not uncommon for ministers to give plenty of latitude to ranking officials in the field—indeed, ministers often have no choice but to do so. Churchill did get heavily involved in other aspects of Palestine's governance, in accord with the normal duties of a British colonial secretary for an administered territory. By the time Congreve issued his circular, however, Churchill's mind was increasingly focused on trying to reconcile Northern and Southern Ireland and reduce Britain's role there. In November 1921, Meinertzhagen recorded in his diary about Palestine, "Winston does not care two pins, and does not want to be bothered about it. He is reconciled to a policy of drift." Later that month, Churchill did not attend a conference of Arabs and Zionists in London that was sponsored by his ministry.[17]

Although far more concerned with various European, Russian, imperial, political, and economic issues, and willing to defer to subordinates on

Middle Eastern issues, which impeded his efforts on behalf of the Zionists, Churchill retained underlying sympathy for the Zionist cause. While some of his supportive comments were made in forums that demanded it, he also publicly touched on themes that were consistent with his prior and subsequent views on the issue, and with his overall worldview: humanitarian concern for scattered Jewry, respect for Jews' historic right to Palestine, and belief that Jews were agents of progress and civilization, particularly compared to the Arabs. He articulated the civilizational theme often spontaneously and always with special enthusiasm; it was one of the most enduring and prominent reasons he supported Zionism.

With the exception of June 1921, when he proposed breaking the government's pledge to the Zionists, Churchill generally was more supportive of Zionism than most other officials, including his aides, especially on key Zionist issues. He certainly was more pro-Zionist than the military in Palestine, whose pro-Arab sentiment was well known. Churchill once commented to the Cabinet on the "chilling disapprobation of the military." He also recognized the pro-Arab sympathies of others in the British administration in Palestine, and he submitted a memo to the Cabinet, written by an aide, which recommended replacing British officials in Palestine who did not support the government's Zionist policy.[18]

Most notably, Churchill demonstrated more concern for ensuring success of the Zionist experiment than Herbert Samuel, a Jew who as a government official first urged the Cabinet to embrace a Zionist policy in 1914–1915, and who then was appointed high commissioner of Palestine in 1920 to replace the British military administration that was found to have encouraged Arab anti-Jewish rioting. An illustration of Churchill and Samuel's differing opinions was their divergent response to the Arab-Jewish clashes in Jaffa in May 1921, which left several hundred dead or wounded. The violence seemed to lead Samuel, who in 1915 had already taken a very patient long-term view of the Zionist movement, to become more intent on avoiding conflict and maintaining support for his administration among Palestinian Arabs than fulfilling Britain's Zionist policy. In his report to Churchill about the riots, Samuel absolved the Palestinian Arabs, whose leaders he considered moderate; sympathized with Arab frustration over their lack of proportional representation; and blamed Jewish immigration for the violence. Samuel sought to suspend Jewish immigration temporarily and then restart it only if the immigrants were carefully selected and if jobs awaited them. The Zionists strongly objected, and even the *Times* opposed the suspension of immigration and urged the administration to be firmer. Lloyd George privately called Samuel "rather weak."[19]

Churchill counseled patience and offered perspective. He wrote to Samuel, "In times like these when few countries present an aspect of tranquility there is no disposition to exaggerate the significance of the inevitable troubles attending the birth of the Jewish National home." He blamed the Arabs more, who aimed at "frightening us out of our Zionist policy." He encouraged Samuel to establish a Jewish police reserve for self-defense and issue them arms. Churchill approved the suspension of immigration at the urging of at least one of his aides but was clearly reluctant to do so, writing to Samuel that "only grave anxiety would I feel have induced you to suspend immigration." As Sidebotham correctly surmised to the Zionist Organization, "I believe he [Churchill] did not like Samuel's action, but he will never openly throw Samuel over." This was another instance of Churchill as minister giving greater deference to the wishes of an official in the field. Indicative of Churchill's sympathy for the Jewish immigrants, he expressed concern to an aide about those Jews who were held up in Vienna, Trieste, and Constantinople en route to Palestine. "We cannot leave them in Vienna," he declared, asking what could be done to accommodate them. The next day he asked Samuel to announce that, as the "first step to re-opening immigration," the immigrants temporarily held up in Constantinople and Trieste be allowed to proceed. Still, Churchill assented to Samuel's proposal to limit the number of immigrants to the ambiguous capacity of Palestine to employ them, which Samuel made public on June 3, 1921. The Zionists vehemently opposed this new policy—Weizmann, who was optimistic about prospects for immigration, privately called Samuel's speech a "negation" of the Balfour Declaration—and it led to a precipitous drop in Jewish immigration. Churchill was apparently unenthusiastic in approving the new policy, since he had an expansive view of Palestine's absorptive capacity, as he declared in the Commons a couple weeks later: "There is no doubt whatever that at the present time the country is greatly under-populated. . . . I see no reason why with care and progress there, there should not be a steady flow of Jewish immigrants into the country, and why this flow should not be accompanied at every stage by a general increase in the wealth." Indeed, he was greatly impressed by the Zionists' ability to develop the land.[20]

While Churchill agreed to these shifts in policy, his intent was to ensure the continuation of Jewish immigration and thus the very viability of the Zionist experiment. For that reason he rejected Samuel's proposal to establish an elected advisory council to British administration, which the Arabs, as the majority of the population, would dominate. Churchill, in accordance with official government policy, insisted on the long-term objective of creating a Jewish national home over any short-term representative institutions. He raised this dilemma in the Commons early in his term and made his choice clear in various venues. He insisted that while the Palestinian Arabs could be permitted some gradual establishment of elective institutions, no institution could be founded that would seek to curtail or end Jewish immigration. As he wrote to one aide, this "avoids the folly of going out of our way to procure a hungry lion and then walking up to him with a plate of raw beef to see how much he would like to take." More formally, Churchill instructed Samuel that "no representative bodies that may be established will be permitted to interfere with measures (e.g. immigration &c.) designed to give effect to principle of a National Home or to challenge this principle." Moreover, he did not believe that the Arabs were ready for democratic government, and he granted self-government to Arabs outside Palestine only out of necessity, not moral obligation. In any case, Churchill considered the timing of Samuel's proposal harmful, as it would appear to reward violence. He also opposed Samuel's proposal for the establishment of an Arab committee that would be the equivalent of the Zionist Organization, which had a special status in the Palestine government.[21]

Samuel wanted to deliver a major speech on Palestine policy on June 3, 1921. Churchill agreed but warned Samuel to be very careful in what he said: "Adhere as closely as possible to the exact wording eventually approved by me." No language was more sensitive than a Jewish "national home," which was the government's stated aim in the Balfour Declaration, as well as the official wording used by the Zionist movement. A "national home" was more substantial than a "centre," a word that Churchill had first used in Manchester and indeed still used but now in conjunction with the former, stronger term. Samuel wanted to use the term "spiritual centre," suggesting a nonpolitical entity and echoing terms he used in his two 1915 memos. Churchill responded that "national home" meant that the "Jewish people scattered throughout the world but whose hearts always turn to Palestine should within the limits fixed by numbers and the interests of the present population *be encouraged to make their home in Palestine* and by their resources and efforts help to develop the country to the advantage of all its inhabitants" (italics added). This statement was strikingly reminiscent of Rabbi Gaster's words to Churchill in 1905: "The heart of the Jew turns to Palestine and no other country in the world." Churchill did not want to dilute Britain's pledge to the Jews, especially in response to the Jaffa violence. Samuel countered that such a formulation might confirm Palestinian Arab fears of immediate Jewish mass immigration and instead stated in his June 3 speech that the Jews "should be enabled to found" in Palestine "their home" and that "some among them" should come to Palestine. In his own speech to the Commons ten days later, Churchill used his more pro-Zionist formulation, one that more adhered to the government's policy, and eschewed Samuel's.[22]

Churchill's defense of Jewish immigration and the foundation of the Zionist experiment extended to the political battle over whether the Jewish immigrants were Bolsheviks. This was no minor matter, as he cautioned Samuel after the Jaffa riots, which were ignited by Jewish Communists, and he told Samuel to "purge" these Communist elements. Even a couple months before the riots Churchill urged the Zionists in Jerusalem to allow into Palestine only "picked men" who were "worthy representatives of Jewry and of the cause of Zionism." But Churchill did not overstate this matter. He consistently maintained that Zionist ranks had few Communists, which he certainly had the credibility to argue based on his own previous anti-Bolshevik demagoguery, including the labeling of Bolsheviks as Jews. Indeed, if he had sincerely meant what he wrote in his 1920 article "Zionism versus Bolshevism," he should have welcomed eastern European Jewish Communists who focused their energy on Zionist activities. He told some Zionist leaders after the Jaffa riots, according to meeting minutes, that, based on his own encounter with Jewish settlers, "they were as far from being 'Red' as could be imagined." He repeated the same point to the Cabinet and at an imperial conference, saying that the "stories of Bolshevism have been much exaggerated." He even presented to the Cabinet a Bolshevik circular of March 25, 1921, sent out to secret international Communist organizations, which accused Zionist organizations of conducting espionage on behalf of the British government and directed Communists to act against Zionists. He also addressed the issue in the Commons in 1922, when defending the electrification concession of Rutenberg, a Russian-born Jew and thus in some minds a Communist: "It is hard enough, in all conscience, to make a New Zion, but if, over the portals of the new Jerusalem, you are going to inscribe the legend, 'No Israelite need apply,' then I hope the House will permit me to confine my attention exclusively to Irish matters."[23]

Beyond any specific policies and away from Parliament, Churchill declared his sympathy for Zionism in many venues and occasions. In the most dramatic moment of Churchill's engagement with Zionism thus far, and ultimately one of the most moving Zionist experiences of his life, he spoke to a crowd of ten thousand Jews at the site of the uncompleted Hebrew University on Mount Scopus in Jerusalem on March 29, 1921. In attendance were many Jewish schoolchildren, along with Herbert Samuel and James de Rothschild. The Ashkenazi and Sephardi chief rabbis of Palestine, Avraham Yitzchak Kook and Yaakov Meir, presented Churchill with a Torah scroll, and Rabbi Kook declared that England, the Jewish national home, and Palestine were all bound together, not only by passing events but by eternal facts consecrated by God. Churchill then announced, in his first pro-Zionist speech since 1908 in Manchester, "My heart is full of sympathy for Zionism. This sympathy has existed for a long time, since twelve years ago, when I was in contact with the Manchester Jews." (Another account, seemingly less accurate, has Churchill stating, "My heart has throbbed with Zionism.") Back in 1908 he also used the phrase "full sympathy" when expressing support for Zionism, suggesting that he retained that earlier sentiment in the far reaches of his mind (or he retained the earlier speech in his files and borrowed from it). Further echoing the vague phrases he had used before, he stated, "I believe that the establishment of a Jewish National Home in Palestine will be a blessing to the whole world, a blessing to the Jewish race scattered all over the world, and a blessing to Great Britain." He then planted a palm tree, assisted by Samuel and Rothschild, while

Hatikvah (The Hope), the Zionist anthem, was sung enthusiastically by the crowd.[24]

Churchill was even more effusive the previous day when he met a Zionist delegation in Palestine. He referred to "the greatness of the ideal" of Zionism, sympathized with the Zionists' challenges, extolled their virtues, and expressed confidence in their success: "I know how great the energy is and how serious are the difficulties at every stage and you have my warmest sympathy in the efforts you are making to overcome them. If I did not believe that you were animated by the very highest spirit of justice and idealism, and that your work would in fact confer blessings upon the whole country, I should not have the high hopes which I have that eventually your work will be accomplished." He repeated the message that same day to a hostile Palestinian Arab delegation, which had harshly protested Zionist activity in anti-Jewish terms. He insisted that he had no inclination or interest to repudiate the Balfour Declaration and terminate Jewish immigration: "It is not in my power to do so, nor, if it were in my power, would it be my wish." He explained why: "We think it will be good for the world, good for the Jews and good for the British Empire. But we also think it will be good for the Arabs who dwell in Palestine, and we intend that it shall be good for them." Several months later, to a skeptical audience at an imperial conference, Churchill announced, "The Zionist ideal is one that claims my keen personal sympathy." And, in an impressive description of a politically unpopular, untested movement, he added that it was "a great experiment which deserves a fair chance."[25]

Churchill continued to believe that the Jews deserved the Holy Land for historical and humanitarian reasons. Most officially, he declared in strong terms in a June 1922 statement known as the Churchill White Paper, which was drafted by Samuel, that the Jews were in Palestine "as of right and not by sufferance," based on their "ancient historic connection." He tried repeatedly to convince the Arabs who disputed Jewish right to the land, and in the process he absorbed a deeper understanding of Zionism. To a hostile Palestinian Arab delegation in the spring of 1921, he defended Zionism on humanitarian and historical grounds: "It is manifestly right that the Jews, who are scattered all over the world, should have a national centre and a National Home where some of them may be reunited. And where else could that be but in this land of Palestine, with which for more than 3,000 years they have been intimately and profoundly associated?" He repeated these ideas to another Palestinian Arab delegation five months later: "This is a country where they [Jews] have great historic traditions, and you cannot brush that aside as though it were absolutely nothing. They were there many hundreds of years ago." He then introduced a new justification, that for the Jews Palestine was a "sacred place": "Many of them go there to be buried in the city which they regard as sacred,—as you regard it as sacred." More important, he argued that the Jews deserved the Holy Land because they had always been devoted to it and always yearned in the Diaspora to live there: "They have always tried to be there." As he told a Zionist audience in Jerusalem in the spring of 1921, "The hope of your race for so many centuries will be gradually realised here."[26]

Whatever historical claims the Jews had to the Holy Land, and Churchill considered them very strong, almost did not matter as much to him as their immediate ability to civilize the land and contribute to the world's progress. The Zionists' phenomenal development of land long left barren by what he perceived to be primitive inhabitants provided them with a renewed title deed to the land. Like the British and other allegedly enlightened white races, he saw the Zionists as agents of civilization and progress. In both public and private, to British politicians and officials as well as Arabs and Jews, Churchill reported on how well the Zionists were developing the land. This perception became a central component of his Zionism, a point he returned to throughout the rest of his life. That he repeated this message regardless of the venue partly reflected his belief in its universal appeal—British imperialists, Palestinian Arabs, and others, he wrongly believed, should all see the value of this gift of the Zionists to themselves and to the world. But mostly he repeated the civilizational argument like a mantra because he felt it so deeply, especially in this time when so much of his dear Victorian civilization had been corrupted.

Churchill saw the Zionists' civilizational achievement firsthand during his eight-day journey through Palestine in March 1921. He plainly stated to a virulently anti-Zionist Arab delegation in Palestine, "This country has been very much neglected in the past and starved and even mutilated by Turkish misgovernment." He then insisted, "You can see with your own eyes in many parts of this country the work which has already been done by Jewish colonies; how sandy wastes have been reclaimed and thriving farms and orangeries planted in their stead." That same day, he told a Jewish delegation that when he returned to London he hoped to relate how the Zionist experiment "is transforming waste places into fertile; it is planting trees and developing agriculture in desert lands; it is making for an increase in wealth and of cultivation; it is making two blades of grass grow where one grew before, and the people of the country who are in a great majority [the Arabs], are deriving great benefit, sharing in the general improvement and advancement."[27]

Churchill witnessed exactly that two days later, on the last day of his trip, when he had a chance to tour more of the country. He saw more clearly what the Jews had accomplished, and was overwhelmed. On March 30, he visited Jaffa, Tel Aviv, Bir Yaakov, and Rishon Lezion. In Tel Aviv, a small young town, he was welcomed by schoolchildren lining flag-filled streets. Bessarabian-born Mayor Meir Dizengoff saluted his distinguished guest and delivered a brief but eloquent speech that outlined what the Zionists had accomplished and sought to achieve: "This small town of Tel-Aviv, which is hardly 12 years old, has been conquered by us on sand dunes, and we have built it with our work and our exertions. It is in this manner that we are determined to render fruitful the land of our ancestors by work, by knowledge and by culture." Despite the Turks and the war, he continued, "we have been able to create such a pretty oasis in the middle of the sandy desert, what cultural values shall we not create under the protection of the Government of His Britannic Majesty [?]" He concluded, "Our most ardent desire is to work in peace, under the shelter of the British flag, at the building up of our National Home, that is to say at our civilizing action in the domains of agriculture, industry, and commerce, for the greatest benefit of all the inhabitants of the country.... The Jewish people will still have to speak its word in the history of civilisation." The conscious determination of these pioneers to civilize their long-barren ancestral land resonated with Churchill; he marveled how the city was "the result of the initiative of its inhabitants in so short a period during which, too, the war had intervened." He then went to Bir Yaakov, a small new pioneer settlement of immigrants from Russia. With Rutenberg interpreting, Churchill asked the immigrants if they were Bolsheviks. They replied that they were not but that they were dedicated to the ideal of labor and to building a society based on self-help and physical exertion. Churchill certainly was impressed.[28]

The highlight of Churchill's tour, which particularly left a lasting impression, was Rishon Lezion ("First to Zion"), the first permanent Zionist agricultural settlement, which was established in 1882 by ten pioneers from Russia. The settlement had been supported at times by Baron Edmond de Rothschild and was visited by Theodor Herzl in 1898. During Churchill's visit, six youths on horseback greeted his car and gave flowers to Mrs. Churchill and Lady Samuel, the high commissioner's wife. The riders then formed a bodyguard for the visiting delegation until they reached the synagogue, where the colony's elders welcomed the British guests. In their collective speech, the elders greeted Churchill in "the name of the Jewish farmer-pioneers of Palestine." They pointed out that they had created a great deal in forty years "through self sacrificing and energy for our common purpose." In 1882, they found the land "deserted" and "serving as a dwelling for jackals," and "now in this very place all kinds of plantations as oranges, almonds, vines, olives etc. are to be found." Additionally, "at present nearly all swamps, rocks and sands became beautiful colonies, gardens and orchards on which we are proud." They were working closely with "our Arab neighbors," who had adopted the Jews' system of agriculture and building, while more remote Arab villages "remained in a primitive state as in former years." This speech, like Dizengoff's, uncannily expressed values that Churchill shared and struck a cord with him. What he saw did so even more. For he then inspected the settlement's wine cellars and was visibly impressed. He enthusiastically declared, "Nothing will stand in your way. You have changed desolate places to smiling orchards and initiated progress instead of stagnation. Because of our belief in you we are supporting the Zionist Movement."[29]

It was a magnificent testimony, apparently made extemporaneously and thus most revealing. Churchill's choice of words was especially telling. His whole worldview was based on the nineteenth-century ideal of promoting progress, and now he had witnessed firsthand the Zionists doing just that. They were collaborators, fellow civilizers in this most important historical mission. His visit concretized and intensified his enthusiasm for Zionism. Later, when he thought of the Zionist enterprise, he often thought of the bronze pioneers and blooming orchards of that young settlement. Rishon Lezion left an impression on Churchill that lasted the rest of his life, and his excitement for it ensured that he would always remain at heart a Zionist.

Upon returning to England, Churchill exuberantly shared his positive impressions both in private and in public. Churchill, Sidebotham noted after a meeting with him, was "enthusiastic" about Jewish colonies in Palestine: "Splendid open air men, he exclaimed, beautiful women; and they have made the desert blossom like the rose." Churchill had even remarked, in Sidebotham's words, that "he had always been sympathetic with Zionism ever since his N.W. Manchester days." After not mentioning Manchester for thirteen years, Churchill now referred to it twice within a month, with the second reference likely sparked by the presence of Sidebotham, who had been an editor at the *Manchester Guardian*. To the Cabinet the following month Churchill "paid a high tribute to the success of the Zionist colonies of long standing, which had created a standard of living far superior to that of the indigenous Arabs." And a month later he told the Commons that anyone who had seen the work of the Zionists in the past twenty or thirty years would now be "struck by the enormous productive results which they have achieved." He insisted that amid the "most inhospitable soil," the Jews of Rishon Lezion had produced the "most beautiful, luxurious orange groves" and "excellent wine." He continued with great force, "I defy anybody, after seeing work of this kind, achieved by so much labour, effort and skill, to say that the British Government, having taken up the position it has, could cast it all aside and leave it to be rudely and brutally overturned by the incursion of a fanatical attack by Arab population from outside. It would be disgraceful if we allowed anything of the kind to take place." He could not imagine Britain standing in the way of the indispensable mission to promote world progress. He then insisted, "I am talking . . . of what I saw with my own eyes." There was no question that this startling rhetoric came from his heart and was based on his trip. He then pointed out how Jewish industry was benefiting the Arabs: "All round the Jewish colony, the Arab houses were tiled instead of being built of mud, so that the culture from this centre has spread out into the surrounding district." This echoed exactly what Chaim Weizmann and the Zionist leadership repeatedly claimed. One week later, Churchill reiterated the same themes to a rather skeptical imperial conference: "It should be remembered that wherever they [the Zionists] have been they have not only created wealth for themselves but for the Arabs around them. Wherever the footprints of the Jew in Palestine are found you have prosperity, progress and scientific methods of cultivation, and where there was a wilderness you now find vineyards. They are very good, energetic agriculturists."[30]

These were astonishing statements, delivered to the mostly unsympathetic Cabinet, Commons, and imperial conference. They were not circumspect or hedged in tentative words, unlike much else that Churchill said about Palestine. When he discussed the civilizational impact of the Zionist venture, Churchill was bold and defiant, and insisted that Britain continue to support this momentous historical endeavor. He spoke no differently about Zionist achievements in what he deemed backward territories than he did about Britain's own achievements in such lands. At the same imperial conference, Churchill expressed his opposition to Britain leaving Egypt and Sudan, as Egyptian nationalists demanded, by citing a similar civilizational argument, describing the territories as "tremendous regions which have been developed out of barbarism by British labour and money."[31] He believed that British development of Egypt and Sudan entitled Britain to sovereignty over those areas, just as he believed Zionist cultivation of Palestine gave the Jews an additional claim to that land (though he did not see the Jews as imperialists). Churchill saw the British and Zionists as kindred spirits, sharing a mission to civilize the world.

Just as Churchill would forever picture Rishon Lezion when thinking about Zionist Palestine, he attached Chaim Weizmann's face to the Zionist movement. And as with the Zionists in Rishon Lezion, Churchill perceived in Weizmann a man with values similar to his own. Weizmann, like many Russian Jewish immigrants of his generation, was devoted to England and its values, including freedom, civil liberty, toleration, moderation, and pragmatism. Weizmann imagined the emerging Jewish state to be just like his romantic image of England (which eventually undermined his position within the Zionist movement in the 1940s), and he believed strongly that the progress of mankind could not ultimately be stymied. Weizmann spoke in a vivid, concrete manner that appealed very much to the British, and he charmed Churchill and many other British politicians. Isaiah Berlin, who knew Weizmann well and was a close observer of his activities with British officials, wrote: "It was this serene and absolute illusion among the statesmen of the world that he was himself a world statesman, representing a government in exile, behind which stood a large, coherent, powerful, articulate community. Nothing was—in the literal sense—less true, and both sides knew it well. And yet both sides behaved—negotiated—as if it were true, as if they were equals. If he did not cause the embarrassment that supplicants so often engender, it was because he was very dignified, and quite free." Berlin continued, "Ministers were known to shrink nervously from the mere prospect of an approaching visit from this formidable emissary of a non-existent power, because they feared the interview might prove altogether too much of a moral experience," thereby leading them to offer unintended concessions.[32] There are in fact records of Churchill sharing such experiences with Weizmann.

Yet, however positively Churchill viewed the Zionists, his overall perception of Jews remained somewhat mixed. He maintained the Disraelian view that Christianity and the civilized Christian world were indebted to the Jews. When presented with a Torah scroll at the Hebrew University site in Jerusalem, he thanked the rabbis for the gift, "which as you have said, contains all the truth which has been accepted by the greater part of the enlightened world, and which is the heritage of Christians and Jews alike." Churchill even went so far as to say, "I shall treasure this present in my family and hand it down to my children after me." He was also appreciative of Jewish support for Britain's effort in the First World War. He remained, however, a bit unsure about the Jews. He believed that the Jews had to prove to him, Britain, and the world that they were worthy of the largesse of this gift of a homeland. He conveyed that apprehension to the Jews in North-West Manchester fifteen years before, in his 1920 article "Zionism versus Bolshevism," and before an audience at the Hebrew University site, when he declared, "You Jews of Palestine have a very great responsibility; you are the representatives of the Jewish nation all over the world, and your conduct should provide an example for, and do honour to, Jews in all countries." Similarly, at Rishon Lezion the next day, he stated that "because of our belief in you we are supporting the Zionist Movement." He was not completely convinced but "believed" the Jews would make a success of their endeavor. Perhaps this was as much as the Jews could ask for, given that a Jewish homeland was a radical modern experiment. The Jews, after all, had a checkered historical image among Westerners, historically were not known to be laborers of the field, and were perceived as being disproportionately involved in Communist movements—indeed, Churchill had repeatedly promoted that last image the past couple of years. A correspondent for the *Zionist Review,* writing about Churchill's trip to Palestine, recognized this leap of faith: "He has stated that his Zionism is based upon his faith in the Jewish people to make good in Palestine—it is only left to us to justify that faith."[33]

Although Churchill was still somewhat uncertain about the Jews, he became certain in his poor regard of the Palestinian Arabs after visiting Palestine, meeting their leaders there and in London, and generally involving himself in the Zionist issue. As a soldier and journalist in Sudan in 1898, he thought Muslims backward, unproductive, and slovenly. He came to view the Palestinian Arabs the same way. If the Jews were agents of progress, the Arabs guaranteed stagnation. He felt that the Arabs' historic ineptitude at developing Palestine automatically disqualified them from governing the land, and he held that view for the rest of his life, though he never suggested that they be kicked off their individual plots. In the summer of 1921 an unidentified person argued in the Cabinet in favor of the Balfour Declaration because, according to the minutes, "the Arabs had no prescriptive right to a country which they had failed to develop to the best advantage." It almost certainly was Churchill. Four days later he echoed those comments to an Arab delegation. In the following year, he explained in the Commons that while the dynamic Jews had "converted" the desert "into gardens," "under centuries of Turkish and Arab rule, they had relapsed into a wilderness. There is no doubt whatever that in that country there is room for still further energy and development if capital and other forces be allowed to play their part." He continued, when defending the Rutenberg concession, to describe forcefully the Palestinian Arabs as hopelessly primitive: "I am told that the Arabs would have done it themselves. Who is going to believe that? Left to themselves, the Arabs of Palestine would not in a thousand years have taken electrification of Palestine. They would have been quite content to dwell—a handful of philosophic people—in the wasted sun-scorched plains, letting the waters of the Jordan continue to flow unbridled and unharnessed into the Dead Sea." It was a startling public denunciation. Churchill also believed the Palestinian Arabs, unlike the Jews, to be unfriendly toward Britain. In 1921 he met a Palestinian Arab delegation in London, and the secretary of the delegation referred to Palestinian Arabs having fought at Britain's side during the war. Churchill asked rhetorically how many had fought in Allenby's army; as Churchill keenly knew, the Palestinian Arabs had in fact supported the Ottoman cause.[34]

The Palestinian Arabs were implacably anti-Zionist, as they made clear through their words and deeds. Churchill slowly came to recognize, or at least acknowledge, this. On his way to Palestine in March 1921, Churchill and his entourage met a tumultuous crowd in Gaza whose chief cries, in Arabic, were "Down with the Jews" and "Cut their throats." Lawrence did not translate these chants, and Churchill was ignorantly pleased with the enthusiastic crowd. Churchill certainly learned the truth about the Palestinian Arabs' feelings when he met with their delegations later during his trip and in London that summer. He also read a commission of inquiry into the Jaffa riots by the British administration in Palestine, which asserted that the Arabs were "generally the aggressors [and] inflicted most of the casualties," and that a "large part of the Moslem and Christian communities condoned it, although they did not encourage violence." He wrote Balfour later that year that "nine-tenths of the [Palestinian] population and an equal proportion of the British officers are marshaled" against Zionism. Churchill, incidentally, liked to wave Palestinian Arab anti-Zionism in front of others when it served other important objectives. He cited it in his warnings in 1921 against an anti-Turk policy, contending that the Turks would utilize Britain's Zionist policy to incite the Palestinian Arabs against the British. And he seemed to emphasize Palestinian Arab hostility to minimize his own responsibility should Palestinian violence continue. In any case, the Palestinian Arabs had good reason to believe resistance paid off. The vagueness and seemingly fundamental contradiction of the Balfour Declaration sowed confusion, the League of Nations did not ratify the Palestine Mandate until July 1922, and the anti-Zionist Allenby administration tolerated if not encouraged sherifian activities in Jerusalem around the time of the 1920 riots. A British court of inquiry that examined the Easter riots in Jerusalem in 1920 concluded that Allenby's approach was wrong and that eastern peoples had to be forced to reconcile to a fait accompli.[35] Samuel's timidity in the face of the Palestinian Arabs' violence, including his temporary suspension of Jewish immigration after the 1921 Jaffa riots, must have only encouraged the Palestinian Arabs even more.

Churchill's belief that the Palestinian Arabs needed to recognize the futility of their opposition, his exasperation with their intransigence and violence, and his disgust with what he deemed their primitiveness and their support for the Ottomans led him to speak very bluntly and impatiently with Palestinian Arab leaders. He did not speak to them respectfully, as he did to Zionist leaders. In a meeting with them in Palestine, he pointedly stated, "The paper which you have just read painted a golden picture of the delightful state of affairs in Palestine under the Turkish rule ... but it had no relation whatever to the truth." When the secretary of a Palestinian Arab delegation in London protested that Arab rights had not been safeguarded, Churchill replied, "I do not admit that is true." When the secretary then claimed Britain had promised them self-government, Churchill responded in exasperation, "No. When was that promised? Never." Churchill became exasperated again the following week, after the delegation refused to meet with Zionist leaders, and spoke to the Palestinian Arabs almost as if they were children: "The British Government mean to carry out the Balfour Declaration. I have told you so again and again. I told you so at Jerusalem. I told you so at the House of Commons the other day. I tell you so now." He continued, "You are not addressing your minds to the real facts of the case." When the Arab delegation argued that Arab rights were being infringed by the Jews, he countered, "We intend to bring more Jews in. We do not intend you be allowed to stop more from coming in." Even when he extended the olive branch and begged the delegation to work with the government, he did so in blunt, pointed, and sarcastic terms: "Do you want to go back to Palestine empty-handed, having spent a while in London, seen some people, had some luncheons and dinners, and that is all?" Churchill might have been in a particularly foul mood in the London meeting because his infant daughter, Marigold, was very sick; she died the next day, less than two months after the death of his beloved mother. But he never had patience for the Palestinian Arabs' rejectionism. He found among them no Michael Collins (the Irish militant-turned-peacemaker with whom Churchill negotiated) and saw no Palestinian

Arab counterpart to the Zionists' Carlsbad Declaration of September 1921, which sought harmonious living with the Arabs. Of course, the Jews had more to gain from magnanimity than the Arabs. Churchill did not even show the Palestinian Arabs the implicit respect that he showed the Jews by calling on them to be worthy of their race, since he never thought much of the Arab race. Other officials in the Colonial Office shared Churchill's disappointment with the Palestinian Arabs and looked down on them as well.[36]

Given what he saw as the Palestinian Arabs' backwardness, unreasonableness, and anti-British attitude, Churchill did not believe they deserved self-determination. In fact, he never cared much for self-determination and had a restricted view of which people deserved it. This was evident even from his rather imperial attitude toward the Jews. He suggested that Britain in Palestine was hosting both the Jews and the Arabs. He referred at an imperial conference to the Jewish Communists as abusing and breaching British "hospitality," even though the British had only been in Palestine since 1917 while Jews, and Arabs, had lived there for centuries.[37]

Unlike some British officials, including some of his close aides, and many Britons in general, Churchill generally did not think much better of the Arabs outside of Palestine and certainly did not romanticize them. He considered all Arabs to be irredeemably backward, wild, and emotional people, incapable of governing themselves responsibly. He was privately wary of the Arabian bedouin leader (and future founder of Saudi Arabia) Abd al-Aziz al-Saud, commonly referred to as Ibn Saud. Churchill opposed installing Ibn Saud in Mesopotamia on the grounds that he "would plunge the whole country into religious pandemonium," and he publicly characterized Ibn Saud's subjects, the fundamentalist Islamic Wahabis, as "intolerant, well-armed, and blood-thirsty." Churchill considered Faisal irritatingly restless and rambunctious, and wrote shortly after installing Faisal in Mesopotamia, "Has he not got some wives to keep him quiet? He seems to be in a state of perpetual ferment." Even British officials who had championed Faisal came to the same conclusion. Churchill's favorite Arab chieftain was Abdullah, whom he privately considered "weak" but agreeable, willing to accommodate Zionism, and a friend to Britain. This perception was largely accurate, at least compared to other Arab leaders, but Lloyd George more presciently doubted that Abdullah would be satisfied with the relatively small territory of Transjordan. Although Churchill might have thought better of the sherifians than of other Arabs, he installed them to rule over the Arab masses not because they were objectively responsible governors or administrators but because he thought he was giving the lowly Arabs what they deserved. At an imperial conference in 1921, Churchill explained that he was installing the sherifians to rule Mesopotamia because they were less costly than the efficient British administration they replaced. "Also," he continued, "there is no doubt that these turbulent people are apt to get extremely bored if they are subjected to a higher form of justice and more efficient administration than those to which they have for centuries been accustomed. At any rate, we have reverted perforce and by the teaching of experience to more primitive methods." Earlier in 1921, Churchill was more blunt in writing Mesopotamia High Commissioner Percy Cox about plans for an Iraqi National Assembly: "Western political methods are not necessarily applicable to the East." This was no more condescending than the attitude held by Faisal himself, who told Lawrence in the spring of 1921, with apparently unintentional self-criticism, that the Mesopotamian masses were "not fitted yet for responsible Government." Faisal thought poorly of the Palestinian Arabs as well. Faisal's rule did not much change Churchill's views of Arab governance; he referred in 1922 to Faisal's "incompetent Arab officials."[38]

Other British Zionists felt the same way about the Arabs, including Lloyd George, Meinertzhagen, and Leo Amery, who helped draft the Balfour Declaration. Weizmann, who acquired many British traits, also looked down upon the Palestinian Arabs and wrote to a colleague in 1921 that "they are fifth rate people." This view was shared by many Jews in Palestine who came from Russia and Europe. The Palestinian Arabs were just as disdainful of the Jews, if not more so. One U.S. official assigned to British forces in Palestine, William Yale, observed in 1918, "The Palestinians will not be intimidated by the Jews, whom for centuries they have looked down upon and despised and considered as inferiors." It was difficult for the Palestinian Arabs, who had been part of the ruling group in the Ottoman Empire, to accept being treated the same as the upstart Jews, let alone being governed by them. This sentiment was particularly true among the majority Muslims, who for religious reasons throughout the centuries felt entitled to rule over Jews. Indicative of this attitude, Samuel reported, a popular Palestinian Arab slogan in the autumn of 1922 was "Government by apes but not by Jews."[39]

Churchill played for time with Zionism. He did not believe he would live to see a Jewish-dominated state, given the numerical advantage of the Palestinian Arabs. (In 1922 there were 488,000 Arabs and 340,000 Jews in Palestine, and he expected no more than 10,000 Jews annually would immigrate to Palestine in his lifetime.) Instead, he hoped to build momentum for the Zionist movement until enough Jews immigrated to shift the demographic balance, which until the flight of European Jews in the 1930s seemed a long way off. He expected to do that by lowering the political temperature, minimizing Jewish-Arab differences, and permitting Jewish prosperity to enrich and pacify the Arabs. Also, he hoped for enough tranquility to complete his ministerial tenure to some acclaim. As he maintained in his first speech about Palestine in the Commons in 1921, he sought "patience, coolness, and a little good fortune."[40]

Despite recognition of growing Palestinian Arab hostility toward Zionism, Churchill still hoped that the Jews and Arabs would get along, just as he hoped the North and South Irish would. In the summer of 1921, after his first encounter with a hostile Palestinian Arab delegation, he told Lloyd George, Balfour, and Weizmann at Balfour's house that he felt confident a modus operandi could be worked out with the Arabs for a few years. He sought to avoid any unnecessary rifts between the two peoples. This was one reason he opposed the creation of a non-Jewish agency in Palestine, as he explained to Samuel in 1921: "It seems to me that it is desirable to avoid as far as possible crystallising distinction between Jews and non-Jews as such." He also tried to convince a Palestinian Arab delegation that they had a lot in common with the Jews: "The Jews are people whose history from immemorial times has been very closely intermingled with that of the Arabs, and often in the most amicable manner." This echoed the view held in Disraeli's Britain that Jews and Muslims felt a special bond; however, while some Jews in the nineteenth century felt this kinship, Muslims did not, and apparently many did not in 1921 either. Also, against Churchill's hopes, Zionist economic development did little to weaken Palestinian Arab hostility. Many Zionists since Herzl, particularly Labor Zionists, had hoped for the same or at least argued the same so as to minimize opposition to their movement.[41]

To ease tension in Palestine, even while firmly maintaining that the Balfour Declaration would not be altered, Churchill exaggerated the time frame for a Jewish state. He suggested to a Palestinian Arab delegation that a Jewish homeland would not emerge for "hundreds of years hence" and encouraged them instead to focus on "what will happen in the next five years." Also, he did not directly or clearly answer their legitimate question of what a "national home" meant and whether it was the same as a state. Even to an imperial conference, albeit an unsympathetic one, he downplayed the imminence of a state: "If, in the course of many years, they [the Jews] become a majority in the country, they naturally would take it over." This differed little from what Balfour had said privately. Churchill also wanted the Zionists to tone down their propaganda, which in various venues he disingenuously held solely to blame for Arab agitation. (Zionist statements certainly had some impact, such as when Weizmann in 1919 told Paris conferees he hoped that seventy thousand to eighty thousand Jews would immigrate annually to Palestine, making that land eventually "as Jewish as America is American or England English.") He wanted the Zionists to remain circumspect. For instance, when Weizmann asked at a mid-1921 meeting attended by Balfour and Lloyd George about illegal gunrunning to defend Jewish settlements and illegal immigration, Churchill replied, "We don't mind it, but don't speak of it." This was no different from his confession to Sidebotham that he was not averse to Jewish settlement in Transjordan but did not want it spoken about. And he was irritated when British politicians aroused the Palestinian Arabs, complaining in 1922 to Balfour that British anti-Zionists had gone about "stirring up these fanatical Arabs," making them more obstinate and causing more bloodshed.[42]

Attempts to calm the Palestinian Arabs frequently aggravated the Zionists, who were often anxious. At the end of 1921, for instance, the Zionists were concerned that Britain might hand the Palestine Mandate over to the French and thereby end their experiment. Churchill wrote to Balfour that he had "been approached by Zionist leaders who are passing through one of their periodic fits of extreme agitation." The Zionists were worried that the British government no longer was committed to the goal of a national home. They were particularly unsettled by Samuel's June 1921 statement that minimized the meaning of a national home, introduced the economic capacity of Palestine as a limiting factor for Jewish immigration, and endorsed the establishment of a representative government. Weizmann undoubtedly had that policy statement in mind when he complained later that summer, "Of the Balfour Declaration nothing is left but mere lip service." The Zionists were even more troubled in June 1922 by the Churchill White Paper, which, unbeknownst to the public, was also drafted by Samuel. This policy paper was based partly on language Samuel had privately advanced for his June 1921 statement, which Churchill rejected, and on a November 1921 draft by senior colonial official John Shuckburgh, which Churchill also had rejected. Yet, Churchill quickly approved the new policy paper upon Shuckburgh's recommendation, and it became known as the Churchill White Paper. The document explicitly refuted Weizmann's controversial declaration in 1919 to make Palestine as Jewish "as England is English." It defined a Jewish national home not as an "imposition" of Jews on the Palestinian Arabs but as "the further development of the existing Jewish community" so that it may become an amorphous "centre in which the Jewish people as a whole may take, on grounds of religion and race, an interest and a pride," where Jews had no political primacy. Immigration would be based on the vague "economic capacity" of the country to "absorb new arrivals." Parts of the White Paper were also sympathetic to the Zionist cause. It formally clarified that McMahon's pledge to Hussein excluded the "whole of Palestine west of the Jordan," maintained that the Balfour Declaration was "not susceptible of change," explained that self-government in Palestine would be established in "gradual stages and not suddenly" due to "special circumstances" of the country (the Palestinian Arabs wanted self-government set up immediately while they were the overwhelming majority), and memorably recognized that Jews were in Palestine "as of right and not by sufferance."[43] It is unclear why Churchill approved this generally weak statement after overriding a similar formulation in 1921. He had defined "national home" far more sympathetically to the Jews both in private correspondence to Samuel and in a speech to the Commons one year earlier. Churchill was at this point was much more detached from the issue than he was for most of 1921; there were far fewer notes back and forth with Samuel. Churchill exuded a sense that he had basically completed what he wanted to do on the matter in 1921, save a speech or two in the Commons, and thus left it to his subordinates to carry on. However significant the Churchill White Paper was for policy, its formulations speak more to Churchill's attitude toward his job than to his views on Zionism. Of course, the Zionists reacted furiously. Weizmann blamed Samuel, while the *Jewish Chronicle* labeled the White Paper the "Churchill Renunciation." Yet, feeling left with no choice, the Zionist Organization accepted the White Paper. The Palestinian Arabs did not, and they also boycotted elections for an advisory council that Churchill supported in which they could be outvoted by a combined vote of Jewish representatives and British officials. The advisory council proposal, in which Arab members far outnumbered Jewish ones, did not please the Zionists either. The Zionists were more pleased when the League of Nations in July 1922 finally ratified the mandate, which embodied the Balfour Declaration in its preamble. This prompted Weizmann to write to Churchill that "Zionists throughout the world deeply appreciate the unfailing sympathy you have consistently shown towards their legitimate aspirations and the great part you have played in securing for the Jewish people the opportunity of rebuilding its national home."[44]

Despite the anger on both sides, particularly from the Arabs, Samuel began his last monthly report before the end of Churchill's tenure as colonial secretary in October 1922 with these striking words: "The country is quiet."[45] It was a great accomplishment for Churchill to complete his responsibility for this land—which was so filled with strife before, during, and after his term—in relative peace.

With the fall of the Liberal-Conservative coalition government in October 1922, Churchill's term as colonial secretary ended, as did his intimate involvement with Zionism for the rest of the decade. When asked at a campaign rally in Dundee whether the Balfour Declaration should be broken, he replied, "I am strongly in favor of holding that Declaration." He lost that election anyway, and then some others. He was miserable; the Liberals, fractured and in decline, were hostile to him, while the Conservatives, led by Stanley Baldwin (who took over in 1923 when Bonar Law died), opposed his inclusion in the government. Finally, in 1924, Churchill won what became a lifetime seat in Epping (which was divided in 1945 and called Woodford). He also managed to endear himself to Baldwin and was appointed chancellor of the exchequer, the second most important post in the government, because Baldwin did not want to give the important portfolio to his rival Neville Chamberlain and because he decided that Churchill would be more damaging and uncontrollable out of the government than in it. Churchill now held the last position his father had held, and on his first day on the job he donned the robes Randolph had worn as chancellor, which had been stored since 1886, and continued where his father had left off.[46]

Churchill tried to make the most of this new lease on political life by solidifying his resurgent position and avoiding the reckless actions that his father took in the position. He generally succeeded, endearing himself over time to many in the Conservative Party, both with his restrained performance in office and with his personal rapport. In 1926, one Conservative Party leader, Samuel Hoare, wrote to Max Beaverbrook, "Churchill practically is the Government. He has got complete stranglehold on the young reactionary Tories who used to move Baldwin about as they liked." Churchill certainly did not want to undermine his resuscitated career by anything he might say or do about Zionism, a movement that was foundering in the mid to late 1920s.[47] He was focused on his new senior position, and it did not much involve Palestinian matters. When a Zionist issue did cross his desk, his ministerial responsibilities argued against lending much support to it. In any case, for the next five years Churchill displayed little warmth toward Zionism, except when speaking to British Jews.

Churchill sought to limit government expenditures as much as possible, as chancellors of the exchequer often do. He remained wary of continued expenditures in Iraq, eager in 1925 for Britain to end its "quixotic philanthropy" and leave that country within a few years. He felt the same sense of economy—with little or no more warmth—toward the other British mandate in the region, Palestine, which he had already made clear to Colonial Secretary Amery in 1924. In 1926–1928, Palestine endured an economic crisis, and the Zionist Organization almost went bankrupt. The closing of Soviet borders undercut immigration as well. In 1927–1928, more Jews emigrated from Palestine than immigrated to it. Britain also experienced economic depression, and Churchill wanted to use the Palestine budget surplus to subsidize some of Transjordan's costs. Yet, he wrote to Amery in 1927, "There is no excuse whatever for Palestine being a burden on the Exchequer of this country. It is quite capable of paying its own way in every respect as most Crown Colonies. I cannot understand why the idea of keeping Palestine in a dole-fed condition at the expense of our taxpayer attracts you." This harsh memo contradicted the facts and contrasted sharply with any prior warmth he had shown toward Zionism as well as with his later view of the matter in the 1930s. In 1928, Weizmann wanted Britain to underwrite a £2 million loan to be negotiated under the aegis of the League of Nations in order to finance the settlement of three thousand Jewish colonists. Churchill flip-flopped on the issue, first supporting it in a meeting with senior officials and Weizmann, then submitting a Treasury memo that opposed it to the Cabinet, and then supporting a revised proposal at a Cabinet meeting attended by an ailing Balfour. Churchill did see some economic value to Palestine, such as acting as a conduit and port for oil produced in northern Iraq; indeed, a pipeline running to the Haifa port was built by a consortium in 1935 and operated until 1948.[48]

Churchill was also very circumspect when addressing Palestine in his memoirs of the First World War. He omitted any reference to the Balfour Declaration or to Zionism at all. In a volume published in 1927, he did refer to British conquest of Jerusalem in December 1917 but only noted that it ended the Turks' "400 years of blighting occupation." The appendix to the fifth volume, published in 1929, contained a five-page "Memorandum upon the Pacification of the Middle East," that reviewed the Middle East in the prior decade, focusing mostly on Iraq and the reduction in costs while practically ignoring Palestine. He portrayed his activities as merely executing the government's policy and not contributing anything to it. Of the Cairo conference decision, based on his staff's recommendation, to separate Transjordan from western Palestine, he wrote, "As regards Palestine, the Conference did little more than confirm the policy previously adopted and still maintained."[49] In fact, it was a far-reaching conference, and Churchill had to convince Lloyd George and others in the Cabinet to adopt its provisions. Churchill certainly saw little political advantage in reminding any Conservatives of his colonial tenure.

Churchill maintained to some extent the mixed views of Jews that he had harbored during the Russian Civil War. In 1928, when British Jews appealed for government funds to relieve those suffering from famine in Soviet Russia, he dictated a letter for his private secretary to sign opposing the request, arguing that those who had opposed the Bolsheviks in the civil war, including Jewish and non-Jewish British servicemen, had "a prior claim upon us than the Jews of Russia, who have not been without influence in bringing about the present lamentable condition of the country."[50] He still considered many of the Bolsheviks to be Jews.

In front of British Jewish audiences Churchill demonstrated greater warmth toward Jews and Zionism. In 1926, reminiscent of his remarks to Manchester Jews in 1906, he attributed singular Jewish fortitude to their religious observance: "The Jewish race experienced oppression through many centuries and it could never have preserved its strength, its integrity, its power . . . but for the sheer anchor to which the Jewish people have been attached, unshakable in their unswerving adherence to the faith of their fathers." When discussing Zionism he focused on three of his favorite themes: the Jews' historical attachment to the land, their success in civilizing it, and Disraeli's dictum. He recalled his visit to Rishon Lezion and other Jewish settlements in 1921: "When I visited Palestine, I had the opportunity of seeing the marvellous work which has been achieved by the Zionists in the reclamation of barren desert wastes and in the creation in the most inhospitable surroundings of smiling lands, with culture, moisture, trees, and wine." He discovered "a magnificent grove of palm trees, planted on a soil which twenty years before had been only a bitter, salt, sandy, blistered desert." He perceived some historical restoration, witnessing "the Jewish community living as it used to live thousands of years ago, agriculturists, horsemen if need be, warriors, carrying on their life in the full continuity of history in the land of their origin." He also quoted Disraeli's adage for the first time since 1920—"The Lord deals with the nations as the nations deal with the Jews"—when he argued that it was vindicated again in the morrow of the First World War. Nations that treated the Jews well (Britain) came out well, while those that treated the Jews poorly (presumably Russia) did not do so well. These sentiments were genuine and heartwarming, but they constituted meaningless rhetoric that ignored pressing realities.[51]

If Churchill, a talented amateur painter, attempted to depict his stands on Zionism in the 1920s pictorially on canvas, the final product would resemble the scattered and splattered swirls of Jackson Pollock. Churchill's views were seemingly all over the place. At times he ignored and even scorned Zionism, and at other times he vehemently endorsed it. As colonial secretary he privately proposed abandoning the Palestine Mandate, impatiently transferred 75 percent of the mandate to an Arabian prince on the wrong premise that the prince and his sherifian family's territorial appetite was satisfied, stood by as a rabid anti-Zionist and anti-British Arab was appointed to a senior Palestinian Muslim post, approved the temporary suspension of Jewish immigration after the Jaffa riots, agreed to limit Jewish immigration based on a vague economic absorptive capacity of the land, and approved a White Paper that diluted Britain's pledge to the Jews and the conception of a homeland. Further, he did not study the issues sufficiently and relied too heavily on subordinates. Indeed, all of these negative actions or nonactions, except for proposing to abandon the mandate at one particular moment, were in response to views held by or actions committed by subordinates. This was particularly true during the last twelve months of his twenty-two-month tenure at the Colonial Office, when he became far less engaged in Palestinian matters, except for his rousing speech in the Commons in July 1922 in defense of the Balfour Declaration and the League of Nations mandate. The Palestinian Arabs remained hostile to Britain's Zionist policy, no matter what Churchill did to assuage their concerns, though they remained more peaceful as his tenure progressed. As chancellor of the exchequer, he was rather indifferent to the desperate plight of the Zionist settlement in Palestine. Mostly, his policies were framed by his paramount concerns with politics and anti-Bolshevism, along with a healthy dose of ignorance, a short attention span, and, in 1921, a rash restlessness to get something accomplished.

And yet, as colonial secretary, Churchill implemented the Balfour Declaration, ensured that Jews retained the right to immigrate to Palestine, privately agreed to illegal Jewish gunrunning, backed the Rutenberg electrification concession, advanced several significant and enduring intellectual defenses of Zionism, insisted to the Palestinian Arabs that they accept Zionism, and allowed the Zionists to establish durable national institutions—all of which set in motion the founding of the State of Israel in 1948.

For some, these conflicting positions reaffirmed Churchill's inconstancy. After his remarks at the Hebrew University site in 1921, his first fully pro-Zionist statement since 1908, the *Jewish Chronicle*—which had been disappointed by Churchill's unfulfilled 1908 promises on domestic Jewish issues and then by his provocative 1920 article "Zionism versus Bolshevism"—was puzzled about where Churchill actually stood on Zionism. It memorably editorialized, "The Colonial Secretary himself, however, is not easy to understand even when his words are most unequivocal. For he is Mr. Winston Churchill—with a record very distinctly equivocal. . . . Where at any moment Mr. Churchill is to be found on any subject, is invariably a puzzle soluble only by an accurate knowledge of political anemography as it affects the prospects and position of—Mr. Churchill."[52]

During Churchill's tenure at the Colonial Office, Zionism had permeated his being at some basic level for the first time, even if he did not fully recognize it and even if he continued to advance or approve ideas and policies that he believed took priority over Zionism. He now came to understand the relevant practical issues surrounding Zionism. He was forced to defend Britain's Zionist policy repeatedly and in the process internalized several key arguments, some of which he had enumerated before, including his view of the Jews, their ancient attachments, and the need to rectify their sadly anomalous condition. His new defense, the civilizational argument, which he took up during and after visiting Palestine, was evidently preeminent in his mind. Adopting yet another Zionist argument, he measured Zionist success, both in and of itself and in its treatment of the Arabs, by how well the Jews developed Palestine. He saw firsthand how well the Zionists had cultivated Palestine, and he became unusually attached to that land. For the rest of his life, Rishon Lezion stuck in his mind as emblematic of Zionist progress. He had many dealings with the Zionists, and while they sometimes aggravated him he considered them, especially their leader, Weizmann, to be moderate people who shared his nineteenth-century values. These experiences only confirmed his view of the Jews as a superior race. Indeed, he never really considered the Russian Jewish immigrants he met in Palestine to be backward, "Asiatic" Russians, but part of an advanced race that was essentially comparable to his. This was the positive flipside of the Russian-Jew distinction he made in the late 1910s that led him then to say nasty things about the Jews. There was no question in Churchill's imaginative mind now that the Zionists were kindred spirits, and that their mission was his mission and Britain's. He was on their side, he had friendly exchanges with them, and his actions or nonactions and the words he uttered—even those that undercut Zionism—generally came from the vantage point of someone in the Zionist camp. He now was forced to choose sides, and he certainly did not favor the Palestinian Arabs, whom he was convinced were primitive, unreasonable enemies of Britain who had lost whatever claims they might have legitimately held to controlling Palestine.

In this new, corrupted postwar world, exemplified by the rise of Bolshevism, Zionism held out hope for a better civilization, based on the values of the Victorian era that Churchill held so dear. In a sense, Zionism was a refutation of Bolshevism, not in the soul of the Jew but in the divergent and more noble vision it offered for the future. This did not make Zionism a primary issue in Churchill's mind along with, say, India. Nor did it mean that he encouraged the definition and development of a Jewish national home that could be wholeheartedly embraced by the Zionists. He certainly was not as attentive or persistent in pushing the movement's agenda as he was with an anti-Bolshevik campaign or other great strategic matters. Instead, he saw Zionism as a cause to be supported as much as reasonably possible. As Churchill embarked on a decade of political isolation, within both his party and his country, these thoughts and beliefs germinated and took firm root.

CHAPTER FIVE

Together in the Wilderness

1929–1939

FROM 1929 TO 1939, Churchill was without a ministerial position for the first extended period since his early days in Parliament. This was quite a turn of events after reaching the heretofore pinnacle of his political career in the prominent position of chancellor of the exchequer. These self-described "wilderness years" were difficult and unsettling for him, especially at the beginning. He grappled with financial demands, especially after losing substantial money in the stock market crash, and as usual turned to writing books and articles to earn money. He even considered retiring from politics to earn a significant full-time income. Adding further to his woes, in 1932 he was injured after being hit by a car while crossing Fifth Avenue in New York City. He told his wife that he did not know if he would ever recover from these physical, political, and financial blows. Conservative Party leader Stanley Baldwin liked him personally, and a shifting group of other Conservative MPs supported him at various times, but Churchill had no firm or consistent political base and remained generally isolated in the Conservative Party and across the political spectrum. His own political stumbles and the ascendancy of Neville Chamberlain to prime minister contributed to his growing isolation.[1]

On the great world issues of the day—India, Germany, Russia—Churchill's views were out of sync with his party and the country. He was seen as dangerous, reckless, and alarmist with his unpopular warnings about the German threat. His judgment was called into serious question, as it had been before and as his father's had been. Following a rousing speech by Churchill after the Anschluss in 1938, when Nazi Germany annexed Austria, a prominent Conservative remarked to an observer, "Oh, the usual Churchillian filibuster; he likes to rattle the sabre and he does it jolly well, but you always have to take it with a grain of salt."[2]

Zionism was one of the world issues that caused Churchill to be ostracized. Britain was moving increasingly away from its Zionist pledge of 1917, while Churchill was embracing it as he never had before. His empathy and support for Zionism solidified, never again reverting to the hostile approach he occasionally took in the late 1910s and 1920s, and he criticized the same anti-Zionist opinions that he had privately expressed in those years. His alienation from the party and country and his lack of ministerial responsibilities unshackled him and led him to think more deeply and express his opinions more candidly. Contributing to his sense of liberation was his relatively diminished hunger for higher office in the early years of this period; at the content age of fifty-five years old in 1929, he had just completed five years of unusual stability in a very high position after years of ambitiously climbing up—and stumbling down—the political ladder.

Moreover, in Churchill's mind, British security and world issues argued for a favorable attitude toward Zionism. Whereas in the late 1910s and early 1920s he considered a pro-Zionist policy to be an obstacle to more important strategic and imperial objectives, he now saw it as beneficial to them. Faced with rising strategic threats from Germany and Italy and weakening imperial control over India and Egypt, Churchill feared that any loosening of British control in Palestine and any reneging on Britain's commitment to the Jews would signal an image of weakness and unreliability that exacerbated those dangers. More directly, for the first time he considered the Jews in Palestine to be strategic assets, while he continued to see the Palestinian Arabs as hostile to Britain and its interests. He and the Jews shared the same enemies, and he viewed their growing strength in Palestine as enhancing British security. He similarly saw the Zionists as allies in the mounting battle of ideas. Churchill believed that Zionists shared the principles of the Victorian world that Britain helped shape, while Palestinian Arabs were the enemies of those ideas, supporting and identifying with some of the forces that corrupted that beloved world. His support for Zionism was heightened by his sympathy for the Jews' plight in the face of Nazi and Arab persecution. For the first time, he saw Zionism as a humanitarian and moral imperative. These views, however, ran counter to the dominant positions in the Conservative Party and the country, and contributed to his alienation from the establishment. Indeed, in addition to the ideological, sentimental, civilizational, strategic, and humanitarian considerations, Churchill felt a personal bond with the Jews and Zionists, who shared his besieged and isolated fate in the British wilderness.

The 1929 election began Churchill's longest stretch out of government and out of favor. The Socialists, headed by Ramsay MacDonald, eked out a narrow victory over the Conservatives. Another election in 1931 led to the formation of a Socialist-Conservative national government, with Conservative leader Baldwin as the dominant player. Even before the 1929 election, Churchill had excluded himself from high office over India. For the next several years, he publicly disagreed with the government on a number of issues, including India, Palestine, free trade (for a time), and Nazi Germany. When the Conservatives won overwhelmingly in 1935, Churchill sought a Cabinet post but was denied one. He then began openly to criticize the government even while secretly wishing to join it. This tactic, or the fear of it, had succeeded before with David Lloyd George in 1917 and Baldwin in 1924, but this time prime ministers Baldwin (1935–1937) and Chamberlain (1937–1940) did not bite. In addition to being out of sync with the Conservative Party and the nation on many foreign policy issues, Churchill increased his isolation by frequently exercising poor political judgment (which was a common liability of his, often to his moral credit), such as when he took the highly unpopular position in 1936 of being overly sympathetic to Edward VIII, who soon after abdicated to marry the soon-to-be divorced American Wallis Simpson.[3]

With the advent of the Socialist-led government in 1929, Churchill became extremely concerned over the future of the British Empire and the progress of civilization. One week after assuming office, MacDonald, with the assent of Baldwin, announced the government's determination to remove all British troops from Egypt, except in the Suez Canal zone. Churchill was furious and later remarked, "It was evident I was almost alone in the House." In public and private, Churchill explained that such a move was a blow to British prestige and honor, and violated its duty to develop the country. After Britain had brought Egypt "from anarchy to civilisation," he argued, the removal of British troops would plunge Egypt into chaos. Similarly, later in the year, when the Conservative shadow Cabinet agreed to support the government's policy to grant dominion status to India, Churchill wrote of the British "rescue of India from ages of barbarism" and "tyranny" and "its slow but ceaseless forward march to civilisation." He also worried that this marked the beginning of the waning not only of the British Empire but also of British strategic influence.[4]

Meanwhile, grave violence erupted in Palestine in late summer of 1929. After a peaceful march by right-wing Jews on the sacred Wailing Wall (which used to surround the ancient Jewish Temple), Muslim agitators, including the mufti of Jerusalem, claimed that the Jews intended to attack the sacred al-Aqsa Mosque (one of the holiest Muslim shrines, located behind the Wailing Wall). The Muslim leaders exhorted their followers to attack Jews in Jerusalem, and from there violence spread to Hebron and elsewhere in Palestine. Over a five-day period, 532 Jews and 178 Arabs were killed and wounded.[5]

The Zionists were shocked, but the MacDonald government was indifferent, if not hostile, to them. Zionist leader Chaim Weizmann could not even immediately secure an interview with the new colonial secretary, Lord Passfield, but met with his wife, Beatrice Webb, who did not understand why the Jews were making such a "fuss." When Passfield finally met with Weizmann, he maintained opposition to mass Jewish immigration into Palestine. In the spring of 1930 a government-established commission concluded that the violence sprung from Palestinian Arab frustration and made recommendations that led to the issuance of the Passfield White Paper, which suspended Jewish immigration as long as there was high unemployment in Palestine. The White Paper further claimed that there was little land available for use by new immigrants, threatened the Zionists with an embargo on additional purchases of land, and disparaged Zionist achievements in Palestine.

The Zionists were outraged and Weizmann, who put his faith in cooperation with the British, resigned as president of the Jewish Agency (the recently formed quasi-government of the Palestinian Jews). Fortunately for the Zionists, the White Paper was attacked by Conservatives, Socialists, and others, and MacDonald backed off. In early 1931, MacDonald issued a letter clarifying that the government felt obligated to facilitate Jewish immigration, which it no longer saw as a threat to non-Jewish residents, and would not interrupt or prohibit immigrants who landed jobs.[6]

The damage was done, however. These events further radicalized both Palestinian Arabs and Jews. Palestinian Arabs had again been shown that violence was rewarded, while the Zionists became more convinced that it was imperative to build up their strength. In 1933, David Ben-Gurion, a leading socialist Zionist and member of the Jewish Agency and Zionist Executive in Palestine, who later became the first prime minister of the State of Israel in 1948, drew this lesson: "We have sinned in this land, in all other lands, we have sinned for two thousand years, *the sin of weakness*. We are weak—that is our crime." While he sought to reverse that, the right-wing Revisionists led by Vladimir Jabotinsky rose in popularity and broke away from the Zionist Organization to form the New Zionist Organization in 1935. Weizmann, who resided in London, and his moderate wing were in eclipse.[7]

Churchill responded immediately to this violence. In a few articles and a speech in 1929 and 1930, he condemned the attack on Jews as "evil" and a "massacre and pillage of a horrible character," and referred to the "nearly 200 cruel murders, for the most part of defenceless people." Yet, however genuine his sympathy for the Jewish victims, his main concern was how the disorder affected British imperial interests. He pinned the timing of Arab violence not on any local factors but on the projection of weakness signaled by the new government's proposal to withdraw from Egyptian cities. He feared that any appeasement of the Palestinian Arabs and their violence would undermine British control in India and Egypt and lead to more bloodshed and destruction. He continued to take a comprehensive view of the region and asserted, echoing a memo he wrote to Lloyd George in 1921, that "the whole of the Middle East is intimately related." Reflecting his view of empires as stabilizing forces, he continued: "Beneath the smooth surface of British rule and the slender garrisons which normally sustain it are smouldering the antagonisms of centuries.... There are always scores to be settled and fanatical thirsts to be slaked." Any appearance of British "lack of willpower... blows like a draught of air on the dull, fierce embers." Churchill wrote his wife that the "Palestine butchery" would repeat itself in Egypt if British troops were withdrawn. He also worried that any weakening of support for Zionism would undercut Britain's standing in the United States, where he continued to perceive large Jewish influence.[8]

Prompted by fear of perceived British weakness and eventual withdrawal or scuttle, Churchill insisted that Britain not give up the mandate in Palestine. This marked a reversal of his position on the issue during the previous decade and forced him to criticize views that he had privately espoused a decade before—not that he recognized or acknowledged any contradiction. It was now a matter of "honour" for Britain to stay in Palestine. Churchill insisted on a point he had ignored in the late 1910s and early 1920s: that unless any other major power accepted the mandate, "anarchy in Palestine and a massacre of the Jews would follow in due course." He dismissed the claim, which he had made repeatedly a decade before, that if not for the Zionist movement Palestine would be easy to maintain. Similarly, he now claimed that Palestine was not a burden on Britain but, with the financial assistance of the Jewish Agency, was "a self-supporting country whose finances balance and are continually expanding." He went further: "There is hardly one of the innumerable territories included in the British Empire which has a better financial record in its relations with the Central Power." The Jews were "entitled to a full and fair chance" to establish a national home and Britain "must not, and will not, weary of its lawful discharge."[9]

Beyond his preoccupation with British imperial interests, Churchill continued to champion Jewish rights to Palestine and extol Zionist virtues. He maintained that the Jews had a historic right to Palestine and commended the Jewish chance "to revive the life and fame of their native land." However, it was the civilizational argument that Churchill most focused on. The conflict with Egypt only intensified his perception of the Arabs as backward and anti-British and strengthened his view of the Zionists as fellow agents of civilization. He again defended Zionism based on the "great wealth and civilisation" it brought to Palestine, and he argued that the Jews had brought the Palestinian Arabs "nothing but good gifts, more wealth, more trade, more civilisation, new sources of revenue, more employment, a higher rate of wages, larger cultivated areas and better water supply—in a word, the fruits of reason and modern science." For that reason he thought Palestinian Arab rights were compatible with a Jewish national home. And there was more for the Jews to accomplish; Churchill went so far as to proclaim, "There is no country of which it can more truly be said than of Palestine 'that the Earth is a generous mother,' and will provide for all her children if they will cultivate her soil in justice and in peace." It was an extremely optimistic assessment of Palestine's agricultural potential, even more positive than anything he said back when he visited Palestine in 1921. He maintained that the "arid plains lack only comparatively simple irrigation works to bloom like a garden." Churchill did not trumpet Zionist success as useful to Britain or her empire but to world progress. Zionism offered powerful civilizational, not imperial, value. The Zionist settlements commanded the support of all civilized people; even if there had been no Balfour Declaration, these communities "would deserve the strong protection and the sympathies of free and enlightened people in every quarter of the globe." This was a very enthusiastic endorsement of the Zionist experiment.[10]

By contrast, the Arabs forfeited their claim to control the land due to their backwardness: "These particular Arabs, numbering scarcely a million, have not in a thousand years done as much to revive and develop Palestine as the Zionist Association have done since the Treaty of Versailles." Churchill had not made such a disparaging comment about Palestinian Arab abilities since his defense of the Rutenberg concession a decade before; he was essentially picking up where he had left off in 1922. But he was not overly concerned about Palestinian Arab opinion since it was "by no means representative of the Arab race. It is only a small fraction." He also argued that the British owed very little to the Palestinian Arabs, pointing out that the "bulk" of the Palestinian Arab "military males served against us in the Turkish Army during the war" and that the Palestinian Arabs "were the conscript soldiers of our Turkish enemy."[11]

Some of Churchill's criticisms were simply aimed at scoring political points. For instance, he now sought to vindicate his tenure as colonial secretary, a tenure he had mostly ignored after it ended. Referring to the momentous conference he organized as colonial secretary, he wrote, "The period of tranquility and progress which Palestine has enjoyed since the Cairo Conference of 1921 has been suddenly and violently disturbed by a fierce explosion of racial and religious passion." He attributed some of this violence to the disbanding, by MacDonald's Socialist government (which had a short term in 1924) of the five-hundred-member police force that Churchill established as colonial secretary. (Under questioning a few years later, however, he privately acknowledged that he too was partly responsible, because he had reduced the force as chancellor of the exchequer in 1925.) Churchill also tweaked the Conservatives by voicing his pleasure that under a Socialist government "the hostile organs of the Conservative Press will not be able to exercise any influence" on Palestine policy.[12]

Throughout the 1930s, Churchill continued to focus on his usual interests in Zionism. He remained captivated by its civilizational value, with his interest during the mid-1930s verging at times on fixation. His unusual attentiveness may have been fueled by the running debates over India and Egypt, as well as by his visceral belief that Britain contributed so much to the advancement of people in these countries—for instance, he wrote privately in 1937 that Britain had to maintain control in India "for our advantage and their salvation." Even for a person with renowned curiosity about matters large and small, Churchill's fascination with the land of Palestine was uncommon. For instance, during an overnight stay in Jerusalem in 1934 while touring the Middle East (his second and last time in the Holy Land), he asked how High Commissioner Arthur Wauchope had successfully dealt with the criminal destruction of fruit trees in Samaria that had been going on for years, and also asked about the level of the Sea of Galilee (Palestine had suffered a drought the previous three years). In reply to Wauchope's response to these detailed inquiries, Churchill wrote, "The results are most encouraging, and thoroughly justify the course you adopted in dealing with the singularly cruel offence of destroying fruit trees in a thirsty land." He also expressed hope that rain would restore the Sea of Galilee to its proper level.[13] He seemed to feel rather proprietary over the land's health, and perhaps only the topography of his Chartwell estate received more detailed attention by him.

As the 1930s wore on, Churchill became increasingly alarmed by the rising German threat to British and European security. From the beginning of Hitler's ascendancy, Churchill considered anti-Semitism integral to Nazi ideology, and he condemned it repeatedly, both in public and in private. Churchill felt deep compassion for the Jews and sought to highlight their treatment as illustrative of the nature of the Nazi regime. In 1932, while Churchill was in Germany researching a book on his ancestor the Duke of Marlborough, it was proposed that he meet Hitler, who had yet to become chancellor. Churchill obliged but Hitler never showed up. Churchill opined to Hitler's aide that Hitler could not build an enduring regime based on anti-Semitism: "Tell your boss from me that anti-Semitism may be a good starter, but it is a bad sticker." (Churchill apparently liked that line and repeated something similar in 1949.)[14]

Once Hitler became chancellor in January 1933 and the Nazi regime began targeting Jews, Churchill stepped up his criticisms. In April 1933, he joined other MPs in condemning the new German ban of Jews from public office. He denounced the Nazi "persecution of the Jews, of which so many Members have spoken and which distresses everyone who feels that men and women have a right to live in the world where they are born" and pursue a livelihood. In September 1935, a Nazi convention in Nuremberg passed two special statutes, known as the Nuremberg Laws, that prohibited sexual relations and marriages between Jews and non-Jews and forbade Jews from employing non-Jewish German women under the age of forty-five. In a series of subsequent regulations, Jews were barred from all official and professional work in Germany. In the following month, Churchill wrote a magazine article, "The Truth about Hitler," in which he condemned the scapegoating of Jews and the virulent anti-Semitism expressed by the regime and by German society as a whole:

> The twentieth century has witnessed with surprise, not merely the promulgation of these ferocious doctrines, but their enforcement with brutal vigour by the Government and by the populace. No past services, no proved patriotism, even wounds

sustained in war, could procure immunity for persons whose only crime was that their parents had brought them into the world. Every kind of persecution, grave or petty, upon the world-famous scientists, writers, and composers at the top down to the wretched little Jewish children in the national schools, was practised, was glorified, and is still being practised and glorified.

He also expressed compassion for the persecuted socialists, communists, and liberals, but his concern was not as deep, nor was it expressed as vividly, as it was for the Jews. Further, he recognized that the Jews were just the beginning, like the canary in the mineshaft. Two years later, in 1937, Churchill came back to the theme of Jewish scapegoating in a newspaper column, assailing "the persecution of the Jews in Germany, the exploitation of anti-Semitism as a means by which violent and reactionary forces seize, or attempt to seize, despotic power."[15]

Later in 1937, in the Commons, Churchill again denounced Nazi anti-Semitism when he declared that "it is a horrible thing that a race of people should be attempted to be blotted out of the society in which they have been born." In early 1938, he wondered in a newspaper column, "Why should religion be the subject of oppression? Why should racial persecution endure?" He was clearly referring to the Jews, particularly in the second question. In the summer of 1938, a few months after the Anschluss, Churchill wrote about Nazi extension of their humiliating anti-Semitic practices to Austria: "It is easy to ruin and persecute the Jews to steal their private property; to drive them out of every profession and employment; to fling a Rothschild into a prison or a sponging-house; to compel Jewish ladies to scrub the pavements; and to maroon clusters of helpless refugees on islands in the Danube; and these sports continue to give satisfaction." He warned the Nazis that by doing this they hurt themselves and weakened their occupation of Austria: "A very serious loss to the already straitened economic life of Vienna is incurred when a busy, ingenuous, industrious community, making themselves useful in a thousand ways, is reduced to a mass of helpless, miserable folk, who nevertheless cannot quite be allowed to starve wholesale." Persecution of the Jews was counterproductive strategically as well, since it antagonized the United States. He acknowledged, however, that persecution of the

Jews did not hurt the Nazis' standing with many Austrian Catholics, who had made "a separate truce for themselves."[16]

By this time, his criticism of anti-Semitism had become integral to his thinking and surfaced even in unforced passing remarks. For instance, in a letter to his son in late 1936 he wrote that the "basis of the Anti Nazi League is of course Jewish resentment at their abominable persecution." And in an early 1938 article he referred to Armand Calinescu, the Romanian prime minister, as "the Jew-baiter, Goga." Along the same lines, in the late-1930s draft proofs of his book *History of the English-Speaking Peoples* (which was not published until 1956), Churchill apparently had the present in mind (as he often did when writing history) when he noted that the seventeenth-century Puritan autocrat Oliver Cromwell restored the Jews to England after they were banished in 1290 for the cynical reason that he considered them "useful." Perhaps most telling of his state of mind about the Jews was what Socialist leader Clement Attlee recalled years later about the often emotional Churchill: "I remember the tears pouring down his cheeks one day before the war in the House of Commons, when he was telling me what was being done to the Jews in Germany—not to individual Jewish friends of his, but to the Jews as a group."[17]

During this period Churchill was conscious of the general mistreatment of Jews, even outside of Nazi countries, though his response depended on the country. For instance, beginning in 1935 Jews were subject to widespread attacks in Poland and Romania. The plight of Polish Jewry drew particular attention and alarm from many in Britain and triggered a protest conference in England in the spring of 1937. However, Churchill politely declined an invitation to deliver a message at the conference for fear of alienating Poland in the struggle with Germany: "I am reluctant to take up a position antagonistic to Poland at this time when our dangers are so great, and we have to pick our steps so carefully. We do not want these people as well as Italy, to go into the Nazi camp." Despite Churchill's genuine concern about the persecution of the Jews, he deemed it subordinate to the strategic threat the Nazis posed to Britain and the Western world. Yet, he was not reluctant to criticize the treatment of Jews by another potential ally against Germany, the Soviet Union. He perceived a rise of nationalism in Stalinist Russia, which meant a turn against the internationalist Bolshevik Jews that

Churchill so roundly attacked fifteen years before. Amid a round of purges by Stalin, Churchill noted in a 1936 article that "these victims were nearly all Jews." He then added, again conveying some ignorance of historical Russian anti-Semitism, "Evidently the Nationalist elements represented by Stalin and the Soviet armies are developing the same prejudices against the Chosen People as are so painfully evident in Germany. Here again extremes meet, and meet on a common platform of hate and cruelty." Churchill again saw a country's treatment of the Jews as a barometer of its regime's morality. He was perhaps willing to criticize Soviet anti-Semitism because, as he told the War Cabinet in late 1939, the Russians "were impervious to words."[18]

Churchill's compassion for the Jews added another dimension to his Zionism. He came to believe it essential that Palestine act as a refuge for persecuted German Jews. In the spring of 1936, he passionately argued in the Commons against offering self-government to Palestine because with a majority of Arabs it would mean the end of Jewish immigration. He powerfully declared that at a time when German Jews were "being subjected to most horrible, cold, scientific persecution, brutal persecution, a cold 'pogrom,'" with "every form of concentrated human wickedness cast upon these people by overwhelming power, by vile tyranny," the Commons could "not allow the one door which is open, the one door which allows some relief, some escape from these conditions, to be summarily closed, nor even allow it to be suggested that it may be obstructed by the course which we take now." Further, with his opposition to Egyptian self-rule evidently in his mind, he explained that the Palestinian Arabs were still incapable of self-government, in contrast to "the progressive vigour that is shown by the Jewish community." These forceful remarks marked a turn in Churchill's thinking about Zionism. He had always understood the movement's general humanitarian benefit, but he now saw its immediate, concrete moral imperative. Nazi persecution was something like Churchill's Dreyfus case, the point at which he came to understand the immediate necessity of Zionism, as Theodor Herzl had forty years earlier. But there were limits to this revelation. Unlike Herzl and many other Zionists, Churchill did not consider Zionism an existential solution to the Jews. Having grown up in awe of European civilization, he was not yet ready to give up on Europe as a safe place for Jews. And like so many unfortunate European Jews, he did not foresee the mass murder that Hitler would unleash on the Jews during the Second World War. But he understood more than ever that the liberties, if not the lives, of many Jews depended upon the refuge that Zionism promised. Not only was Zionism a cause seeking to right historical wrongs and advance the civilization, but it was now in his eyes also a movement of great humanitarian urgency. Perhaps it is not surprising that in 1936 Weizmann, after renewing his acquaintance with Churchill on an airplane, remarked that Churchill was "quite sound."[19]

In the spring of 1936, Palestinian Arab leaders, in a bid to end British rule—which appeared weaker amid Italian and Nazi aggression and propaganda—and halt soaring Jewish immigration resulting from Nazi persecution (the Palestinian Jewish population doubled to 355,000 during 1932–1935), triggered a violent revolt that lasted three years. Churchill wrote his wife that the Palestine situation was "grievous." The British government established a royal commission headed by Robert Peel to examine the causes of the Arab revolt and the future of the Palestine Mandate. The commission interviewed people in Palestine and London. Churchill was called as a witness in the spring of 1937 and was told his testimony would be kept confidential. He spoke so freely that afterward he regretted what he had said and requested that some remarks not appear in the secret permanent record. None of his evidence was used in the commission's report.[20] Given the confidential setting and the extent and nature of the questioning—very pointed questions about Palestine and slanted against Zionism—this testimony presents the most candid and comprehensive record available of his views toward Zionism for this or any period.

Churchill gave a spirited defense of Zionism to the Peel Commission. He evidently was still interested in imperial matters but was more concerned with how those imperial conflicts affected the more fateful strategic challenges posed by the rising European Fascist powers of Germany and Italy. Civilizational matters remained crucial, but strategic concerns dominated his mind. He was now fixated on strengthening British resolve after years of what he perceived to be utter weakness and bungling in the face of one Fascist triumph after another. He was getting particularly anxious over Mussolini's ambitions in the Mediterranean. These concerns added a strategic dimension to his Zionism; he now believed it important to Britain to have the Palestinian Jews as allies and to be perceived as keeping its pledge to the Jews.

As much as Churchill sympathized with the Jews' plight, he did not base his support for Zionism on it. As he pointed out to the Peel Commission, Nazi treatment of the Jews made the matter "more poignant" but was not the source of British responsibilities. Instead, Churchill placed "enormous importance" on the upholding of Britain's wartime pledge to the Jews, for which "we gained great advantages in the War." He made the same point publicly as colonial secretary in 1921–1922, but now it took on wider significance. He worried that if Britain reneged on its commitment to the Jews it would create an image of unreliability and weakness, which would be compounded if Britain lost control over the situation in Palestine and was forced to withdraw. He emphasized the need to recreate the gendarmerie that he claimed worked so well in the early 1920s. He insisted that Britain reassert control and work out arrangements with the Jews and Arabs in Palestine from strength. He contended that if Britain did not put down the guerrilla campaign directed at British officials, then it would have to concede as it had in Ireland. Or as he pointedly put it, "If British mastery disappears you had better be quit of the whole show." If that happened, British control in Egypt and India would be undermined. In the late 1910s and early 1920s, Churchill saw British possession of Palestine as diverting scarce resources and undercutting British imperial interests, but now he saw it as essential for maintaining those other, more important imperial possessions. An image of feebleness and inconstancy had even greater strategic consequences: it whetted the appetites of the emergent belligerent powers of Germany, Italy, and Japan and undercut the chance for sorely needed alliances with Russia and the United States. The United States would be particularly put off by a betrayal of the Jews, whom Churchill believed had great influence in that country. He felt that the Balfour Declaration during the First World War had been a "potent factor on public opinion in America."[21]

British withdrawal from Palestine would trigger another undesirable imperial and strategic consequence: it would immediately create a void that would be filled by an Italy eager to claim the Mediterranean as its own, thus jeopardizing British naval access to Egypt and India. Mussolini played both Arab and Jewish sides as a means of gaining a foothold into Palestine; he reached out to the Jews while also broadcasting to the Middle East that he was a friend of Islam. Churchill suggested that the Jews could get along with the Italians but that the Arabs would not, indicating that it was strategically important for Britain to get along with the Zionists and that the Arabs had a lot to lose by backing the Fascist powers.

Churchill considered Palestinian Jews to be Britain's allies and Palestinian Arabs to be its enemies. He insisted to a skeptical commission member that the Palestinian Arabs had sided with the Ottomans in the First World War and "filled the armies against us and fired their rifles and shot our men." The only friends among the Arabs had been the sherifians. Churchill correctly predicted that the Palestinian Arabs would again side with Britain's enemy in a future war. Indeed, within a few months of Churchill's testimony, Palestinian Arab demonstrators carried flags and photographs of Hitler and Mussolini in celebration of their prophet Muhammad's birthday, and the mufti declared his admiration of the new Germany and sought German friendship in return. Many in the Arab world joined the Nazis in hating Jews and congratulated Hitler over the Nuremberg racial laws. Many Arabs, within Palestine and without, saw opportunity in Britain's decline and in its Palestine troubles; the Syrians and Iraqis, for example, considered Palestine part of their own country. Churchill rejected a suggestion by a commission member that Britain's conflict with Palestinian Arabs was alienating other Arabs. "I think it is much exaggerated," he claimed. "I have heard it so often."[22]

Beyond strategic concerns, Churchill saw other "merits" to Zionism, and he dwelled on them at greater length at different points of the testimony. Unlike some of the commission members, Churchill believed that the Jews had a legitimate historical claim to Palestine. He took exception to one commission member referring to the Jews in Palestine as a "foreign race." Churchill replied, "A foreign race? Not at all." The Jews "had" Palestine "before that indigenous population [the Arabs] came in and inhabited it." But, as often was the case with Churchill, he fixated on the future. Here he focused on the Jewish race's ability to further the cause of civilization in Palestine. In response to a commissioner's statement that the Arabs felt pushed aside, he said plainly, "It is a question of which civilization you prefer." To him, it was no contest.[23]

Echoing what he had said as colonial secretary, Churchill relentlessly stressed that the Arabs in Palestine did nothing with the land and thus forfeited any right to control its destiny. He claimed that in "the time of Christ the population of Palestine was much greater, when it was a Roman province," intimating that Palestine prospered under Western, or at least non-Arab, rule. (He did not mention that the Romans depopulated much of the area shortly thereafter by killing and exiling hundreds of thousands of Jews.) Matters changed with the Arab invasion six hundred years later: "When the Mohammedan upset occurred in world history and the great hordes of Islam swept over these places they broke it all up, smashed it all up. You have seen the terraces on the hills which used to be cultivated, which under the Arab rule have remained a desert." Thus, for more than twelve hundred years, Palestine remained a backward wilderness. While claiming to have "great regard for Arabs," Churchill also asserted that "where the Arab goes it is often desert." When one commission member disputed that and contended that the Arabs were "doing a lot" with their plantations, Churchill dismissively replied, "I am very glad to hear it." Churchill believed that the undeveloped state of the land suited the Arabs fine: they "lived fairly easily in a flat squalor typical of pre-war Turkish Empire provinces." In other words, like most people he deemed backward, the Arabs of Palestine were satisfied with their lowly existence and did not aspire to more or have any interest in progress. (This primitiveness, he maintained, was not unique to the Palestinian Arabs but a common trait of all Arabs. When a questioner countered, referring to the Moors, that the Arabs had created a good deal of "civilization" in Spain before the Christians conquered it, Churchill snapped, "I am glad they were thrown out.") For this crime against human advancement, civilizational justice demanded that the Arabs lose their right to govern the land. The "injustice" in Palestine was not Jewish immigration but "when those who live in the country leave it to be a desert for thousands of years." He asked rhetorically about the Zionists, "Why is there harsh injustice done if people come in and make a livelihood for more and make the desert into palm groves and orange groves? Why is it injustice because there is more work and wealth for everybody? There is no injustice." He felt Jewish immigration thus benefited the local Arabs. [24]

At one point Peel stated that the Arabs would not be persuaded to support Jewish immigration simply out of perceived economic advantage, but Churchill evinced little interest in what the Arabs thought. He felt the Arabs must accept the Balfour Declaration and submit to Jewish immigration and eventual control since it would further progress in the world: "If I were an Arab I should not like it, but it is for the good of the world that the place should be cultivated and it never will be cultivated by the Arabs." He vividly explained that he viewed Zionism in a wider, civilizational context and considered the Zionists to be fellow civilizers: "I do not admit that the dog in the manger has the final right to the manger, even though he may have lain there for a very long time. I do not admit that right. I do not admit, for instance, that a great wrong has been done to the Red Indians of America, or the black people of Australia. I do not admit that a wrong has been done to those people by the fact that a stronger race, a higher grade race, or, at any rate, a more worldly-wise race, to put it that way, has come in and taken their place." This was a brutally honest and revealing pronouncement, one Churchill never made in public.[25]

Churchill was adamant about maintaining Jewish immigration into Palestine. He was less concerned with the number of Jews allowed to immigrate in a given year than with maintaining overall stable growth. He remained opposed to Arab self-government, since it would undermine Jewish immigration: the "Mandate over-rides the self-governing institutions," he insisted. "[The] self-governing aspect," he continued, "although important, is not superior but inferior to the prime obligation in the declaration under which we went into this country"—namely, to establish a Jewish national home. Yet, despite his concern for the European Jews suffering Nazi persecution, he wondered whether too many Jews had immigrated to Palestine from Europe and unnecessarily provoked the Arabs. He hoped the Jews would do a better job of reconciling with the Arabs and believed that Arab hostility would be overcome. He never considered the Jews "entitled" to bring into Palestine as many immigrants as the economy could absorb "no matter what other consequences arose"—Britain was ultimately responsible for such decisions—but "it must be made clear our loyalty is on the side of bringing in as many as we can." When asked whether he had ever envisioned four hundred thousand Jews in Palestine, as there were in 1936, he replied, "Yes, certainly. I hoped for it." When told by Peel that the Jews would soon outnumber the Arabs, Churchill replied that the "conception undoubtedly was" that the Jewish population "should not in any way be restricted from reaching a majority position." He insisted that it "would not be right" and "would be contrary to the whole spirit of the Balfour Declaration if we were to declare that in no circumstances, however naturally it might arise, would we contemplate a Jewish majority." Indeed, a Jewish majority had been his goal since the early 1920s.[26]

Churchill was pressed repeatedly by the hostile commissioners about his vision of Palestine's future. He unabashedly and unequivocally proclaimed his support for the eventual creation of a Jewish state that would include an Arab minority. Although the mainstream Zionists had thus far avoided public discussion of a Jewish state, Churchill asserted that "certainly we committed ourselves to the idea that some day, somehow, far off in the future, subject to justice and economic convenience there might well be a great Jewish State there, numbered by millions, far exceeding the present inhabitants of the country and to cut them off from that would be wrong." He said at another point in the testimony, "We are always aiming at the fact that, if enough Jews come eventually it may be a great Palestinian State, in which the large majority of the inhabitants would be Jews." He added that this would not happen for "a century or more." At another point he declared that if over "the generations or the centuries" the Jews settled in Palestine and acted correctly with the Arabs, "it was contemplated and intended that they might in the course of time become an overwhelmingly Jewish State." He noted that he did not mean a Jewish religious state, but a state in which the Jews were a majority. His hope was that this "great idea" would be realized.[27]

Since a Jewish state was not expected to emerge for a long time, the British mandate in Palestine would need to last a long time. Churchill did not imagine the British leaving at the very moment the Jews constituted a majority of the country; instead, he envisioned the British mission completed and the Balfour Declaration fulfilled only when "it was quite clear the Jewish preponderance in Palestine was very marked, decisive, and when we were satisfied that we had no further duties to discharge to the Arab population, the Arab minority." Churchill felt that

Britain, which was the "judge" of when to give up the mandate, should do so when it "cannot carry it any further." Whereas during the First World War he often could not wait to get rid of the mandate, now he did not think the mandate had endured long enough for its success to be assessed. "What is seventeen years?" he asked. He envisioned not changing policy for "another fifty or hundred years." He conceived of a permanent mandate for the foreseeable future.[28]

The Peel Commission issued its report in July 1937. It argued that there was no common ground between Arabs and Jews, one being "predominantly Asiatic in character, the other predominantly European," and believed that a government on behalf of both groups could not evolve. It thus made a radical recommendation in favor of a two-state solution, which effectively discredited continuation of the British mandate. The commission recommended a truncated Jewish state spanning much of the coastal area north of Gaza to Galilee, and an Arab state comprising the rest of western Palestine, including the Negev desert, and much of what is now the West Bank. Transjordan would be on the eastern part of Palestine, and Britain would retain as a mandate control over Jerusalem and a corridor to the sea. The territory allotted to the Jews amounted to about 20 percent of remaining Palestine excluding Transjordan, or 5 percent of Mandated Palestine that was referred to in the Balfour Declaration. There would be an exchange of population between the Palestinian Arab and Jew states. In addition, Jewish immigration would be limited to twelve thousand annually for five years. The British government immediately accepted the report's recommendations.[29]

For the Zionists, this was a very mixed bag. For the first time a British body was explicitly calling for a Jewish state in Palestine, and not just the vaguer "national home." It was an extremely small state, however, and was very limited in its short-term population growth. This plan divided the Zionists; Jabotinsky and the Revisionists rejected the tiny allotment of land, while Weizmann saw it as the high point of his collaboration with Britain and a vital step closer to the dream of an independent Jewish state. Ben-Gurion saw even a truncated state as a springboard for expansion. In any case, the Palestinian Arabs rejected partition, since they opposed any Jewish state in Palestine.[30]

Many Gentile Zionists were opposed to partition as well, considering it a concession to violence. Josiah Wedgwood, a Liberal-turned-Labour MP and Gentile Zionist, captured this opinion well in a letter to Churchill in the spring of 1937: "This is an admission of failure, scuttle, & the end of British expansion in those parts. Both new countries will curse us for all & hate us in future. . . . The prestige of GB [Great Britain] goes into the mud: & all for want of a little resolute rule such as our forbears would have seen thro' [through] with courage & success."[31]

Churchill opposed partition because he did not think it would resolve the Arab-Jewish conflict in Palestine and because it would worsen Britain's strategic position. He sympathized with the Jews' plight and many Zionists' reluctant willingness to accept even a truncated state. He wrote in the *Jewish Chronicle* that he could "readily understand" that "after ages of dispersion and oppression" the Jews desired "a coherent Jewish community and rallying point for Jews in every part of the world." Instead of constant disputes with British officials and annual immigration quotas, he recognized, "here will be a responsible Government" that would be independent. He was not happy with the Peel Commission's borders, believing that a Jewish state should be larger and should certainly include the Negev desert. This marked the first of many times over subsequent years that he would make that point, which was certainly the Zionist view.[32]

More important, however, Churchill thought creating two small states would create an "electric atmosphere" leading to more violence and instability, repeating the error of the Paris treaties following the First World War. As he wrote in the *Jewish Chronicle,* "The assumption which underlies the Commission's Report that, once States, however small or primitive, have become members of the League of Nations their troubles are ended, they never do any wrong themselves and will never be molested, is, to say the least of it, premature." The movement of Palestinian Arabs out of the Jewish area to the Arab territory would lead to many confrontations. The Zionists would not be satisfied with their small area, and the Palestinian Arabs would not permit any encroachments on their territory. "Certainly the Arabs will, from the outset, be on the alert against the slightest encroachment. The Arabs, children of the desert, are always armed and can rapidly improvise a fighting power. . . .

Every measure the Jewish State takes for its defence will look like a design for aggression." Britain would not be able to keep the peace in such a situation and would appear weak, and the conflict would invite Italian penetration into Palestine on the side of the Palestinian Arabs. Along those lines, he told Henry Melchett, an English Zionist activist, of his opposition to Wedgwood's idea to hold a plebiscite for making a Jewish State a "seventh dominion" of the British Empire, fearing that it would lead the Arab states to hold similar plebiscites to join an Italian Empire. It was better, Churchill thought, for the Arabs and Jews in Palestine come to their own temporary agreement that would "afford to the present generation a measure of peace, prosperity and happiness." He wrote Leo Amery that, as bad as the situation was, partition "will only make everything much worse." More succinctly, he wrote Herbert Samuel that partition was "folly."[33]

Churchill made it abundantly clear in various settings how much he tied Zionism to his larger strategic concern—the threat of Nazi Germany and the Fascist nations—which had increased his own isolation in the Conservative Party and the nation. In mid-1937, Weizmann proposed a dinner party at the home of Archibald Sinclair (a Liberal, and long-time friend and former aide of Churchill), which was to be attended by other Zionists and prominent Britons but which had to accommodate Churchill's schedule. Churchill did not disappoint as the main guest. Apparently drunk, Churchill told Weizmann, "You know you are our master—and yours, and yours," pointing to other members of the party, "and what you say goes. If you ask us to fight we shall fight like tigers." He told Weizmann that partition was wrong and was proposed only out of weakness. He went on to fulminate against the Conservative government, which he considered untrustworthy and "a lot of lily-livered rabbits." He thought it shameful how the government had let down the Jews in the past. Still, the Jews had to "persevere, persevere, persevere," just as Britain had to against the German threat. Churchill also remarkably told Weizmann (according to Weizmann), who had pointed out that they saw each other only once in ten years, "Yes, I am afraid to see you. After every meeting I am depressed for ten days, and I have to work for my living."[34]

Churchill reiterated the same themes the next day in a meeting with the Palestinian Zionist leader David Ben-Gurion. "Right away,"

Ben-Gurion recorded in his diary, "Churchill jumped up and said: Our entire tragedy is that we have a weak government. The Baldwins are idiots, totally lacking in talent, etc. If England is to be dependent on them, she is lost." Churchill added, in apparent reference to Britain's abdication crisis involving Edward VIII, during which he was hurt politically, "They are concerned only with deposing and crowning kings, while Germany is arming and growing stronger, and we are slipping lower and lower." "But this situation will not last long," Churchill stated presciently. "England will wake up and defeat Mussolini and Hitler, and then your hour will also come." First things first; only after the Fascist powers were defeated could Britain permit termination of the mandate. The Nazi threat was evidently most on his mind, even when speaking to Zionists, and he often saw the Zionist struggle through that lens. A few months later, he wrote a former colonial aide that he did not believe partition would work. He added, "We are oppressed by so many larger burdens that I could wish we had only Palestine and its troubles on our hands."[35]

While debating the Peel Commission report in the House of Commons in the summer of 1937, Churchill reiterated many of these themes. He stated that the governance of Palestine "is a problem where all the world is looking to see whether Great Britain behaves in an honourable manner, in a courageous manner and in a sagacious manner." Britain should not do anything, he thought, to undermine an image of strength before the Nazis and its allies. Palestine now had far more strategic importance, if indirect, than it ever had. In a newspaper column two days after his Commons speech, Churchill suggested that people should not overreact and that the situation in Palestine was significantly improving. Referring to his visit to Palestine in 1934, he wrote, "I was delighted at the aspect of the countryside. The fine roads, the new buildings and plantations, the evidences of prosperity, both among Jews and Arabs, presented on every side, all gave a sense of real encouragement." He recommended a tactical retreat to defuse Arab anger: lowering the political temperature, as he had suggested in the early 1920s, and moderating the influx of Jewish immigrants. "Too much current was put on the cables. And the cables have fused. That may be a reason for mending the cables and reducing the current. It is surely no reason for declaring that electricity is a fluid too dangerous for civilisation to handle." Again, he counseled "perseverance." Churchill was so greatly identified with Jews and Zionism during this time that, in the spring of 1937, he was invited to be the main speaker at a fund-raising dinner for Hebrew University. He politely and rather distantly declined.[36]

The partition debate was soon superseded by events in Palestine, Britain, and Europe. The European situation was severely degenerating. Hitler and his troops rolled into Vienna in March 1938, and in September Chamberlain and French Prime Minister Edouard Daladier met with Hitler and Mussolini in Munich—neither Stalin nor Czechoslovakian president Edvard Benes was invited—and agreed that, in order to avert war, Germany would get the Sudetenland, the strategic heights of the nascent Czechoslovakian state and the center of its Skoda military factories. The Czech government reluctantly agreed. Nonetheless, six months later, German troops marched unopposed into Czechoslovakia. Meanwhile, the Nazis intensified their persecution of the Jews. Six weeks after Munich, on the night of November 9 (later called Kristallnacht, or the Night of Broken Glass), two hundred synagogues in Germany, Austria, and the Sudetenland were set ablaze, hundreds of Jewish businesses were destroyed, thirty thousand Jews were sent to concentration camps, and twelve hundred Jews were murdered. Poland also became more hostile to its three million Jews. Churchill, his own credibility under attack by Chamberlain, cited Kristallnacht in a speech as demonstrating the absurdity of the prime minister's post-Munich optimism: "The words were hardly out of his mouth before the Nazi atrocities upon the Jewish population resounded throughout the civilised world."[37]

Meanwhile, violence intensified in Palestine. By August 1939, three years of violence had resulted in 6,768 casualties, including 2,394 Jews, 3,764 Arabs, and 610 British. Hundreds of the Arab casualties were victims of Haj Amin's intent to consolidate power. After initially cracking down on some of the Arab leadership and maintaining twenty thousand troops in Palestine, by late 1938 the British began to relax their pressure on the Arabs and to curtail Jewish immigration. The Chamberlain government established the Woodhead Commission, which concluded that the Peel plan was unfeasible and recommended instead Arab and Jewish states linked in economic union, with the Jewish state comprising less than 5 percent of western Palestine and less than 1 percent of Mandated Palestine, an even smaller area than the Peel Commission's parsimonious allocation. The government invited Zionists, Palestinian Arabs, and representatives of Arab states, including Yemen, to a conference in London, which commenced in early 1939—though the Arabs refused to sit in the same room as the Jews. The conference was inconclusive and marked a departure from recent British policy by sanctioning intervention of various states into territory controlled by Britain. It signified a return to a pan-Arab approach to Palestine, which only complicated matters further and led to further bloodshed.[38]

In late 1938 in the Commons, Churchill denounced the "tragedy in Palestine," where blood was shed, economic revival dashed, and Britain humiliated. He also welcomed the partition plan's demise. He made the rather startling declaration that "few things are more important at the present time than for the British Empire to have a plan for the settlement of Palestine," because what happened in Palestine affected British control in Egypt and India, and influenced Britain's image in Europe. He maintained that the mandate was successful in quieter times and wondered, "Are we to conclude that British administration in Oriental lands is no longer capable of facing a storm?" He also asked whether "our gift in the Orient" was sustainable. Churchill proposed limiting Jewish immigration, conceding that too many European Jews had immigrated and thus unnecessarily aggravated the Palestinian Arabs. Intent to defuse the violence and bolster Britain's image without appearing to break Britain's pledge to the Jews, he recommended, based on a plan by Samuel, that Jewish immigration be limited to the natural annual increase of the Arab population plus 10,000 for ten years, which in effect meant approximately 30,000–35,000 Jewish immigrants per year. At this rate, Jews would not gain a majority "within the compass of our short lives." If the Palestinian Arabs would not agree to such an arrangement and not "cease to wage war upon the Crown of Britain," then he asserted that Britain should remove any limitation on Jewish immigration, look to the "strong armament of the Jewish population," and rely on increasing Jewish power, which was a good deal stronger than he used to think, for British administration, thereby freeing up needed British troops. Or as he put it privately to Amery and Weizmann, "If the Arabs refused to accept that, then we should wash our hands of them, bring in all the Jews we could, arm them, and liberate the British troops now in Palestine." Churchill thought a "settlement" in Palestine was possible, and essentially wanted Britain to pursue it on the back of Palestinian Jewish force.[39]

Like Churchill, Chamberlain also viewed Palestine in a wider regional and global context. However, he drew opposite conclusions to Churchill's, as he did about the emerging global conflict. With the European situation deteriorating, war looming, and the London conference having been unproductive, Chamberlain sought to strengthen Britain's strategic position by appeasing the Arabs thereby relieving Arab pressure. Here pragmatism merged with principle, since Chamberlain was in fact anti-Semitic and anti-Zionist. Based on the recommendations of the Committee of Imperial Defence, chaired by John Shuckburgh, a pro-Arab former senior official in Churchill's Colonial Office, the Chamberlain government issued a seminal White Paper on Palestine in May 1939. The White Paper limited Jewish immigration for five more years to seventy-five thousand, after which time there would be no further immigration "unless the Arabs of Palestine are prepared to acquiesce in it"; prohibited the sale of Arab land to Jews; and envisioned an independent Arab state in ten years but no Jewish state. In effect, the White Paper thwarted efforts to establish a safe haven for Jews fleeing Europe and tried to preclude a Jewish majority from materializing in Palestine. The mandate then would have created another Arab state instead of a Jewish national home, which was its intended purpose. The White Paper passed the Commons but led to some division in Conservative ranks, while Liberal and Labour parties declared that they were not bound by this policy in any future government they formed. The government won the vote 268–179, but its overall parliamentary majority of 248 was reduced in the vote to 89. Two Cabinet ministers and 110 backbenchers abstained, while more than 20 Tories voted against it, including Churchill. Amery warned that the Zionists would fight back, and Wedgwood hoped the Zionists would break the law. In fact, a few months later, at a Zionist congress in Geneva, Ben-Gurion proclaimed, "The Jews should act as though they were the State of Palestine, and should so continue to act until there will be a Jewish State there." Even the Permanent Mandates Commission of the League of Nations determined that the White Paper contradicted the League mandate under which Britain had legal authority to rule Palestine.[40]

Churchill had generally avoided criticizing the Chamberlain government for its Palestine policy, instead framing his views in more constructive terms. That changed with the White Paper, which enraged him, and he delivered a devastating speech lambasting the government in the parliamentary debate before the vote, which apparently had an impact on the vote totals. Reflecting his mood, he asked to have lunch with Weizmann on the day of the debate, and showed the Zionist leader his speech shortly before he delivered it. Churchill saw the White Paper, as did the government, primarily through the lens of the European crisis and denounced the White Paper in the Commons as another aspect of the government's appeasement policy that proclaimed British betrayal and weakness and that emboldened Britain's enemies in Europe and the Middle East. He asked incredulously, "Is our condition so parlous and our state so poor that we must, in our weakness, make this sacrifice of our declared purpose? . . . What will our potential enemies think?" He responded to his own question, asserting that enemies would think, "This is another Munich." Nothing was more damning in his eyes. He further warned that these acts of appeasement "will later on have to be retrieved, as it will be retrieved, by additional hard exertions." He maintained that the appeasement would alienate potential and existing friends, implicitly referring to Soviet Russia and the United States, whom he sought to bring together in alliance. "You are not going to found and forge the fabric of a grand alliance to resist aggression," he warned, "except by showing continued examples of your firmness in carrying out, even under difficulties, and in the teeth of difficulties, the obligations into which you have entered." Weizmann, who shared much of Churchill's worldview, also saw the European and Middle Eastern conflicts as intertwined and interpreted British government policy in both areas as reflecting a lack of national will, imagination and desire to live, along with a feeling of exhaustion and fear of the future. Both Weizmann and Churchill thought a new vigorous attitude was required.[41]

Churchill maintained his perception of the Palestinian Jews as strategic assets who shared the same Italian and German enemies. In 1938 in the Commons, he contended that the Jews in Palestine were stronger than the Arabs there. He now reminded the Commons how the Palestinian Jews had provided "important help" to the Allies during the

First World War. He made these assertions about Palestinian Jewish strength outside the larger strategic context, but the fact nevertheless was not lost on him as the Nazi threat became more imminent. His thoughts paralleled what his South African friend Jan Christian Smuts privately wrote at the time of the White Paper, which Amery forwarded to Churchill: "Please . . . prevent abandonment of Jews and Balfour policy. If real trouble comes Jews in Palestine and elsewhere will prove reliable friends."[42]

Churchill was particularly concerned that the White Paper undermined Britain's standing with the United States, where he believed the Jews were influential as he believed they were in the First World War. As recently as 1937 Churchill had tried to persuade the pro-German Duke of Windsor—who had abdicated the throne in 1936 and had just dined with Hitler in Germany—not to sail to the United States on a German ship with the argument that there "are millions of Jews in the United States and they have a great deal of influence there." Now Churchill alluded to this power as another reason for pillorying the White Paper: "What will be the opinion of the United States of America? Shall we not lose more—and this is a question to be considered maturely—in the growing support and sympathy of the United States than we shall gain in local administrative convenience, if gain at all indeed we do?" In fact, the U.S. government did take note. In 1938 President Franklin Roosevelt asked Secretary of State Cordell Hull why the British were "reneging" on their "promise" to give Palestine to the Jews, and then in 1939 Roosevelt, urged on by many domestic protests, declined to support the White Paper on the grounds that it contravened the original mandate.[43]

Aside from its impact on the European crisis, Churchill condemned the White Paper on its own terms. He saw it as a betrayal of the Jews, considering the provision allowing the Arab majority to veto Jewish immigration to be a "breach," "abandonment," and "repudiation" of the Balfour Declaration. It was a "melancholy occasion," one that marked the "end of the vision, of the hope, of the dream." He thought the government, as the ultimate authority in Palestine, had the right to adjust immigration, as he proposed in late 1938, but had "no right whatever" to "wash their hands of it, to close the door." He pointed out to the Commons something that many apparently no longer recalled or understood, that Britain had addressed its pledge in the form of the Balfour Declaration to the Jews outside of Palestine. And now those Jews, at least those in central Europe, desperately sought refuge from persecution: "This pledge of a home of refuge, of an asylum, was not made to the Jews in Palestine but to the Jews outside Palestine, to that vast, unhappy mass of scattered, persecuted, wandering Jews whose intense, unchanging, unconquerable desire has been for a National Home." As he had argued since 1936, Jewish immigration to Palestine was now an urgent humanitarian necessity.[44]

Churchill continued to emphasize the civilizational value of Zionism at a dark time in the world when barbaric ideologies were ascendant and menacing. He had told the Commons in late 1938, "The Jews were coming in a steady stream, bringing with them . . . wealth, development and civilisation." Now he applauded Zionist achievements in the Commons, declaring that the Jews had "made the desert bloom," "started a score of thriving industries," and "founded a great city on the barren shore." Even Malcolm MacDonald, the secretary of state for dominion affairs, acknowledged the Zionists' civilizational value. In particular, Churchill remained proud of the Rutenberg electrification project. And all of these achievements, Churchill insisted, also benefited the Arabs: "So far from being persecuted, the Arabs have crowded into the country and multiplied till their population has increased more than even all world Jewry could lift up the Jewish population." He wondered incredulously, "Now we are asked to decree that all this is to stop and all this is to come to an end." He did not understand how the government could turn its back on what he considered a great movement, which held precious ideals that were unfortunately in global retreat, when the Jews were developing Palestine just as hoped: "It is stranger still that we should turn away when the great experiment and bright dream, and the historic dream, has proved its power to succeed." The government's attitude represented an ideological scuttle from what Britain supposedly held dear. He quoted Neville Chamberlain's statement two decades earlier that the Zionists had the task "to build up a new prosperity and a new civilisation in old Palestine, so long neglected and mis-ruled." Churchill then added, "Well they have answered his call. They have fulfilled his hopes." He concluded his speech powerfully and with absolute astonishment: "How can he find it in his heart to strike them this mortal blow?" His words and tone were reminiscent of his powerful defense of the Rutenberg concession and the mandate in 1922.[45]

Churchill's comments against the White Paper had a personal component as well. He suggested that the system he put in place as colonial secretary had succeeded, and now the government was pulling the plug on it all. The government was in a way betraying him as well as the Jews. He had been making occasional public references to his experience in the region for a few years, which marked a break from his virtual silence after leaving the Colonial Office. In the debate over the Peel Commission report in 1937, he mentioned "having studied the question as far as I can and having some personal connection and responsibility for it." And in 1938 he referred to "having sat at the Colonial Office on these sort of matters about Palestine." He now went further, portraying the White Paper as a personal betrayal: "As one intimately and responsibly concerned in the earlier stages of our Palestine policy, I could not stand by and see solemn engagements into which Britain has entered before the world set aside for reasons of administrative convenience or—and it will be a vain hope—for the sake of a quiet life." Such capitulation was certainly a cardinal sin in the eyes of such a restless battler. Churchill recommended that Chamberlain, who had voted for the Balfour Declaration, "stand by" the Zionists "in the days of his power."[46]

As much as Churchill's respect and sympathy for the Jews had strengthened, his opinion of the Palestinian Arabs and their cause had worsened. He could not understand why the Arabs were indulged when they, in contrast to the Jews, reaped more than history owed. He argued that "elsewhere over vast regions inhabited by the Arabs independent Arab Kingdoms and principalities have come into being such as had never been known in Arab history before." More specifically, he did not understand why the government favored the Palestinian Arabs who historically had been hostile to Britain and its interests (fighting for the Ottomans in the First World War, for instance), and still were. He expressed great frustration with the perverse strategic choices made by the government of favoring enemies over allies. He exclaimed, "We are now asked to submit—and this is what rankles most with me—to an agitation which is fed with foreign money and ceaselessly inflamed by Nazi and by Fascist propaganda." Perhaps reflecting his complete exasperation with the Palestinian Arabs, in 1938 he got into a big argument with

Malcolm MacDonald, the new colonial secretary, in the lobby of the House of Commons. MacDonald recalled the argument several decades later: "He told me I was crazy to help the Arabs, because they were a backward people who ate nothing but camel dung." While these might not have been Churchill's exact words, the gist of the comment jibed with what he had thought of the Palestinian Arabs at least since encountering them in the early 1920s. The Jews, including his early backer in Manchester, Nathan Laski, and Weizmann, expressed their gratitude to Churchill for so strongly opposing the White Paper.[47]

Churchill's speech about the 1939 White Paper culminated a decade of growing consciousness on his part about Zionism. He began the period focusing on the historic, humanitarian, and civilizational aspects of Zionism and seeing it through the lens of British imperial interests. He ended the decade seeing Zionism through the lens of Britain's strategic interests, but his viewpoint was also imbued with a concrete, deep sense about Zionism's moral imperative and civilizational value. In addition, he felt a great bond with the Zionists; their enemies were his enemies, their friends were his friends, ideologically, strategically, and politically. There is no question that world events played a large role in this deeper attachment. Nazi persecution of the Jews, the radicalization and pro-Fascism of Palestinian and regional Arabs, the mounting Fascist threat, along with his own political isolation all contributed to Churchill's more intense feelings in favor of Zionism. But it also appears that these events unlocked a sentiment about Zionism that he did not always express. What Isaiah Berlin wrote about Moses Hess's Zionism in the 1860s appears apt as well to Churchill's Zionism in the 1930s: "He gave expression to a dominant conviction which he had for many years repressed, and which finally proved too strong to stifle, and felt at peace." Churchill's decade in the wilderness, detached from all the details, deadlines, and complications of governing, seems to have been very conducive to such a transformation. Indeed, he may never have seen Zionism or world events any more clearly than he did during this time. What Churchill wrote in a 1931 essay about the biblical Israelite leader, Moses, seemed to apply to him as well: "Every prophet has to come from civilization, but every prophet has to go into the wilderness. He must have a strong impression of a complex society and all that it has to give, and then he must serve periods of isolation and meditation. This is the process by which psychic dynamite is made."[48] The timing for this psychic explosion was remarkably fortunate for the Zionists. It occurred on the eve of another world war, which again accelerated their march toward statehood, and on the eve of Churchill's becoming prime minister and one of the most powerful men in the world. Thus, at the very time when he ascended to the zenith of his political power and obtained a position from which he could help the Zionists in a significant way, Churchill reached the apogee of his Zionism.

CHAPTER SIX

Champion in War

1939–1945

ON SEPTEMBER 3, 1939, Britain and France rose to the defense of Poland, which was suffering the onslaught of fifty-eight German divisions, and the world found itself at war for the second time in two decades. Prime Minister Neville Chamberlain, whose appeasement policy was in shambles, sought to boost his credibility by appointing Churchill first lord of the Admiralty and a member of the War Cabinet. Then on May 10, 1940, after Chamberlain lost political support and resigned following a failed British assault on Norway and a punishing German attack on France and Belgium, Churchill achieved a lifelong dream and became prime minister, heading a national unity government.

Churchill, recognizing that this was a pivotal time in the destiny of Jews, Zionism, the world, and himself, conveyed his determination to be good to the Jews and their causes. He relayed this to Chaim Weizmann early in the war and, for the first time since 1926, invoked Disraeli's dictum that the Lord deals with the nations as the nations deal with the Jews. Now, when Britain was fighting for its life and liberty, all hell was raging across the globe, and Jews were falling victim to genocide in Europe, Churchill believed it was no time to mistreat the Jews, and he had no inclination to do so anyway. This contrasted with the attitude of most British officials and with the rising anti-Semitism among the British public, along with the general indifference exhibited by the U.S. government, including President Franklin Roosevelt.

Publicly and privately, Churchill expressed great concern for the plight of European Jews. Discerning the Nazi mass murder of Jews early on, he publicly condemned it and warned the perpetrators on several occasions. He privately supported a few efforts to help beleaguered European Jews—he even once advocated the bombing of the Auschwitz-Birkenau death camp or the railroad tracks leading up to it—but he generally gave the matter little thought and did not follow through on the proposals he engaged. Winning the war was his overwhelming priority, and he generally opposed compromising wartime principles or diverting badly needed wartime resources to such efforts, to the extent he gave them any consideration. Also, few in the War Cabinet shared his sympathy for the Jews, and there was a limit to which he would fight over matters of ultimately subordinate importance. It did not help that the British Jews were not better organized or more assertive.[1]

Churchill was far more proactive and aggressive pursuing Zionist objectives. While he did not speak about Zionism in public or seek to overturn the controversial 1939 White Paper, he privately encouraged his colleagues to allow more Jewish immigration into Palestine, aspired to arm the Palestinian Jews so they could defend themselves against the Arabs, and eschewed any semblance of balance in the treatment of Palestinian Arabs and Jews. Further, he doggedly and passionately pursued a Middle Eastern diplomatic settlement that would establish a Zionist state in Palestine within a loose Arab-led federation after the war. He had more bureaucratic and diplomatic wiggle room in this undertaking than in providing any help for European Jews (which entailed greater mobilization of the political-military apparatus). Also, it was a long-standing diplomatic cause of Churchill's that did not conflict much with the war effort but involved for him principles that transcended Palestine and the Jews. Yet, his quest for a pro-Zionist regional settlement marked a radical departure from his two-decade-long approach of waiting for the Jewish population to become a majority in Palestine over the course of generations before permitting a Jewish state to emerge. It also marked an emphatic (private) rejection of the 1939 White Paper and the anti-Zionist policy championed by Chamberlain, Halifax, and others in the War Cabinet. Churchill sought to use his new supreme authority to finish the job he had begun twenty years before as colonial secretary and address the needs of desperate Jews toward whom he felt great compassion, some debt, and a strong bond. He managed to achieve tentative War Cabinet approval for his plan in 1944, but the plan unraveled soon after because of Saudi antagonism, American equivocation (if not disapproval), rising political opposition, strategic demands, and his own feelings of frustration and depression.

It was not just what Churchill did or sought to do about Zionism but how he went about it that was significant. Until the last months of the war, he did not revert to the approach he took when last in government of keeping his head down and taking a detached view of the League of Nations mandate. He sincerely and unequivocally championed Zionism before British and U.S. officials, though always behind the official veil away from the public eye so as to minimize political and diplomatic conflict. Indeed, Churchill battled anti-Zionist and (according to him) anti-Semitic ministers, military officers, and civilian officials with gusto over Zionism. This was partly a function of his new superior governmental position. More important, his renowned Zionism and philo-Semitism were qualities that distinguished him from the rest of British officialdom, and he relished conflict with an establishment that had never accepted him and always viewed him as an unstable, dangerous man with erratic judgment. He felt vindicated over his prewar pro-Zionist policy as he did over his prewar anti-Nazi policy; these two foreign policy issues remained intertwined in his mind as they had been in the 1930s. In the wilderness and now back out he and the Zionists remained together, and, despite his meager wartime record on behalf of European Jews, these years marked the zenith of his Zionism.

Churchill served in and then headed a government that was generally hostile to Jews and Zionism, and this was not a conducive environment for him to accomplish a great deal on behalf of either cause even if he had been determined to do so. Few Cabinet ministers actively shared his pro-Zionist views; Conservative Leo Amery was the most notable. Liberal Archibald Sinclair was also a Zionist but he was not much of a force. Churchill's Conservative colleagues were overwhelmingly anti-Zionist. Many Socialists sympathized with Zionism, but Labour ministers generally did little to promote the cause during the war, except perhaps Home Secretary Herbert Morrison, and Labour head and deputy prime minister Clement Attlee was at this point anti-Zionist. In addition, there was a rise of anti-Semitism and xenophobia among the populace during the war, and these sentiments were outright rampant throughout the ranks of the Foreign Office, Colonial Office, military, and other branches of the bureaucracy. Several senior Cabinet ministers, such as Lord Moyne (Walter Guinness), who held various portfolios, and Foreign Secretary Anthony Eden, disliked Jews and were anti-Zionist. These officials regularly communicated a cold indifference to the Jews' fate in Europe and elsewhere, and a steely determination to keep them out of Palestine no matter the dire consequences. They did not believe that the Jews deserved a homeland in Palestine and did not wish to upset the Arabs for strategic and other reasons.[2]

Churchill fully recognized the attitudes of these officials and considered their anti-Zionism a result of their anti-Semitism and not of the more lofty reasons they cited. He often lumped the two "isms" together, as when he warned Edward Spears, a Conservative MP who headed the mission in Lebanon and Syria during most of the war, "against drifting into the usual anti-Zionist and anti-Semitic channel which it is customary for British officers to follow." Churchill made the same point in 1944 in a letter to Colonial Secretary Oliver Stanley addressing the question of who should become the new Palestine high commissioner: "It is especially important that the person chosen should not be infected with the usual anti-Semitism of British officials and soldiers in that part of the world." He distrusted and was contemptuous of British officials involved in Palestine policy, whom he considered slaves to their parochial, anti-Semitic prejudices and ignorant of wider issues.[3]

Far from being inhibited by such official attitudes, Churchill was emboldened by them. Weizmann wrote that in 1943 Churchill explained that of every fifty officers who came back from the Middle East only one spoke favorably of the Jews, "but that has merely gone to convince him that he was right." In many of his dealings with officials Churchill exuded an air of incredulity, a conviction that his sympathies toward the Jews and Zionists were self-evidently correct and that the opposing views of anti-Zionist and anti-Semitic officials were absurdly wrong. This was in stark contrast to Churchill's previous stint in power, in the 1920s, when, with the exception of his civilizational argument, he was far less confident and far more deferential to the subordinates who were considered experts. As colonial secretary, he was less knowledgeable about the region and served in a politically subordinate position during a tenuous political period of his life. Since then, he had increasingly seen the establishment's intensifying anti-Zionism as often irrational, obsessive, reckless, and an important part of its woefully misguided worldview during the 1930s, which depicted him as a dangerous, unstable alarmist. The establishment never considered Churchill one of its own, and his Zionism was part of the larger reason why he was such a politically isolated figure in the 1930s. The battles he waged with other officials over Zionism during the Second World War were essentially a continuation of the disagreements he had with the establishment over world issues in the prior decade. Weizmann, whose ideals often paralleled Churchill's own, understood the situation well, and once during the war, when Churchill complained about the anti-Zionism of some of his advisors, Weizmann asserted, "You must remember, Sir, that those who are against us are against you too."[4] Churchill certainly agreed.

Churchill made abundantly clear his disgust with the establishment's anti-Semitism and anti-Zionism. In late 1939, the War Cabinet considered sending instructions to Lord Lothian (Philip Kerr), the ambassador to the United States, that Britain would not "whittle down" the 1939 White Paper to secure American Jewish support for the Allied cause. Churchill, then first lord of the Admiralty, wrote a scathing memo to the War Cabinet in response, framed by his characteristic perspective: "The one thing he [Lothian] ought not to say is that with the world in flux and the life of every European nation and the British Empire hanging in the balance, the sole, fixed, immutable inexorable fact was that Jewish immigration into Palestine would come to an end after five years in accordance with the White Paper." In June 1940, when Britain resolved to stand alone against the Fascist powers, Churchill, now prime minister, was similarly irked by bureaucratic opposition to his plan to arm the Jews in Palestine so that highly trained British troops stationed in Palestine (and needed to protect the Jews) could return to Britain in its hour of need. He bitterly and incredulously complained to Colonial Secretary George Lloyd about the many officials who, as Churchill saw it, were prepared to risk the overriding goal of survival for the sake of a pro-Arab obsession: "I think it is little less than a scandal that at a time when we are fighting for our lives these very large forces should be immobilized in support of a policy which commends itself only to a section of the Conservative Party." After his plan to arm Palestinian Jews was postponed, Churchill in 1942 shared with the anti-Zionist Colonial Secretary Viscount Cranborne (Robert Arthur James Gascoyne-Cecil) his thoughts of vengeance against some civilian and military officials: "It may be necessary to make an example of these anti-Semite officers and others in high places. If three or four of them were recalled and dismissed, and the reasons given, it would have a very salutary effect." Perhaps he had such thoughts in mind when he briefly considered appointing Weizmann the new British high commissioner of Palestine in 1944, a position held by the pro-Zionist Herbert Samuel in the 1920s. Had that appointment gone forward, it would have resulted in a furor among the Palestinian Arabs matched only by an uproar among British officials.[5]

The Holocaust, the systematic and genocidal murder of approximately six million Jews by the Nazi regime and its collaborators, highlighted Churchill's attitude toward Jews and contributed to his grappling with the Zionist issue. As the German army moved east after attacking the Soviets in June 1941, the SS *Einsatzgruppen* (mobile killing units) began killing thousands of Jews. Hitler ordered the systematic extermination of all Jews under German control, and from October 1941 on, all Jews were forbidden from leaving the German sphere. From June through December 1941, five hundred thousand Jews were murdered. In December 1941, the Nazis set up the first of the extermination camps, Chelmno, in a part of Poland annexed to Germany, where Jews were killed in mobile vans. On January 20, 1942, fifteen high-ranking officials from various German bureaucracies, including the Foreign and Justice Ministries, met at a brief conference in the Wannsee suburb of Berlin to work out a more efficient system for the "final solution" of the Jews in order to ensure no "recreation of Jewry." Thereafter, Jews from across Europe were deported to newly built extermination camps and murdered in gas chambers. News of the massacres began trickling out in July 1941 in some New York Yiddish dailies and spread to the major news outlets.[6]

Churchill quickly recognized the uniqueness of the Nazis' murder of the Jews, based on signal intelligence reports, which he had devoured for years. In August and September 1941, Churchill received from Bletchley Park, the British government's code-breaking center, twenty-five summaries of decrypted signals from the non-Nazi German police force, the *Ordnungspolizei*, which oversaw the newly occupied territories. Churchill apparently asked specifically for the Ordnungspolizei's execution reports to Berlin and circled the number of Jews murdered. British intelligence was not able to intercept the reports of larger massacres committed by the SS Einsatzgruppen. Churchill seemed to make his first public allusion to the growing mass murder of Jews in a broadcast to the nation on August 24, 1941, upon returning from a meeting with Roosevelt, where they signed the Atlantic Charter, a statement of war principles. Discussing Hitler's onslaught against Russia, Churchill declared, "As his armies advance, whole districts are being exterminated. Scores of thousands—literally scores of thousands—of executions in cold blood are being perpetrated by the German police-troops upon the Russian patriots who defend their native soil." He added starkly, "We are in the presence of a crime without a name." Despite the Bletchley reports, Churchill may not have specifically mentioned the Jews for fear of tipping off the Germans to the supersecret intercepts, though his reference to "police-troops" may have made the Germans suspicious anyway. (The following month a German general ordered that the execution reports be sent more securely by courier instead of transmitted by radio.) Also, Churchill may not yet have felt that he had conclusive evidence of Nazi intentions. That changed a few days later, and by mid-September, after more signal intelligence reports flowed in, there no longer was any doubt in his mind or among the Bletchley analysts.[7]

In November, armed with indisputable secret evidence and further press reports, Churchill explicitly singled out the Jews as victims of mass murder and continued—despite questionable domestic appeal—to identify them as the first victims of Nazism and as a lens through which to view Hitler's regime. In a message to the *Jewish Chronicle* on its centenary—the first message ever sent by a British prime minister to a Jewish newspaper—he gave the Jews their due for being the primary target of Hitler's hatred and persecution: "None has suffered more cruelly than the Jew of the unspeakable evils wrought on the bodies and spirits of men by Hitler and his vile regime. The Jew bore the brunt of the Nazis' first onslaught upon the citadels of freedom and human dignity." His message offered the beleaguered Jews something to live for, seemingly alluding to the postwar Zionist plans he was at that time quietly pursuing: "Assuredly in the day of victory the Jew's sufferings and his part in the struggle will not be forgotten." This was a dramatic promise, one he did not keep. He then quoted from a Longfellow poem, "Retribution," suggesting that the Nazi crimes would be avenged. In mid-1942, Churchill echoed some of these themes in a statement to a huge crowd at Madison Square Garden protesting Nazi outrages. He again proclaimed the Jews "Hitler's first victims" and asserted that he and Roosevelt had resolved nine months earlier "to place retribution for these crimes among major purposes of this war." In contrast, Roosevelt sent a message to the Garden crowd expressing sympathy "with all victims of Nazi crime" but did not single out the Jews.[8]

As the scope of the Nazi death machine expanded and intensified, so did Churchill's rhetoric against it. In the autumn of 1942, one day after the London *Times* reported that four thousand French Jewish children had been deported to the Auschwitz death camp, he declared in the Commons, "The cruelties, the massacres of hostages, the brutal persecutions in which the Germans have indulged in every land into which their armies have broken have recently received an addition in the most bestial, the most squalid and the most senseless of all their offenses, namely, the mass deportation of Jews from France, with the pitiful horrors attendant upon the calculated and final scattering of families." Around the same time, he issued a statement to a public gathering that the "systematic cruelties" and "vile crimes" perpetrated against the Jews were "amongst the most terrible events of history."[9]

Despite his rhetoric and the early Bletchley reports, Churchill asked as late as mid-December 1942 at a War Cabinet meeting if the reports of wholesale massacre of Jews in Poland were true. Eden replied that there was no confirmation but that it appeared so. At the time, the British government was sifting through more reports of mass murder of the Jews and was being pressed by Jewish, Polish, and other groups to make an official statement on the matter. The government drafted a statement, which many Allied governments issued jointly on December 17, 1942, that "condemned in the strongest possible terms this bestial policy of cold-blooded extermination" and vowed retribution for those responsible. After Eden read the statement in the Commons, James de Rothschild, MP, spoke emotionally about the Jews' suffering, and members rose for a moment in silence. The statement represented an exception to general official indifference. Most British officials were reluctant to focus on the mass murder of Jews, and British sympathy for Jews waned during 1943. Indeed, British anti-Semitism remained potent throughout the war.[10]

Churchill went even further rhetorically during Nazi deportation of Hungary's eight hundred thousand Jews to Auschwitz-Birkenau in 1944, when he unequivocally told Eden, "There is no doubt that this is probably the greatest and most horrible crime ever committed in the whole history of the world," and vowed retribution. He made a similar remark in the Commons in early 1945, calling the reported murder of three and a half million Polish Jews "one of the most horrifying acts of cruelty, probably the most horrifying act of cruelty, which has ever darkened the passage of man on the earth." Here, however, he perversely framed the mass murder as part of Hitler's plan to destroy the Polish race, arguing that because Russia had saved the Polish race from complete destruction by the Germans, Russia had a right to the more favorable Curzon Line as its border with Poland. But this argument was merely a convenient point for defending the Yalta agreement: Churchill knew the truth about the Holocaust, and he knew how cynical Stalin had been about Polish life during the Warsaw uprising in 1944 (when Soviet troops stopped advance toward Warsaw and allowed German massacre of revolting Poles).[11]

In April 1945, as extermination camps were being liberated by advancing Allied armies, the world became more vividly aware of the Holocaust's enormity through extensive press reports and newsreels. Churchill received and distributed to the Cabinet reports and photos directly from U.S. General Dwight D. Eisenhower, the commander of Allied forces in Europe who visited the death camps. Churchill declared in the Commons, "No words can express the horror which is felt by His Majesty's Government and their principal Allies at the proofs of these frightful crimes now daily coming into view." At Eisenhower's invitation, Churchill sent a delegation of parliamentarians to visit the camps and gather "first-hand proof of these atrocities." He expressed his outrage in letters to his wife over the next two days: "Here we are all shocked by the most horrible revelations of German cruelty in the concentration camps." "Intense horror has been caused by the revelations of German brutalities in the concentration camps. They did not have time to cover up their traces."[12]

Not all British officials grasped the significance of, or were especially moved by, the murder of six million Jews. Five months after the German surrender, when more gruesome facts became known, Ernest Bevin, the foreign minister in the postwar Socialist government, wrote a British diplomat that the Jews "have gone through, it is true, the most terrible massacre and persecution," and then added with stunning indifference, "but on the other hand they have got through it and a number have survived."[13] Not surprisingly, Churchill later accused Bevin of being an anti-Semite.

Beyond words of sympathy and promises of postwar deliverance and retribution, Churchill expressed his compassion for the Jews more concretely. He sought to grant Jews vengeance against the Nazis by forming a special Jewish brigade to fight within the Allied command in Europe and march all the way to Berlin, even though Jews already were serving in Allied armies. This proposal reflected his persistent belief that anti-Semitism was integral to Nazism and that the Jews were unique victims of Hitler. (Some British officials wanted the brigade to fight the Japanese.) Churchill had to lobby the United States for this and overcome resistance from the War Office. He insisted in 1944 to P. J. Grigg, secretary of state for war, "I cannot conceive why this martyred race, scattered about the world, and suffering as no other race has done at this juncture, should be denied the satisfaction of having a flag" and sending a "message to go all over the world." Such a brigade was formed, but it did not fight the Nazis until shortly before the German surrender in 1945. Along the same lines, Churchill told Weizmann in 1943 that he would hand Hitler over to the Jews, an incredible promise that would have faced stiff opposition from Churchill's compatriots as well as the Russians and many others who thought they deserved Hitler's hide.[14]

Despite the horror he felt, Churchill did not focus very much on the Holocaust or ways to combat it, and he fobbed off on the Foreign Office many appeals and delegations seeking help. In fact, many of his cardinal wartime principles conflicted with possible efforts to save Jewish lives. He opposed any major relaxation of the economic blockade of Nazi-occupied Europe, sought to avoid any unnecessary actions that might create dissension with the Soviets, and rejected negotiations with the Germans on the subject. In 1943, after seeing a Foreign Office memo on approaching Germany and other enemy governments to grant leave to Palestine for a few hundred Jews, he expressed his displeasure to Eden: "Surely we ought not to have any special negotiations with the German Government on such a matter?" And in 1944, he rejected Weizmann's request of support for a Zionist official going to Hungary to explore a deal for Hungarian Jews amid their deportation to Auschwitz. He instructed Eden, "On no account have the slightest negotiations, direct or indirect, with the Huns." Even if he was inclined to do so, Churchill understood that a distrustful Stalin would fiercely object, viewing it as a possible means of betrayal. Ultimately, Churchill felt, as he wrote Zionist activist Henry Melchett amid the extermination of Hungarian Jewry in 1944, that the "principal hope [for] terminating" the horrible crimes against the Jews "must remain the speedy victory of the Allied Nations." Churchill was not alone in his refusal to focus on saving European Jews; few Jews in the United States or Palestine devoted much attention or effort to rescuing them, and many questioned the practicality of doing so.[15]

At least twice Churchill considered using military force to impede Nazi extermination of the Jews. At the end of 1942, General Wladyslaw Sikorski, prime minister of the Polish government-in-exile, requested that the Polish Air Force be allowed to bomb some targets in Poland related to German persecution. Churchill asked Chief of the Air Staff Charles Portal to consider Sikorski's request, and also to undertake two heavy bombing raids on Berlin in January 1943 and drop leaflets warning Germans that attacks were in "reprisal for the persecution of the Poles and Jews," according to their meeting minutes. Nothing came of this request.[16]

Another instance was more significant but ended the same way. In June 1944, a few weeks after D-Day and almost three years after first receiving reports of the mass slaughter of Jews, Churchill read a brief but detailed report about the deportation to Auschwitz-Birkenau of Hungarian Jews, along with some suggested responses—bombing the railroad tracks from Hungary to Auschwitz-Birkenau, bombing Auschwitz-Birkenau, and bombing government buildings in Budapest. Evidently upset, Churchill scribbled on the report, "What can be done? What can be said?" Eden initially was not eager for Britain to do anything, and responded that further public warnings could make the "anti-Jewish atrocities worse," without explaining how it could get any worse for the Jews. A few days later, Eden passed along Weizmann's request that Britain bomb the Auschwitz-Birkenau death camp and the railways leading up to it, and recommended that Churchill write Stalin about it. Churchill replied immediately to Eden, "Get anything out of Air Force you can and invoke me if necessary. Certainly appeal to Stalin." He did not specify what he wanted to be bombed exactly. The next day, Churchill indicated that he wanted the request to go from Eden to Soviet Foreign Minister Vyacheslav Molotov, rather than from himself to Stalin. He also made clear that he supported a declaration warning the Hungarians, regardless of whether it be British, Russian, or British-American-Russian, adding, "I am entirely in accord with making the biggest outcry possible." Churchill agreed to Eden's suggestion of a public declaration by Stalin alone (or with the United States). Eden passed along Churchill's instruction to urge some bombing to Air Secretary Archibald Sinclair and was surprised that "this ardent Zionist" (who had hosted a Zionist dinner party in 1937 that included Weizmann and Churchill) was wary. In the end, nothing happened, and a junior Foreign Office official sent Weizmann the negative decision on September 1. On September 6, British Air Marshall Norm Bottomley wrote Lieutenant General Carl Spaatz of the U.S. Strategic Air Forces that the Foreign Office advised against such bombing, so "we are taking no further action at the Air Ministry and I suggest that you do not consider the project further." The United States never seriously considered bombing the camps or the railways leading up to them. Also, there is no record that Churchill, who was abroad at the end of August and apparently was not told of the adverse decision, followed up on the matter internally or ever discussed it or any similar idea with Stalin or Roosevelt.[17]

There were other, easier means of helping the Jews beyond disrupting the Nazi death machine, as important as that goal should have been. One of these means was to provide a sanctuary in Palestine to fleeing European Jews; in that way, the British response to the Holocaust was directly linked with Zionism. Even when the Jews had a chance to flee Europe—especially before October 1941 and after mid-1944, when Soviet troops began liberating eastern Europe—there was virtually no place for them to go. The United States left 90 percent of its immigration quotas unfilled, several Latin American countries denied any entrance, Turkey denied transit rights, and Britain severely restricted Jewish immigration. Palestine was the only viable sanctuary. However, the British sought to prevent or at least minimize Jews entering Palestine as well. Formally, British policy was driven by the White Paper of 1939, which limited Jewish immigration into Palestine for five years (until March 31, 1944) to seventy-five thousand, but even that was too permissive for some officials, and the government suspended legal Jewish immigration many times early in the war. The Colonial and Foreign Offices often forced Jews who managed to escape for Palestine to return to Europe, so as to discourage future immigrants. The government decided in late 1940 to deport those Jews who managed to reach Palestine without a permit, so-called illegal immigrants, to the island of Mauritius, 4,500 miles away in the Indian Ocean, where they were to remain for the duration of the war. This policy was slightly modified in mid-1942 to allow illegals who reached Palestine to remain there; however, in order to minimize its actual implementation, the new policy was not announced. In mid-1943, the War Cabinet decided to permit Jewish immigration into Palestine beyond the White Paper's 1944 deadline until the limit of seventy-five thousand immigrants was reached, but it did not announce this policy either until later in the year. These relative liberalizations of immigration policy had little practical effect, however, since Germany had sealed off Europe by this time. And when in 1944 the Soviets conquered southeastern Europe and a flood of Jewish immigrants tried to come to Palestine, the British government prevented many of them from entering. British officials were so successful in impeding Jewish immigration that by March 31, 1944, twenty thousand of the seventy-five thousand slots were still open, and the White Paper quota was not filled until December 1945—seven months after the end of the European war and almost one year after Auschwitz-Birkenau was liberated by Soviet troops.[18]

The White Paper of 1939 epitomized British anti-Zionism and served as a key barrier to a Jewish state in Palestine. As such, it persisted as one of the most controversial subjects in the Palestine dispute. Churchill remained viscerally opposed to the White Paper; in missives to various officials he referred to it as "treachery and bad faith on our part towards the Zionists" and a "gross breach of faith." He also considered it a violation of his own policy as colonial secretary—"a breach of an undertaking for which I was prominently responsible." In late 1939, when Churchill was first lord of the Admiralty, he had made a promise to Weizmann through his aide Brendan Bracken: "Look here—does not Dr Weizmann trust me? Tell him I am on the watch with regard to his affairs, and that I should resign from the War Cabinet if it does anything contrary to the Mandate. Tell him to trust me." Yet, while he argued against adherence to the White Paper in the Chamberlain government, he never threatened to resign over it, and as prime minister he never tried to overturn it. Even if he was inclined, he knew he was isolated within the government on this issue. No matter how much he opposed the White Paper, there was a limit to which he would expend political capital on such a subordinate and divisive matter. In 1943, he explained his characteristically rigid fixation, especially during war, on the paramount priorities: "Everything for the war, whether controversial or not, and nothing controversial that is not *bona fide* needed for the war."[19] Guided by that principle, he sought to remove the White Paper as a source of contention, whether domestic or international.

While Churchill opposed any public defense of the White Paper, both he and his government curtly made clear in statements and notes that it remained the government's policy. Harold Laski correctly wrote to Churchill in 1943 that the basis of British policy in Palestine was "the very White Paper you have condemned." Churchill privately denied Laski's claim and insisted to Weizmann in 1943 that the government maintained the policy "for the time being in the exigencies of war" and that "it runs until it is superseded." Ten days later Churchill made the same point to the War Cabinet: "I do not feel that the fact that we make no new declaration now in any way compromises or commits those who have opposed the White Paper of 1939. Faced with the emergencies of war, we have left the question where it stood. We are free, as a new Government, to review the entire field at the end of the war." And so the policy remained in place for the rest of the war. Churchill's primary goal was to prevent Palestine from interfering with the general war effort; as he told the War Cabinet in 1943, "Our chief aim at the present time should be to keep the situation as quiet as possible and to avoid bringing the Jewish-Arab problem into undue prominence."[20]

This argument in favor of the status quo, particularly concerning public pronouncements, cut both ways, and Churchill wielded it both before and after becoming prime minister as a means to oppose strong affirmation of the White Paper or other anti-Zionist proposals by various officials. He often insisted that such ideas would upset domestic politics during the war, conscious that many Labourites and Liberals and even a number of Conservatives expressed pro-Zionist sympathies, as evidenced by the White Paper vote in 1939, and he was sensitive to the government's political support. Perhaps more persuasively, he also argued in the War Cabinet that defending or enforcing the White Paper would adversely affect relations with the United States. He saw no reason to upset such vital diplomatic and strategic ties over a subordinate policy, especially when he too opposed it. As reports of mass murder of European Jews began to mount by late 1941 and early 1942, American Jews intensified their demands against the White Paper, arguing for open entry of Jewish refugees into Palestine and for a Jewish state there. The British surely noted how this activism was affecting the U.S. government when in mid-1942 Roosevelt proposed to the British that Palestinian Arabs be offered money and land near Aleppo, Syria. American Zionists raised the political pressure—and irritated Churchill—in 1943 by publishing ads containing excerpts of Churchill's 1939 speech blasting the White Paper. U.S. opposition to the White Paper, as well as U.S. support of Jewish immigration and a Jewish commonwealth in Palestine, cut across party lines and peaked in the election year of 1944. This provoked a number of anti-Zionist British officials to agitate for greater affirmation of the White Paper, which Churchill blocked. In response to such a suggestion by Halifax, who was ambassador to the United States, Churchill asserted pointedly, "Surely we are not going to make trouble for ourselves in America and hamper the President's chances of reelection for the sake of this low-grade gasp of a defeatist hour." He noted that Halifax, his anti-Semitic, anti-Zionist, pro-appeasement political rival, was "as usual on the wobble." Churchill threatened to condemn the White Paper publicly if Halifax defended it.[21]

Beyond the debate over the White Paper and its impact on other vital matters, Churchill took issue with a some specific arguments from other civilian and military officials on why Jewish immigrants should not be allowed into Palestine. He disregarded the concern that it would upset the Arabs, particularly the Palestinian Arabs, since he judged them irredeemably hostile to Britain and its interests. When General Archibald Wavell, commander in chief in the Middle East, argued in late 1940 that permitting survivors of the *Patria* vessel (a Mauritius-bound ship which had been sabotaged by Zionists to keep the Jewish immigrants on board in Palestine, accidentally killing 240 Jewish passengers) to remain in Palestine would disastrously undermine Arab confidence in Britain, Churchill responded skeptically, "If their attachment to our cause is so slender as to be determined by a mere act of charity of this kind it is clear that our policy of conciliating them has not borne much fruit so far." Also, Churchill dismissed the argument that enemy agents lurked among the Jewish refugees. Although he was for decades fixated on intelligence reports and issues and often suspicious about the presence of enemy agents, he related to Colonial Secretary Lloyd that "the Jewish authorities themselves, as Weizmann can assure you, would be most efficient and vigilant purgers in this respect." Military intelligence reported in the middle of the war that no agents were found among the Jewish immigrants, and this finding remained true for the rest of the war. Additionally, Churchill differed from his colleagues in his belief that Britain shared a responsibility to help the beleaguered Jewish refugees. For example, he stressed to Wavell about the *Patria* survivors, "Personally I hold it would be an act of inhumanity unworthy of the British name to force them to re-embark." Around the same time, he lectured the Colonial Office that Britain had "to consider their promises to the Zionists, and to be guided by sentiments of humanity towards those fleeing from the cruellest forms of persecution." Some officials were not so guided. The anti-Zionist Lloyd, for instance, complained in 1941 that Churchill repeatedly asked him, "What are you doing to my Jews?"[22]

Although Jewish immigration into Palestine was not a matter Churchill usually focused on or controlled, when he did focus on it he consistently tried to facilitate Jewish entry into Palestine. At the end of 1939 and early 1940, as first lord of the Admiralty, he instructed that naval vessels should not be used to interdict ships suspected of carrying illegal Jewish immigrants to Palestine and objected strenuously to a policy of treating these refugees as criminals and denying them sanctuary. He demanded that the colonial secretary tell him how "these wretched people" were to be treated and where they were to be sent. In late 1940, as prime minister, he agreed to the Colonial Office proposal to deport

Palestine-bound Jewish refugees to Mauritius, unaware that the high commissioner of Palestine had proclaimed that they could never return to Palestine (apparently to deter other Jews from seeking refuge in Palestine). After learning of the high commissioner's prohibition, he objected in a heated War Cabinet meeting—as such meetings often were regarding Jewish immigration to Palestine—and the prohibition was eventually abandoned after the war. He also succeeded in getting the *Patria* survivors freed in Palestine and having interned refugees in Mauritius treated more humanely—he opposed their being "caged up" in camps with barbed wire and guards.[23]

In early 1942, at the instigation of his son, Randolph, Churchill objected to the continued internment and harsh living conditions of Jewish refugees in Palestine from the *Darien II,* a decrepit ship from Romania via Turkey filled with almost eight hundred Jewish refugees that went to Palestine against British wishes. In a note to Colonial Secretary Moyne, he used the explosive term "concentration camp," with all its Nazi connotations, borrowing language from a Jewish Agency memo. Moyne disagreed, and on February 16 Churchill raised the matter to the War Cabinet, where, in the words of the War Cabinet secretary, he "strongly urged" the release of the Jewish internees, arguing that there was "a strong case for releasing them and that many of them might become soldiers or workers on the land or in industry." He did not think this would risk a wave of new Jewish immigrants because the circumstances had changed since the government decided to divert illegal Jewish immigrants to Mauritius in late 1940. Taking up the Zionist argument, Churchill asserted that now "that the whole of South-Eastern Europe was in German hands this risk must be greatly diminished." Moyne countered by citing the case of the *Struma*—an unseaworthy vessel from Romania with 769 Jewish refugees that Turkey refused to let dock unless Britain admitted the refugees into Palestine—as evidence of the imminence of more illegal immigrants. The War Cabinet postponed a decision until Minister of State Oliver Lyttelton's opinion was ascertained, but the government eventually released the *Darien II* Jews from internment.[24]

The *Struma* Jews were less fortunate. The War Cabinet did not directly address that issue at the February 16 meeting, and the Turks towed the immobilized vessel out to the Black Sea, where it sank on

February 25, 1942, for reasons unclear. All but one person perished, provoking international indignation. Churchill seemed mostly in the dark about the circumstances surrounding the *Struma*. During much of the discussions with the Turks, Churchill was in the United States mapping war strategy with Roosevelt. (The Japanese had bombed Pearl Harbor on December 7, 1941, and Hitler declared war on the United States four days later.) On February 13, after Churchill's return to Britain, Eden wrote him about the *Struma* situation but did not mention the horrible conditions on the ship or the Turks' deadline for decision. Eden also implied that the ship should be routed to Mauritius, when in fact he and Moyne wanted it returned to Romania. It is likely that when Moyne brought up the *Struma* at the February 16 War Cabinet meeting in connection to the *Darien II*, Churchill did not appreciate the gravity of the situation but conflated the issues of the two ships and figured that both would be resolved when Lyttleton sent in his views. It did not help Churchill's focus that on the prior day Singapore fell, and over seventy thousand armed troops surrendered to the Japanese—an event he later described as the "worst disaster and largest capitulation in British history." Much of the three-hour War Cabinet meeting on February 16 was spent discussing Singapore and how to respond to it in public. In his diary entry for that day, the pro-Zionist Amery only mentioned the War Cabinet discussing Singapore and did not refer to the *Darien II* or *Struma*.[25]

There were some other instances when Churchill encouraged a more sympathetic policy toward Jews seeking refuge in Palestine. In late 1942, when more press and political attention was being paid to the Holocaust, the Colonial Office proposed, in response to a Jewish Agency request and despite Foreign Office objections, that 5,000 Jewish Bulgarians—4,500 children and 500 adult women—be admitted into Palestine. An evidently surprised Churchill replied excitedly to Colonial Secretary Oliver Stanley, "Bravo!" and obtained War Cabinet approval as well. In the end, however, Germany blocked the Bulgarians from carrying it out. In mid-1943, Churchill forcefully and successfully urged the War Cabinet to oppose naval searches of ships to find illegal Jewish immigrants, to extend Jewish immigration into Palestine beyond the March 1944 deadline, and to allow illegal immigrants into Palestine up to the limit established by the 1939 White Paper.[26]

Churchill also contributed to what little the Allies did to provide sanctuary to European Jewish refugees outside of Palestine. In the spring of 1943, the British and U.S. governments, under domestic pressure to help alleviate Jewish suffering—and also intent to relieve pressure on Spain so it would re-open its Pyrenean frontier to the influx of escaping British military personnel—convened a conference at Bermuda to address settling wartime refugees. The conferees agreed not to make the refugee issue exclusively about Jews and took Palestine off the table as a refuge. They recommended housing refugees in camps in North Africa. Eden considered Bermuda successful but its paltry results only deepened Jewish despair. On the eve of the Bermuda conference, Churchill urged his colleagues to support making the ex-Italian colonies of Eritrea and Tripolitania into "Jewish colonies affiliated, if desired, to the National Home in Palestine." He thought such a formulation an appealing compromise, one that addressed Jewish humanitarian needs without violating the 1939 White Paper and without declaring Palestine closed to Jews. Churchill made the same proposal to an indifferent and skeptical Roosevelt in Washington in May 1943, arguing that it would take the "strain off the National Jewish Home in Palestine . . . without prejudice to the more permanent policy" in Palestine. More than a month later he pleaded with Roosevelt that the issue had become more urgent and conveyed a sense of personal responsibility in a letter: "Our immediate facilities for helping the victims of Hitler's anti-Jewish drive are so limited at present that the opening of the small camp proposed for the purpose of removing some of them to safety seems all the more incumbent on us." Soon after, he and Roosevelt agreed to move refugees in Spain, some of whom were Jewish, to North Africa, and Churchill noted, likely for Roosevelt's benefit, that this provided "a solution for our difficulties in Spain." These camps came to shelter tens of thousands of non-Jewish refugees and only two thousand Jewish refugees. Roosevelt told Churchill that the Jews sheltered in North Africa would be returned to their original European countries after the war, while Churchill had considered leaving the Jews there to form some sort of colonies affiliated with a Jewish national home in Palestine.[27]

Churchill also consistently sought to ensure that Jews already in Palestine remained safe and strong. This issue came to the fore early in the war when Churchill sought to bring many British troops home from Palestine to defend Britain against a possible German invasion. Since this meant increasing the vulnerability of Palestinian Jews to Arab attack, he wanted to arm the Jews. In late 1939, when he served in the subordinate position of first lord of the Admiralty, he recommended arming both Palestinian Arabs and Jews, but after becoming prime minister in 1940 he repeatedly urged his colleagues to permit the Palestinian Jews to defend themselves and no longer raised the idea of arming the Palestinian Arabs. He was repeatedly rebuffed by other officials, including from the Colonial Office and the military. Although he promised not to let Weizmann down and to "see the thing through," the War Cabinet rejected the idea in the autumn of 1941, and he eventually gave up on it in mid-1942, though Churchill's prodding seemed to force an end to British disarmament of the Palestinian Jews. Churchill was chiefly motivated by strategic, humanitarian, and Zionist concerns, including the interest to enhance Palestinian Jewish leverage over the Palestinian Arabs, which he explicitly expressed to Weizmann at the beginning of the war. But given the War Cabinet's broad anti-Zionism, he usually emphasized the strategic value—that Palestinian Jewish military strength bolstered Britain's capability to defend Palestine. (Italy and then Germany threatened Palestine from North Africa in 1940 and 1941, and Italy even bombed Tel-Aviv and Haifa in September 1940.) As he told the War Cabinet in early 1940, when he was first lord of the Admiralty, the Zionists "were the only trustworthy friends we had in that country," and therefore Britain should build up a "strong" Palestinian Jewish military force. He went so far as to assert to one minister that the more the Jews could defend themselves, "the safer we shall be." Eventually, more than twenty-five thousand Palestinian Jews served in the British Army.[28]

During the war, Churchill continued to see the same historical and civilizational advantages to Zionism that he had for decades. He wanted the Jews, restored to their historical homeland, to regain equal status with other nations of the world. He promised Weizmann in 1943 that after victory "we shall have to establish the Jews in the position where they belong." That same year, he notably used the phrase "Jewish national home" several times. He unequivocally conveyed to his colleagues that Palestine historically belonged to the Jews. In a note to the anti-Zionist

Moyne in early 1942 urging that interned Jewish immigrants from the *Darien II* be absorbed into Palestine, Churchill provocatively wrote, "I suggest that you let them join their compatriots in Palestine." By using "compatriots" instead of the less controversial "co-religionists" Churchill was suggesting that the Jews were a nation whose homeland was Palestine. He was even more provocative and personal in a 1944 War Cabinet discussion of Hungarian Jewish refugees. Churchill pugnaciously declared to Cranborne, in words that Amery recorded in his diary, that the Jews "had as good a claim to it [Palestine] as he [Cranborne] had to Hatfield," a town in Hertfordshire from which Cranborne's family had long hailed. The anti-Zionist Cranborne was no doubt shocked by this aggressive remark, as other War Cabinet members must have been.[29]

Churchill also continued to see the Zionists as civilizing agents and the Palestinian Arabs as backward, and he initially hoped others in the government might agree. One of his arguments to the War Cabinet in early 1940 against proposed anti-Zionist land restrictions was that they would stymie the progress of civilization in Palestine. Churchill's close South African friend and ideological kinsman Jan Christian Smuts relayed a similar view to Weizmann in 1943. Smuts, in Weizmann's account, "could not understand what the British saw in the Arabs," and then referred to the Jews by stressing that "the essence of humanity was in Palestine." Weizmann certainly needed no convincing, as he shared Churchill's civilizational outlook. The Zionist leader, for example, told U.S. State Department officials in 1943, according to a report of the meeting, "It is impossible to have a dynamic group [the Jews], constituting about one-third of the population, which has built up modern Palestine, subjected to a backward majority [Palestinian Arabs], and this is, in his [Weizmann's] opinion, a misconstruction of democracy in its real sense." Weizmann then immediately added, correctly, referring to Churchill, "The abnormalcy is being realized by some statesmen, particularly by the Prime Minister."[30]

Zionism was also important to Churchill's strategic vision. He valued the Palestinian Jews' fidelity and strength in Palestine, as well as the impact a pro-Zionist policy had on the views of American Jews toward Britain. The exaggerated image of Jewish political power had been widely shared on both the political Left and Right in Britain for years, and often derived from anti-Semitic feelings. Churchill, however, generally saw it more neutrally, as established fact. The Jews, particularly Weizmann, shrewdly encouraged this exaggerated image, as they had during the First World War. Churchill cited the power of American Jewry to argue against a proposal to restrict Jewish purchases of land in Palestine in late 1939. He often equated appeasing American Jews with appeasing the United States. He suggested placating American Jews as a means of enhancing the support for President Roosevelt, who was Britain's "best friend." He often framed Palestine issues in terms of whether Britain wanted to appease the United States or the Arabs and attributed little value to the latter. After Britain crushed a pro-Nazi revolt in Iraq in 1941, Churchill rebuffed a proposal to confirm the 1939 White Paper by stating, "I am quite certain that we should lose in America far more than we should gain in the East." Churchill was also concerned with courting American Christian Zionists. He hoped to use alleged American Jewish influence (and their hatred of Nazi Germany) to secure U.S. aid before Pearl Harbor and then, once the United States entered the war, to maintain good ties with Britain's new powerful ally. This was most evident shortly after he became prime minister in May 1940. Only a few days after the Dunkirk evacuation of British troops from France, which signaled Britain's determination to fight the Nazis alone if necessary after France's impending capitulation, Churchill wanted Weizmann to go immediately to the United States and convince American Jews to throw their weight behind helping Britain. Churchill, fixated on victory, sought to employ all possible weapons on Britain's behalf and was incredulous that other officials did not want to do the same. He reminded his colleagues to focus on the overwhelming objective and not cause problems for the Palestinian Jews. Disraeli's dictum had very immediate, practical relevance for Churchill.[31]

Despite Churchill's great sensitivity to Roosevelt's alleged political demands, he often put himself in the strange position of reminding the president of the political importance of appeasing American Jews. In 1943, shortly after the Bermuda conference on refugees, Churchill discussed various Zionist schemes with Roosevelt. Vice President Henry Wallace recorded in his diary that "Churchill remarked that there were more Jews than Arab votes in the Anglo-Saxon countries and we could not afford to ignore such practical considerations." Yet, Roosevelt did not seem to take the subject very seriously, perhaps because he took for granted overwhelming American Jewish support, or perhaps because he feared a pro-Jewish policy was unpopular with most other Americans, who were increasingly anti-Semitic. After introducing to Churchill a State Department plan to spread the Jews out thinly around the world, so that they would not be concentrated in Palestine, Roosevelt cracked that he had tried that in Marietta, Georgia, and Hyde Park, New York (where he owned homes), by adding four or five Jewish families at each place but did not think the locals would object if no more were added. Similarly, at Yalta in early 1945, when asked by Stalin if he intended to make concessions to Ibn Saud at an upcoming meeting, Roosevelt replied that he might offer to give him the six million Jews in the United States. Churchill never made such jokes about Jews, while Roosevelt often flip-flopped over Jewish and Zionist issues. As Cordell Hull, Roosevelt's secretary of state, noted, "In general the President at times talked both ways to Zionists and Arabs, besieged as he was by each camp." He was also besieged by the Jewish and anti-Semitic camps.[32]

Underlying Churchill's pro-Zionist views and policies was not simply a preference for the Jews and Zionists but a continuing indifference and at times hostility toward the Palestinian Arabs. This was evident at a pivotal War Cabinet meeting in July 1943, when the government approved extending the White Paper deadline past March 31, 1944, and establishing a committee to examine partition. Churchill gave an impassioned pro-Zionist plea on various matters, "brushing the Palestine Arab case on one side as wholly irrelevant and trivial," Amery recorded in his diary. Churchill believed there was little cost to alienating the Arabs, whom he considered enemies of Britain, with the exception of Abdullah and Ibn Saud (who were enemies of each other). Many Arabs, including the Jerusalem mufti, were pro-Axis, which Hitler and Mussolini encouraged. Churchill often couched his private pro-Zionist statements with derogatory comments about the Arabs and Arab loyalties.[33]

Another reason Churchill was indifferent to Arab concerns was that he believed that despite their enmity the Arabs respected strength and would fall in line once Britain demonstrated its power. In early 1941, when German forces were threatening Greece and were expected soon to attack North Africa, Wavell requested postponement of the plan to form a Palestinian Jewish division lest it make the Arabs more receptive to Axis propaganda and complicate his military campaigns. Churchill relented but wrote Moyne that Wavell was overreacting as he had over the *Patria:* "All went well, and not a dog barked. It follows from the above that I am not in the least convinced by all this stuff. The Arabs, under the impression of recent victories, would not make any trouble now." Yet, one month later the Arabs offered a fresh challenge to Britain, despite the government's decision to hold off forming a Palestinian Jewish force (and while continuing to enforce the White Paper). In the spring of 1941, Rashid Ali al-Gailani, a leading Iraqi politician, took power, overthrew the pro-British regent, and declared war on Britain. Iraq, which suffered through numerous governments after Faisal's accession to the throne in 1921, had been a promoter of pan-Arabism for years. Churchill, overriding Wavell's objections, ordered the rebellion crushed, which it was the following month, despite help from German planes that arrived via Vichy Syria. Ali fled to Germany. So did the mufti of Jerusalem, a promoter of the rebellion who had been in Baghdad since 1939 and was subsidized by the Iraqi government (which had also sent arms to him and Palestinian Arab radicals during their revolt in 1936–1939). The rebellion only confirmed Churchill's view of the Arabs as hostile to Britain. He never forgot their open betrayal and referred to it often. Churchill once remarked sharply, in an April 1943 note to the War Cabinet, that with the exception of Ibn Saud, who was neutral, and Abdullah "the Arabs have been virtually of no use to us in the present war. . . . They have taken no part in the fighting except in so far as they were involved in the Iraq rebellion against us." He felt, therefore, that the Arabs had "created no new claims upon the Allies, should we be victorious." At a lunch at the White House the following month, Wallace recorded, "Churchill cussed out the various Arabian leaders and pointed especially at their failure to come through with substantial help of any kind."[34]

When Churchill became colonial secretary in 1921, he essentially viewed his role in Palestine as constructing a political framework that implemented policies and principles established by others. For the following two decades, he recommended maintaining that framework while it remained in Britain's interest and until the Jews eventually reached a majority. A Jewish state was seen as a real but distant goal. In its broad outline, this was a status quo approach. As prime minister during the

Second World War, Churchill was in a position to affect Palestinian policy again and was energized by a strong desire to help the Zionists. He actively worked behind the scenes to secure a pro-Zionist regional settlement based on ideas proposed by others that would replace the increasingly anachronistic 1922 League of Nations mandate and the despised 1939 White Paper and fulfill the aim of the 1917 Balfour Declaration. In the First World War, the British Cabinet considered it necessary to support Zionism publicly—indeed, the public declaration was the basis for the policy. Churchill, however, reflecting different realities in Britain and the Middle East, as well as his own diplomatic approach, was averse to any public official pronouncements, either in support of or hostile to Zionism. He often acted coy in private official circles to minimize arousal of the overwhelming anti-Zionist forces inside the government. He preferred to keep these forces at bay as much and as long as possible to provide himself with more maneuvering room to pursue a settlement.[35]

Churchill did garner tentative War Cabinet approval of his pro-Zionist Middle East plan in early 1944, and he hoped to gather the support of Roosevelt and Ibn Saud, with which he would have overruled any future popular or official domestic opposition. This approach was not unusual. Churchill pursued bolder diplomatic initiatives with far less Cabinet consultations or support—such as in 1941, when he publicly pledged full material support for the Soviet Union after it was attacked by Germany, and in 1953, during his second premiership, when he pursued a summit with the new Soviet leadership following Stalin's death. Churchill did not discuss his plan at any formal conferences with Stalin and Roosevelt, but he wanted it formally addressed at a postwar conference of victors, which had become a tradition following previous major European conflicts.

Churchill did not often think it necessary to explain why he was pursuing a pro-Zionist Middle East settlement, certainly not to the anti-Zionist officialdom that had rejected him and now was supposed to serve him. Zionism was integral to him now, and he fervently wanted to see a Jewish state, within limits. As we have seen, during the war he referred here and there to why he supported Zionism—historical, civilizational, humanitarian, and Disraelian imperatives; antipathy toward the Arabs, particularly the Palestinian Arabs; and the strategic need to appeal to American and Palestinian Jews and to align politically with the United States. Churchill also certainly recognized the strategic and diplomatic benefit that would accrue to Britain, whose decline as a world power vis-à-vis the United States and Russia became ever more clear to him, by forging a comprehensive settlement in the Middle East. Notably, Churchill began his quest for a grand pro-Zionist Middle Eastern settlement in response to strategic issues in the spring of 1941, before he recognized the mass murder of Jews afoot in eastern Europe in September 1941. The Holocaust did have some impact on his plans, however, since he partly reacted to the growing militancy of the Zionists that resulted from it. More directly, Churchill also believed that Jewish suffering in Europe should be redeemed by a Jewish homeland in Palestine.

A few months after the war began, in December 1939, Churchill told Weizmann that he supported a postwar Zionist state with three to four million Jews, repeating an idea and population range he had raised in 1920, which in turn echoed a proposal and population range advanced by Herbert Samuel in 1915. However, Churchill was not really giving any thought to Middle Eastern postwar plans at this time; he mentioned it only to curry favor with Weizmann as the Zionist leader embarked on a trip to the United States, which Churchill deemed crucial to deepening American support for Britain's cause. Others were, however, pondering postwar Middle Eastern matters. In the 1920s and 1930s, many Zionists took the pan-Arabist view that if the Palestinian Arabs were, in Elie Kedourie's words, "submerged in a wider Arab entity," and thus less anxious, there would be no more conflict with them. After the British government rejected partition in 1938, there was growing support in Zionist circles for a Jewish entity within a large Arab federation consisting at least of Transjordan and Syria. Ibn Saud was reportedly interested in heading such a federation, and discussions among various parties ensued in 1939 and 1940. In November 1941 at Weizmann's behest, Churchill's principal private secretary, John Martin (who had served as secretary to the Peel Commission), met with Hugh St. John Philby, a controversial Arabist of questionable reliability, who reported that Ibn Saud was willing to permit the Jews to have Palestine in return for being allowed to rule a regional federation and a payment of £20 million.[36]

Churchill began seriously considering the postwar Middle East in 1941 in response to pressing strategic challenges. After Britain survived the Battle of Britain in the summer of 1940 without a German invasion, the war's focus turned to the Mediterranean. By late 1940, British forces were fighting in Greece and Africa, and in the spring of 1941 German troops overpowered British positions in North Africa while the pro-Nazi Rashid Ali rebelled in Iraq. German designs on Syria were also feared. Churchill worried that an Arab rebellion against Britain coupled with direct German occupation in the region would imperil Britain's whole position in the Middle East, including in Egypt, the Suez Canal (and thus India), and the Abadan refineries in Persia.[37] None of these concerns led him to appease the Arabs at the Jews' expense, as most British officials were inclined to do. Instead, he sought to rally some Arabs and shore up the support of the Jews in Palestine and in the still-neutral United States. All this led him to consider redrawing the political map of the region.

Churchill made his first broad proposal in March 1941, on the eve of another Weizmann trip to the United States. He barged in on a Weizmann-Bracken meeting to tell his old Zionist friend that he supported the formation of a regional federation that included a Zionist state and that was ruled by Ibn Saud, who would be the "Boss of the Bosses." He offered to broker such a settlement and assured Weizmann, "I will see you through." He also stated that their thoughts were 90 percent the same, that he was constantly thinking about Zionism, and that he felt a "twist in his heart" whenever he saw his old friend—echoing his remark in 1937 that he was afraid to see Weizmann because it left him depressed. Churchill asked Weizmann to keep their talk confidential though suggested he raise the issue with Roosevelt; the Zionist leader did not do so when he met with the U.S. president.[38]

In May, Churchill advanced a more considered proposal in a memo he gave to Eden for comment. Churchill suggested that if the French army in Syria remained pro-Vichy, Britain should assert that the French mandate in Syria had lapsed and proclaim an independent Syrian state in permanent alliance with Turkey and Britain. In the following months, Churchill wrote to Eden in favor of Lebanese and Syrian independence, and also of "Arab independence." This recalled the First World War strategy of offering independence to rally Middle Eastern peoples to Britain's side, and the language suggested that era's pan-Arab conception. Still, after all these years of involvement and concern with the region he acknowledged that he was not expert on all the related matters and was unsure of the feasibility of such a plan, and he suggested that the "Islamic authorities" should comment. He raised the idea he had just discussed with Weizmann of making Ibn Saud "general overlord," or "Caliph," of Iraq and Transjordan. Churchill characterized Ibn Saud as the "greatest living Arab," who had "given long and solid proofs of fidelity," although he failed to mention that the "fidelity" had been partly based upon British subsidies. Churchill had come a long way from his negative view in the early 1920s of Ibn Saud, or he at least felt that Ibn Saud—who had ruled over much of Arabia since ousting Hussein ibn Ali (head of the sherifians) in 1924 from the Hejaz region of Arabia, was sitting on increasing oil riches, and remained neutral during the war (thus retaining some leverage with each side)—was the Arab leader who must be dealt with. This favorable view of Ibn Saud somewhat reflected the attitude of other British officials, who were in awe of the Bedouin. In 1942, for instance, a report by the War Cabinet's Middle East standing subcommittee referred to Ibn Saud's "honourable character" and described him as a "proved friend of Britain." In 1943, one senior colonial official considered him "the outstanding Arab of his generation." None of these views suggested sufficient respect for Ibn Saud's Hashemite rival and Britain's closer friend, Abdullah, emir of Transjordan. It was self-evident to Churchill that this gift of a federation would have to be contingent upon Ibn Saud's acceptance of a Jewish state in Palestine. He declared that in return for "giving these very great advancements to the Arab world, we should, of course, negotiate with Ibn Saud a satisfactory settlement of the Jewish problem; and, if such a basis were reached, it is possible that the Jewish State of Western Palestine might form an independent Federal Unit in the Arab Caliphate." He envisioned this Zionist entity rather liberally: "This Jewish State would have to have the fullest rights of self-government, including immigration and development, and provision for expansion in the desert regions to the southward, which they would gradually reclaim." Churchill seemingly wanted to offer the whole of western Palestine to the Zionists, including the Negev in the south, and exclude a separate entity for the Palestinian Arabs. This did not contravene the mandate but did serve as a rejection of the Peel Commission's 1937 partition plan, which he had never supported. Unlike other officials, he believed that Britain had leverage over the Arabs and not the other way around, and he wanted to use some of that leverage to establish a Jewish state. Shortly after Churchill delivered his memo, Eden made clear that he opposed a postwar Zionist state and thought that, while greater Arab unity was to be encouraged, a federation that included Ibn Saud and the rival sherifians/Hashemites would be unstable. The Colonial and Foreign Offices and the War Cabinet overwhelmingly shared Eden's views and consistently opposed Churchill's plan. In the following month, the War Cabinet rejected Churchill's plan.[39]

Nevertheless, this was a breakthrough proposal. For several years Churchill had spoken about a Jewish state as a distant goal, as had Weizmann, but now he considered it a very real short-term objective. Broadly, his plan was based on the sherifian/pan-Arab conception propounded after the First World War by T. E. Lawrence and other Arabists in the Colonial and Foreign Offices, in which a respected Arab chieftain would impose control over Palestinian Arabs. More specifically, it resembled Samuel's 1920 proposal of an independent Jewish government in Palestine as part of a loose Damascus-based Arab federation headed by Hussein's son, Faisal. But in the two decades since Samuel's proposal, the official establishment, including some of the same officials, had turned increasingly against any program that might lead to the creation of a Jewish entity in Palestine, even one that was part of a broad Arab federation, which many officials favored as well. Churchill's plan envisioned a totally new Middle East, one that was fundamentally opposed to the Middle Eastern ideas held by the establishment.

Although the strategic necessity of shoring up Palestinian and American Jewish support might have initially contributed to Churchill putting forth his pro-Zionist plan, that motive was not the basis of the plan, and he did not even frame it that way to the anti-Zionist Eden, which certainly would have been more persuasive. Churchill's relentless pursuit of the plan away from the public eye, and beyond the period when Palestine and the Middle East were vulnerable to Nazi penetration and attack and American Jewish support was deemed critical, suggested that he was following deep convictions. He strongly believed that there was now an opportunity to achieve his long-held aspiration for a Jewish homeland in Palestine.

A couple of months after the War Cabinet rejection, Churchill revived his idea following more problems with the Free French in Syria, supposedly increased interest from Ibn Saud, growing reports from

Bletchley Park of Nazi murders of Jews in eastern Europe, and intensified Zionist preoccupation with a state. When the Free French did not promise Syrian and Lebanese independence, or any concessions to these countries that Britain wanted, Churchill recommended to the War Cabinet in the late summer of 1941 that Britain break with the Free French and reach a general settlement with the Arabs based on granting Syrian independence and a Jewish state. Eden and Moyne opposed this, and Churchill postponed further consideration of the matter. But with the Jewish tragedy unfolding in Europe and Zionist leaders becoming more demanding in public of their postwar needs, the issue did not go away. The following month, Churchill got Amery, who was secretary of state for India and Burma, on board with his plan by enlisting the efforts of Indian High Commissioner Firaz Khan Noon, who met Weizmann at Churchill's suggestion. Churchill discussed his plan at the War Cabinet but, as the minutes recorded, distanced himself from the idea: "The Prime Minister referred to the suggestion that had been made that Ibn Saud should become King of an Arab Federation; and that provision should be made for an autonomous Jewish State, with reasonable room for expansion." Apparently alluding to the Weizmann-Noon talks, Churchill noted that this "suggestion had been well received by Dr Weizmann." Churchill asked that Amery, Eden, Moyne, and Oliver Lyttelton, the minister of state for the Middle East and a member of the War Cabinet, discuss the matter. He wrote the four of them that this plan "is full of interest and indeed the best I can think of." However, among the four only Amery supported the plan, and yet another effort on Churchill's part came to nought. Churchill remarked to Moyne, "It is much better now however to get on with the war." Yet, five days later, Churchill intimated continued interest in a postwar Jewish state with his public statement: "Assuredly in the day of victory the Jew's sufferings and his part in the struggle will not be forgotten."[40]

The plan was temporarily shelved but Churchill remained defiantly supportive of a Zionist state. A few days after the War Cabinet's rejection, he wrote Cabinet Secretary Edward Bridges, "I may say at once that if Britain and the United States emerge victorious from the war, the creation of a great Jewish state in Palestine inhabited by millions of Jews will be one of the leading features of the Peace Conference discussions. The Liberal and Labour Parties will never agree to the pro-Arab solutions which are the commonplace of British Service circles; nor, so long as I remain in British public life, will I." This private statement was striking. Churchill articulated in no uncertain terms, and with no ulterior motive, that the long time frame—generations or centuries—he had envisioned only a few years earlier for a Jewish state to emerge was emphatically a relic of the past. He foresaw a Jewish state to be part of the new postwar order, and he did not care at all what the anti-Zionist establishment felt. A few months later he met Weizmann, whose upcoming trip to the United States interested Churchill very much. When Weizmann said that after the war the Zionists wanted a state consisting of three to four million Jews in Palestine, Churchill replied, "Yes, indeed, I quite agree with that."[41] This time when Churchill expressed support for a Zionist state on the eve of Weizmann's trip to the United States, he did so in the context of active effort on the Zionists' behalf.

Churchill did not actively pursue his plan for a Zionist state and regional settlement in 1942. He certainly faced continued opposition. In January 1942, the War Cabinet's Middle East standing subcommittee, chaired by former aide John Shuckburgh of the Colonial Office, issued a report concluding that an Arab federation was impractical given little Arab interest, as well as jealousies and religious and geographic differences among possible Arab members. And an Arab federation headed by Ibn Saud that included a Jewish state was determined to be especially quixotic: "We cannot regard such a suggestion as deserving of serious consideration." The subcommittee thought "a man of Ibn Saud's high spirit and honourable character could not be bribed or cajoled into taking a step which every Arab would regard as a shameful surrender of Arab interests." Another obstacle to approval of Churchill's controversial plan, at least earlier in the year, was his diminished leverage within the War Cabinet. After the shocking defeats in Singapore and Tobruk, along with other setbacks, he faced calls to cede direction of the war to someone else and relinquish the minister of defense portfolio, which he held simultaneously with the premiership. He retained the portfolio but felt obliged to make some changes in ministerial appointments. Yet another obstacle to active pursuit of the pro-Zionist plan was that Churchill had other priorities at this time. The Japanese attack on Pearl Harbor in December 1941 and the entrance of the United States into the war transformed the strategic landscape and war planning. Also, Germany's advance into Egypt, spearheaded by General Erwin Rommel, led to more time spent formulating plans for the evacuation of Palestine than deliberating the future policy toward it.[42]

Still, Churchill quietly pondered his pro-Zionist plan. He spoke about it with U.S. Treasury Secretary Henry Morgenthau, a leading Jew in the Roosevelt administration. As Weizmann wrote in a letter in June 1942, "Morgenthau is as sound as ever and he has told me that he had a talk with Churchill on Palestine and the latter has mentioned to him his 'plan' about Ibn Saoud, etc. The same was confirmed to me by [British Field Marshall John General] Dill." Perhaps with this in mind, Weizmann wrote to Rabbi Stephen Wise, an American Jewish leader, a couple weeks later, "We have one great friend in England, the Prime Minister." A couple of months later, Churchill was in Cairo and discussed with Spears a federation of four states in the Middle East, three of which would be Arab and one Jewish. From Cairo he also wrote Roosevelt of his concern that the latter's proposed message on the anniversary of the Atlantic Charter regarding self-government for all Asian peoples would undermine British rule in India. He added, perhaps believing this would be more persuasive, "Here in the Middle East the Arabs might claim by majority that they could expel the Jews from Palestine, or at any rate forbid all further immigration." He asserted emphatically, "I am strongly wedded to the Zionist policy, of which I was one of the authors." Churchill did not need to make such a strong personal comment about Zionism to make his point, but his remarks jibed with what he told Spears and with what he told a colleague earlier about the Atlantic Charter. In any case, Churchill's concern was not theoretical; a member of his own government, Moyne, suggested in the House of Lords one month later that a Zionist state conflicted with the Atlantic Charter. Churchill wrote one other time during the war of being "wedded" to Zionism, and that was in a note to Moyne in 1941.[43]

In that ardent Zionist spirit, Churchill expressed words of encouragement to Weizmann, who was despondent over both the lack of progress in the Zionist movement and personal problems such as the death of his son from action in the Royal Air Force. At the suggestion of his aide Martin, Churchill sent a private message (drafted by Martin) to Weizmann on November 2, 1942, the twenty-fifth anniversary of the Balfour Declaration, which read, "My thoughts are with you on this anniversary. Better days will surely come for your suffering people and for the great cause for which you have fought so bravely." This message, which was certainly unnecessary, attested to the special personal relationship Churchill had with Weizmann and to the special bond he felt toward a movement that had inspired him for much of his long and meandering political career.[44]

Churchill renewed his pursuit of alternative plans for the Zionists in 1943, in response to growing international focus on the genocide of European Jewry and on Jewish refugees from Europe, intensification of Zionist diplomatic and political activity, and assorted meetings and conferences in Britain and North America. In January 1943, Weizmann and other Zionist leaders met with the U.S. State Department's Near Eastern Division, and Weizmann referred to the "Prime Minister's plan" involving Ibn Saud. Under-Secretary of State Sumner Welles and other officials thought it an excellent idea and asked whether Weizmann was prepared to discuss it with Ibn Saud; Weizmann was, under the right circumstances. After the meeting, Weizmann insisted to Isaiah Berlin, who then served in the British Embassy in Washington, that the plan was Churchill's and that he (Weizmann) was not overly optimistic about it but thought it promising. Berlin reported to Halifax that Weizmann's wife, Vera, "who has considerable influence with her husband," opposed the Saudi plan because she thought it overestimated Ibn Saud's influence. Also, she thought sending Weizmann to Arabia would only increase suspicions among Americans, Britons, Arabs, and Jews. At another meeting at the State Department in March, Weizmann minimized Ibn Saud's written opposition to the federation but backed off a bit from the plan, believing it premature for him to meet Ibn Saud. Still, one senior colonial official at this time referred to the plan as "Dr. Weizmann's 'Ibn Saud' project."[45]

Eden certainly was distressed over Weizmann's January meeting with the State Department, fearing that the Zionists, and perhaps even Churchill, were seeking to make an end run around him and other anti-Zionists in the British government by enlisting U.S. support for a pro-Zionist federation scheme. Reflecting both his anxiety and perhaps a lack of trust in Churchill on the matter, Eden even insinuated that Churchill had given Weizmann permission to discuss his plan with the United States (which Churchill did in 1941). Churchill, offended, sharply replied, "Dr. Weizmann has no authority to speak in my name. At the same time I expressed these views to him when we met some time ago, and you have often heard them from me yourself." He then added a line he would repeat often when he temporarily backed off from his plan: "I regard all discussions on these points as premature at present and only liable to cause dissension."[46] He knew there was nothing to be gained from arguing with Eden.

Yet, Churchill was in no mood to suspend his Zionist agenda. Spears recorded in the spring of 1943 that Churchill "laid down his Zionist policy in the most emphatic terms. He said he had formed an opinion which nothing could change. He intended to see to it that there was a Jewish state. He told me not to argue with him as this would merely make him angry and would change nothing." Reflecting this new temper, Churchill used the term "national home" on several occasions with his colleagues and Roosevelt in describing Jewish Palestine, after not using the term much, if at all, since 1939. Groping about for ways to help the Zionists, he conveyed to Roosevelt in Washington in May, according to Wallace's diary, his support for the "development of Trans-Jordania for the Jews." Churchill intimated the same idea to Weizmann several months later. This radical proposal was more generous to the Zionists than his federation plan whereby the Jews would only receive western Palestine. Although Abdullah, the leader of Transjordan, remained the most pro-British Arab ruler in the region, the new proposal seemed to reflect the same lack of respect for him that was inherent in the federation plan, in which he would in effect be subordinate to his (and his family's) bitter Saudi rival. In any case, Roosevelt asked Churchill to agree to cohost an Arab-Jewish conference to help resolve the Zionist issue.[47]

A few days after Churchill met with Roosevelt in Washington and discussed Palestine, Roosevelt received a stridently anti-Jewish and anti-Zionist letter from Ibn Saud, who maintained that Palestine was a "sacred Moslem Arab country" that "belonged to the Arabs" and that the period when the Jews "occupied it" was "full of massacres and tragedies." He accused the Jews of seeking to "exterminate the peaceful Arabs" and expressed hope that the Allies would not "evict" the Arabs and install "vagrant Jews who have no ties with this country except an imaginary claim which, from the point of view of right and justice, has no grounds except what they invent through fraud and deceit." Ibn Saud also argued that a "religious animosity" had existed between Jews and Muslims since the birth of Islam and the "treacherous behavior of the Jews towards Moslems and their Prophet." This letter was reminiscent of the truculent pronouncements of the Palestinian Arabs that Churchill faced in the early 1920s, and it supported one of Eden's arguments against Churchill's federation scheme. U.S. Ambassador John Winant informed Churchill about the letter, diplomatically explaining that Ibn Saud expressed "his opposition to the creation of a Jewish state in Palestine or any further increase in that country of Jewish influence." Roosevelt, in reply to his "Great and Good Friend" Ibn Saud, expressed his wish that Arabs and Jews come to a friendly understanding over Palestine before the war was over and pledged not to make any important decisions about Palestinian "without full consultation with both Arabs and Jews."[48]

Roosevelt remained intrigued by Churchill's pro-Zionist regional scheme during a meeting with Weizmann in June 1943 and suggested that the Arabs were "purchasable," in Weizmann's subsequent paraphrase. Weizmann agreed that he had heard the same, perhaps alluding to Philby's 1941 report. Roosevelt decided to explore Ibn Saud's interest by sending Lieutenant Colonel Harold Hoskins to meet with him. Hoskins, who was born in the Levant to a missionary couple and was profoundly pro-Arab and anti-Zionist, was in the Office of Strategic Services and had recently returned from an exploratory tour of the Middle East. The British approved Hoskins's meeting with Ibn Saud despite wariness among some officials over increasing U.S. involvement in Arabia at Britain's expense. There was also some British skepticism of the value after Ibn Saud had told General Patrick Hurley, another U.S. presidential envoy, in May that he opposed a Zionist state and declared, "I hate the Jews more than anyone. My religion and my Islamic belief make it inevitable that I should." In the summer of 1943, Hoskins reported to Roosevelt after his meeting that Ibn Saud remained opposed to a Jewish state in Palestine but extolled the Arabian chieftain's virtues. The president, Hoskins recounted, was influenced by this report and took a decidedly anti-Zionist stance. Roosevelt, claiming to have seen reports that European Jews wanted to return after the war to their countries of origin and not move to Palestine, said that he was working on settling some Jews in Colombia and was leaning toward the idea of a trusteeship for Palestine that would be shared by all three major religions—Muslims, Jews, and Christians. Roosevelt appeared to have changed his mind yet again about Zionism. By contrast, Churchill was unmoved and shrugged off Hoskins's report when he read of it in the autumn of 1943. He also rebuffed a Foreign Office request to meet with Hoskins: "Alas I cannot see him. My opinions on this question are the result of long reflection and are not likely to undergo any change. I will talk to the President about it when we meet."[49]

The United States and Britain discussed for several months issuing a joint declaration welcoming a wartime Arab-Zionist agreement and pledging to make no final decision about Palestine until after the war and only after consultations with both Jews and Arabs—in effect what Roosevelt wrote to Ibn Saud. The Zionists, who wanted their issue considered by the Allies immediately, opposed such a statement, and the U.S. War Department eventually nixed it. A couple of weeks later, at the Anglo-American Quebec Conference in August, Roosevelt and Churchill privately agreed to hold the Palestine question "in abeyance," according to meeting minutes, and assess it as the war unfolded. A few months later, at the Tehran conference of the Big Three—Stalin, Roosevelt, and Churchill—Palestine was not discussed. Roosevelt "triumphantly" told his Cabinet that the subject of Palestine "had not even been mentioned."[50]

Although Britain and the United States refrained from any joint action, the British government was busy formulating its own policy. On July 2, 1943, the War Cabinet convened a pivotal meeting to consider a number of papers on Palestine. Churchill considered the meeting significant and reprimanded Cabinet Secretary Edward Bridges afterward for not fully capturing his pro-Zionist statements and the pro-Zionist decisions made by the War Cabinet, insisting that the necessary corrections be made in a revised version of the minutes (which they largely were). Indeed, at this meeting Churchill was very passionate about Zionism and scored important successes with his colleagues.[51]

The anti-Zionists made their case first. Colonial Secretary Stanley called the Palestinian Jews "totalitarian, aggressive & expansionist," in the words of Deputy Cabinet Secretary Norman Brook, and accused them of "trying to run a state w'in [within] a state v. [very] much on Nazi lines." This was a tough accusation, especially considering what the

Nazis were doing to the Jews in Europe. Churchill changed the tenor of the discussion by issuing an ardent defense of Zionism. According to the meeting minutes, he insisted that the Balfour Declaration be carried out, describing the 1939 White Paper as "a breach of that solemn undertaking" and arguing that "at the proper time it would, in his view, be our duty to show that we were not prepared to be driven off solemn undertakings which we had given." Or as Churchill put it afterward to Bridges, "The record should certainly bear on its face my reminder of the pledges we had given to the Zionist Association and my view that the White Paper is a breach of those pledges, and of our duty to redeem them if strength be given us at the end of the war." Brook's extemporaneous notes convey a more powerful statement, with Churchill declaring, "I'm committed to creation of a Jewish National Home in Palestine. Let us go on with that; and at end/war we shall have plenty of force with which to compel the Arabs to acquiesce in our designs. Don't shirk our duties because of difficulties." He had no interest in letting Arab opposition get in his or the Zionists' way. Amery recorded in his diary a similarly strong tone: "Winston then took up the theme, dominating and overriding all faint murmurings of dissent with an all out assertion of the Jewish case both as regards Palestine and in its broader aspects" and dismissing the Palestinian Arab case altogether. Churchill also strongly supported the arming of Palestinian Jews; according to the minutes, he "was glad that the Jews were well armed." He got the War Cabinet to agree that the British administration in Palestine should not disarm the Palestinian Jews unless it enforced the same against the Palestinian Arabs.[52]

Churchill's vigorous comments led Home Secretary Herbert Morrison (Labour), Secretary of Air Sinclair (Liberal), and Amery to make a number of pro-Zionist comments. Morrison suggested that a Jewish national state include Transjordan. Amery proposed partition as recommended by the Peel Commission, and Churchill agreed despite repeatedly scorning partition in the late 1930s. The Zionists put the anti-Zionists on the defensive, leading Chancellor of the Exchequer Kingsley Wood (Conservative) to complain that the discussion was one-sided and assumed no Arab case. The War Cabinet decided to establish a committee to consider the long-term policy for Palestine, with Churchill in charge of nominating the members. The committee's point of departure was the 1937 Peel partition plan, and it also considered developing the Negev and establishing satellite Jewish settlements in North Africa, all of which Churchill had promoted. These War Cabinet decisions—to establish a committee to study Palestine policy with partition as the point of departure, permit Jewish immigration into Palestine beyond the White Paper's deadline, allow fleeing Jews to enter Palestine against the quota, and ensure no disarming of the Palestinian Jews—prompted Amery to exalt in his diary, "On the whole a great day for the Jews if they had known of it—perhaps some day they may include Winston with Balfour (and to some extent myself too) as one of their real friends."[53]

Two days after this critical War Cabinet meeting, Churchill hinted at his efforts, and at his growing belief that a Jewish state was necessary to redeem the Holocaust, when he wrote to Harold Laski, a Labour leader and son of his old friend and supporter Nathan Laski, "I have never forgotten the terrible sufferings inflicted upon the Jews; and I am constantly thinking by what means it may lie in our power to alleviate them, both during the war and in the permanent settlement which must follow it." A few months before, Weizmann had written to Churchill that the mass murder of Jews could be redeemed only by establishing a Jewish state in Palestine. A few weeks after his note to Laski, Churchill circulated to the War Cabinet a memo written by Smuts, which argued that the mass murder of European Jews added urgency after the war to the establishment of a Jewish state in Palestine or of sanctuaries in North Africa, or both, and that addressing Jewish claims was essential to a fair postwar settlement and an appropriate rejection of Hitlerism. Churchill noted to the War Cabinet that he agreed with Smuts.[54]

Churchill designated the Labourite Morrison to chair the Cabinet Committee on Palestine. As home secretary, Morrison had been apprehensive about Jewish immigration into England because he claimed it fueled domestic anti-Semitism. But he had been sympathetic to Zionism since he visited Palestine in 1935, and spoke out strongly against the White Paper in the parliamentary debate in 1939. Other members of the committee included pro-Zionists Amery and Sinclair, along with anti-Zionists Stanley, Lord Privy Seal Cranborne, and Minister of State Richard Law (Andrew Bonar Law's youngest son), who acted as the Foreign Office's point person in opposing establishment of a Jewish state. Moyne, the minister of state resident in the Middle East, was subsequently added, somewhat tilting the committee to the anti-Zionist side, though its instructions had a pro-Zionist point of departure. Eden objected to the inclusion of Amery, whom he did not respect, but Churchill rebuffed his foreign secretary with some sarcasm: "It is quite true he [Amery] has my way of thinking on this point, which no doubt is to be deplored, but he has great knowledge and mental energy." The committee began deliberations in late summer 1943.[55]

In late October, amid this momentum toward bureaucratic consensus on partition and a Jewish state, Churchill shared an especially warm meeting with Weizmann and quoted the old Disraeli saying (slightly modified in this account of the meeting), "God deals with the nations as they deal with the Jews." This was the first time he had invoked the adage regarding Zionism—after quoting it in 1905, 1920, and 1926 regarding Russian treatment of Jews—and it reflected his determination to obtain official British approval of a Jewish state. He also seemed to be thinking along those lines when he told Weizmann that he would soon plunge "into the pie and extract a real plum." A couple of months later, after the Big Three conference in Tehran, Churchill similarly hinted to the press, "We shall, however slowly, fulfill our pledge to the Jews."[56] Progress was in fact being made toward that goal.

At the end of 1943, Morrison's committee on Palestine submitted a draft plan that endorsed Churchill's current support for partition. The committee recommended four states: a "Jewish State"; a "Jerusalem Territory" controlled by the British government (it was referred to both as a "state" and a "territory"), which would include the Lod airstrip, deemed important for postwar imperial air communications; a truncated Lebanon; and "Greater Syria," composed of Syria proper, the area in Lebanon south and east of Sidon, Transjordan, and certain Arab areas of Palestine. (Lebanon and Syria were part of the League of Nations French mandate.) These four states would form an "Association of Levant States." The British government would control the Negev while its development potential was independently explored. The French, the British, and possibly the Americans would guarantee the integrity of the states and would have treaty rights to maintain military facilities, including naval and air, in the area. The Jewish state would include key commercial cities, such as Haifa and Tel Aviv, and superior agricultural land, but its size would be reduced by almost five hundred square miles, or 25 percent, from what the Peel Commission recommended. The committee believed that the Palestinian Arabs, who would be left with a generally undeveloped area, would prefer to join with Syria in a state than with Transjordan. The committee recognized that Ibn Saud would oppose creation of a Greater Syria, which he would see as a large Hashemite federation, but believed his "personal animosities" should not stand in the way of a "statesmanlike redistribution" of the Levantine territories. In the possible, but hoped unlikely, event that the Jews would agree but the Arabs in Palestine and outside would oppose the plan, the committee recommended that the government go ahead with it anyway.[57]

Overall, the report was sterile, as written products of bureaucratic committees seeking consensus often are. It emphasized what was considered practical and did not extol Zionist virtues or mention British pledges to the Jews. It approached the distribution of land mostly through an economic lens, gave the Jews land only where they already predominated in population with less room to grow through immigration. Nor did it address how the Jews could reasonably defend their allotted land, which was very narrow, from attacking Arab forces. The report did not betray a deep understanding of the politics and interests of different Arab lands and leaders beyond the Hashemite–Ibn Saud rivalry. It saw Palestine in a pan-Arab lens and unlike the Peel Commission did not believe the Palestinian Arabs should get their own state. (In fact, neither the Balfour Declaration nor the mandate envisioned an Arab state in western Palestine.) Of course, the Palestinian Arabs rejected the Peel plan in 1937, and the Arabs in Syria and Transjordan also opposed a separate Arab state in Palestine since they coveted that land too. Also unlike Peel, the committee did not envision a significant transfer of population. U.S. cooperation here was not considered especially essential and was generally minimized. Richard Law of the Foreign Office dissented, believing that the Arabs would never accept this plan and that it would not settle the Palestine conflict.[58]

Churchill finally got the draft government report he coveted. He insisted to Eden and Attlee that "some form of partition is the only solution." He quibbled with some of the territorial details: the British-controlled Jerusalem territory was unnecessarily large at the expense of the Jews; the Huleh salient (in the northeast of Galilee) might be given to the Arabs with territorial compensation paid to the Jews; and the Jews should possess the Negev (as he had maintained at least since 1937).[59] In this plan, the Palestinian Arabs would be enveloped in an Arab area, and thereby supposedly neutralized. This partition plan did not jibe with Churchill's suggestions earlier in 1943 for Jewish development of Transjordan and conflicted with his 1941 proposal for the Zionists to receive all of western Palestine. Generally, Churchill was not especially focused on borders and other details. For him the key, at least at first, was the creation of a Zionist political entity, and some sort of Arab federation, both of which he sought as colonial secretary in the early 1920s.

Churchill won a significant victory in his march toward a proZionist regional settlement when the War Cabinet considered the report on January 25, 1944. The minutes record that the "general view" was that the Morrison plan was "as good as any that could be devised and was fair to all parties concerned." Churchill went further and claimed the plan "had been of the greatest value in clarifying the whole position." The War Cabinet "approved" the Palestine committee's plan "in principle" on the condition that the details would be further fleshed out. Churchill hoped that would happen by the time Germany was defeated, and the Cabinet decided not to publicize the plan or act on its general outlines "until after the defeat of Germany." Although somewhat conflicted, Churchill raised the idea of sharing the plan with Roosevelt and Weizmann, but his colleagues convinced him otherwise. Both Churchill and his colleagues were uncertain how a leak of the War Cabinet's decision would affect Roosevelt's reelection. Churchill certainly wanted to share the good news with Weizmann after speaking vaguely about the federation plans for several years; he wanted to demonstrate to his old Jewish friend, whose opinion and moral authority he respected and sometimes feared, that he was indeed fulfilling his commitments to the Jews and following Disraeli's dictum.[60]

A new strategic situation, and a slightly different plan, permitted Churchill to change his mind on partition and support it. Despite what he told the War Cabinet, Churchill was in fact prepared to have this plan forced on the Palestinian Arabs. For on the very same day that the War Cabinet met, he wrote General Hastings Ismay, chief of staff to the minister of defense (Churchill), that even if the Palestinian Arabs reacted violently to partition, the Jews were stronger and could defeat them. "Obviously," he continued, "we shall not proceed with any plan of Partition which the Jews do not support."[61] This alone did not change his calculus since even in 1938 he supported helping the Palestinian Jews force a settlement on the Palestinian Arabs yet still opposed partition. Then, Churchill feared partition would be unstable and would lead to more Palestinian Arab-Jewish violence that a reeling Britain could not handle, further undermining Britain's international standing and adding another uncertain element to the regional and international equation. Now, after several years of his premiership and mounting British victories on the battlefield, these no longer were concerns. Indeed, as he made clear at the War Cabinet meeting on July 2, 1943, he was now prepared to use British power to compel the Palestinian Arabs to agree to his plan for the area, as the Morrison committee report also suggested. This would certainly be possible after the war with Churchill as prime minister, which he expected to be. Although Churchill did not address postwar territorial adjustments, as prime minister he certainly figured to give the Zionists a lot of leeway to push out from their tiny area delineated by the Morrison committee. What he wrote Ismay, and what he said in 1938 and at the 1943 War Cabinet meeting, all suggested that he was mostly concerned, within limits, with what the Zionists thought and disregarded Palestinian Arab considerations if they were not in his opinion reasonable and accommodating. He never said or wrote anything during the war, or even in the 1930s, that indicated any concern for the Palestinian Arabs, whom he considered backward enemies of Britain. Indeed, Churchill indicated on several occasions during the war that he thought the Jews deserved all of western Palestine if not more. He reasoned that what was important in the near term, at a minimum, was for the Zionists to establish a recognized state. And this War Cabinet vote was a significant victory toward that goal, and an official repudiation of the government policy guided by the 1939 White Paper.

Dangers, however, lurked in the government and in the Middle East that would help undermine this progress. For the next nine months, Morrison's committee continued to elaborate on its partition plan, which gave anti-Zionist officials further opportunity to argue against the concept and its particulars. Moyne convened a conference in April 1944 of regional officials, who gave vent to more opposition to the plan. All this managed to delay any further consideration at the Cabinet level until the autumn of 1944. Also, attacks by an extremist Zionist group, the Irgun, agitated Churchill and complicated his domestic challenges. He warned Melchett in the spring of 1944 that he would "wash his hands" of the whole matter if these attacks continued.[62]

On November 3, 1944, Bridges submitted to Churchill the final report of the Cabinet Committee on Palestine. The committee, as in late 1943, again favored partition and the establishment of four separate states: a Jewish state, a Jerusalem-based state, Lebanon and Greater Syria. However, given that Abdullah would never agree to be part of a Greater Syria, that proposal was suspended until he died. For the foreseeable future, therefore, the committee recommended that Arab Palestine and Transjordan join into an Abdullah-ruled "Southern Syria." The change effectively suspended indefinitely the proposal for an Association of Levant States, which was now considered a long-term policy. This draft more clearly recommended and emphasized the establishment of a Jerusalem-based state controlled by Britain that would "safeguard for ever the Holy City." The generally sterile, bureaucratic report reserved its only passionate language for this proposal, which "deserves, in our opinion, pride of place in a project which is otherwise one of expediency." In another instance of the committee's focus on British concerns, the report stipulated that the Jewish and Southern Syrian states would sign treaties with Britain, which would "guarantee the State frontiers and be granted the facilities necessary for the safeguarding of British strategic interests." The Galilee would now go to Southern Syria, while the Negev would still be controlled by the British government until its development potential was independently explored. Churchill did not fully agree with this report: he preferred that the Negev go to the Jews, was not very keen on the size or perhaps even existence of the British-controlled Jerusalem-based state, and thought that Roosevelt's and Ibn Saud's opinions should be given much greater consideration. Still, the report gave Churchill the minimum of what he needed—namely, a recommendation that a Jewish state, among a couple of others, be established as soon as possible. The report, however, did not circulate to the War Cabinet; that awaited Eden's submission of his own memo—expected to oppose partition—after he returned from a trip to the Middle East.[63]

The day after receiving Bridges's note and the Morrison committee report, Churchill met with Weizmann, who had wanted to see the prime minister before traveling to Palestine. Coming on the heels of

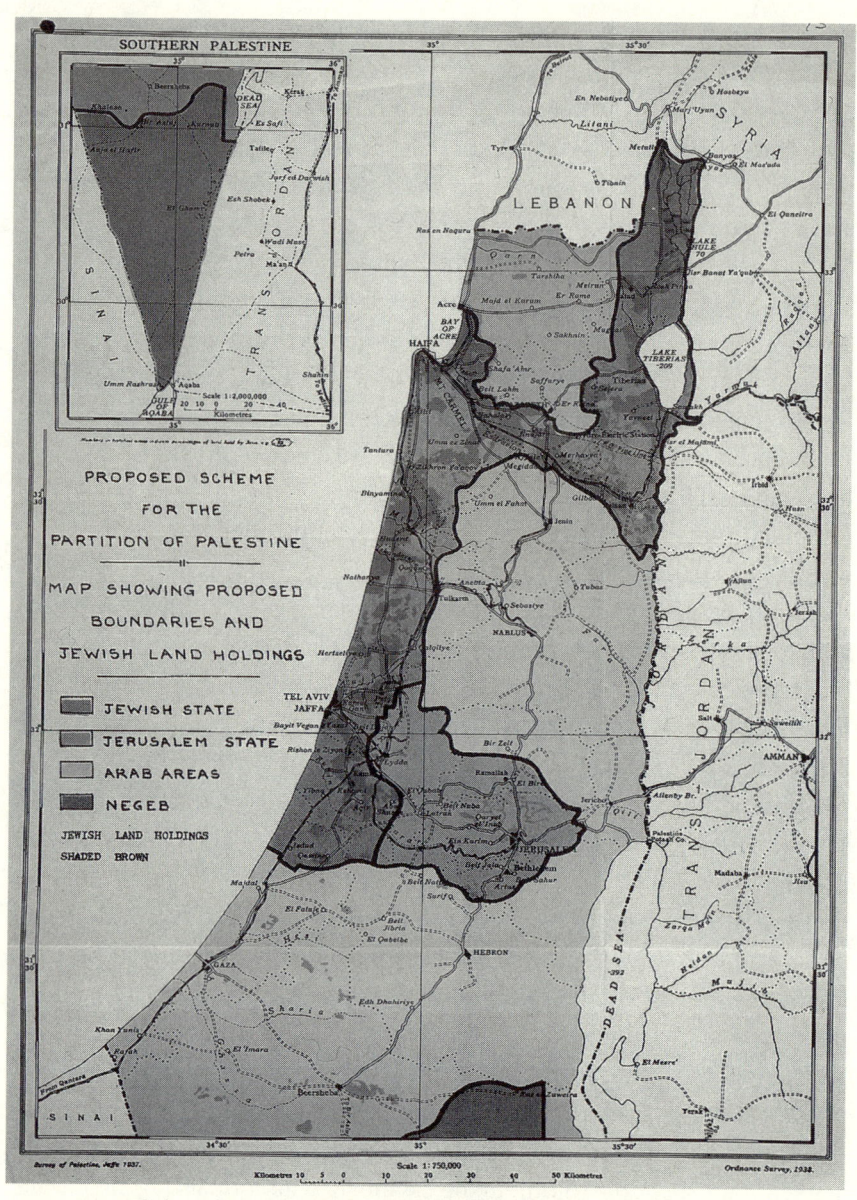

MAP 3 Map of plan of British Cabinet Committee on Palestine, October 1944. PREM 4/52/1, p. 75. Reprinted by permission of The National Archives.

the Morrison committee report, Churchill's determination to establish a pro-Zionist Middle Eastern settlement reached a peak of sorts at a two-hour lunch with Weizmann on Saturday, November 4, which was also attended by Churchill's aide Martin and brother Jack. Weizmann was intent on trying to nail down an agreement on Palestine as the war's end neared and was concerned that the Jews would be allocated little land in any partition scheme that he believed was being contemplated. Churchill acknowledged that a Cabinet committee consisting of some pro-Zionists had been formed but insisted that it would not lead to any statement about Palestine policy until after the end of the war with Germany and probably after a postwar general election. Churchill maintained that although the Jews should receive all of Palestine, including the Negev, they should still accept partition if that was not possible. While he recognized that a large number of Jews would need to immigrate to Palestine after the war, he maintained his faith in European civilization and believed that the continent might not be as inhospitable to Jews after the war as Weizmann feared. Churchill was very worried about obtaining support for his pro-Zionist plan and repeatedly asserted that there were many anti-Zionists among Conservatives and military personnel. That might have emboldened his own Zionism, but it complicated his efforts and was more significant than any support he perceived among Labour and Liberal MPs. Churchill emphasized the absolute need to involve the United States in solving the Palestine problem and asserted, "If Roosevelt and I come together to the Conference Table, we can carry through all we want." This suggested that with U.S. support he could overcome any Soviet or perhaps even Arab opposition, or circumvent the opposition of anti-Zionist officials in his own government, as Eden had feared Churchill would do. However, Churchill became concerned that the U.S. government was not sufficiently pro-Zionist, or as Weizmann put it later in a letter, Churchill "seemed worried that America was more or less academic in its attitude." Indeed, in his own personal encounters, Churchill often felt compelled to persuade Roosevelt to be more sympathetic to the Jews and Zionists, and he must have wondered if the Zionists had as much political clout in the United States as he thought or as he avowed to his anti-Zionist colleagues. Several times he expressed to Weizmann his surprise at the anti-Zionism of some American Jews, such as Bernard Baruch, the financier and confidante of U.S. presidents whom Churchill befriended years earlier. Weizmann countered that those Jews who were against Zionism also stood against Roosevelt and Churchill, which Churchill acknowledged, even though Baruch, for one, was a prominent confidante of both leaders.[64] Undoubtedly, the unreliability of American Jews and the U.S. government weighed on Churchill as he pursued a Zionist agenda among his largely anti-Zionist colleagues.

Churchill and Weizmann came away from their meeting emboldened. Weizmann gave a favorable report to his colleagues and wanted to go see Roosevelt, with whom he hoped to "clinch matters." For his part, Churchill on that very day pressed, in the words of one Foreign Office official, for an "urgent discussion by the Cabinet" of the Morrison committee's revised report. Reflecting his enthusiasm, on the following day Churchill made the unusual proposal to Roosevelt that Palestine should be considered a location for the upcoming meeting of the Big Three: "I am somewhat attracted by the suggestion of Jerusalem. Here there are first-class hotels, government houses, etc., and every means can be taken to ensure security." In such a setting, Churchill likely would have raised the postwar regional settlement that he and his government were contemplating. Roosevelt demurred and the meeting was held at Yalta three months later.[65]

Two days after his meeting with Weizmann, Churchill's ardor for a pro-Zionist settlement suffered a grievous setback—not at the hands of the United States or the Arabs but by the actions of the Zionists themselves. On November 6, 1944, in Cairo, members of the extremist Stern Gang assassinated Moyne, the British resident minister in the Middle East. This followed a number of other Stern Gang attacks, including a failed assassination attempt that summer on High Commissioner Harold MacMichael. Churchill expressed his outrage in the Commons at the "shameful crime" in very measured words and tone, and in very personal terms. As the leading Zionist in Britain, a status that certainly did not enhance his political popularity, he also portrayed the killing as a personal betrayal: "It has affected none more strongly than those like myself who, in the past, have been consistent friends of the Jews and constant architects of their future." Indeed, the assassination was not the work of a movement that he had repeatedly argued was advancing civilization. He continued, "If our dreams for Zionism are to end in the smoke of assassins' pistols, and our labours for its future to produce only a new set of gangsters worthy of Nazi Germany, many like myself will have to reconsider the position we have maintained so consistently and so long." Proceeding in an equally personal way, he felt gratified that Weizmann, "a very old friend of mine," and Ben-Gurion assured that this evil would be eradicated. Recognizing that the whole Zionist movement should not be punished for the sins of a few, Churchill took no reprisals against the Zionists; he rebuffed the recommendation of the Foreign Office and others to suspend immigration lest it unnecessarily unite the Palestinian Jews against Britain and undermine the focus on rooting out the terrorists. (His aide, Martin, made the latter argument to him.) He also maintained strategic perspective and rejected the military's request to postpone redeploying troops from Palestine to Italy in order to search for illegal arms held by Jews. Churchill told the War Cabinet that the Jewish Agency was preparing to act against the extremists, and if it did not he was prepared reluctantly to suspend Jewish immigration. The most significant immediate consequence for British policy occurred behind the scenes: Churchill decided a few days after the assassination to postpone War Cabinet debate on the Morrison committee's partition plan, which Churchill had urgently sought and which already had been put on the agenda and circulated to War Cabinet members. The postponement led to a permanent shelving; the War Cabinet never did debate the final draft of the plan. One week after Churchill's remarks in the Commons on the assassination, the *Jewish Chronicle* editorialized that for all Churchill has done for liberty and in the fight against tyranny and injustice, Jews everywhere "love him" and "always will." And his judicious statement only strengthened that sentiment.[66]

Yet, the assassination took some air out of Churchill's Zionist balloon. Since his sympathy for Zionism was primarily based on moral, sentimental, and personal reasons and less on strategic purposes, it was an immoral event with no strategic implication that diminished his concern for it. The cost for this sentimental project had risen, and he began again to voice opinions that echoed his views of the late 1910s and early 1920s. In January 1945, the Chiefs of Staff wrote a memo to the War Cabinet requesting postponement of any announcement for partition of Palestine until after the war when it could reinforce troops in Palestine; they considered the government's Palestine policy the most important factor for internal security in the Middle East. Churchill wrote to Ismay that he did not oppose the memo's circulation to various Cabinet ministers but that he did not agree with its recommendation. This was not surprising. What was surprising was how Churchill expressed his opposition. He wrote that reinforcements were not needed since Britain should not be responsible for maintaining daily law and order in the region: "Suppose a lot of Arabs kill a lot of Jews or a lot of Jews kill a lot of Arabs, or a lot of Syrians kill a lot of French or vice versa, this is probably because they have a great desire to vent their spite upon each other. . . . We really cannot undertake to stop all these blood-thirsty people slaying each other if that is their idea of democracy and the New World." It was best to hold on to key strategic locations and "utter wise words in sonorous tones." Only decrees by the three victorious Great Powers, Russia, Britain, and the United States, might stop the civil wars that would ensue in the region. "We are getting uncommonly little out of our Middle East encumbrances and paying an undue price for that little," he continued. The substance and language reflected his complete exasperation with the political difficulties and violence in the region, including Palestine, especially after British troops just finished fighting off Communist guerrillas in the nearby Greek civil war in the name of democracy. It was particularly remarkable that for the first time he equated the suffering of Palestinian Jews with the Arabs, and showed no concern for the safety of the Jews. At the same time, he also did not show much concern for the troublesome French in Syria. In any case, he asked Ismay not to share his note with what he considered incidental remarks ("*obiter dicta*"), and in the end Churchill did not even send the note.[67]

Churchill's mood showed in smaller ways as well. He demurred from sending Weizmann a seventieth birthday wish in late November 1944, as the Zionists had requested, and simply scribbled "no message" to an aide. When in late January 1945 Weizmann requested that Churchill arrange a meeting for him with Stalin, Churchill asked Eden for his view, knowing full well what his anti-Zionist foreign minister would say. Eden on cue replied that it was would be "unwise" since it would encourage the Arabs and Jews to play off Russia against Britain. (Actually, Stalin managed that feat, with British assistance, by supporting the Zionists in their war against Britain and the Arabs in 1948 and by recognizing the Jewish state.) When Eden asked Churchill to express his regret to Weizmann, Churchill curtly scribbled back, "Please do so yourself."[68]

However much Churchill detached himself personally from the Zionists and their suffering, he coolly continued his diplomatic quest on their behalf. He had too much invested and maintained his perspective. At the Big Three conference at Yalta in February 1945, Churchill told Roosevelt, according to the president's account to Stephen Wise, "Don't talk about the White Paper or Regulations—but we will let the Jews come in." This was reminiscent of his comment to Weizmann in 1921 about illegal Jewish immigration and gunrunning. He wanted to help the Zionists but still sought to minimize unnecessary political controversy before the war's end. Wise correctly replied to Roosevelt that the bureaucracy would stymie Churchill's wishes. Churchill must have made other comments to Roosevelt that were pro-Zionist and sympathetic to the Jews, since one month later, when Hoskins asked Roosevelt if Palestine was discussed at Yalta, the president said no, and then added, "Mr. Churchill is as strongly pro-Zionist as ever and, among other ideas, Mr. Churchill wanted to put the Jews into Libya." That was an idea Churchill first raised in 1943. Wise claimed that Roosevelt told him that the Big Three agreed at Yalta to hand over Palestine to the Jews, but there is no official record of this or even of any discussion of the matter, except Stalin's ambiguous and disingenuous remark to Roosevelt that he was a Zionist "in principle."[69]

Right after Yalta, and a few days after Roosevelt's own meeting with Ibn Saud, Churchill arrived in Egypt and drove into the desert to meet Ibn Saud at an oasis hotel for lunch. At the grave risk of compromising some of Britain's interests in Middle Eastern oil, Churchill pressed Ibn Saud to accept a Jewish state, apparently along the lines of the federation scheme that he had promoted since 1941, even though the Morrison committee did not emphasize Ibn Saud's role. Churchill reported to the War Cabinet that he "pleaded the case of the Jews with His Majesty but without, he [Churchill] thought, making a great deal of impression, Ibn Saud quoting the Koran on the other side, but he [Churchill] had not failed to impress upon the King the importance which we attached to this question." Churchill likely did not want to belabor the failed meeting in his War Cabinet report, and we learn more from Ibn Saud's account to the U.S. minister to Saudi Arabia, William Eddy, a fervently anti-Zionist

Arabist cousin of Hoskins who also was born in the Middle East to a missionary family in Lebanon, and who later worked for the Arabian oil company Aramco. According to Ibn Saud's account to Eddy, which essentially rings true, Churchill reminded Ibn Saud that Britain had subsidized him for twenty years and assisted in stabilizing his regime by holding off potential enemies at his borders. Ibn Saud recounted the gist of Churchill's pan-Arab argument: "Since Britain had seen me through difficult days, she is entitled now to request my assistance in the problem of Palestine where a strong Arab leader can restrain fanatical Arab elements, insist on moderation in Arab councils, and effect a realistic compromise with Zionism." But Ibn Saud would have none of that and replied that it would be heretical, that "I could not acquiesce in a compromise with Zionism much less take any initiative." He also warned Churchill that the Arabs were determined to fight the Jews over Palestine. Churchill refused Ibn Saud's request to halt Jewish immigration but assured him that he would oppose any plan of immigration that would drive Arabs out of Palestine or deprive them of a livelihood. Not surprisingly, Ibn Saud did not like Churchill, who did not help his cause by insisting to the teetotaling Muslim fundamentalist that he held it to be an absolutely sacred rite to smoke tobacco and drink alcohol before, during, and after all meals, and in the intervals in between.[70]

This encounter with Ibn Saud was surely a disappointment to Churchill. After all those years of helping Ibn Saud, including during the war, and even praising him in public, Churchill had called in his chit on behalf of Zionism. He wanted Ibn Saud to rein in the extremists and accommodate a Zionist entity in Palestine. Churchill might have been encouraged, as other British officials were, by movement toward Arab unity in 1944, which culminated in the establishment of the Arab League in the spring of 1945. But there was nothing in this development toward Arab unity that suggested a more accommodating stance to Zionism. Certainly, Ibn Saud did not give any such signal, and he remained the same religious extremist that Churchill perceived decades earlier. Even if Ibn Saud was inclined to agree to a deal that Churchill proposed, he had little money (the petrodollars did not roll in until after the war) and a weak hold over the religious tribes across the vast Arabian desert, let alone over the Palestinian Arabs. Ibn Saud's easy dismissal of Churchill's proposal also reflected how much Britain's leverage with the

Arabs had diminished since the First World War. Back then, Faisal was open to Zionism, and Ibn Saud was a relatively compliant recipient of British subsidies that Churchill helped arrange. Although Britain still controlled a good deal of the Middle East, Churchill could no longer effectively wield the "big stick," as Ibn Saud termed it. The Arabian chieftain instead looked to the ascendant United States for support, and perhaps also a means to gain some leverage over Britain, which supported his enemies, the sherifian rulers in Transjordan and Iraq. Nevertheless, Churchill sought to maintain good relations with Ibn Saud, so he papered over his rejection in a post-Yalta speech in the Commons and praised Ibn Saud as a "famous ruler" and "remarkable man" who acted with great loyalty toward Britain, especially early in the war. Churchill did not disclose the details of his proposal but still maintained that Ibn Saud's "aid will be needed at the close of the war in reaching a solution of the problems of the Arab world and of the Jewish people in Palestine."[71]

Ibn Saud had little incentive to accommodate Churchill when only a few days earlier the more powerful Allied leader, Roosevelt, had been far less demanding concerning Zionism and the Jews. Roosevelt had just won his fourth term in office a few months earlier and had less reason to be concerned about American Jewish opinion, while he and his government were increasingly preoccupied with Arabia's promising petroleum potential as U.S. reserves appeared to be in decline. Although Roosevelt had felt confident a month before that he could convince Ibn Saud to come to some agreement on Zionism, Ibn Saud made clear shortly before the meeting to a U.S. legation that their friendship would end if the United States preferred the Jews, who were "accursed in the Koran as enemies of the Muslims until the end of the world." When they finally met on U.S.S. *Quincy* in the Suez Canal, Roosevelt set an accommodating tone by suspending his chain-smoking in Ibn Saud's presence. He also tried somewhat to dissuade Ibn Saud from his anti-Zionism. According to his translator, Roosevelt expressed the wish that the Arab countries would permit ten thousand European Jews to immigrate into Palestine after the war. When Ibn Saud rejected even that small request, Roosevelt focused on ingratiating himself. He reacted positively to Ibn Saud's recommendation that surviving European Jews return after the war to their homes or move to Axis countries. Also, Roosevelt, according to U.S. minutes of the meeting, "wished to assure His Majesty that he would do nothing to assist the Jews against the Arabs and would make no move hostile to the Arab people." The president distanced himself from pro-Zionist remarks made by other U.S. politicians and even suggested that the Arabs should do a better job of making their case because "many people in America and England are misinformed." The president also made a point of disparaging Britain, the United States' close wartime ally and growing rival over Middle Eastern oil, confirming British suspicions about U.S. intentions in the region. Ibn Saud was understandably ecstatic after this meeting.[72]

Roosevelt gave conflicting reports of his meeting and the conclusions he drew, depending on his audience. He told Baruch and Wise that he did not like Ibn Saud and was displeased with the meeting. And he told Hoskins that he was not impressed with Zionist development of Palestine beyond the coastal plain (which he observed from his airplane), that the more numerous Arabs in Palestine and in its neighboring lands would emerge victorious over the Palestinian Jews, and that he supported a State Department draft plan for making Palestine an international territory for Jews, Christians, and Muslims. Perhaps most significant was his off-the-cuff assessment to Congress: "On the problem of Arabia I learned more about that whole problem, the Moslem problem, the Jewish problem, by talking with Ibn Saud for five minutes than I could have learned in the exchange of two or three dozen letters."[73] However much Churchill had misjudged Ibn Saud's view toward Zionism before their meeting, he was dead-on in the pessimistic assessment of Roosevelt's attitude that he conveyed to Weizmann a few months earlier.

Ibn Saud completed what the Stern Gang assassins initiated: Churchill's disillusionment with arranging a pro-Zionist Middle Eastern settlement. In addition to the usual opposition from the British military, Eden, the Foreign Office, the Colonial Office, and various other anti-Zionist officials, more important players were turning out to be unaccommodating: the Zionists were misbehaving, the Arabs were hostile, and the Americans were unreliable. Further, the domestic political risks had grown too great. The Moyne assassination had undermined whatever little support for Zionism remained in Parliament or throughout the country. Churchill eventually recognized that despite pro-Zionist resolutions, support for Zionism was ebbing among the Socialists.

Attlee was now firmly anti-Zionist, believing Palestine belonged to the Arabs, and became exasperated during the war with talk about Jewish suffering and using Palestine as a refuge for Jews. Even had Churchill considered ignoring Ibn Saud and pressing ahead for a Jewish state—which he did not—the forces arrayed against it seemed to him too great. Without U.S. support, or a respected Arab chieftain willing or able to control the Palestinian Arabs, any effort appeared to him useless. He remained supportive of Zionism, but he could not muster much passion for a vexing sentimental issue that caused him great disappointment and embarrassment, offered scant prospect of near-term success, and posed significant substantial political opposition, all while he was beginning to battle depression. So he kept his distance and parried all inquiries from pro- and anti-Zionists, planning to address the issue again in a postwar peace conference.[74] He focused on other pressing matters instead, such as ending the war and trying to limit and counter the growing Russian threat that was causing him tremendous anxiety.

Churchill even kept his distance from the numerous desperate pleas from the politically moderate Weizmann, who was at wits' end and in serious political trouble within the Zionist movement for his faith in the British. In one dramatic plea after the German surrender but before the postwar British election, Weizmann begged, "This is the hour to eliminate the White Paper, to open the doors of Palestine, and to proclaim the Jewish state." Churchill simply replied, "There can, I fear, be no possibility of the question being effectively considered until the victorious Allies are definitely seated at the Peace table," by which he later explained meant "the Peace Table in Europe unless the Japanese war comes to an end beforehand." Churchill was not referring to the Potsdam conference that emerged in July 1945 but to a peace conference in the grand spirit of previous postwar conferences. Perhaps the closest Churchill came at Potsdam to addressing Zionist concerns was when he discussed with Stalin and President Harry Truman the former Italian colonies in North Africa and noted that the Jews were not interested in them. On that day in the conference discussions, he mostly fixated on the more strategically significant fate of Poland and Soviet control over eastern Europe. Churchill left Weizmann high and dry, which likely explains Weizmann's rather perfunctory letter to him after his stunning electoral loss.[75]

Churchill's immediate solution was to revive an idea he had broached to David Lloyd George in 1921—to get the United States to take responsibility for Palestine. This was as unrealistic in 1945 as it was in 1921. He began to ruminate on the idea in early 1945, and as Potsdam approached he focused on the strategic benefits of the United States taking Palestine over. As in the late 1910s and early 1920s, and unlike in the 1930s, Churchill, in contrast to the Chiefs of Staff, saw strategic value in disengaging from Palestine. He saw it as a useful means to entangle the United States in a region where Britain had many interests but declining power: "I believe we should be the stronger the more they are drawn into the Mediterranean." And by demonstrating no inclination to keep the mandate, Britain would burnish its image as a selfless power and further convince the United States of their shared values, in contrast with an imperialist Soviet Russia that needed to be contained at the impending Potsdam summit. He wrote to the Chiefs of Staff and Colonial Secretary Stanley, "I am not aware of the slightest advantage which has ever accrued to Great Britain from this painful and thankless task." Churchill could have written the same thing about himself. He felt he had achieved nothing in his quest to arrange a postwar pro-Zionist regional settlement except to become more disappointed in the postwar world. He added, "Somebody else should have their turn now." But he also understood a few weeks later that no one else in the government would follow where he left off. When he left Potsdam in the middle of the conference after the British electoral returns came in, one aide asked whether he wanted to give newly elected Labour Prime Minister Clement Attlee the comments by the Colonial Office and Chiefs of Staff on the proposal for the United States to take over Palestine. Churchill replied, "I will keep them. They have no interest."[76]

In spite of all of Churchill's efforts during the war, the Zionists essentially found themselves in the same political position at the end of the war as before the war: White Paper immigration restrictions intact, and an anti-Zionist, pro-Arab British government in place that sought to retain control over Palestine. It is not what Churchill had envisioned from as early as 1941 to as late as 1945. His passionate pursuit of a pro-Zionist regional settlement was ultimately a personal quest, one that emanated from a desire to complete what he had begun in 1921, if not in 1906.

The quest was also based on a deep Disraelian conviction to do right by the Jews and redeem their suffering at this most precarious moment in their history, along with his longstanding desire to do what he considered right by history and civilization, and to some extent advance British strategic interests. At a deep level, Zionism was for him a litmus test; support for it meant a commitment to one's pledges, fidelity to one's allies, determination to hang tough, adherence to nineteenth-century liberal values and to the principles of civilization that he held so dear; and an expansive view of the world's possibilities.

Unfortunately for him and the Zionists, Britain no longer shared those values and attitudes. Whereas Churchill's own support for Zionism was cresting, the country had moved far away from the Balfour Declaration of 1917. Since then, Britain had weakened, and it increasingly clung to the Arabs for help, or at least eagerly sought to avoid their antagonism, which meant breaking Britain's pledge to the Jews. This was in Churchill's view symptomatic of what was wrong with the country. He thought he had steered Britain back to his ideals during the Second World War, but the country was no longer in the same position to implement those ideals or impose them on others. The Britain that Churchill had so admired had changed irreversibly since the First World War. Ibn Saud recognized this change, and his rejection of Churchill's plan buried it in a way that British bureaucratic opposition and Moyne's assassination had not. Churchill mistakenly pinned all his hopes on an Arabian Wahhabi leader whom he had previously considered a dangerous extremist. Churchill did this despite Ibn Saud's repeated comments since 1943 clearly expressing vehement opposition to a Jewish state and despite a lack of evidence that Ibn Saud had the power to impose control over the Palestinian Arabs even if he wanted to. This was an unusual instance when Churchill cared what an Arab thought of Zionism, though he was somewhat encouraged by the Zionists to pursue this scheme.

Why did Churchill insist on a Saudi-led federation when partition could well have been achieved by simply forcing it on the Palestinian Arabs, as he was clearly prepared to do in cooperation with the Palestinian Jews and the pro-British Abdullah, who was eager to grab as much of Palestine as he could? Indeed, the Morrison committee report suggested as much as a last resort and minimized Ibn Saud's role in the regional solution. But Churchill remained wedded to two key objectives from his days as colonial secretary in the early 1920s, a Jewish state and a loose regional Arab federation, which he became convinced required Ibn Saud's support and leadership. Unfortunately, these two goals were no longer compatible. He was committed to the post–First World War pan-Arab plan in the hopes that it would stabilize the region, but the Arabs in the region were more fractured and shared a greater antipathy toward Zionism—and had become more covetous of Palestine and eager that other Arabs states not grab it—than he recalled from twenty-five years earlier. They were also more nationalistic and more expressive of their interests. Moreover, Churchill could only practically impose a solution on the Palestinian Arabs and ignore Ibn Saud with the cooperation of the United States, just as he considered American cooperation essential in solving other major world issues. But that support was lacking. At a crucial moment, Roosevelt betrayed his oft-expressed (and oft-contradicted) support for Zionism and made clear that he was more intent on achieving influence in Arabia, preferably at Britain's expense.

At that point, Churchill simply deemed the practical, diplomatic, political, and psychological demands too great to do much on Zionism's behalf until after the war. He felt the need to distance himself from Zionism partly, and ironically, because it was never more integral to his being. In the end, Churchill did not fulfill his wartime promise to redeem the Jews' unique suffering at the hands of the Nazis. Yet, the Second World War marked the pinnacle of his Zionism.

CHAPTER SEVEN

Zionist at the End

1945-1955

THE MAGNITUDE OF THE HOLOCAUST LED MANY JEWS around the world to believe that they urgently required their own state in Palestine. Their prospects were promising: there was international sympathy for the Jews; the Palestinian Jews had contributed troops and other support to the Allied cause, developing military skill and national cohesiveness in the process; and the new British government was headed by a Labour Party that consistently declared its strong support for Zionism. However, the new prime minister, Clement Attlee, was anti-Zionist, while Foreign Secretary Ernest Bevin was outright hostile to Jews and Zionism, and they, like Neville Chamberlain and Lord Halifax in the 1930s, saw British interests served by a pro-Arab policy.

Even Churchill, now leading the Opposition, did not consciously feel the urgency of founding a Jewish state. For the first few years following the end of the war, he maintained the detachment that had begun after his meeting with Ibn Saud in early 1945. He remained above the fray, distancing himself from the increasingly intense international diplomatic activity and violence on the ground, and acting more as an observer than as one of the main protagonists of the Zionist saga in the first half of the twentieth century. He was tired physically and mentally, and he had no interest in engaging an issue that had dashed his many earnest efforts and hopes. Moreover, in Churchill's mind larger forces were generally unfavorable to Zionism, and he gave them priority. One of those top priorities was a fervent desire to become prime minister via the ballot box (for the first time) and defeat the diminutive and despised Attlee. Championing a Zionist state while Palestinian Jews were violently clashing with British soldiers was not a means to unite the anti-Zionist Conservative Party nor defeat Attlee and his popular anti-Zionist policy. Pushing a Zionist agenda also conflicted with his overarching foreign policy goal of maintaining close relations with the United States in order to buttress Britain's global position and strengthen the West against Soviet Russia. At times, Churchill seemed decidedly Arabist in his views, though he never derogated the Palestinian Jews as he did other native peoples battling Britain for independence at this time, such as the Egyptians and Indian Hindus. Indeed, deep down, Churchill still cared a great deal about the Jews and about Zionism, and he felt guilty over his aloofness.[1]

From late 1948, seven months after Israel became a state, until 1955, when he retired from his second premiership (1951–1955) and active politics, Churchill returned to his old ways and expressed strong pro-Zionist sentiments. Larger issues supported such a shift. Politically, Zionism became less politically toxic as it became evident that the Attlee-Bevin policy had failed. He also considered a pro-Zionist stance advantageous to Britain's imperial interests; after India's independence in 1947, his imperial focus shifted more to the dispute with Egypt, and he saw Israel as an ally in that conflict. And the United States was an important backer of the new Jewish state. Generally, he saw Israel as a strategic ally in the Middle East and the world. Although it took him several months, Churchill recognized quicker than most in Britain the past, present, and future significance of the State of Israel for the Middle East and the world, and he urged his compatriots to embrace the new Jewish state, which he now considered, as he had envisioned fifty years earlier, a great milestone in the history of the world.

After the war, tens of thousands of Jews who had survived the Holocaust were desperate to immigrate to Palestine. In addition to those languishing in displaced-person camps, many were particularly eager to flee Poland, where a postwar pogrom claimed hundreds of Jewish lives. Attlee and Bevin, however, turned their backs on the Labour Party's repeated promises to the Zionists (including the 1944 resolution, "Let the Arabs be encouraged to move out as the Jews move in"), downplayed Jewish suffering, closed off Palestine indefinitely to Jewish immigration, appeased Arab peoples, opposed a Zionist state, and (in line with the military's thinking) sought to maintain control over Palestine as a strategic asset. Shortly after becoming prime minister, Attlee received from President Truman the Harrison report, which detailed the horrendous conditions of Jews in European displaced-person camps and recommended that one hundred thousand Jews be allowed to immigrate to Palestine. Furious, Bevin recommended the establishment of an Anglo-American Committee of Inquiry to study the matter and co-opt the United States, and he explicitly staked his political future on its findings. In May 1946, the committee recommended the forming of a binational state and the immediate admission into Palestine of one hundred thousand Jews. Although Attlee was opposed, Truman endorsed the committee's findings and emphasized that it de facto abrogated the 1939 White Paper's restrictions on immigration. Anglo-American discussions led to the Morrison-Grady plan, which effectively called for the end of Jewish immigration into Palestine and the creation of semiautonomous Jewish and Arab regions under British trusteeship. On October 4, 1946, the eve of Yom Kippur and one month before the U.S. midterm elections, Truman expressed his opposition to this plan, called for more liberal immigration into Palestine, and hinted at support for partitioning Palestine into Jewish and Arab states.[2]

Meanwhile, violence was heating up in Palestine, particularly between the Jews and the British, raising the costs for continued British control of Palestine. In February 1947, Bevin implicitly acknowledged defeat by announcing that Britain would submit the Palestine issue to the United Nations without recommendation, and he scathingly attacked Truman to much applause in the Commons, accusing the president of allowing domestic politics—in other words, Jewish political influence—to determine U.S. policy. In August 1947, the U.N. Special Committee on Palestine recommended partition and admittance of 150,000 Jewish immigrants over two years. The U.N. General Assembly endorsed partition on November 29 by a vote of 33–13, with the United States (over State Department opposition) and the Soviet Union supporting the plan and ten countries, including Britain, abstaining. The

Zionists accepted partition, but the Arabs, including those in Palestine, rejected it. A Palestinian Arab-Jewish war ensued. On May 14, 1948, as the last British high commissioner left Jerusalem, the Jews in Palestine declared the establishment of the State of Israel. The United States recognized the new state but Britain did not. The new Jewish state then fought a war for survival against attacking Arab countries—including Syria, Transjordan, Egypt, Lebanon, and Iraq, and expeditionary forces from Yemen and Saudi Arabia—which ended in victory for Israel in January 1949.[3]

For almost one year after his stinging electoral defeat in July 1945, Churchill gave no major address on Zionism or any subject of the Middle East, despite the fast-paced events of the period and Chaim Weizmann's many pleas. Nor did he bring any motion in Parliament condemning the government's policy in Palestine or its handling of Jewish immigrant ships. He did not say much privately either. Weizmann, who staked his whole political career on the goodwill of England, was furious at Churchill's silence and inactivity at this critical moment for the Jewish people. In the autumn of 1945, Churchill declined Weizmann's request to meet, saying that he was not meeting many people those days and was sure Weizmann would understand. Weizmann retold this to a fellow British Zionist and exclaimed, "Well, as a matter of fact, I don't understand at all!" And in 1946, Churchill rejected a plea from Weizmann by claiming, "There is nothing that I personally can do in the matter," a questionable statement given that he headed the Opposition Conservative Party. He then added that Zionism "continues to be of profound interest to me," which, if true, was not generally apparent.[4]

Churchill did quietly express his support for Zionism here and there. In early 1946, when asked at a press conference in Miami Beach about the Palestine conflict, Churchill gave the impression, according to one reporter, that although Palestine used to be a very important subject to him he did not want to say very much. Still, Churchill noted, "As you know, I have been a Zionist from the very beginning" and when asked about the 1939 White Paper, he quickly replied, "Oh, I have always been opposed to it." A couple of months later, while attending a dinner party at the home of his old American friend Bernard Baruch, he reiterated that he was a Zionist and tried to convince his Jewish host to be one too. And a few months after that, Churchill, upon learning of the government's plan to disarm the Jews in Palestine in order to end terrorist attacks against British subjects, reminded Attlee that if effective the plan "carries with it the obligation to protect them from the Arabs."[5]

Churchill's general detachment was partly attributed to the depression he had suffered since Yalta. He went to Lake Como, Italy, to decompress and convalesce and wrote his wife of how happy he was not to read a newspaper or deal with worldly worries but to focus instead on painting: "This is the first time for very many years I have been completely out of the world." After obsessing about the postwar situation until only recently, he now felt "a great sense of relief which grows steadily, others having to face the hideous problems of the aftermath."[6] Even when he returned from vacation he did not publicly discuss many foreign issues. For almost a year after the election, Churchill directed most of his talks to his main preoccupations: politics, the United States, Russia, and Europe. He was disinclined to address such a frustrating subordinate issue as Zionism.

Churchill also recognized that Zionism was political dynamite. He headed a Conservative Party that did not support a Zionist policy; Robert Boothby was the only other Zionist in the shadow government. Although Palestine policy was at times a useful basis to criticize the Attlee government, it was not an issue that united Conservatives and would not help ride them back to power. Churchill acknowledged to his wife and the Commons his isolation from the Conservatives on Zionism. Although his stature and historical legacy were secure, he was not overly popular in the Conservative Party in general, and never really had been, and his Zionism was one of the reasons. This is evident from a diary account by Henry Channon, Conservative MP, of a 1948 lunch held in Churchill's honor by Conservatives on the publication of the first volume of his Second World War memoirs, which recounted the litany of mistakes that led to the war. The Conservatives, already disparaged by critics for Chamberlain's disastrous appeasement policy, were unhappy with Churchill's historical indictment. Channon wrote, "His [Churchill's] reception was tepid but not in the least unfriendly— though gone is the rapture of yesteryear. I think that the Party resents both his unimpaired criticism of Munich, recently published, and his alleged pro-Zionist leanings." That Churchill's "leanings" toward Zionism were "alleged" demonstrates that his new lukewarm or negative public stances on Zionism, whether completely genuine or not, had taken root. Moreover, that Channon lumped Zionism with Munich as major issues of contention demonstrated the remarkably intense anti-Zionist feeling among Conservatives. Churchill also had to contend with a general public that was increasingly anti-Semitic and supported the Attlee government's anti-Zionist policy, especially as violent clashes with the Palestinian Jews (including some macabre Jewish attacks on British soldiers, and the Irgun bombing of the King David Hotel in Jerusalem, which killed many British officials) and diplomatic disputes with the United States escalated. Even the ardent Zionist Richard Meinertzhagen was so furious in mid-1946 over Zionist extremists kidnapping several British officers that he recorded in his diary, "They must be released without condition before I again turn to Zionism."[7] Churchill took these popular feelings fully into account when he addressed the Palestine issue.

Amid mounting British conflict with Egypt, hugely unpopular British-Zionist clashes in Palestine, and announcement of the Morrison-Grady plan, Churchill turned his attention back to Zionism and the region for the first time since the war. In a few speeches in the Commons from spring through autumn of 1946, Churchill reverted to many of the cautious and non-Zionist themes he had articulated in the 1920s and begun to reiterate in 1945. He argued in favor of "a Jewish national home in Palestine, with immigration up to the full absorptive capacity," blamed "friction" on excessive Jewish immigration and demands, and derided Britain's experience in Palestine: "We have discharged a thankless, painful, costly, laborious, inconvenient task for more than a quarter of a century." He also partly blamed Zionist extremism on the Labour Party for making strong pro-Zionist declarations and speeches and then, when in power, dashing Jewish hopes and causing "deep and bitter resentment." To a lesser extent, the same could have been asserted about Churchill's own broken wartime promises, made somewhat cryptically to the Jews in public and more explicitly in private to Weizmann. In a deleted passage of a letter he sent to Attlee, Churchill hinted that Britain no longer was obligated to uphold the mandate, noting that the Palestine Mandate had originated in the "now defunct League of Nations." He suggested publicly, as he did privately in early 1945, that Britain no longer needed to protect the Palestinian Jews and no longer was responsible for them. That now was the United Nations' duty. Had Britain terminated the mandate in 1921, as Churchill had once privately recommended, it may well have crippled the development of the nascent Zionist experiment. But now, ironically, that public suggestion served the Zionists' desire to be left alone to form a state, although that was not Churchill's intent. In both instances, he was focused only on Britain's interests and gave little consideration to Zionist needs.[8]

Regarding those British interests, Churchill believed that the security, strength, and prestige of the waning British Empire was best upheld by not wasting precious resources—both human and financial—in Palestine that should instead be dedicated to preserving British control over Egypt and India. Attlee sought to achieve the opposite: to cling to Palestine while loosening control over Egypt and India. Churchill was dumbfounded at this inversion and perversion of priorities, and he was all about prioritization of thought and action. Attlee's plan made no sense from a humanistic standpoint either; evacuation from India alone would lead to a civil war that would dwarf "anything that could happen in Palestine," making bloodshed in the latter appear "microscopic." Churchill likened the situations in India and Egypt versus that in Palestine to "wars of elephants compared with wars of mice."[9]

These imperial considerations fed into strategic concerns. While Churchill believed it vital to retain India, Egypt, and other existing British imperial possessions despite disapproval in the United States and elsewhere, he opposed any new policy that unnecessarily smacked of high-handed imperialism or that made Britain seem Soviet-like in its international ambitions. Churchill feared that such an image would blur the East-West ideological divide, which he was determined to sharpen and highlight in order to help persuade the United States to join an Anglo-American alliance against the Soviets. This fear, for instance, partly explained why he opposed at this time the establishment of a trusteeship of Cyrenaica (in modern Libya) to protect the Suez Canal: "We shall be immediately represented . . . as a greedy, grasping nation, playing at power politics and demanding territories formerly owned by others for the sake of our own designs upon Egypt." And it was this point that he made in arguing against the government's plan to evacuate Egypt and depend upon continued control of Palestine as a place from which to dominate the Suez Canal. He believed that this would dangerously transform Britain's image from an honorable, disinterested enforcer of the League of Nations' Palestine Mandate to a covetous imperialist. He was perplexed at why the government would risk all that by digging in its heels in a messy territory that was a sideshow on the world stage. He thundered, offering vintage perspective: "Now, apparently, the one place where we are at all costs and at all inconveniences to hold on and fight it out to the death is Palestine, and we are to be at war with the Jews of Palestine, and, if necessary, with the Arabs of Palestine. For what reason? Not, all the world will say, for the faithful discharge of our long mission but because we have need, having been driven out of Egypt, to secure a satisfactory strategic base from which to pursue our Imperial aims." Undermining relations with the United States also dashed any chance for American cooperation in Palestine, which he considered essential to Britain's extracting itself from Palestine with any dignity while maintaining its pledges to the Jews. He confided to a former military advisor, Alan Brooke, "All idea of America being brought into Palestine to help, on account of their Jewish interests, seems to me also to be destroyed by the Government's policy. How can the United States be expected to send troops or aid to an establishment which will in future be represented as the British *place d'armes* in Palestine, in order to dominate or terrorize Egypt?" Without U.S. cooperation and involvement, he maintained that Britain should "resign our Mandate, as we have, of course, a perfect right to do."[10]

This intent to align Palestine policy with the United States and ensure that it did not drive a wedge into Anglo-American relations was the one constant in Churchill's attitude toward Palestine and was behind most of the conflicting opinions he expressed over various proposed plans. For instance, he sided with Bevin on restricting immigration yet considered the Anglo-American Commission "a step in the right direction," despite its call for one hundred thousand Jews to immigrate to Palestine. He also supported the Morrison-Grady plan, which contradicted the Anglo-American Commission report. He acknowledged that the priority of ensuring U.S. support for Britain's Palestine policies meant a weak attachment to any particular program: "It is far more important that there should be [Anglo-American] agreement than that there should be this or that variant of the scheme." He even minimized the importance of partition or the federation scheme he pushed so strongly during the war: "I will not try to examine the various schemes of partition or cantonisation which have been put forward, nor would I dwell on that idea, which I always championed, of a wider union—an Arab-Jew federal system of four or five States in the Middle East."[11]

Given his changed attitude toward Zionism and the popular political hostility toward it, Churchill minimized his previous involvement, portraying himself as a passive colonial secretary, as he did during his colonial tenure. He asserted that "it fell to me to define" the mandate, for which he received "the approval of the then Cabinet and Parliament," and that he drafted the 1922 White Paper only "for the approval of the authorities of the day." What he did take credit for was coining the phrase "economic absorptive capacity" as the limit for Jewish immigration, which he figured would be popular in the current anti-Zionist climate. Actually, it was Herbert Samuel who suggested that concept and who also drafted the 1922 White Paper. As part of Churchill's public repositioning, he went out of his way to embrace some aspects of the popular anti-Zionist Attlee policy. He made a point of proclaiming that he concurred "entirely" with the government that Britain should not be expected to bear the burden alone of the Anglo-American Commission report. He also connected with popular sentiment by chafing at the United States and other nations that "sat on the sidelines and criticised our shortcomings with all the freedom of perfect detachment and irresponsibility." This sentiment was genuine, and he had expressed it privately near the end of the war and before Potsdam. Over the years, particularly in the late 1910s and 1920s, he often became irritated by what he considered ignorant, irresponsible, holier-than-thou criticism leveled by a detached United States. This populist approach somewhat undercut his more considered opinion that Britain should act in tandem with the United States over Palestine.[12]

Even on the issue of Jewish immigration into Palestine, about which he had been consistently adamant for several decades, Churchill strained to align himself with the Attlee-Bevin policy. He repeated his criticism of the 1939 White Paper, but in far more subdued language and by explaining only that it failed to fulfill Britain's obligations. He still recognized Palestine's recent value as a sanctuary for downtrodden Jews, but now that the Nazis were defeated, he ascribed less humanitarian value to it. He did not see it as solving what he now called a "Jewish problem" and "Zionist problem." He derided the idea that there was enough room in Palestine for those Jews in Europe wishing to leave, "or that they could be absorbed in any period which it is now useful to contemplate." Reflecting his frustration with Zionism and disgust at Palestinian Jewish attacks on British personnel in Palestine, he uncharacteristically claimed, "The idea that the Jewish problem could be solved or even helped by a vast dumping of the Jews of Europe into Palestine is really too silly to consume our time in the House this afternoon." Despite the Holocaust, he maintained his hope in a liberal European civilization: "I am not absolutely sure that we should be in too great a hurry to give up the idea that European Jews may live in the countries where they belong.... Are we not to hope that some tolerance will be established in racial matters in Europe...? It is quite clear, however, that this crude idea of letting all the Jews of Europe go into Palestine has no relation either to the problem of Europe or to the problem which arises in Palestine." When Sidney Silverman, a Labour MP and a Jew, questioned whether European Jewish survivors of the Holocaust "who regarded a country in Europe as nothing but the graveyard and cemetery of all his relatives, friends and hopes should be compelled to stay there," Churchill lamely and irrelevantly responded, "I am against preventing Jews from doing anything which other people are allowed to do." At this time, Churchill believed a revitalized continent was essential to fighting the emerging Cold War, and he wanted Europe to become as unified and anti-Soviet as possible. He was becoming increasingly fixated on the concept of a "United States of Europe," asserting that Europe was a "noble continent" and the "fountain of Christian faith and Christian ethics," and even considered becoming president of an organization called the Pan-European Union. In his mind, this was no time to disparage (western) Europe or question its ethical vitality.[13]

Despite this non-Zionist tone, Churchill reaffirmed his support for Zionism though he acknowledged "this is not a very popular moment to espouse it." He explained that after the many new Arab entities Britain established after the First World War, Jews were entitled to their small slice of land too: "It was little enough, indeed, that we had asked for the Jews—a natural home in their historic Holy Land." He also continued, in a more subdued way, to recognize Jewish talent to civilize and enrich the land of Palestine, benefiting both Jews and Arabs, and he pointed out that "Zionists and the Palestine Jews" stood "vehemently and undividedly" with Britain in the crucible of war. And he wanted the Jews to know, amid all the Zionist-British violence in Palestine, that Britain "alone" had "steadfastly carried" Zionism "forward across a whole generation to its present actual position, and the Jews all over the world ought not to be in a hurry to forget that." He still cared what the Jews thought, whether for political reasons (British Jews), tactical reasons (Palestinian Jews), strategic reasons (American Jews), or mystical reasons (Disraeli's dictum). He privately told Attlee that partition, which Churchill came to promote during the Second World War, was the only solution and that Britain must fulfill its "pledges" to the Jews by giving the mandate back to the United Nations. Yet, these pro-Zionist statements were largely drowned out by the rest of his message.[14]

Churchill now portrayed the Arabs, even the Palestinian Arabs, in a more favorable light, and emphasized that he was one of their great friends. It undoubtedly was politically advantageous to do so, might have helped Britain's position in the Middle East (including vis-à-vis the United States), and might also have appealed to Indian Muslims (who opposed the anti-British Hindu nationalists). He no longer denigrated the Palestinian Arabs as primitive, nor did he compare them poorly to other Arabs but instead lumped them all together. Churchill now claimed that Britain had protected the Jews in Palestine from the hostility of the much stronger "Arab forces" who emerged from the First World War with "so much distinction and credit from the struggle against the Turks." He had rarely delivered such a compliment before and certainly never lumped the Palestinian Arabs with such pro-Allied heroism. He suggested that Britain, with the aid of his handpicked subordinate T. E. Lawrence, that "champion of Arab rights," had treated the Arabs very well, "which so great a race deserves and requires." He never before considered the Arabs, whether in Palestine or outside, a great race, but always saw them as a retrogressive force in the world. Churchill paid "tribute" to the "splendid king," Ibn Saud, as a strong ally during the Second World War, neglecting to mention how the fundamentalist Arabian leader remained mostly neutral during the war and also sabotaged his grand wartime scheme to achieve a lasting pro-Zionist regional settlement. Churchill even voiced concern about how the Arabs and Muslims had been "alarmed and estranged" by Britain's Zionist policy, which contradicted his emphatic wartime dismissals of any such notion. In fact, he now attributed the 1941 Rashid Ali revolt in Iraq not to Arab betrayal, which he communicated repeatedly and heatedly during the war, but partially to Britain's Zionist policy: "No doubt our Zionist policy may have led, in part, to the divergence of Arab sentiment."[15] This was Churchill as Arabist, and it was false, unnatural, disingenuous, and antithetical to almost everything he thought earlier. He never again gave much consideration to Arab or Muslim concern or reaction to Britain's involvement in Zion.

The Attlee-Bevin government continued to dig in its heels over Palestine, despite intensifying violence with the Zionists, while deciding in 1947 to withdraw from India and to support Muslim-Hindu partition and the creation of an independent India and Pakistan as new British dominions, thereby ending 200 years of political power and 130 years of general supremacy in the Indian subcontinent. Demonstrating further erosion of British power, in March 1947 the United States felt compelled to take over Britain's effort to help the Greek government against Communist insurgents and hold the line in Turkey. Perceiving a political opening for an attack on the Attlee government, Churchill in late 1946 and 1947 publicly castigated it for inverting foreign policy priorities, threatening the survival of the British Empire, undermining Britain's position in the world, endangering relations with the United States, and pursuing a policy that was costly in terms of blood, treasure, and honor. He thundered incredulously, "To abandon India, with all the dire consequences that would follow therefrom, but to have a war with the Jews in order to give Palestine to the Arabs amid the execration of the world, appears to carry incongruity of thought and policy to levels which have rarely been attained in human history." He was astonished that the government was expending three to four times as many troops in Palestine (a total of one hundred thousand) as in India even though Palestine did not have "a twentieth part of the importance of India." He was dismayed by such a waste of resources during an acute economic period in Britain. Using a favored word at this time, he declared, with characteristic perspective, " 'Scuttle,' everywhere is the order of the day—Egypt, India, Burma. One thing at all costs we must preserve: the right to get ourselves world-mocked and world-hated over Palestine, at a cost of £82 million." As in the economically challenging late 1910s and early 1920s, Churchill wanted the government to focus on stabilizing and developing the existing imperial territories at the expense of Palestine: "There is a great difference between British territory built up and held for generations and a mandate which we accepted." He caustically summarized the government's approach as "a vacuum, a gaping void, a senseless, dumb abyss—nothing." This attack accompanied a slight shift back toward the Zionist camp, not only in criticism of warring with the Jews but also when he stated, "I have always supported the Zionist movement."[16]

Churchill was so critical of the Attlee government that he increasingly minimized the Zionists' share of blame for the violence. He again attributed some of the violence to Jewish resentment at the Socialist Party's breaking its promises to the Zionists and breaking the country's "pledges" to them. He sympathetically noted in early 1947, "I hate this quarrel with the Jews," and claimed that while "I hate their methods of outrage," Zionist outrages were perpetrated only by a "small, fanatical, desperate minority." And he remained astonished that Britain was "fighting the Jews in order to give the country to the Arabs," again suggesting that Palestinian Arabs did not deserve to govern Palestine, which is how he had always felt. Whatever his misgivings about supporting the Zionists at this time, they had nothing to do with the Palestinian Arabs, whom he never liked. These remarks were politically troubling for some of his anti-Zionist colleagues. Shortly thereafter, following a parliamentary debate on Palestine policy, one Conservative MP recorded in his diary that fortunately Churchill was not in the chamber due to his brother's death so "we were spared a speech from him which might well have caused trouble"—apparently for the Conservatives—"in view of his Zionist attitude."[17]

Meanwhile, Churchill generally conveyed mixed messages over Jewish suffering. The horror of the Holocaust evidently permeated his consciousness. In a vision he had in late 1947 of a conversation with his father, Churchill cited the genocide of the Jews in describing the great bloodshed of the Second World War: "Seven million were murdered in cold blood, mainly by the Germans. They made human slaughter-pens like the Chicago stockyards." It remained for him a unique event in history. Yet, only a few months earlier, in the summer of 1947, Churchill said nothing publicly when for two days Jewish property was attacked and looted in Liverpool, London, Glasgow, and other cities in response to Palestinian Jewish extremists abducting and hanging two British sergeants.[18] Churchill's silence stood in contrast to 1911 when as home secretary he quickly dispatched troops to protect Jews during riots in Wales. Perhaps the political climate at this time was not very conducive to defending live Jews in public.

Churchill's shift back toward the Zionists remained limited and seemed geared toward scoring political points against Attlee. Indeed, Churchill said nothing in public or private after the partition plan was passed by the United Nations on November 29, 1947, or even after the State of Israel was declared on May 14, 1948. The Jews had reestablished sovereignty and normalcy in their ancient homeland after almost two thousand years of persecution and exile. And yet, incredibly, the historical profundity seemed lost on Churchill, even though he had begun to envision this very event more than forty years before and had striven to achieve it during much of the Second World War. He also did not voice any consternation that this new state was having to fight for its very existence against more than five Arab armies, one of which, Transjordan, was supported and directed by the British government. He said nothing after Britain's U.N. representative, Alexander Cadogan, refrained from using the word "Israel" and refused to support a U.N. truce in June 1948 until it was clear the Arab side was exhausted. Even Weizmann gave up on Churchill. In June 1948, as an embattled Jerusalem's fate hung in the balance, Isaiah Berlin made an offer to Weizmann, the newly elected president of Israel, to approach Churchill and urge an attack on the Socialist government's policy. Weizmann, however, advised against disturbing his old friend.[19]

Churchill did prepare a statement after Israeli independence in which he criticized the government for allowing the British-led and subsidized Transjordanian forces to shell Jerusalem. (Those forces, called the Arab Legion, then grabbed Jerusalem and what was supposed to be Arab Palestine under the U.N. partition plan.) However, he based his argument partly on the legalistic reason that it violated the alliance treaty with Transjordan. He also declared, "I never conceived it possible that the Government, in carrying it [the mandate] out, would not show the strictest impartiality between Jew and Arab." This was not exactly a rousing declaration in favor of the new Jewish state. Further, his statement did not address the Bernadotte plans of the summer and autumn of 1948, which would have undone many of Israel's conquests and stripped it of Jerusalem, Lod, and the Negev, as well as significantly undermined its independence. At any rate, he did not issue the statement. And when in the summer of 1948 Churchill, the leader of the Opposition, was asked by Brendan Bracken to intervene again in a debate about Israel, he responded lamely and disingenuously, "I cannot do any more on Palestine. Events must take their course."[20] Churchill remained disengaged from the fast-moving, momentous events occurring on the ground and in the diplomatic corridors around the world.

What did engage Churchill was the Attlee-Bevin government's willingness to risk its relations with the United States over Palestine when the main event in world affairs was the mounting Soviet threat. The State of Israel was established during the Berlin crisis, when the Soviets blockaded the former German capital in a test of wills with the West. Churchill feared that the Soviets intended to grab Western Germany and perhaps western Europe, and he raised the idea of threatening the Soviets with nuclear attack if they did not withdraw the blockade. This was clearly not a time to look weak and cause unnecessary rifts with the United States. At a Scottish Conservative Party conference two weeks after Israeli independence, Churchill blasted the Labour government's "lack of mental grip" regarding Palestine, and was bewildered that it had become "involved in a dispute with the United States at a time when good relations are indispensable to us, and when no one can gain from any divergence or differences except the Soviet Government and the Communist 5th Columns in every part of the world." At the annual Conservative Party conference in the autumn, which certainly was not filled with Zionists, Churchill again addressed Palestine, but only to lash out at the Attlee government's disastrous policy.[21]

There was much calculation in Churchill's public indifference toward Zionism, and it tugged on his conscience. In July 1948, two months after the establishment of the State of Israel, Churchill bluntly confided to Walter Elliot, a pro-Zionist Conservative, that the charged political atmosphere prohibited his engagement: "The Palestine position now, as concerns Great Britain, is simply such a hell-disaster that I cannot take it up again or renew my efforts of twenty years." He then strained to say defensively, "It is a situation which I myself cannot help in," despite heading the Opposition. More honestly, and significantly, he added that it was a subject that he "must, as far as I can, put out of my mind." If he was not going to do anything for the Zionists, despite his longstanding attachment to their cause, he sought to ease his sense of shame by not even thinking about it. That explained why he hardly discussed Palestine in private. Still, he could not fully separate himself mentally or emotionally. In a private discussion in the autumn of 1948 with Robert Boothby and his son-in-law Christopher Soames, Churchill congratulated the former for standing up for the Zionists when he did not: "You were quite right to write to *The Times* protesting against the shelling of Jerusalem." He then insisted, "We have treated them [the Zionists] shamefully. I will never forgive the Irgun terrorists. But we should never have stopped immigration before the war." By referring to the 1939 White Paper, which was by now an irrelevant issue, he was able to cite an example of a time when he stood steadfastly on behalf of Zionism and thereby absolve himself from the shame of his postwar disengagement and inactivity on the Zionists' behalf. When Soames said British opinion was pro-Arab, Churchill retorted, "Nonsense. I could put the case for the Jews in ten minutes." But Churchill had not really done so since the war. He never even saw Weizmann in the crucial years after 1944. Churchill protested that Weizmann was too fascinating to talk to and thus took up too much of his time. This excuse obviously was disingenuous, and Boothby countered pointedly that Weizmann thought the reason was because he represented "Conscience." Indeed, that interpretation jibed with several of Churchill's earlier comments to Weizmann, such as his 1937 statement that he was afraid of seeing the Zionist leader because it left him depressed for ten days and his 1941 remark that he got a "twist in his heart" whenever he saw his old friend, with whom he shared so many values and views. Churchill knew that Boothby and Weizmann were right, and he did not bother to respond.[22]

British officialdom, notably, felt neither shame nor guilt but huge relief at no longer having to accord respect to Weizmann or Zionism. Isaiah Berlin, who was close to Weizmann and to the situation, contended that Weizmann was "a tragic, formidable and politically embarrassing figure. It had always been a somewhat daunting, not to say punishing, experience both for ministers and their officials to meet the full impact of Weizmann's terrifying indignation." Now the Colonial Office treated Weizmann icily, the Foreign Office (including junior officials) indulged their Arabism and snubbed him, and Bevin in particular treated him rudely. This was Weizmann's reward for his life-long faith in England and its commitment to the Jews; he was punished by Palestinian Zionists for clinging to a romantic image that was a relic of a vanished age.[23]

Shortly thereafter, Churchill radically changed his whole approach to Zionism as now embodied in the new State of Israel. At the end of 1948, during the foreign affairs debate in the Commons, he noted, almost incidentally, that the establishment of the Jewish state was "an event in world history." This was a watershed statement that echoed what he said in 1908. The abject failure of the Attlee-Bevin policy emboldened Churchill to lash out at the government. He rehashed old criticisms and argued that he had supported partition as a means of securing a national home for the Jews, which was supported by the United States, and "would, of course, have taken into account the legitimate rights of the Arabs." The last statement was disingenuous, since the Arabs rejected partition and since Churchill did not care about the Palestinian Arabs nor lament that they did not achieve their own state (after Transjordan grabbed the West Bank for itself). Further demonstrating a lack of concern for the Palestinian Arabs, whom he believed had little claim to self-rule, he asserted that "we had the power and the chance to impose and enforce—I must use that word—a partition settlement in Palestine," and that the recent Israeli victory over neighboring Arab states demonstrated how "easy" it would have been for the Jews to "have enforced an effective partition after the German defeat." Here he was apparently expressing regret for not encouraging the Jews to do just that instead of relying on Ibn Saud's support in 1945. Bevin had more substantially "misjudged" Jewish strength, and Churchill intimated that anti-Semitism had in part skewed Bevin's thinking. He said of the government, "Their whole treatment of the Palestine problem has been a lamentable tale of prejudice and incapacity." This was a remarkable public statement, and it was in line with what he said and wrote privately during the war about most British military and civilian officials involved in the Palestine conflict. He reduced a difference in opinion to something very basic and personal: anti-Semitism. It was the only way to explain what he considered to be an irrational and reckless policy. He wanted the government to shake off its illusions, "face the facts," abandon the "sulky boycott," and recognize a Jewish state as the Soviets and Americans already had, which would enhance British influence and reduce the chance for disputes with the United States.[24] This was the wartime Churchill speaking, a persona that had been missing in action for four years.

In early 1949, the new State of Israel had defied overwhelming odds and defeated its Arab enemies to win its war of independence. It only had 750,000 Jews (and 150,000 Arabs) versus 30 million Arabs in the five main countries it fought. Israel signed armistice agreements with Egypt and then other neighboring Arab states (though the Arabs refused to sign peace agreements), in which it retained 21 percent more land than it was allotted in the 1947 partition plan that the Arabs rejected. Still it remained a tiny country, and Jerusalem was divided between Israel and Transjordan. Israel held its first elections and established a functioning parliament and government.[25]

In the autumn of 1945, a few months after becoming foreign secretary, Bevin wrote a confidential telegram in which he complained that British policy, including under Churchill, had focused on the "kings, princes or pashas," and he wanted instead to focus on appealing to the "people." In fact, in a region of kings, princes, and pashas, who had slim claims to legitimacy, Israel was the only country where the people ruled. Its democratic government was headed by a socialist prime minister, David Ben-Gurion. And yet despite these apparent virtues, Bevin had worked very hard to prevent the establishment of this state, did not recognize the state diplomatically, and strongly opposed its government. Bevin's concern with the "people" revolved around Arab people, and he sought to maintain British influence in the region through close relations with Arab countries.[26]

The Attlee government was stuck, paralyzed by its own past policies and unable to face new realities. Bevin, the Foreign Office, and the Chiefs of Staff were, for instance, still mired in the First World War–era perception of the Zionists as Communists who were interested in aligning themselves with the Soviets. Bevin shared with the United States his opinion that Jewish immigrants came mostly from Communist countries where they were exposed to Communist philosophy. British intelligence supported this view, reporting that Jewish refugees from eastern

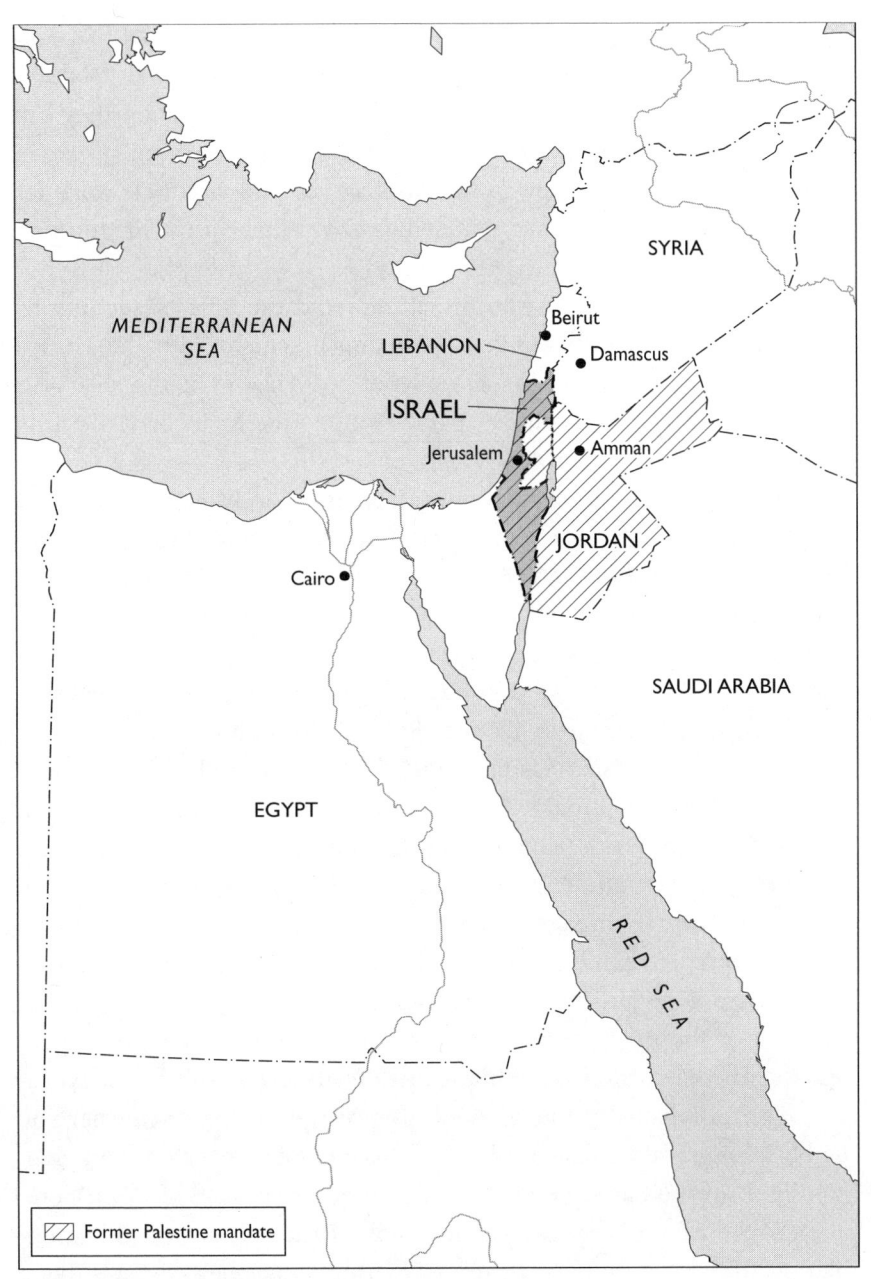

MAP 4 State of Israel and region, 1949. Drawn by Bill Nelson.

Former Palestine mandate

Europe included indoctrinated Communists. Bevin explained to a Foreign Office official in 1947 that this contributed to Soviet support for partition: "I am sure they are convinced that by immigration they can pour in sufficient indoctrinated Jews to turn it into a Communist state in a very short time. The New York Jews have been doing their work for them." Bevin must have had misgivings about this comment, since he told the official to burn the letter (a carbon copy survived).[27] In fact, it was the anti-Soviet Bevin who unwittingly did the Soviets' bidding by undermining British credibility, provoking a schism with the United States over a subordinate issue, and not realizing what the shrewder Stalin did: that leverage could be gained among the Arabs by supporting a Jewish state.

Bevin's policy was resoundingly discredited, and Churchill believed that for the good of domestic politics, strategic interests, and moral imperatives, Britain should be friendly toward and supportive of the powerful new Jewish state which he considered part of the Western orbit. A new era had dawned in the Middle East, and Churchill believed Britain should not be stuck in the past but should deal with the new realities, which happily aligned with his own deep-seated sentiments.

Ironically, an embarrassing British-Israeli military incident in early 1949 led Churchill to make these points in public. The Israelis downed several Royal Air Force planes flying with Egyptian air squadrons on reconnaissance over Israeli positions at the close of the Arab-Israeli war, provoking Bevin to threaten Israel. In an emergency debate in the Commons, Churchill abandoned his tentativeness over Zionism and offered a full-throated endorsement of the significance of the State of Israel. It was one of the most forceful pro-Zionist addresses he ever delivered, and the first since the 1939 White Paper debate. He smelled political advantage and relished personal vindication in yet another area where he had been politically isolated. Churchill blasted Bevin's "astounding mishandling" of the Palestine problem and memorably said of Bevin's creation of the Anglo-American Commission of Inquiry, on which he publicly gambled his political future, "No more rash bet has ever been recorded in the annals of the British turf." He attacked Bevin very personally since the foreign secretary was so personally identified with the government's policy. Churchill openly called him an anti-Semite: "All this is due, not only to mental inertia or lack of grip on the part of the

Ministers concerned, but also, I am afraid, to the very strong and direct streak of bias and prejudice on the part of the Foreign Secretary. I do not feel any great confidence that he has not got a prejudice against the Jews in Palestine." He declared that Bevin was "wrong, wrong in his facts, wrong in his mood, wrong in the method and wrong in the result," and that "no one has been proved by events to be more consistently wrong on every turning-point and at every moment than he." Bevin pursued a "policy of folly, fatuity and futility the like of which it is not easy to find in modern experience." In the process, Bevin pushed Britain into opposition against the United States, Russia, and Palestinian and world Jews without even helping the Arabs. As a result, British influence was "at a minimum." In a further humiliation for "poor old Britain ... we find ourselves shot down in an air skirmish, snubbed by the Israeli Government."[28]

To maximize his political gain, Churchill credited the Conservative Party for doing the most to build up a Jewish national home in Palestine, noting that "many of us have always had in mind that this might some day develop into a Jewish State." This statement was specious, since the Conservative Chamberlain-Halifax policy in the late 1930s sought to undermine the emergence of a Zionist state. He more accurately asserted that the "Conservative Party has done a great task over twenty-five years, with Parliaments which had a Conservative majority, in trying to build a Jewish National Home in Palestine." Labour governments, including those in 1924 and 1929–1935, had not been pro-Zionist, while the governments headed by the Liberal David Lloyd George in coalition with a majority of Conservatives from 1916 to 1922, as well as Churchill's own wartime government, had been the best for Zionism. However much Churchill sought to capitalize politically on the Labour government's failure in Palestine, there was nothing false in these comments. This speech was a milestone, and Churchill never felt sheepish again about his Zionism.[29]

Churchill was now far more engaged and expansive than he had been in prior speeches on Palestine. He expressed shock that Bevin dismissively compared the lack of diplomatic relations with Israel to lack of relations with Indonesia, accusing Bevin of confusing a great ancient race with a bit player in world civilization. Churchill now enthusiastically stressed that the founding of the State of Israel was of great historical significance: "[The] coming into being of a Jewish State in Palestine is an event in world history to be viewed in the perspective, not of a generation or a century, but in the perspective of a thousand, two thousand or even three thousand years. That is a standard of temporal values or time values which seems very much out of accord with the perpetual click-clack of our rapidly-changing moods and of the age in which we live. This is an event in world history. How vain it is to compare it with the recognition, or the claims to recognition by certain countries, of the Communist banditti which were resisting in Malaya or of the anarchic forces which the Dutch are trying to restrain in Indonesia."[30]

The ancient past always captivated Churchill and, to him, justified the Jewish claim to Palestine. He recognized that although the Jews had been scattered around the world for two thousand years, they had "always been there" and had "lived in Palestine for thousands of years side by side" with the Arabs. He did not cite the Holocaust as an additional reason for why the Jews needed their own state, because his Zionism predated that recent tragedy and also because he had not given up hope on Europe as a hospitable place for Jews. He also maintained faith in the enigmatic Jewish endurance, as expounded by Benjamin Disraeli. Churchill wrote in 1951 about the Jews and Greeks, "Personally I have always been on the side of both, and believed in their invincible power to survive internal strife and the world tides threatening their extinction." Still, he did not totally ignore the Holocaust, as he mostly had since the end of the war, and he expressed hope that the Negev desert would provide a "refuge to the survivors of the Jewish community who have been massacred in so many parts of Europe."[31]

As usual, Churchill also enthusiastically justified Zionism for its civilizational accomplishments. He believed that the Jews deserved the Negev, an area of some international dispute, more than the primitive Arabs, who kept it a barren desert after it "once held great cities and nourished important populations." He added, "The Jews, by the gift they have and by the means which they do not lack, have a way of making the desert bloom. Those who have seen it can testify," as he could from his 1921 trip. He contended that the Arabs, by contrast, "with all their dignity and grace, are primarily the children of the desert, and where they dwell, in this part of the world at least, and for the most part, the desert lands do not become reclaimed while the Arab control is complete over them." He categorized the Arabs as backward, uncivilized people: "One has only to look up to the hills that once were cultivated and then were defaced by centuries of medieval barbarism, to see what has been accomplished." Jewish efforts, he continued, had been "amazing" in bringing "back into economic usefulness lands which the world cannot afford to leave lying idle." He remained fixated with the development of this small patch of earth. And Jewish progress advanced the lot of the Palestinian Arabs as well, thus fulfilling the spirit of the Balfour Declaration. He argued, "The idea that only a limited number of people can live in a country is a profound illusion; it all depends on their co-operative and inventive power. There are more people today living twenty storeys above the ground in New York than were living on the ground in New York 100 years ago." This was a far more expansive view of Zionist immigration and development than he espoused as late as 1946.[32]

Otherwise, Churchill was not overly concerned with the fate of the Palestinian Arabs. He did not mourn Transjordan's conquest of land designated for a Palestinian Arab state as specified by the 1947 U.N. partition plan. His own wartime plan for a federation did not include such a state, and neither did the Balfour Declaration or mandate. He blamed the Palestinian Arab refugee problem on the Palestinian Arabs and their fellow Arabs. He argued, in line with the official Israeli view, that after the Arab nations attacked and tried "to extinguish the Jewish National Home, all this Arab population fled in terror to behind the advancing forces of their own religion." He acknowledged that their "condition is most grievous" but maintained that it would be alleviated only when a "lasting peace," about which he was hopeful, was established between Arabs and Jews. In reality, while many Palestinian Arabs did voluntarily flee, many also were expelled by Israelis. Churchill might well have been resigned to the wartime displacement of people, given how many millions of Germans, Poles, Jews and others in Europe lost their property during and after the Second World War only a few years before. In any case, he was not terribly sympathetic to the Palestinian Arab plight.[33]

Churchill continued to distinguish the Palestinian Arabs from some of the other Arabs, particularly Abdullah, whom Churchill installed as head of Transjordan and who remained for him a source of pride. Even when Abdullah attacked the nascent Jewish state, Churchill asserted that "no fault can be alleged against him." He was certain that Abdullah wanted peace and patronizingly blamed Bevin for not instructing Transjordan on what to do. It is unclear whether Churchill meant what he said here or knew more than he suggested. He very well might not have been aware that Bevin had in fact encouraged Transjordan in early 1948 to use the British-led Arab Legion at a minimum to capture the areas designated for the Palestinian Arabs, including the West Bank, and seemingly also Jerusalem, which was designated for international control despite British opposition. (In discussions with other Arabs, Bevin apparently suggested he wanted the Jewish state destroyed.) At the very least, Bevin pursued an aggressive and risky strategy. Indeed, Abdullah coveted all of Palestine, as he and his family long had. Still, Churchill had good reason to think that compared to other Arab leaders Abdullah was moderate; he maintained frequent secretive contact with Israeli leaders, shared with the Israelis a common enemy in Haj Amin and a suspicion of other Arabs, respected Zionist dynamism, and agreed to a draft peace agreement with Israel in 1950.[34]

The Zionist debate was over in Churchill's mind, and he never questioned Zionism's value again. Israel, he believed, was a vibrant, militarily strong, democratic, liberal, civilized, historically correct, Western-oriented state that was a natural ally of Britain.

When Churchill was elected prime minister in October 1951, he sought to achieve the close relations with Israel that he had called for in Opposition. But he faced a similar situation to that during the Second World War, when the rest of bureaucracy, including the Conservative Party, Foreign Office, and military, were all generally hostile toward the Zionists. The Chiefs of Staff, for instance, did seek Israeli military cooperation in defense of the region against the Soviets, but within limits. In a memo to the Cabinet Defense Committee in the spring of 1953, they wrote, "Arab goodwill is essential to the success of our plans and is more important than that of Israel. Co-operation with Israel must be subordinated to our plans for the defence of the area as a whole, and must be within the limitations imposed by the needs to avoid antagonising the Arabs." Churchill, who took the defense minister portfolio as he did during the Second World War, did not agree. Nor did he agree with the Foreign Office, telling Evelyn Shuckburgh, Foreign Secretary Anthony Eden's personal private secretary, in 1955 that the department was "riddled with

Bevinism." He maintained that Bevin was prejudiced, noting to an official in 1953 that Bevin "had a strain of anti-Semitism in his thought." He insisted that Bevin "put the Foreign Office in on the wrong side when Israel was attacked by all the Arab States."[35]

Churchill sought to reorient Britain's foreign policy in the Middle East by embracing Israel and utilizing it for Britain's strategic benefit. Broadly, he thought support for the Zionists would help Britain maintain support from the United States. He told a conference of Commonwealth prime ministers in 1955, "Israel is a force in the world & a link w [with] the USA." He had held this view since the First World War.[36]

More immediately, Churchill thought Israel could bring Britain greater leverage in its intensifying dispute with Egypt. Out of power, he opposed the Attlee-Bevin policy of supporting Egypt against Israel. Twice in 1950 he called on the Attlee government to stop its support of the Egyptians, including selling them 110 jets intended "to enable them to face the new State of Israel," and to oppose the Egyptian blockade of oil tankers through the Suez Canal destined for the Israeli port of Haifa. After becoming prime minister, Churchill reversed British policy toward Egypt and Israel, viewing the former as an enemy and the latter as an ally. He believed Israel and Britain shared a common interest in containing if not attacking the Egyptians, who were intent on eliminating British control of Suez, where eighty thousand British troops were stationed. In the autumn of 1951, Egyptian Prime Minister Nahas Pasha unilaterally abrogated the 1936 Anglo-Egyptian Treaty, the legal basis for British troops in Suez, and the Convention of 1899, which validated the Anglo-Egyptian Condominium over Egypt's former colony Sudan. Shortly after, Churchill insisted with a clenched fist to Eden, "Tell them [the Egyptians] that if we have any more of their cheek we shall set the Jews on them and drive them into the gutter, from which they should never have emerged." The conflict with the Egyptians led him to denigrate them, as he often denigrated native peoples fighting imperial British control.[37]

In early 1952, Anglo-Egyptian relations worsened. The Egyptian government did not intervene as mobs destroyed various foreign and ethnic (including British and Jewish) establishments. In the summer, there was a coup, and some military officers, now headed by Mohammed Neguib, took power. Churchill was keen to use the new Jewish state as leverage in increasingly intense Anglo-Egyptian negotiations. He explained to two senior Foreign Office officials, Selwyn Lloyd and William Strang, in the spring of 1953 that "Israel is the most powerful fighting force in the Middle East and may come in very handy in dealing with Egypt if [Egyptian strongman] Neguib attacks us. We ought never to have allowed the obstruction in the Suez Canal of oil for Haifa." A few days later he bluntly explained to Strang that Israel was an asset to be publicly embraced and that it should not be disparaged in a naive and futile attempt to appease Egypt: "I do not mind it being known here or in Cairo that I am on the side of Israel and against her ill-treatment by the Egyptians. The idea of selling Israel down the drain in order to persuade the Egyptians to kick us out of the Canal Zone more gently is not one which attracts me." And a couple of weeks later, Churchill told the Cabinet Defense Committee that a strong Israeli military "would constitute a useful deterrent against Egyptian aggressive aspirations and the possibility of such forces being built up would be a useful factor in our present negotiations with the Egyptian Government." He also saw domestic political value in his new approach to the region, hoping to garner support for his Egyptian policy from pro-Israel Socialists and Liberals, who would not otherwise support him: "We have probably got to have a showdown with Neguib, and Israel will be an important factor both *Parliamentary* and military. We must not throw away any important card we have in our hand."[38]

Churchill also sought a departure from Bevin's policy regarding Jordan. (Abdullah changed the country's name from Transjordan in 1949.) Bevin had encouraged Abdullah's 1948 drive into Palestine (which contributed to other Arab states joining in to minimize Abdullah's advantage), provoking a war with Israel, while Churchill wanted Israel and Jordan, Britain's two close regional allies, to make peace. He told an Israeli diplomat in 1950 that Abdullah was the only reliable and stable Arab ruler (notably excluding Ibn Saud), and he urged the Attlee government that year to reconcile two old friends of Britain, Abdullah and Weizmann. His hopes were dashed when Abdullah was murdered in 1951 by a supporter of Haj Amin. Churchill lamented in the Commons that Abdullah, a "champion" of the Arabs and "friend" of the Jews, might have reconciled the two peoples.[39] An Israeli-Jordan peace accord would have contributed to regional stability and enhanced British influence in the region. Churchill was also hoping to avoid a terrible dilemma some day of being called to fulfill Britain's 1948 obligation defend Jordan against Israel; he certainly did not want British troops fighting against the nascent Jewish state.

Generally, Churchill felt constrained from acting fully upon his pro-Israel views. He had aged since the war and had far less zest to combat the bureaucracy over subordinate matters. He even lacked the energy to achieve his most dear project during his second administration: a summit with the new post-Stalin Soviet leadership. When that pursuit essentially died in late 1953, partly due to U.S. opposition, he confided to his physician Lord Moran about U.S. Secretary of State John Foster Dulles, whom he disliked, "Ten years ago I could have dealt with him. Even as it is I have not been defeated by this bastard. I have been humiliated by my own decay." The Israeli issues Churchill faced were no longer existential but relatively mundane, and he took practically no initiative in dealing with them, often deferring to the Foreign Office. A fortnight after his election in 1951, he replied to a memo by his long-time aide Lord Cherwell, "I am keeping your paper about the Middle East which contains many unpleasant truths. I have had to agree to Anthony [Eden]'s proposals. They will probably lead to a deadlock." After Chancellor of the Exchequer Rab Butler and Eden wrote in 1952 of their opposition to an Israeli request for a £20 million loan, Churchill did not seek to convince them otherwise but replied in resignation, "I am so sorry no help can be given." (Eden, like Butler, argued in favor of an Israel that was neither excessively weak nor strong, a view he must have regretted during the 1956 Suez War debacle when as prime minister he allied with Israel against Egypt, just as he likely came to regret his 1954 memo to Churchill claiming that the "gravest danger to the Middle East remains the possibility of a break-out by Israel.") Churchill also allowed the bureaucracy to block many of his own initiatives. In 1953, he suggested to the Foreign Office that Britain retaliate against Lebanon for its secondary boycott of Israel, but when the Foreign Office opposed, Churchill quickly retreated and agreed to what Lloyd termed "vigorous representation."[40]

Churchill was able, however, to take the hard edge off of the bureaucracy's plans. In 1953, Israel requested to be consulted about Suez negotiations, and senior Foreign Office official Lloyd suggested a "colourless reply." Churchill responded that he wanted a stronger reply in light of

Israeli strategic importance in the Egyptian matter, and he strengthened the revised reply. Similarly, in 1954, after receiving a message from Israel on some matter, he directed the Foreign Office to "draft a civil answer for my consideration." More substantively, Churchill fended off any steps that would bring Britain to blows with Israel. Amid Israeli-Jordanian border skirmishes in 1953, Eden wanted to meet Jordan's request for British troops, and Churchill confided to Moran the next day, "Now the F.O. [Foreign Office] wants a war with Israel. Ernie Bevin apparently made a treaty with Jordan. I don't want war." Churchill had a different agenda and proposed stationing troops in both countries in order to stop the fighting: "One Armoured brigade divided equally between Palestine and Trans-Jordania with the agreement of both as a security against aggression." This was an intriguing and rather shocking proposal given Britain's earlier pledge to Jordan, but it would have ensured that British troops would not fight Israel. And during further Israeli-Jordanian clashes in 1954, Churchill rejected a recommendation of disclosing to Jordan how Britain concretely intended to assist it in any major conflict with Israel. He did not want to invite the possibility of an Anglo-Israeli military clash.[41]

Whether or not he pushed pro-Israel policies, Churchill radiated great pride and vindication over his longstanding support for Zionism. In 1952, he told the U.S. Congress, "From the days of the Balfour Declaration I have desired that the Jews should have a national home, and I have worked for that end. I rejoice to pay my tribute here to the achievements of those who have founded the Israelite State." While perhaps he saw political gain in praising Zionism in the United States, he repeated the sentiment, though more reservedly, in the less receptive House of Commons in 1953. His most forthright and enthusiastic statement was delivered spontaneously to the Washington Press Club in 1954: "I am a Zionist. Let me make that clear. I was one of the original ones, after the Balfour Declaration, and I have worked faithfully for it. I think it a most wonderful thing that this community should have established itself so effectively." After pointing out Zionism's humanitarian and civilizational benefits, he repeated, "I think it's a wonderful thing." However favorable, these statements were inaccurate; he expressed no support for Zionism right after the Balfour Declaration of 1917, although he did in 1908 and then next in 1921. Churchill exuded the same general enthusiasm for Zionism in private conversations with Americans, often to less receptive audiences. When Churchill dined at the White House at the end of Truman's presidency in January 1953, his aide Jock Colville unsympathetically described the scene in his diary: "After dinner Truman played the piano. Nobody would listen because they were all busy with post-mortems on a diatribe in favour of Zionism and against Egypt which W. [Winston] had delivered at dinner (to the disagreement of practically all the Americans present, though they admitted that the large Jewish vote would prevent them disagreeing in public)."[42]

Churchill made sure to tell the Israelis of his joy over their new state. In late 1951, shortly after his election as prime minister, he wrote to President Weizmann, "The wonderful exertions which Israel is making in these times of difficulty are cheering to an old Zionist like me. . . . Every good wish my old friend." In perhaps his last contact with an Israeli official while prime minister, Churchill met in February 1955 with Israeli Ambassador Eliahu Elath, who drafted the following report to his government: "He [Churchill] took joy in the establishment of our State and expressed his confidence in its splendid future. He went on to say: you are a nation of ideals and that is the greatest thing in the life of both the community and the individual."[43]

Churchill always saw Zionism as standing for ideals that were loftier than pure nationalism. One of those ideals was adherence to the Bible that was so pivotal to Western civilization. He told Elath in 1950 that he admired how the Jews had faithfully guarded the biblical heritage in the past and implored the "free Jewish nation," in Elath's words, to "preserve close association with the book; Israel must guard the people's spiritual and moral inheritance." This pronouncement, which echoed his injunctions to Manchester Jews fifty years before, could have been spoken by the Herzl-era cultural Zionist philosopher Achad Ha'am. In a 1955 meeting with Elath, Churchill even inquired about the Western Wall, Judaism's holiest site, which stands in the Old City of Jerusalem, and which Israeli Jews were forbidden to access by Jordanian officials. This focus on the Bible and religious sites reflected his belief that the Jews were a great ancient race and his satisfaction that they had returned to their ancient religious homeland. In 1952, he praised his old friend Weizmann, who had just died, by asserting that he "led his people back into their promised land, where we have seen them invincibly established as a free and sovereign State." He always suggested, when he thought about it, that Jerusalem belonged to the Jews, and he told one Foreign Office official in early 1955, "You ought to let the Jews have Jerusalem; it is they who made it famous." He privately conveyed to the Israelis what he said publicly in the late 1940s, that the emergence of a Jewish state was important not only for Jewish history but also for world history. He relayed that to Elath in 1950, and in 1954 he wrote Israeli Prime Minister Moshe Sharett amid skirmishes with Jordan, about the "great experiment in your country which as you know I have always regarded as one of the most hopeful and encouraging adventures of the 20th century."[44]

Another ideal which Churchill was happy to see fulfilled was of Israel serving as a refuge to persecuted and scattered Jewry. In the politically charged environment in Britain and Palestine in 1946, he had minimized the importance of a haven for Jews in Palestine, even though he considered that important since 1906 and then vital in the 1930s and early 1940s. But both he and the political situation had begun to mellow. He was undoubtedly further sensitized to this matter when more became known about the Holocaust, and he became excited over the astonishing influx of Jewish refugees that flooded Israel from eastern European and Muslim countries—doubling the Israeli population by mid-1953 and nearly tripling it by 1956. In 1950, according to Elath, "Churchill spoke movingly eloquent on the sufferings of the Jews throughout history," and in 1955 he told Elath that he admired how Israel had absorbed many refugees. He expressed the same sentiment in the U.S. Congress in 1952, and then in Washington in 1954 Churchill also applauded Israel for affording "a refuge to millions of their coreligionists who had suffered so fearfully under the Hitler, and not only Hitler, persecution." This immigration explosion must have been particularly satisfying for him since he had worked hard in the 1920s as colonial secretary to ensure continued Jewish immigration and had envisioned a Jewish majority back then when it seemed highly unlikely.[45]

Churchill continued to take unusual interest in Israeli development of the land and its advancement of civilization. Like David Ben-Gurion (Israel's prime minister for most of 1949–1963), Churchill was very focused with development of the Negev desert, seeing it as an essential area for settlement. In 1949 in the Commons he warned against begrudging

Israelis their "fair share of the deserts of the Negeb.... I have always felt that the Negeb should afford a means of expansion to the Jewish settlers in Palestine and offer future prospects to Zionist movements." He followed that up by asking Elath in 1950 about Israeli plans to develop the Negev. And he wrote the Foreign Office in 1952 of his complete objection to an Arab proposal for Israel to give up the Negev: "Surely there can be no question of Israel being asked to give up the Negeb, as its development might afford the only means of sustaining their great population of refugee immigrants." As late as early 1955, a month before retiring as prime minister, he told one Foreign Office official that large numbers of refugees ought to be settled in the Negev. He also referred to the Negev when he spoke in 1952 to the U.S. Congress of his hope of refugees helping "convert deserts into gardens" and when he mentioned to the Washington Press Club "turning the desert into fertile gardens and thriving townships."[46]

Churchill's public and private remarks beginning in late 1948 suggest that his cool attitude toward Zionism from February 1945 was only a temporary, partially calculated funk. Unfortunately for the Zionists, that funk occurred at an extremely inopportune time. He betrayed them in their hour of need, and said and did nothing on their behalf for almost four key years, while they were fighting for their existence. He had betrayed his own values, and he felt ashamed. But from late 1948 on, all the elements of his old vigorous Zionism returned—historical, humanitarian, civilizational, strategic, personal, and romantic. He saw the establishment of the State of Israel as a great historical event, just as he had imagined in 1908.

Less than two months before the end of his term as prime minister, which was for all intents and purposes the end of his career and in some ways even his life, Churchill made a point of reminding the Israeli ambassador that he remained a friend of the Israeli people. According to Elath, he insisted "that he will continue to see to it that no evil befalls Israel." This echoed what he relayed to Weizmann in 1939 shortly after the Second World War began. At this most poignant moment in his life, he asserted that he was "happy that future generations would thereby know that the sons of the prophets dwelling in Zion were among his many well-wishers from all over the world."[47] This was a remarkable statement, one that was pregnant with deep consciousness about the past and the future, and one that few, if any, other British politicians would have made or conceived. It attested to the fact that for half a century Churchill remained devoted to Disraeli, the Jewish people, and their nationalist aspirations.

Conclusion

WINSTON CHURCHILL FULLY ENGAGED THE WORLD. He lived and breathed it, his moods were frequently affected by it, and he desperately wanted to shape it. He deeply felt an obligation to posterity, to contribute his part to the progress of civilization. Churchill did not accept the status quo but impatiently battled to fashion a better a world. This anxious and restless urgency to act, so uniquely mixed with creative thought and imagination, was evident in a 1916 letter to his wife from the western front in the First World War criticizing the government from which he had just resigned in disgrace: "How easy to do nothing. How hard to achieve anything. War is action, energy, & hazard. These sheep only want to browse among the daisies." The same attitude was conspicuous when he rebuffed David Lloyd George's criticism of his 1919 anti-Bolshevik crusade: "I cannot help feeling a most dreadful & ever present sense of responsibility. Am I wrong? How easy for me to shrug my shoulders & say it is on the Cabinet, or on the Paris Conference. I cannot do it." Churchill was not only eager to act but was usually prepared to act alone, or, as he said about Britain in 1940, "to stand alone in the breach."[1]

All this was predominantly true about grave matters of war, peace, and empire, such as his unpopular crusade against the Bolsheviks in 1919–1920, his unsung battle in the 1930s to contain Nazi Germany, his provocative 1946 "Iron Curtain" speech in Fulton, Missouri, his bid to keep India as part of the empire in the 1930s and 1940s, and his solitary quest for a summit and settlement with the new post-Stalin Soviet leadership in 1953. The same was also true, although less frequently and less intensely, regarding Zionism. Indeed, the lonely struggle to advance civilization that defied public opinion and went awry of the establishment was to him most compelling and sublime.

Churchill always focused on the supreme challenges in his mind and sought to maintain perspective. Within the overall objective of advancing civilization, his preeminent concerns, which often took on sentimental overtones, were mostly strategic, imperial, and political. Since he rigidly prioritized his goals, these larger concerns shaped his mood and attitude toward Zionism, a subordinate, nonstrategic, nonimperial, largely sentimental cause he championed only intermittently until the early 1930s, when it became integral to him and his worldview. During some periods, the larger context shaped his attitude adversely. For several years after the First World War, his fixation on his vulnerable political position, the Bolshevik threat, the danger of self-determination, and the need to conserve financial and military resources led to a more negative attitude toward Jews and Zionism. The paramount issues also worked against Zionism in the first years after the Second World War, for a different set of reasons. However, at other times they facilitated or encouraged a more pro-Zionist stance. In the first years of his career, Zionism's political resonance with Churchill's constituents in North-West Manchester led him to embrace it. And in the 1930s, when politically unshackled, Churchill determined that adhering to the Balfour Declaration and demonstrating toughness with the Palestinian Arabs would bolster Britain's position in Europe and imperial territories. Beginning in 1949, various larger aspirations, including political and strategic concerns, snapped Churchill out of his non-Zionist mood and allowed him to complete his last six years of his career as a dependable, if less forceful, Zionist.

However subordinate, Zionism remained an important, largely sentimental concern that fit into Churchill's worldview. His romantic love of the past, determination to right historical wrongs, and broad devotion to religious values contributed to his supporting the restoration of the Jews to their ancient homeland. He also was devoted to his father and his father's principles, attitudes, and friends. This encouraged Churchill's comfort with Jews on a personal level, a respect for them and their abilities, and compassion for their plight. And it led him to the teachings of Benjamin Disraeli, from whom he learned several lessons: that Jews were a great race, that Jews and their ideas contributed substantially to Western civilization, and that God dealt with countries as they dealt with the Jews. These convictions made Churchill more favorably disposed to the Jews and their causes, and his own encounters with them only reinforced that predilection. He invoked the adage that he attributed to Disraeli, "The Lord deals with the nations as the nations deal with the Jews," not only when warning other nations against mistreating Jews but also when discussing with Chaim Weizmann in 1943 his support for partition and a Jewish state. He evidently felt an added mystical imperative to support Zionism so that God would be good to him and to Britain. He somewhat confirmed that in 1955 when he told the Israeli ambassador that he was gratified that Israelis were among his supporters. Less mystically or mysteriously, Churchill also came to view the Zionists as strategic and ideological allies, which became especially important beginning in the late 1930s. Earlier in the 1930s, he came to share a personal identification with the Zionists, one that lasted basically for the rest of his life; their friends were his friends, their enemies his enemies, and their values his values. The Jews reciprocated this affection. Indeed, after voting heavily for him in 1906 in North-West Manchester, the Jews and the Zionists remained perhaps Churchill's most consistent and reliable supporters, in England and abroad, during his long, tumultuous, and often unpopular career.

Churchill also believed that Zionism advanced the cause of civilization, which was always the overriding preoccupation in his worldview. The imperative of spreading civilization transcended race and geography and was integral to his very core. He believed that the Zionists shared his own nineteenth-century values, and he viscerally identified with their attempts to develop and civilize Palestine. He became completely convinced of this from his interactions with Weizmann and from his visit in 1921 to Palestine, where he witnessed the barrenness of the Arab areas compared to the flourishing, developed Jewish settlements, such as Rishon Lezion. He became certain that the Zionists shared his mission of civilizing the world. Just as many in Britain believed in the nineteenth century that restoration of the Jews to Palestine would benefit the human race by precipitating the Second Coming, Churchill believed it would benefit the human race by advancing Western civilization. In his opinion, this sealed Jewish claims to govern Palestine. Churchill viewed other countries and causes the same way. He believed that Britain was not only a country but a leading champion of certain cherished principles and of a certain way of life. As he said most poetically from London during the Battle of Britain in 1940, "We are fighting *by* ourselves alone; but we are not fighting *for* ourselves alone. Here in this strong City of Refuge which enshrines the title-deeds of human progress and is of deep consequence to Christian civilization...."[2] He thus was consumed with enhancing the security of Britain and the British Empire, not only for nationalist reasons, which he valued in and of themselves, but because he always considered it essential to the progress of civilization. He came to view U.S. security and power the same way.

In many ways Churchill's advocacy of Zionism required far more imagination and intellectual courage than his various lonesome campaigns on behalf of vital strategic causes for which he is better known. When he warned against the Bolshevik or Nazi threat, most others disagreed with his judgments and predictions, but the overall objective—the security of Britain and its empire—was clear and widely shared. The same was not true about Zionism, an international political movement that did not formally begin until 1897 (at least in the West) and that intended to restore a Jewish state to Palestine after almost two millennia. It seemed to many Britons—Gentile and Jew alike—a ludicrous goal that defied much historical and current thinking and, in the 1930s and beyond, one that conflicted with Britain's strategic interests. The dream of a Jewish state in Palestine seemed in 1908 and 1921 more far-fetched than the Nazi threat in 1936 or the post-Stalin Russian promise of 1953. Indeed, his prescient prediction in 1908—a mere eleven years after the First Zionist Congress and when the issue was barely a blip on the world screen—of the reemergence of a Jewish political entity in Palestine was a more remarkable feat than any of his farsighted prophecies about Great Power issues. By the 1930s, if not earlier, Churchill became conscious that Zionism was integral to, and comfortably fit within, his worldview and that he was right about that cause as he had been about so many other, graver world issues.

Churchill championed Zionism despite his lack of expertise and deep historical understanding of the movement and of the Middle East. Although he emphasized the importance of history to understanding statecraft, his historical knowledge was generally more restricted to British, European, and American subjects, about which he had also written extensively. His knowledge of Russian history was shakier, but he compensated for that by closely observing current events from various sources. He knew even less about Jewish and Arabic history and current events, and he had no interest in seeking a subtle understanding in these matters as he did in more important subjects. But he developed a comfort level with the Zionist and Palestinian issues during his eighteen months as colonial secretary in the early 1920s, when he was more impressionable and heavily dependent upon his aides, who themselves were not experts in the region (and in fact were often wrong in their judgments). He learned the most during his short visit to Palestine in 1921, when he came face-to-face with Palestinian Jews and Arabs, and regional Arabs; his views of these groups and some individuals did not change much after that. He built on that foundation, albeit imperfect, and acquired greater expertise in the 1930s by closely observing Palestinian events and engaging colleagues and Zionists in regular discussions. His extraordinary interest in the minutiae of the land in Palestine in 1934 demonstrated his growing inquisitiveness about the subject. His involvement in the partition debate in the late 1930s and his pursuit of a pro-Zionist regional settlement during the Second World War reflected his greater knowledge and confidence about Zionist issues. Where hard facts failed him, he relied on his generally static understanding of the Jewish and Arab races, which his own personal encounters and experiences confirmed. Still, he never gained the expertise about Palestine and Israel that he achieved with Soviet Russia, let alone Germany or France. He rarely displayed profound, complex thought about Palestine and the Middle East or the comprehensive sharp analysis and brilliant prescience that he exhibited with more critical subjects. Generally, Churchill was less innovative and his mind less nimble when considering Zionist and Middle Eastern issues. Yet, he often knew more than most of his colleagues and subordinates about Zionism and Palestine/Israel, and generally demonstrated superior intuition and judgment.

Churchill disliked the Arabs, particularly the Palestinian Arabs, for many of the same types of reasons he favored the Jews and Zionists—racial, religious, historical, humanitarian, civilizational, strategic, and personal. He was not captivated by some romantic image of Arabs, whether nomadic or pastoral, as other Britons were. Instead he considered them a lowly race, backward, lacking imagination and morality, indifferent to the progress of civilization, immoderate, and largely hostile to British and Western interests. His encounters with Arabs and their issues, in the First and Second World Wars and in 1921, contributed to and confirmed that view, particularly regarding the Palestinian Arabs. His interest and support for pan-Arabism, in the late 1910s and early 1920s and during the Second World War, was partly a reflection of his secondary consideration of Palestinian Arabs.

During most of his career, Churchill repeatedly sounded the alarm about the present and near-term future. His habitual expressions of foreboding led many to dismiss him as a sensational Cassandra, and his lapses into depression may have contributed even further to his sense of doom. He certainly perceived a world full of drama and color. Yet, while Churchill believed there would be some low points, such as during and after the First World War, the Bolshevik Revolution, and the Nazi period, he felt confident that the general direction of history was upward. It was a Whig view of history, one propounded by several nineteenth-century historians he had read, such as the renowned Thomas Babington Macaulay. Thus, he believed with varying degrees of certainty that the Communist government in Russia would inevitably crumble, and even expressed that conviction during the dire Berlin crisis in the late 1940s. Similarly, he had faith that the Zionists would right a historical wrong by governing their ancient homeland and continuing to develop and civilize the land. Churchill insisted that people should not give up in their quest for liberty and progress; they must, as he often said, be "unflinchable" and carry on "to the end." However much he reacted to events in Russia and Palestine and tried to shape them, he trusted that time eventually served the cause of peace and progress. Good would triumph, and civilization would continue to advance.

Churchill appeared on the surface a bundle of contradictions: an aristocrat who espoused democracy; a democrat who distrusted the masses; a Briton and an American; a Conservative and a Liberal; a statesman who believed supremely in power yet indulged sentimental interests; a pragmatist who adhered to Disraelian romantic and mystical injunctions; a man of steely determination who was prone to emotional outbursts; a historian who often lacked historical understanding; a perennial and often depressive pessimist with broad, robust optimism; a restless champion of the long view; a nineteenth-century man who helped shape the twentieth century; a nostalgic Victorian who embraced new, seemingly far-fetched causes; a fervent believer in liberal civilization who allied himself with Fascists and Communists; a scourge of Nazis who forgave Nazi criminals; a rabid anti-Communist who tried to destroy the Soviet Union in one world war and embraced it as an ally in another; a cold warrior who fervently pursued a settlement with Soviet Russia; a Zionist who often abandoned Zionism; a philo-Semitic champion of Zionist land development who delivered most of Palestine to Arabs he deemed primitive and hostile; an anti-Wahhabi who relied on Ibn Saud; and on and on. Contemporaries and historians seized on these ostensible inconsistencies to question Churchill's mental stability, judgment, and convictions. These critics often raised the same questions regarding his evolving interest in, and support of, the eccentric, romantic, and largely sentimental movement of Zionism. Indeed, Churchill was not always an advocate of Zionism, but the cause became firmly rooted in his worldview and remained very much a part of his complex core being.

NOTES

ABBREVIATIONS
CAB   Cabinet Records, The National Archives, Kew, U.K.
CHAR   Chartwell Papers, Churchill Archives Centre, Churchill College, Cambridge, U.K.
CHUR   Churchill Papers, Churchill Archives Centre, Churchill College, Cambridge, U.K.
CO   Colonial Office Records, The National Archives, Kew, U.K.
CZA   Central Zionist Archives, Jerusalem, Israel
FO   Foreign Office Records, The National Archives, Kew, U.K.
FRUS   *Foreign Relations of the United States*, U.S. State Department. (For individual listings, see bibliography under U.S. State Department.)
GP   Gaster Papers, Mocatta Library, University College, London
MUN   Ministry of Munitions Records, The National Archives, Kew, U.K.
PREM   Prime Minister's Office Records, The National Archives, Kew, U.K.
WO   War Office Records, The National Archives, Kew, U.K.

INTRODUCTION
1. CAB 24/126, p. 196; Gilbert, *Winston S. Churchill: The Stricken World*, 584; Gilbert, *Winston S. Churchill: "Never Despair,"* 557–558; Rhodes James, *Winston S. Churchill: His Complete Speeches, 1897–1963* (hereafter cited as Rhodes James, *Speeches*), 8: 8327, 8432.
2. Berlin, "Weizmann," 43–62; Berlin, "Origins of Israel," 150; Berlin, "Chaim Weizmann's Leadership," 192.
3. The term "colonist" alone is used in this book to mean simply "settler," and "colony" means "settlement," without any imperial connotation unless

otherwise stated. That was generally how the Zionists and Churchill used the terms regarding Zionism. Churchill quoted in Rhodes James, *Speeches,* 7: 7779; Churchill, *My African Journey,* 42. Also see Howard Sachar, *History of Israel,* 27, 34, 47, 48, 53, 60, 64; Churchill, *Marlborough,* 1: 66.
4. Israel Zangwill quoted in CHAR 10/7, p. 4. Also see Berlin, "Origins of Israel," 161; Berlin, "Weizmann," 43.

CHAPTER 1. CHURCHILL'S WORLDS

1. Gardiner quoted in Gardiner, "Mr. Churchill," 56, 60. Conservative MP was Rab Butler, quoted in Colville, *Fringes of Power,* 122. Shaw quoted in Gilbert, *Winston S. Churchill: "Never Despair,"* 253. Steevens quoted in G. W. Steevens, "The Youngest Man in Europe," *Daily Mail,* December 2, 1898, reprinted in Eade, *Churchill,* 63, 66. Also see Rhodes James, *Churchill: A Study in Failure,* 17–18; "Clearing the Air," *Economist,* May 26, 1945, 686; "British Policy" (editorial), *Guardian,* June 4, 1945; Carr, *Conditions of Peace,* xxii; Berlin, "Churchill," 17; Rhodes James, *Speeches,* 6: 6009, 7: 7572.
2. Churchill quoted in Churchill, *My Early Life,* i; Gilbert, *Winston S. Churchill: Companion Documents* (hereafter cited as Gilbert, *Companion*), 4/3: 1536; Churchill, "Britain's Security Is the Vital Issue," *Evening Standard,* May 3, 1937, reprinted in Churchill, *Collected Essays,* 3: 302. Also see Carr, *Conditions of Peace,* xviii; Berlin, "Churchill," 9; Bowler, *Invention of Progress,* 14.
3. Churchill quoted in Churchill, *Marlborough,* 1: 72; Gilbert, *Companion,* 4/3: 1504–1505; Rhodes James, *Speeches,* 1: 28, 908; Churchill, *River War,* 1: 14–17, 25, 2: 248–249; Hyam, *Elgin,* 503–504. Also see Bowler, *Invention of Progress,* 3; Beloff, *Britain's Liberal Empire,* 32–33; Churchill, "Dictatorship on Its Trial," reprinted in Churchill, *Collected Essays,* 2: 206; Churchill, *World Crisis: 1911–1914,* 185; Hyam, *Elgin,* 49, 50, 226, 505; Churchill, *Great Democracies,* 293–294; Churchill, *Story of the Malakand Field Force,* 315
4. Max Beloff notes that in 1921, when Churchill was forty-seven years old, the sight of a nonwhite on a British street would cause a child to stare. Churchill quoted in Churchill, *Story of the Malakand Field Force,* 9, 11; Churchill, *River War,* 1: 17, 25, 2: 248; R. Churchill, *Winston S. Churchill: Companion* (hereafter cited as R. Churchill, *Companion*), 1/2: 750; Churchill, *My African Journey,* 36, 42. Also see Berlin, "Weizmann," 34; Berlin, "Churchill," 7–8; Churchill, *River War,* 1: 14–16; Churchill, *My African Journey,* 29, 127; Anderson, *Race and Rapprochement,* 12–13, 18–39, 47–49, 69–72; Addison, *Churchill: The Unexpected Hero,* 123, 125; Roberts, *Eminent Churchillians,* 211–212; Marsh, *A Number of People,* 150; Hyam, *Elgin,* 357–359; Churchill, *Marlborough,* 1: 66; Beloff, *Britain's Liberal Empire,* 358n1.
5. Churchill quoted in Churchill, *My Early Life,* 33. Also see Churchill, *World Crisis: 1911–1914,* 4; R. V. Jones, "Churchill and Science," 427–441; Soames, *Winston and Clementine,* 65; Churchill, "Looking Back on Sixty Years," *News of the World,* January 13, 1935, reprinted in Churchill, *Collected Essays,* 3: 127–134.

6. Churchill entitled the account of his vision "Private Article," but it was known among family as "The Dream." Churchill quoted in Churchill, *My Early Life*, 32; Churchill, "Looking Back on Sixty Years," *News of the World*, January 13, 1935, reprinted in Churchill, *Collected Essays*, 3: 132. Imaginary conversation with Randolph Churchill quoted in Gilbert, *Winston S. Churchill: "Never Despair*," 372. Also see Gertrude Himmelfarb, "The Roar," *New Republic*, November 26, 2001, 28; Rhodes James, *Speeches*, 1: 25; Gilbert, *Churchill: A Life*, 165.
7. Castlereagh quoted in Webster, *Congress of Vienna*, 121. Also see Churchill, *World Crisis: 1911–1914*, 40–41, 52–53; Rhodes James, *Speeches*, 3: 2925–2926; Churchill, *Age of Revolution*, 275–276; Churchill, *Great Democracies*, 5–7; C. C. Webster, *British Diplomacy*, 231, 361–362, 366–367; C. Webster, *Cambridge History of British Foreign Policy*, 472; Kissinger, *World Restored*, 164; Hertslet, *Map of Europe by Treaty*, 1: 375.
8. Churchill quoted in R. Churchill, *Companion*, 1/2: 937–938; Rhodes James, *Speeches*, 1: 783, 2: 1085. Also see R. Churchill, *Companion*, 2/1: 73; Rhodes James, *Speeches*, 1: 78–85, 731, 783, 2: 1086; R. Churchill, *Companion*, 1/2: 751; Beloff, *Britain's Liberal Empire*, 72, 108–109, 119; Jenkins, *Churchill*, 155; Soames, *Winston and Clementine*, 96.
9. Churchill, *World Crisis: 1911–1914*, 33; R. Churchill, *Winston S. Churchill: Young Statesman*, 524–533; Addison, *Home Front*, 126.
10. Churchill quoted in R. Churchill, *Companion*, 1/2: 937, 947. Also see Beloff, *Britain's Liberal Empire*, 44–46, 113–114; Seeley, *Expansion of England*, 18, 62; R. Churchill, *Companion*, 1/1: 597–600, 1/2: 938, 1012; Rhodes James, *Speeches*, 1: 550.
11. Churchill quoted in Churchill, "4 August, 1914: A Nation Transformed," *Daily Mail*, August 4, 1933, reprinted in Churchill, *Collected Essays*, 1: 309; Gilbert, *Companion*, 4/2: 1005. Also see Blake, *Unknown Prime Minister*, 288–289; Beloff, *Britain's Liberal Empire*, 278–279; Gilbert, *Companion*, 4/1: 417–418; J. Thompson, *Russia, Bolshevism, and the Versailles Peace*, 196–197; Rhodes James, *Speeches*, 5: 4668; Churchill, "Looking Back on Sixty Years," *News of the World*, January 13, 1935, reprinted in Churchill, *Collected Essays*, 3: 127.
12. Churchill quoted in Churchill, *My Early Life*, 65; Churchill, *World Crisis: The Aftermath*, 454, 459. Also see Churchill, *World Crisis: 1911–1914*, 2–3; Soames, *Winston and Clementine*, 222–223; Gilbert, *Companion*, 4/2: 1054.
13. Churchill quoted in Soames, *Winston and Clementine*, 391. Also see Gilbert, *Companion*, 4/1: 418–420, 550, 4/2: 1190–1194; Soames, *Winston and Clementine*, 295–298, 303; Rhodes James, *Speeches*, 6: 6011; Diggins, *Mussolini and Fascism*.
14. Churchill quoted in Gilbert, *Companion*, 4/2: 1192; Churchill, "Britain's Foreign Policy," *Weekly Dispatch*, June 22, 1919, reprinted in Churchill, *Collected Essays*, 1: 217; Churchill, *World Crisis: The Aftermath*, 75; Gilbert, *Winston S. Churchill: The Stricken World*, 228; Churchill, "Fantastic Trial in Moscow,"

Daily Telegraph, December 4, 1930, reprinted in Churchill, *Collected Essays,* 2: 211. Also see Gilbert, *Companion,* 4/2: 1251–1252, 4/1: 550; Ulam, *Expansion and Coexistence,* 112; Rhodes James, *Speeches,* 3: 2917–2927, 3011.

15. Churchill quoted in Rhodes James, *Speeches,* 3: 3024. Also see Gilbert, *Winston S. Churchill: The Stricken World,* 346–349, 430; Rhodes James, *British Revolution,* 2: 145–146; Beaverbrook, *Politicians and the War,* 28; Blake, *Unknown Prime Minister,* 233–235; Carlton, *Churchill and the Soviet Union,* 31.

16. Churchill quoted in Rhodes James, *Speeches,* 6: 5927. Also see Gilbert, *Companion,* 4/1: 613; Churchill, *Age of Revolution,* 225; Strom, *Uncle Give Us Bread;* Rhodes James, *Speeches,* 6: 6426; Churchill, "Enemies to the Left," September 4, 1936, in *Step by Step,* 44–46; Churchill, "The Communist Schism," October 16, 1936, in *Step by Step,* 53–56; Churchill, "The Creeds of the Devil," *Sunday Chronicle,* June 27, 1937, reprinted in Churchill, *Collected Essays,* 2: 394–397; Soames, *Winston and Clementine,* 417; Ulam, *Stalin,* 361, 364–366, 395, 399–409; Ulam, *Expansion and Coexistence,* 183, 244–245; Gilbert, *Winston S. Churchill: 1922–1939,* 720–724, 740; Soames, *Winston and Clementine,* 391; Charmley, *Churchill: The End of Glory,* 332.

17. Churchill quoted in Gilbert, *Winston S. Churchill: 1922–1939,* 738. Also see Gilbert, *Companion,* 5/3: 448; Gilbert, *Winston S. Churchill: 1922–1939,* 738, 777, 983–984, 1053–1054, 1068; Charmley, *Churchill: The End of Glory,* 335, 559–660; Barnes and Nicholson, *Empire at Bay,* 547; Roberts, *Holy Fox,* 149–167; Addison, *Home Front,* 70; Edmonds, "Churchill and Stalin," 311; Churchill, "Towards a Pact with Russia," *Daily Telegraph,* June 8, 1939, reprinted in Churchill, *Collected Essays,* 1: 444–446.

18. Churchill quoted in Churchill, *Great Contemporaries,* 61. Also see Churchill, "Dictatorship on Its Trial," in Churchill, *Collected Essays,* 2: 206–208; Rhodes James, *Churchill: A Study in Failure,* 385–386; Addison, *Home Front,* 105, 161; Addison, *Churchill: The Unexpected Hero,* 49–50; Rhodes James, "The Enigma," 17; Soames, *Winston and Clementine,* 330; Churchill, *Lord Randolph Churchill,* 823; Churchill, *World Crisis: The Aftermath,* 124, 128–129.

19. Churchill quoted in Winston Churchill, "Lloyd George's War Memoirs, Volume 3," *Daily Mail,* September 21, 1934, reprinted in *Collected Essays,* 3: 97; Rhodes James, *Speeches,* 1: 82; Gilbert, *Companion,* 4/2: 872; Churchill, *World Crisis: The Aftermath,* 120, 128. Also see Churchill, *World Crisis: The Aftermath,* 42, 47, 66, 121, 194–196, 211–212, 446; Gilbert, *Winston S. Churchill: The Stricken World,* 10–11; Gilbert, *Companion,* 3/2, 1467–1468; Rhodes James, *Speeches,* 3: 2643, 2645; Gilbert, *Companion,* 4/1: 423; Palmer, *History of the Modern World,* 688; J. Thompson, *Russia, Bolshevism, and the Versailles Peace,* 385–386; C. Webster, *Congress of Vienna,* iii, 147–148.

20. In the heated postwar election of 1918 Churchill did offer support for the League. Churchill quoted in Churchill, *World Crisis: The Aftermath,* 188, 202, 450; Rhodes James, *Speeches,* 3: 2334, 2821, 2875–2876; Churchill, "Britain's Foreign Policy," *Weekly Dispatch,* June 22, 1919, reprinted in Churchill, *Collected Essays,* 1: 215. Also see Ulam, *Expansion and Coexistence,* 103; Rhodes James, *Speeches,* 3: 2642, 2822, 2925–2926, 3019; Churchill, *World Crisis:*

The Aftermath, 136–138, 159, 259; Soames, *Winston and Clementine*, 293; Gilbert, *Winston S. Churchill: The Stricken World*, 290.

21. Churchill quoted in Rhodes James, *Speeches*, 5: 4676; Churchill, *India*, 83–85; Soames, *Winston and Clementine*, 399; Churchill, "Britain's Security Is the Vital Issue," *Daily Mail*, November 12, 1935, reprinted in *Collected Essays*, 1: 355. Also see Gilbert, *Winston S. Churchill: The Stricken World*, 71; Churchill, "Looking Back on Sixty Years," *News of the World*, January 13, 1935, reprinted in Churchill, *Collected Essays*, 3: 127–134; Edwardes, *Last Years of British India*, 3; Beloff, *Britain's Liberal Empire*, 254, 297–299, 346–347; Soames, *Winston and Clementine*, 408; Louis, "Introduction," 12.

22. Churchill quoted in Churchill, *Second World War: Gathering Storm*, 492. Also see Walters, *History of the League of Nations*, 15–29; Beloff, *Britain's Liberal Empire*, 267–268; Knock, *To End All Wars*, 37; Churchill, *World Crisis: The Aftermath*, 146–147, 161; J. Thompson, *Russia, Bolshevism, and the Versailles Peace*, 368–387; Rhodes James, *Speeches*, 3: 2582, 2642, 2926, 5: 5220; Gilbert, *Companion*, 4/1: 613; Cowles, *Winston Churchill*, 240.

23. Churchill quoted in Rhodes James, *Speeches*, 3: 2673; Churchill, *World Crisis: 1911–1914*, 124. Also see Gilbert, *Companion*, 4/3: 1540–1541; Churchill, "Britain's Foreign Policy," *Weekly Dispatch*, June 22, 1919, reprinted in Churchill, *Collected Essays*, 1: 214–217; Beloff, *Britain's Liberal Empire*, 334, 360; Addison, *Churchill: The Unexpected Hero*, 126–129; Gilbert, *Companion*, 5/1: 1030–1035; Soames, *Winston and Clementine*, 331–332.

24. Churchill quoted in Rhodes James, *Speeches*, 7: 7254. Also see Rhodes James, *Speeches*, 7: 7241, 7521; Gilbert, *Winston S. Churchill: "Never Despair,"* 365–372, 391.

25. Churchill quoted in Moran, *Churchill*, 273, 311. Also see Storr, "The Man"; "Churchill 'on Point of Collapse' near War's End: Depressed British PM Took Security Risks: Censor," *Ottawa Citizen*, September 5, 1999; Gilbert, *Winston S. Churchill: "Never Despair,"* 49, 125, 185; Churchill, *Second World War: Triumph and Tragedy*, 583; Rhodes James, *Speeches*, 7: 7141.

26. Churchill quoted in Soames, *Winston and Clementine*, 511, 512–513, 530; Millis, *Forrestal Diaries*, 35. Also see *FRUS 1945: The Conference of Berlin*, 1: 64–78.

27. Churchill quoted in Churchill, *Second World War: Triumph and Tragedy*, 439; Colville, *Fringes*, 563. Also see Gardiner, "Mr. Churchill," 63; Berlin, "Churchill," 6; Churchill, *Second World War: Closing the Ring*, 112, 115; Harriman and Abel, *Special Envoy*, 225–226; Bryant, *Triumph in the West*, 101; PREM 3/355/8–9; PREM 3/396/14; PREM 3/399/6; PREM 3/397/3; Charmley, *Churchill's Grand Alliance*, 102; Ulam, *Stalin*, 581, 585, 593, 596–598, 601, 644; Soames, *Winston and Clementine*, 503, 506; Churchill, *Second World War: Triumph and Tragedy*, 133–134, 198–199, 402–409, 439, 442–445, 449–453, 483; Gilbert, *Winston S. Churchill: Road to Victory*, 1235; Carlton, *Churchill*, 130–131; Rhodes James, *Speeches*, 7: 6943; CAB 65/48/157; Gilbert, *Companion*, 4/2: 1192; Kitchen, *British Policy*, 150; Ben Fenton, "The Secret Strategy to Launch Attack on Red Army" and "Churchill's Plan for a Third

World War against Stalin," *Daily Telegraph*, October 1, 1998; Richard Norton, "Churchill Had Plans for Surprise Attack on Russia in 1945," *Guardian*, printed in the *Pittsburgh Post-Gazette*, October 3, 1998; Ulam, *Rivals*, 7–11, 23–24.

28. Churchill quoted in Gilbert, *Winston S. Churchill: Road to Victory*, 1235. Also see Churchill, *Second World War: Triumph and Tragedy*, 433–434, 498–499; Rhodes James, *Speeches*, 7: 7112, 7117; Colville, *Fringes*, 593; Rhodes James, *Anthony Eden*, 307; Moran, *Churchill*, 295–299.

29. Churchill quoted in Churchill, *Second World War: Triumph and Tragedy*, 498; Rhodes James, *Speeches*, 7539. Also see Rhodes James, *Speeches*, 6: 6474, 7214–7219, 7291, 7645, 7724, 7773, 7791–7795, 7798, 7801–7810, 7819, 7840, 8: 8048; Ulam, *Stalin*, 629–630; Gilbert, *Winston S. Churchill: "Never Despair,"* 154–155, 161, 371, 444; Anderson, *Race and Rapprochement*, 69; Riasanovsky, *History of Russia*, 68–71.

30. Churchill quoted in Rhodes James, *Speeches*, 7: 7291, 7307–7308, 7353, 7379, 7722. Also see Colville, *Fringes*, 478; Rhodes James, *Speeches*, 7: 7228, 7352–7354, 7722; Leffler, *Preponderance of Power*, 1; Churchill, *Second World War: Gathering Storm*, 15.

31. Churchill quoted in Childs, *Britain since 1945*, 19–20; Soames, *Winston and Clementine*, 545, 553. Attlee quoted by Churchill in Rhodes James, *Speeches*, 8: 8262. Also see Wheeler-Bennett, *Action This Day* 96; Gilbert, *Winston S. Churchill: Road to Victory*, 1223; Reynolds, *Brittania Overruled*, 186; Colville, *Fringes*, 433, 476; Gilbert, *Winston S. Churchill: "Never Despair,"* 233, 246, 369, 973; Rhodes James, *Speeches*, 7: 7241, 7278, 7379–7381, 7484, 7487, 7524, 7900, 8: 8135, 8402; Soames, *Winston and Clementine*, 537, 540–541; Boyle, *Churchill-Eisenhower Correspondence*, 167; Thorne, *Allies of a Kind*, xxiii; Moran, *Churchill*, 390; CAB 129/49 c.(52)10; CAB 129/52 c.(52)166; International Monetary Fund, *International Financial Statistics* 8, no. 7 (July 1955); Rhodes James, *Speeches*, 8: 8298–8299, 8459.

32. Churchill quoted in Gilbert, *Winston S. Churchill: "Never Despair,"* 362, 371; Rhodes James, *Speeches*, 7: 7588, 8: 7944, 8507; Colville, *Fringes*, 482. Also see Rhodes James, *Speeches*, 7: 7768–7769, 7777, 7792–7801, 8: 7985, 8630; Gilbert, *Winston S. Churchill: "Never Despair,"* 362, 369; Colville, *Fringes*, 482, 683; Boyle, *Churchill-Eisenhower Correspondence*, 167; Churchill, *Second World War: Triumph and Tragedy*, 431–432; Moran, *Churchill*, 475.

33. Churchill quoted in CAB 129/61/C(53)194. Also see Rhodes James, *Speeches*, 7: 7214, 7300, 7342, 7350, 7396–7397, 7589, 7799, 7807, 8: 7943–7944, 7985, 8254–8258, 8296, 8475–8485; Ulam, *Rivals*, 198; Knight, *Beria*, 185; PREM 3/430/8; Soames, *Winston and Clementine*, 556; Churchill, *Second World War: Triumph and Tragedy*, 198; Gilbert, *Winston S. Churchill: "Never Despair,"* 119, 422, 691–692; Moran, *Churchill*, 456; PREM 419; Boothby, *My Yesterday, Your Tomorrow*, 212; Gilbert, *Winston S. Churchill: Road to Victory*, 999–1000; PREM 3/66–67; *FRUS 1952–54*, 5: 1761; Colville, *Fringes*, 654, 683.

34. Churchill quoted in Rhodes James, *Speeches*, 8: 8199–8200; Gilbert, *Winston*

S. Churchill: "Never Despair," 1009. Also see Woodward, *Documents on British Foreign Policy*, 3: 577, 580–581, 585; Kimball, *Churchill and Roosevelt*, 3: 632; Truman and Ferrell, *Off the Record*, 31–32, 35, 45; PREM 3/430/11; *FRUS 1945: The Conference of Berlin*, 1: 68, 94–95, 265–266; Gilbert, *Winston S. Churchill: "Never Despair,"* 28n2, 167; Rhodes James, *Speeches*, 7: 7161, 7330, 8: 8197–8198; Winston S. Churchill, *Second World War: Grand Alliance*, 594; Wheeler-Bennett, *Action This Day*, 96; Colville, *Fringes*, 672; Moran, *Churchill*, 436; Ambrose, *Eisenhower*, 2: 21.

35. Churchill quoted in Rhodes James, *Speeches*, 7: 7798. Also see Moran, *Churchill*, 459; Rhodes James, *Speeches*, 7: 7032–7033, 7380–7381, 7982–7983; Gilbert, *Winston S. Churchill: "Never Despair,"* 249.

36. Some historians, such as John Lewis Gaddis and Jonathan Rosenberg, contend that Russian detonation of an atomic bomb in 1949 brought Churchill to reconcile himself with Russian Communism and emphasize peaceful coexistence over threats of force. Churchill quoted in Rhodes James, *Speeches*, 7: 7285, 7806–7807, 8: 8224. Attlee quoted in Butler and Pelly, *Documents on British Policy Overseas*, 364, 573–574. Also see Rhodes James, *Speeches*, 7: 7288–7290, 7307, 7808–7810, 8: 8214–8215; Bullen, *Documents on British Policy Overseas*, 529–530; Churchill, *Second World War: Triumph and Tragedy*, 433–434; Rosenberg, "Before the Bomb and After," 171–193; Gaddis, "Conclusion," 260–271.

37. Churchill quoted in Rhodes James, *Speeches*, 8: 8603.

CHAPTER 2. "THE LORD DEALS WITH THE NATIONS AS THE NATIONS DEALT WITH THE JEWS"

1. Mitchell Cohen, *Zion and State*, 71.
2. Berlin quoted in Berlin, "Origins of Israel," 143. Also see Ben-Sasson, *History of the Jewish People*, 802–803; Howard Sachar, *History of Israel*, 18–20; Gilbert, *Exile and Return*, 3–12; Morris, *Righteous Victims*, 4.
3. Gilbert, *Exile and Return*, 13–25; Berlin, "Benjamin Disraeli," 275; Berlin, "Jewish Slavery and Emancipation," 164, 166–170, 174–179.
4. Roth, *History of the Jews*, 1, 9, 23, 90, 91, 149, 157–158, 171, 241, 242–243, 246, 248–250, 265, 259; Roth, *Essays and Portraits*, 266, 269, 274, 284; Finestein, *Short History of Anglo-Jewry*, 9, 24, 88; Rubinstein, *History of the Jews*, 36–40, 46, 48, 76, 121; Howard Sachar, *Modern Jewish History*, 44, 98–99; Palmer, *History of the Modern World*, 166, 452–453, 568–570; Ben-Sasson, *History of the Jewish People*, 802–803; Hertzberg, *Zionist Idea*, 22; Roth, *Benjamin Disraeli*, 84, 92, 125; Black, *Social Politics of Anglo-Jewry*, 8; Modder, *Jew in the Literature*, 193; Jenkins, *Gladstone*, 305.
5. Kedourie quoted in Kedourie, *England*, 82. Churchill quoted in R. Churchill, *Companion*, 1/2: 1231. Also see Bermant, *Cousinhood*, 217–219; Ragussis, *Figures of Conversion*, 1–13, 15–56, 263–264, 281; Handley, "Introduction," xiii; Defries, *Conservative Party Attitudes*, 199; Allfrey, *Edward VII*; Black, *Social Politics of Anglo-Jewry*, 9; Roth, *Essays and Portraits*, 286–294; Poliakov, *Suicidal Europe*, 187–188.

6. In his famous biography of Disraeli, Robert Blake perpetuates Victorian stereotyping, stating that Disraeli's financial incompetence was "certainly un-Jewish." Blake, *Disraeli*, 3, 11, 50, 503; Berlin, "Disraeli," 257, 260, 268; Roth, *Benjamin Disraeli*, 57–58, 67, 85, 86, 142–145, 174; Blake, *Disraeli's Grand Tour*, 125; Ragussis, *Figures of Conversion*, 9; Endelman, "'A Hebrew to the End,'" 113–114; Kissinger, *Diplomacy*, 148–149; Finestein, *Short History of Anglo-Jewry*, 132; Garrard, *English and Immigration*, 86, 89; Feldman, *Englishmen and Jews*, 102; "Jews and the General Election," *Jewish Chronicle*, October 21, 1908, 5; Lewis, "Pro-Islamic Jews."

7. Disraeli quoted in Beaconsfield, *Tancred*, viii, 149; Beaconsfield, *Coningsby*, 250; *Hansard Parliamentary Debates*, 3rd ser., vol. 133 (1854), 962, 969–970. Berlin quoted in Berlin, "Disraeli," 260. Also see Berlin, "Disraeli," 263–264, 274, 275; Roth, *Benjamin Disraeli*, 83; Lewis, "Pro-Islamic Jews," 403; Beaconsfield, *Tancred*, ix; Beaconsfield, *Coningsby*, 213, 220, 366; Beaconsfield, *Lord George Bentinck*, 355; Ragussis, "'Secret' of English Anti-Semitism," 296; Kedourie, *England*, 82; Lewis, "Pro-Islamic Jews," 403; Roth, *Essays and Portraits*, 12, 14.

8. Reverend Damer and Randolph Churchill quoted in Foster, *Lord Randolph Churchill*, 30. Also see Foster, *Lord Randolph Churchill*, 66; R. Churchill, *Companion*, 2/1: 487–490; Ferguson, *World's Banker*, 855, 857, 886; Allfrey, *Edward VII*, 177, 178.

9. Randolph Churchill quoted in "Lord Randolph Churchill on the Situation in Egypt," *Morning Post*, December 19, 1883, 2. Also see Rothschild, *Dear Lord Rothschild*, 26, 30; *Hansard Parliamentary Debates*, 3rd ser., vol. 278 (1854), 1445–1455; Foster, *Lord Randolph Churchill*, 136, 217; Rabinowicz, *Winston Churchill on Jewish Problems*, 85, 202n12; Keay, *Spoiling the Egyptians*; Ferguson, *World's Banker*, 833–838; Roth, *Benjamin Disraeli*, 137; Churchill, *Lord Randolph Churchill*, 1: 226; Jennings, *Speeches*, 1: x, 70–85; "Jews' Free School Dinner," *Jewish Chronicle*, May 23, 1884.

10. Foster, *Lord Randolph Churchill*, 9–10, 59–60, 115, 118, 132; Churchill, *Lord Randolph Churchill*, 1: 30, 68, 256–257, 273.

11. Randolph quoted in *Hansard Parliamentary Debates*, 3rd ser., vol. 278 (1854), 1445, 1447, 1451; "The Late Lord Randolph Churchill," *Jewish Chronicle*, February 1, 1895, 9. Disraeli quoted in Disraeli, *Lord George Bentinck*, 365. Also see *Hansard Parliamentary Debates*, 3rd ser., vol. 278 (1854), 1439–1455; "Jews' Free School Dinner," *Jewish Chronicle*, May 23, 1884, 3.

12. Churchill quoted in Churchill, *My Early Life*, 8; Gilbert, *Winston S. Churchill: "Never Despair,"* 366.

13. Churchill quoted in Churchill, *My Early Life*, 45–46; Allfrey, *Edward VII*, 281–282. Also see Gilbert, "'The Most Horrible Crime,'" 5; Gilbert, speech on November 2, 2001, at Chapman University, Orange, CA, televised on C-Span on December 8, 2001; Gilbert, *Churchill: A Life*, 61, 180, 181, 185; Allfrey, *Edward VII*, 134, 167, 176, 178–180, 199, 230, 249, 255, 271, 278–279; Rubinstein, *History of the Jews*, 131–132.

14. Churchill quoted in Churchill, *Great Democracies*, 285; Churchill, *Second World War: Closing the Ring*, 471. Also see Churchill, "Moses," 213.
15. Neither Cecil Roth nor Oskar Rabinowicz could find Disraeli using this phrase, and neither could I. Churchill quoted in "Protest Meetings," *Jewish Chronicle*, December 15, 1905, 31. Also see Rabinowicz, *Winston Churchill on Jewish Problems*, 198n90; Roth, *Benjamin Disraeli*, 82.
16. Churchill quoted in R. Churchill, *Companion*, 1/2: 976; CHAR 28/27, p. 55. Also see Howard Sachar, *Modern Jewish History*, 230–233.
17. Churchill's son, Randolph, and Roy Jenkins estimate that 6.5 percent of the electorate (740 out of 11,411) was Jewish, while John Garrard claims 8.7 percent (1,000 Jews). Addison, *Home Front*, 62; R. Churchill, *Winston S. Churchill: Young Statesman*, 113; Jenkins, *Churchill*, 108; Garrard, *English and Immigration*, 86, 122n3; Alderman, *British Politics*, 69, 75; Defries, *Conservative Party Attitudes*, 16.
18. In an interview cited in his obituary, Isaiah Berlin suggests that as a Jew, he always was made to feel as an outsider. Marilyn Berger, "Isaiah Berlin, Philosopher and Pluralist, Is Dead at 88," *New York Times*, November 7, 1997. Churchill quoted in Rhodes James, *Speeches*, 1: 684, 685.
19. Churchill quoted in "The Aliens Bill in Committee," *Jewish Chronicle*, July 1, 1904, 17; "The Aliens Bill," *Jewish Chronicle*, June 3, 1904, 9; CHAR 4/1, p. 35. Balfour quoted in Finestein, *Short History of Anglo-Jewry*, 139. Also see Morris, *Righteous Victims*, 24–25; Alderman, *British Politics*, 66; Rubinstein, *History of the Jews*, 95; Finestein, *Short History of Anglo-Jewry*, 131; Rabinowicz, *Winston Churchill on Jewish Problems*, 165; R. Churchill, *Companion*, 2/1: 356; "The Working of the Aliens Act," *Jewish Chronicle*, December 28, 1906, 11; "The New Government and the Jews" (editorial), *Jewish Chronicle*, December 15, 1905, 11; Rabinowicz, *Winston Churchill on Jewish Problems*, 49–63; Reinharz, *Chaim Weizmann*, 274, 488n96; Poliakov, *Suicidal Europe*, 195.
20. Harry Samuel quoted in "Abandonment of the Aliens Bill," *Jewish Chronicle*, July 15, 1904, 21. Churchill quoted in "The Aliens Bill," *Jewish Chronicle*, December 2, 1904, 12; R. Churchill, *Companion*, 2/1, 358. Also see R. Churchill, *Companion*, 2/1, 359, 646–647, 2/2: 763; *Hansard Parliamentary Debates*, 4th ser., vol. 148 (1904), 860, 875; Rabinowicz, *Winston Churchill on Jewish Problems*, 58–59; Rhodes James, *Speeches*, 1: 984.
21. Churchill quoted in "Protest Meetings," *Jewish Chronicle*, December 15, 1905, 31; "The Aliens Act," *Jewish Chronicle*, October 13, 1905, 20; "Manchester," *Jewish Chronicle*, May 17, 1907, 32; CHAR 4/22, p. 9. Also see Rabinowicz, *Winston Churchill on Jewish Problems*, 79; "Mr. Winston Churchill and the Aliens Act," *Jewish Chronicle*, January 19, 1906, 33; "The Naturalisation Fee," *Jewish Chronicle*, August 2, 1907, 17; CHAR 4/22, pp. 2, 5, 7, 8, 11.
22. Charles Churchill quoted in Kobler, *The Vision Was There*, 63–64. Disraeli quoted in Blake, *Disraeli's Grand Tour*, 67; Howard Sachar, *History of Israel*, 21. George Eliot quoted in Handley, "Introduction," xiii, 496–497. Also see S. Cohen, *English Zionists*, 5–6; Finestein, *Short History of Anglo-Jewry*, 36, 93,

186; Kobler, *The Vision Was There*, 16, 18, 59–60, 89–91; C. Webster, *Foreign Policy*, 1: 761–763; Howard Sachar, *History of Israel*, 20, 22; Fromkin, *Peace to End All Peace*, 268–269; Berlin, "Weizmann," 35–36; Shepherd, *Zealous Intruders*, 107; Gilbert, *Exile and Return*, 28; Blake, *Disraeli's Grand Tour*, 65, 112, 131–132; Roth, *Benjamin Disraeli*, 74.

23. Hess presaged other Zionists who identified with Italian nationalists, such as Vladimir Jabotinsky, the twentieth-century leader of the Revisionist Zionists, who idolized Giuseppe Garibaldi. David Bergman brought this to my attention. Hess quoted in Hess, *Rome and Jerusalem*, 39, 101–102. Also see Berlin, "Life and Opinions," 213, 217, 218, 220–222, 224, 227–228, 230–232, 237, 244, 249, 250; Hertzberg, *Zionist Idea*, 36–38; Hess, *Rome and Jerusalem*, 28–29, 92,111; Howard Sachar, *History of Israel*, 11; Katz, *Vladimir (Ze'ev) Jabotinsky*, 1: 33.

24. Hertzberg, *Zionist Idea*, 33–37, 42–44; Berlin, "Weizmann," 37–38; Berlin, "Origins of Israel," 150–152; Gilbert, *Exile and Return*, 38, 40–43; Howard Sachar, *History of Israel*, 13–17.

25. Herzl quoted in Herzl, *Jewish State*, 37–40, 43; Hertzberg, *Zionist Idea*, 50. Also see Hertzberg, *Zionist Idea*, 46, 48; Howard Sachar, *History of Israel*, 36–44; Morris, *Righteous Victims*, 20–21; Herzl, *Jewish State*, 16, 20, 25–26, 109, 111; Lowenthal, *Diaries of Theodor Herzl*, 210, 224, 245; Berlin, "Weizmann," 33.

26. Herzl quoted in Lowenthal, *Diaries of Theodor Herzl*, 224; Bein, *Herzl*, 369. Rothschild quoted in S. Cohen, *English Zionists*, 89. Also see Finestein, *Short History of Anglo-Jewry*, 144–146; Howard Sachar, *History of Israel*, 44–52; Lowenthal, *Diaries of Theodor Herzl*, 240, 268; Morris, *Righteous Victims*, 23; Hertzberg, *Zionist Idea*, 229; Peretz, "God That Did Not Fail."

27. Herzl quoted in Howard Sachar, *History of Israel*, 53. Also see Howard Sachar, *History of Israel*, 52–56, 59–63; Lowenthal, *Diaries of Theodor Herzl*, 374, 395, 398, 440; Poliakov, *Suicidal Europe*, 195; Peretz, "God That Did Not Fail."

28. A late 1905 article in the *Manchester Courier* that discussed various Jewish nationalist schemes, including those of Herzl, was sent to Churchill and remained among his papers, but it is unclear whether he ever read it. Churchill quoted in "The East African Project," *Jewish Chronicle*, December 23, 1904, 11. Also see CHAR 10/7; *Hansard Parliamentary Debates*, 4th ser. vol. 136 (1904), 561–579.

29. Israel Zangwill quoted in CO 533/24, p. 141; "Mr. Winston Churchill and the Aliens Act," *Jewish Chronicle*, January 19, 1906, 33. Churchill quoted in R. Churchill, *Companion*, 2/1, 495–496. Also see S. Cohen, *English Zionists*, 85; Finestein, *Short History of Anglo-Jewry*, 145; Reinharz, *Chaim Weizmann*, 278; Gilbert, *Exile and Return*, 62; Alderman, *British Politics*, 93; CHAR 10/7, p. 4; CHAR 10/5; *Hansard Parliamentary Debates*, 3rd ser., vol. 278 (1854), 1446.

30. Zangwill quoted in CHAR 10/7, p. 4. Also see S. Cohen, *English Zionists*, 86, 124, 148, 251.

31. Churchill quoted in Hansard *Parliamentary Debates*, 4th series, vol. 49 (1906), 642; R. Churchill, *Companion*, 2/1: 552–553. Zangwill quoted in CHAR 10/13, p. 4. Also see CHAR 10/13, p. 4; Hertzberg, *Zionist Idea*, 203; CO 533/24, p. 138.
32. Churchill quoted in Churchill, *My African Journey*, 32, 127. Also see Churchill, *My African Journey*, 59; Hyam, *Elgin*, 408; Safran, *Israel*, 20.
33. Reinharz, *Chaim Weizmann*, 276–277, 279; Stein, *Balfour Declaration*, 150.
34. Moses Gaster quoted in CHAR 10/5, p. 2. Also see Harry Sachar, "Dr. Moses Gaster," 125–126; CHAR 10/5, pp. 3–4; CHAR 4/13.
35. Gaster quoted in CZA A203/149. Churchill quoted in Churchill, *Second World War: Closing the Ring*, 470. Also see Bayme, "Jewry and Judaism," 412.
36. A letter from David Lloyd George, sympathetically expressing an apology for his absence, was also read at the meeting. Adam Smith's *The Theory of Moral Sentiments* (1759) ushered in English philosophical and literary discussion about "sympathy"; I am grateful to Michael Hurwitz for bringing this to my attention. Gaster quoted in CZA A203/180. Churchill quoted in GP. Also see "English Zionist Federation: Annual Meeting," *Jewish Chronicle*, February 7, 1908, 25.
37. In response to Churchill's initial draft, Gaster expressed the hope that the "views which I then expressed" in their recent conversation "and which I recognize in the concluding part of your letter, will commend themselves also in our time to the English Government." Gaster's message then prompted a new draft and Marsh's note. Churchill's son Randolph revealed the deleted paragraph in 1964. Churchill quoted in GP; "Zionist Demonstration: Dr. Gaster Speaks," *Jewish Chronicle*, February 7, 1908, 26. Deleted passage quoted in "Sir Winston Was for Zionism in 1908," *Jewish Chronicle*, December 18, 1964, 1. Also see "Manchester Zionists," *Manchester Courier*, February 3, 1908; CZA A203/278.
38. Churchill quoted in Rhodes James, *Speeches*, 1: 984–985, 1012; "North-West Manchester Election: The Vote—Some Moralisings," *Jewish Chronicle*, May 1, 1908, 13; R. Churchill, *Companion*, 2/2: 782. *Jewish Chronicle* report on election eve in "The North-West Manchester Election," April 14, 1908, 11. Also see Alderman, *British Politics*, 79–82; R. Churchill, *Winston Churchill: Young Statesman*, 114, 249; "The North-West Manchester Election," "Among the Jewish Electors," and "The Haham and Mr. Winston Churchill," *Jewish Chronicle*, April 24, 1908, 10–13; Defries, *Conservative Party Attitudes*, 93–94, 102.
39. Churchill quoted in Rhodes James, *Speeches*, 2: 1100; GP. Dulberg quoted in Joseph Dulberg, letter to the editor, *Jewish Chronicle*, April 10, 1908, 15. *Jewish Chronicle* report on Churchill loss in "North-West Manchester Election: The Vote—Some Moralisings," *Jewish Chronicle*, May 1, 1908, 13. Also see CHAR 4/13; CHAR 4/17, p. 41; "Mr. Churchill at Manchester," *Jewish Chronicle*, October 16, 1908, 8; *Daily Mirror*, October 15, 1908, 8–9.
40. The Churchill papers for his early Dundee years contain no letters from

obvious Jewish constituents and none discuss Jewish issues. Tony Paterson's *A Seat for Life*, the only study dedicated to Churchill's representation of Dundee, makes virtually no reference to any Jewish or Zionist issue being raised by constituents. *Jewish Chronicle* quoted criticism in "Mr. Winston Churchill's Promises" and "Unfulfilled Pledges" (editorials), *Jewish Chronicle*, October 21, 1910, 5–6. Also see CHAR 5/1–6, 10, 11; Paterson, *A Seat for Life*, 13; Alderman, *British Politics*, 82; Addison, *Home Front*, 64; "Mr. Winston Churchill and the Aliens Act," *Jewish Chronicle*, October 21, 1910, 16; "Mr. Churchill's Opportunity" (editorial), *Jewish Chronicle*, February 18, 1910, 18; "The Administration of the Aliens Act," *Jewish Chronicle*, February 25, 1910, 20; "The Home Office and the Aliens Act," "Concessions," and "Appeals" (editorials), *Jewish Chronicle*, June 10, 1910, 5–6; "At Home" (editorial), *Jewish Chronicle*, September 30, 1910, 17; "The Shops Bill," *Jewish Chronicle*, October 6, 1911, 21; "The Home Secretary and Sunday Closing" (editorial), *Jewish Chronicle*, October 13, 1911, 7; "The Shops Bill," *Jewish Chronicle*, June 10, 1911, 11; "The Need for a Receiving House" (editorial), *Jewish Chronicle*, December 1, 1911, 8.

41. Churchill quoted in R. Churchill, *Companion*, 2/2: 1244. Also see Feldman, *Englishmen and Jews*, 359–361, 366–370; Michael Cohen, *Churchill*, 40–41; R. Churchill, *Companion*, 2/2: 1245; Churchill, "Battle of Sidney Street," 41–47; Addison, *Home Front*, 122; R. Churchill, *Winston S. Churchill: Young Statesman*, 424–425; Rabinowicz, *Winston Churchill on Jewish Problems*, 167–170, 172; "The Government and the Outbreak" and "In the Affected District," *Jewish Chronicle*, August 25, 1911, 11; "The Anti-Jewish Riots in Wales," *Jewish Chronicle*, October 20, 1911, 15.

42. The government's investment brought an outstanding return; by one account the shares still owned by the state had appreciated 240,000 percent by 1987, eight years before the state sold its last shares of British Petroleum (now BP). Churchill quoted in Rhodes James, *Speeches*, 3: 2317–2318. Watson Rutherford quoted in *Hansard Parliamentary Debates*, 5th series, vol. 63 (1914), 1229. Also see G. Jones, "British Government and the Oil Companies"; Jack, "Purchase of the British Government's Shares"; Henriques, *Marcus Samuel*, 46; CAB 37/115; Rhodes James, *Speeches*, 3: 2306–2319; "Reaping the Rewards of Tough Decisions," *Financial Times*, March 20, 1987; "Britain Sells Last Shares in British Petroleum," *New York Times*, December 6, 1995.

CHAPTER 3. "ZIONISM VERSUS BOLSHEVISM"

1. S. Cohen, *English Zionists*, 124, 148, 251.
2. Samuel quoted in CAB 37/123, 43. Asquith quoted in Asquith, *Memories*, 2: 71, 78. Also see Kedourie, *Anglo-Arab Labyrinth*, 55, 57; Samuel, *Memoirs*, 142–144; Kedourie, *Chatham House*, 52–53; Bowle, *Viscount Samuel*, 170–177; Fromkin, *Peace to End All Peace*, 269–270; Stein, *Balfour Declaration*, 103–116; Asquith, *Memories*, 2: 261; Asquith, *Letters to Venetia Stanley*, 306, 321, 406, 477–478, 600; Berlin, "Weizmann," 36–37; Gilbert, *Companion*, 3/1: 691n1.

3. David Lloyd George quoted in Gilbert, *Companion,* 3/1: 670; Asquith, *Letters to Venetia Stanley,* 477. Asquith quoted in Asquith, *Letters to Venetia Stanley,* 478. Churchill quoted in CAB 22/1, pp. 76–78. Also see Gilbert, *Winston S. Churchill: 1914–1916,* 320; CHAR 26/2; Gilbert, *Companion,* 3/1: 605, 611, 665–666, 659, 671, 713; Churchill, *World Crisis: 1915,* 198; Kedourie, *England,* 30; Fromkin, *Peace to End All Peace,* 137, 139; Stein, *Balfour Declaration,* 109; Asquith, *Memories,* 78.
4. Churchill's missive on Belgium and Palestine was written on March 19, 1915. Kedourie, citing V. H. Rothwell, wrongly attributes this note to Grey. Weizmann in his memoirs placed his meeting with Churchill around March 1916, which was impossible since Churchill was then serving on the western front and no longer first lord of the Admiralty. Their encounter had to have taken place around March 1915. Churchill quoted in FO 800/88, p. 332. Also see Kedourie, *Anglo-Arab Labyrinth,* 56; Rothwell, *British War Aims,* 26; Morris, *Righteous Victims,* 7; FO 800/88, p. 271; Asquith, *Memories,* 82; Fromkin, *Peace to End All Peace,* 140; Weizmann, *Trial and Error,* 172–173; Lloyd George, *War Memoirs: 1915–1916,* 49–50; Stein, *Balfour Declaration,* 119–120n15; CHAR 13.
5. Gilbert, *Winston S. Churchill: 1914–1916,* 448–826; Gilbert, *Winston S. Churchill: The Stricken World,* 1–31; Gilbert, *Companion,* 3/2.
6. The key McMahon letter to the sherif was dated October 24, 1915. Kedourie, *Anglo-Arab Labyrinth,* 3, 61–137; Kedourie, *England,* 50–57, 80, 99–100, 110, 112–117, 120–122, 135, 153, 159; Feith, "Palestine and Zionism," 216–217, 219; Gilbert, *Companion,* 4/2: 1305n2; Gilbert, *Winston S. Churchill: 1914–1916,* 200; Gilbert, *Exile and Return,* 86–91; Howard Sachar, *History of Israel,* 92–96; Morris, *Righteous Victims,* 69, 76–77; Lloyd George, *Peace Conference,* 2: 724.
7. Gilbert, *Exile and Return,* 85–86, 96–97, 105, 110; Howard Sachar, *History of Israel,* 98–99, 102–107, 112–115; CAB 23/245; Stein, *Balfour Declaration,* v, 28, 328, 543, 551–552, 572–573, 605–606; Sykes, *Israel,* 20–22, 26–28; Beloff, *Britain's Liberal Empire,* 262–263; Meinertzhagen, *Middle East Diary,* 9; Black, *Social Politics of Anglo-Jewry,* 357; Finestein, *Short History of Anglo-Jewry,* 80; S. Cohen, *English Zionists,* 238, 239, 243–244, 276, 295; Berlin, "Weizmann," 36–37; Poliakov, *Suicidal Europe,* 190–191; Lloyd George, *Peace Conference,* 2: 733.
8. Balfour Declaration reprinted in "The Charter of Zionism," *Zionist Review* 1, no. 8 (December 1917), 121. Balfour quoted in CAB 23/261; Meinertzhagen, *Middle East Diary,* 9. Also see Sykes, *Israel,* 22–27; Morris, *Righteous Victims,* 86; Howard Sachar, *History of Israel,* 107–112; Hansard Parliamentary Debates, 5th ser., vol. 99 (1917), 382; Stein, *Balfour Declaration,* 562; "A Jewish Triumph" (editorial), *Jewish Chronicle,* November 9, 1917, 5–6; "Retrospect and Prospect" (editorial), *Zionist Review* 1, no. 8 (December 1917), 122.
9. Gilbert, *Exile and Return,* 110; Howard Sachar, *History of Israel,* 111; Stein, *Balfour Declaration,* 559, 472–573.

10. Gilbert, *Exile and Return*, 122–123; Howard Sachar, *History of Israel*, 117; Feith, "Palestine and Zionism," 227; Laqueur and Rubin, *The Israel-Arab Reader*, 35; Gilbert, *Winston S. Churchill: The Stricken World*, 482, 660; Gilbert, *Companion*, 4/2: 1337n1.
11. Samuel quoted in CHAR 15/157C, p. 273. Joynson-Hicks quoted in "Some Appreciations," *Zionist Review* 1, no. 8 (December 1917), 138; Churchill quoted in Rhodes James, *Speeches*, 3: 2584. Lloyd George quoted in Lloyd George, *War Memoirs: 1917*, 97–98. Also see MUN 5/131/1000/88; CHAR 15; "Some Appreciations," *Zionist Review* 1, no. 8 (December 1917), 128–142; Gilbert, *Churchill and Zionism*, 6; Holland, "British Empire," 134.
12. There is no mention of the Balfour Declaration among Churchill's constituent papers at this time. CHAR 5/19.
13. CAB 23; Gilbert, *Companion*, 4/1: 153–226; Grigg, "Churchill and Lloyd George," 103–104; Beaverbrook, *Politicians and the War*, 25–28; Blake, *Unknown Prime Minister*, 56, 233–235; Rhodes James, *Churchill: A Study in Failure*, 116–117, 120; Rhodes James, *British Revolution*, 2: 112, 130.
14. J. D. Gregory quoted in Gilbert, *Exile and Return*, 120. Austen Chamberlain quoted in Defries, *Conservative Party Attitudes*, 5. Also see Gilbert, *Winston S. Churchill: The Stricken World*, 229, 400–411, 342n2; Holmes, *Anti-Semitism*, 141–143; Poliakov, *Suicidal Europe*, 198–200, 209, 212; Rabinowicz, *Winston Churchill on Jewish Problems*, 87, 176; Fromkin, *Peace to End All Peace*, 468–469; Cesarani, *Jewish Chronicle*, 136; Gilbert, *Exile and Return*, 126; Marsden, *Protocols*; Ben-Sasson, *History of the Jewish People*, 981–982; Ulam, *Bolsheviks*, 437; "Jews Denounce 'Protocols of Zion,'" *New York Times*, December 1, 1920, 17; Kadish, *Bolsheviks and British Jews*, 12; Rhodes James, *Speeches*, 3: 3005.
15. Churchill quoted in Gilbert, *Companion*, 4/1: 444, 4/2: 860. Jenny Churchill quoted in Gilbert, *Companion*, 3/2: 1368. Also see Defries, *Conservative Party Attitudes*, 199.
16. Churchill quoted in Rhodes James, *Speeches*, 3: 2822, 2919, 3136; Churchill, "Zionism versus Bolshevism," *Illustrated Sunday Herald*, February 8, 1920, reprinted in Churchill, *Collected Essays*, 4: 28; Gilbert, *Companion*, 4/2: 1010, 1012, 4/3: 1657, 1699, 1874. Also see Ulam, *Bolsheviks*, 375; Ben-Sasson, *History of the Jewish People*, 979; Feith, "Palestine and Zionism," 223–224; CHAR 22/7; Gilbert, *Churchill and Zionism*, 6; "Churchill and the Jew-Bolshevist Lie," *Jewish Chronicle*, January 9, 1920, 9.
17. Churchill quoted in Gilbert, *Companion*, 4/2: 912, 4/1: 677; Churchill, "Zionism versus Bolshevism," 4: 27. Poliakov, *Suicidal Europe*, 88–134, 172–173, 314–315; Rabinowicz, *Winston Churchill on Jewish Problems*, 89–92; Ulam, *Bolsheviks*, 375, 457; Berlin, "Weizmann," 40.
18. Churchill quoted in Churchill, "Zionism versus Bolshevism."
19. Churchill's personal military assistant Archibald Sinclair contributed notes to Churchill's article on such issues as the role of Jewish Bolsheviks, the alleged immunity of Jewish buildings to Bolshevik ruthlessness, and non-Jewish Russian hatred of Jews. Churchill quoted in Churchill, "Zionism

versus Bolshevism." Also see Gilbert, *Companion*, 4/2: 1028–1029; N. Webster, *French Revolution*, 20–21, 492–497.

20. "Mr. Churchill, Zionism, and the Jews" (editorial), *Jewish Chronicle*, February 13, 1920, 8; "Mr. Winston Churchill and Zionism" (editorial), *Zionist Review* 3, no. 11 (March 1920), 175.

21. Disraeli quoted in Disraeli, *Lord George Bentinck*, 357–358. Weizmann quoted in Stein, *Balfour Declaration*, 348–349; Meinertzhagen, *Middle East Diary*, 14. Berlin quoted in Berlin, "Weizmann," 48–49.

22. Gilbert, *Companion*, 4/2: 1032.

23. Churchill quoted in Gilbert, *Companion*, 4/2: 1249. Also see Gilbert, *Winston S. Churchill: The Stricken World*, 488; Gilbert, *Companion*, 4/2: 937–939, 959–960, 1119–1120; R. Churchill, *Companion*, 1/2: 750; CHAR 24/1; Rhodes James, *Speeches*, 3: 2951; CHAR 17/4, p. 12; Lewis, *Emergence of Modern Turkey*, 241–242.

24. Churchill quoted in Gilbert, *Companion*, 4/2: 938. Also see Gilbert, *Companion*, 4/2: 959, 992, 1249–1250, 1260–1261n1, 1267, 1272; Gilbert, *Winston S. Churchill: The Stricken World*, 498; CO 732/4; Kedourie, *England*, 52–53; Kedourie, *Chatham House*, 74; "Treaty of Sèvres: General Staff Views on Modification of Terms," War Office, February 16, 1921, CO 732/4, p. 15; Fromkin, *Peace to End All Peace*, 429–430, 432, 460, 465.

25. Churchill quoted in Gilbert, *Companion*, 4/2: 938–939. Also see Gilbert, *Winston S. Churchill: The Stricken World*, 482, 484, 492n1; Gilbert, *Companion*, 4/2: 937; Kedourie, *England*, 197; Stein, *Balfour Declaration*, 606–620.

26. Churchill quoted in CHAR 16/34, pp. 25. Also see Meinertzhagen, *Middle East Diary*, 79–89; CHAR 16/34, pp. 48–51; Kedourie, *Chatham House*, 57, 402–403n15.

27. Churchill quoted in Gilbert, *Companion*, 4/2: 938; Gilbert, *Winston S. Churchill: The Stricken World*, 71.

28. Churchill quoted in Gilbert, *Companion*, 4/2: 1119–1120, 1267. Also see Fromkin, *Peace to End All Peace*, 439; Gilbert, *Companion*, 4/2: 959; Kedourie, *England*, 149, 165, 175.

29. Hussein quoted in Howard Sachar, *History of Israel*, 120. Faisal quoted in Howard Sachar, *History of Israel*, 121. Also see Kedourie, *Anglo-Arab Labyrinth*, 314; Kedourie, *England*, 142, 151–152, 156, 172; Morris, *Righteous Victims*, 76, 78; Howard Sachar, *History of Israel*, 122; Stein, *Balfour Declaration*, 641–643; *Documents Relating to the Palestine Problem*, 17–18, 20; Fromkin, *Peace to End All Peace*, 435–439; Kedourie, *Chatham House*, 57.

30. Churchill quoted in Gilbert, *Companion*, 4/2: 1120, 1199, 1304. Also see Fromkin, *Peace to End All Peace*, 387, 452–453; Dilks, *Chamberlain*, 276; Gilbert, *Companion*, 4/2: 1119, 1123, 1261–1262; Kedourie, *England*, 182, 190, 193, 208, 209, 211; Rhodes James, *Speeches*, 3: 2947–2948, 2950.

31. Churchill quoted in Gilbert, *Companion*, 4/2: 939, 1250, 1261; Rhodes James, *Speeches*, 3: 3102. Also see Gilbert, *Companion*, 3/1: 671; Robinson and Gallagher, *Africa and the Victorians*, 462–472.

32. Rhodes James, *Speeches*, 3: 2951.

33. Weizmann quoted in CZA Z4/10287. Also see CHAR 22/3, p. 58; "Palestine under the Colonial Office" (editorial), *Zionist Review* 4, no. 10 (February 1921), 178.

CHAPTER 4. "SMILING ORCHARDS"

1. Churchill quoted in CHAR 22/2, p. 59; Gilbert, *Companion*, 4/2: 1296; CHAR 17/2, 9. Curzon quoted in Gilbert, *Companion*, 4/2: 1298. Also see Gilbert, *Companion*, 4/2: 1349, 4/3: 1539–1543; Addison, *Home Front*, 218–219.
2. "Arabist" is used in this book to refer to someone who favors Arab interests. That is its more popular meaning. The term can mean, and used to mean exclusively, a specialist or scholar in Arab culture, history, language or literature. Lewis, "Question of Orientalism," 49.
3. Younger quoted in Michael Cohen, *Churchill*, 111. Ormsby-Gore quoted in Michael Cohen, *Churchill*, 137–138. Churchill quoted in Rhodes James, *Speeches*, 3: 3342. Also see Michael Cohen, *Churchill*, 110–112, 137–138; Alderman, *British Politics*, 193n115; Gilbert, *Winston S. Churchill: The Stricken World*, 527, 599, 648, 650; Barnes and Nicholson, *Empire at Bay*, 425; Rhodes James, *Speeches*, 3: 3344–3346; Sykes, *Israel*, 18–19; Hurwitz, "Churchill and Palestine," 21–23; Reguer, "Rutenberg," 692–697.
4. Churchill quoted in Gilbert, *Companion*, 4/2: 1346; CO 732/5, p. 63; CHAR 17/15, p. 164; Rhodes James, *Speeches*, 3: 3089, 3118; CAB 32/2; CHAR 17/11. Also see "Mr. Churchill on Economy," *Times* (London), February 15, 1921, p. 12; "Mesopotamia and Mr. Churchill," *Times* (London), February 23, 1921, p. 11; CZA Z4/14841 I; Gilbert, *Winston S. Churchill: The Stricken World*, 3n1, 24–25n3; Gilbert, *Companion*, 4/3: 1630; Fromkin, *Peace to End All Peace*, 470, 499.
5. Churchill quoted in CO 733/14, p. 53; CZA Z4/1841 I; Rhodes James, *Speeches*, 3: 3096, 3263, 3343. Also see Gilbert, *Companion*, 4/2: 1345, 1371–1372, 4/3: 1585–1586; Gilbert, *Winston S. Churchill: The Stricken World*, 624, 642–645; Rhodes James, *Speeches*, 3: 3095–3111, 3264, 3342–3351.
6. Churchill quoted in Rhodes James, *Speeches*, 3: 3350. Also see Sykes, *Israel*, 77–78; CO 733/14, p. 53; Gilbert, *Companion*, 4/3: 1588–1589; Reguer, "Rutenberg," 691–692.
7. Churchill quoted in Rhodes James, *Speeches*, 3: 3096, 3110; Gilbert, *Companion*, 4/3: 1491, 1498. Lloyd George quoted in CAB 23/42. Also see Gilbert, *Companion*, 4/3: 1489–1490, 1499–1502; Stein, *Balfour Declaration*, 606–607; CAB 23/42; CAB 32/2; Sykes, *Israel*, 20; Beloff, *Britain's Liberal Empire*, 284.
8. The editor, Thomas Marlowe, quoted in Gilbert, *Companion*, 4/3: 1478. Beaverbrook quoted in Gilbert, *Companion*, 4/3: 1478, 1807. Chamberlain quoted in Gilbert, *Companion*, 4/3: 1814. Also see Gilbert, *Winston S. Churchill: The Stricken World*, 690–698.
9. Some have questioned the authenticity of portions of the Meinertzhagen diaries as contemporary records. Churchill quoted in H. Young, *Independent Arab*, 324. Young quoted in Marsh, *Number of People*, 399. Weizmann quoted

in CZA Z4/868. Meinertzhagen quoted in Meinertzhagen, *Middle East Diary*, 33. Also see Gilbert, *Companion*, 4/2: 1295, 1299–1300, 1320–1321; Gilbert, *Winston S. Churchill: The Stricken World*, 514, 582; CAB 32/2; Rhodes James, *Speeches*, 3: 3100, 3111; Addison, *Home Front*, 72; CHAR 17/4, p. 13; Lockman, *Meinertzhagen's Diary Ruse*, 1–3; Gilbert, *Companion*, 4/3: 2122, 2125; Mack, *Prince of Our Disorder*, 314; Wilson, *Lawrence of Arabia*, 645–646, 1117n6; Lawrence, *Seven Pillars of Wisdom*, 393; Klieman, *Foundation of British Policy*, 248; Fromkin, *Peace to End All Peace*, 498.

10. Curzon quoted in Kedourie, *Chatham House*, 79. Kedourie quoted in Kedourie, *Chatham House*, 77–78. Also see Kedourie, *England*, 179, 193; Gilmour, "Unregarded Prophet," 60–68.

11. Churchill quoted in CHAR 17/2, pp. 3–4. Also see CHAR 17/2, p. 13; CHAR 17/11; Gilbert, *Companion*, 4/2: 1295; CO 732/4, p. 171.

12. CAB 24/126, pp. 166–167.

13. McMahon quoted in Klieman, *Foundation of British Policy*, 229n68. Also see Gilbert, *Companion*, 4/2: 1314; Kedourie, *England*, 179–180; Gilbert, *Winston S. Churchill: The Stricken World*, 502–503, 537–541; CAB 24/126, p. 133, 174; CZA Z4/10287; Klieman, *Foundation of British Policy*, 96, 228; CHAR 17/13A; Fromkin, *Peace to End All Peace*, 441–443; Jenkins, *Churchill*, 360; Rhode James, *Speeches*, 3: 3070–3083.

14. Churchill quoted in CO 732/5, p. 63; CAB 32/2. Also see CO 732/5, p. 65; Kedourie, *England*, 209–212; Kedourie, *Chatham House*, 249–256.

15. Churchill quoted in Busch, *Britain, India and the Arabs*, 474; CAB 24/126, pp. 171, 173. Abdullah quoted in CAB 24/126, p. 172. Herbert Sidebotham quoted in Gilbert, *Winston S. Churchill: The Stricken World*, 584. Also see Kedourie, *England*, 207; Busch, *Britain, India and the Arabs*, 467–474; CAB 24/126, 166, 174; Kedourie, *Chatham House*, 215;

16. Lloyd George quoted in Gilbert, *Companion*, 4/2: 1407–1408. Kedourie quoted in Kedourie, *Chatham House*, 214. Also see CAB 24/126, pp. 166–167; *Documents Relating to the Palestine Problem*, 8–10; Feith, "Palestine and Zionism," 240; Klieman, *Foundation of British Policy*, 123, 231–235; CHAR 17/7, pp. 88–89; Wilson, *Lawrence of Arabia*, 642; CAB 32/2; Sykes, *Israel*, 76–77.

17. Meinertzhagen quoted in Meinertzhagen, *Middle East Diary*, 112. Also see Meinertzhagen, *Middle East Diary*, 97–98; CHAR 17/4, p. 51; Morris, *Righteous Victims*, 103; Gilbert, *Winston S. Churchill: The Stricken World*, 583, 638–641, 665–748; Kedourie, *Chatham House*, 58–69; CO 733/17A, p. 422; Klieman, *Foundation of British Policy*, 201; Michael Cohen, *Churchill*, 122.

18. Churchill quoted in CO 733/14, p. 53. Also see CO 733/13, pp. 156–163; Gilbert, *Companion*, 4/3: 1589, 1614; CO 733/15, pp. 246–247, 249–251; CZA Z4/868.

19. Lloyd George quoted in Meinertzhagen, 105. Also see Fromkin, *Peace to End All Peace*, 447–448; CO 733/3, 153–160; CO 733/5; CZA Z4/868; CO 733/16, p. 267; Wasserstein, *Herbert Samuel*, 256; Gilbert, *Companion*, 4/3: 1476, 1559.

20. Churchill quoted in CZA Z4/868; CO 733/3, p. 180; CO 733/13, p. 557; CO 733/16, pp. 135–136; Rhodes James, *Speeches*, 3: 3107. Sidebotham quoted in CZA Z4/868. Weizmann quoted in Meinertzhagen, 104. Also see CO 733/3, pp. 181, 267–268, 289–291, 363–364, 309, 410; "Is This the End?" (editorial), *Jewish Chronicle*, June 10, 1921.
21. Churchill quoted in CO 732/5, pp. 89, 95. Also see CO 733/3, pp. 157–160; CO 733/16, pp. 135–136, 269–270; CO 732/5, p. 78; Gilbert, *Winston S. Churchill: The Stricken World*, 585–589, 615–616; CO 733/3, pp. 157, 290, 307, 364, 381, 387–391, 410; Gilbert, *Companion*, 4/3: 1484, 1496n1, 1559; Klieman, *Foundation of British Policy*, 174–175, 183; CAB 32/2; FO 371/6342, p. 205.
22. Churchill quoted in CO 733/3: 291, 363. Samuel quoted in CO 733/3: 360–361; Sykes, *Israel*, 70. Also see CO 733/3: 364.
23. Churchill quoted in CO 733/13, p. 557; CAB 24/126, p. 196; CZA Z4/1841 I; CAB 32/2; Rhodes James, *Speeches*, 3: 3349. Also see Gilbert, *Winston S. Churchill: The Stricken World*, 568; FO 371/6342, p. 205.
24. Churchill quoted in CAB 24/126, p. 196; "Mr. Churchill in Palestine," *Jewish Chronicle*, April 1, 1921, 25. Also see "Mr. Churchill in Palestine," *Zionist Review* 5, no. 1 (May 1921), 4; Gilbert, *Winston S. Churchill: The Stricken World*, 563–564.
25. Churchill quoted in CAB 24/126, pp. 193, 196; CAB 32/2, p. 767.
26. Churchill White Paper quoted in CO 733/34, p. 328. Churchill quoted in CAB 24/126, p. 193; Gilbert, *Companion*, 4/3: 1613. Also see Gilbert, *Winston S. Churchill: The Stricken World*, 563–564.
27. Churchill quoted in CAB 24/126, 194–195.
28. Tel Aviv, founded in 1911, is now Israel's largest city. Meir Dizengoff quoted in CHAR 17/20, pp. 9–10. Churchill quoted in "Mr. Churchill in Palestine," *Zionist Review* 5, no. 1 (May 1921), 4. Also see Gilbert, *Winston S. Churchill: The Stricken World*, 573.
29. Rishon Lezion grew to 140,000 residents in 2002. Rishon Lezion elders quoted in CHAR 17/20, pp. 13–15. Churchill quoted in "Mr. Churchill in Palestine," *Zionist Review* 5, no. 1 (May 1921), 4. Also see Steven Erlanger, "15 Killed by Suicide Bomber," *New York Times*, May 8, 2002, 14; Howard Sachar, *History of Israel*, 29–34, 48.
30. Sidebotham quoted in CZA Z4/1841 I. Churchill quoted in FO 371/6342, p. 205; Rhodes James, *Speeches*, 3: 3108; CAB 32/2. Also see Fromkin, *Peace to End All Peace*, 446.
31. CAB 32/2.
32. Berlin quoted in Berlin, "Weizmann," 62. Also see Berlin, "Weizmann," 43, 49, 52, 54–55, 61–62.
33. Churchill quoted in CAB 24/126, p. 196; "Mr. Churchill in Palestine," *Zionist Review* 5, no. 1 (May 1921), 4. *Zionist Review* comment in "Mr. Churchill in Palestine," *Zionist Review* 5, no. 1 (May 1921), 5.
34. Unidentified comment in Cabinet in CO 733/14, p. 159. Churchill quoted in Rhodes James, *Speeches*, 3: 3347. Also see Gilbert, *Companion*, 4/3: 1592, 1612; CAB 24/126, 193; Kedourie, *Chatham House*, 74.

35. Arab shouts quoted in Gilbert, *Winston S. Churchill: The Stricken World*, 558. Commission inquiry cited in CO 733/5, pp. 304–305. Churchill quoted in CHAR 17/10, p. 25. Also see CO 733/13, p. 557; CO 733/3, 627; CHAR 17/10, p. 25; FO 371/6342, p. 204; Gilbert, *Companion*, 4/3: 1491; Rhodes James, *Speeches*, 3: 3106, 3263; CO 733/14, p. 53; Gilbert, *Winston S. Churchill: The Stricken World*, 642–645; Kedourie, *England*, 153; Kedourie, *Chatham House*, 57, 402–403n15.
36. Churchill quoted in Gilbert, *Companion*, 4/3: 1610–1613, 15. Also see CO 733/3, p. 625; CO 733/7, p. 206; CO 733/19, p. 580; Gilbert, *Winston S. Churchill: The Stricken World*, 566, 628, 682; CO 733/15, p. 68; CAB 24/126, 194, 196; Gilbert, *Companion*, 4/3: 1592–1601, 1614, 1616; CO 733/15, pp. 269, 275–276.
37. Churchill quoted in CO 733/13, p. 557. Also see CAB 32/2.
38. Churchill quoted in CO 732/4, p. 170; Rhodes James, *Speeches*, 3: 3102; CHAR 17/15, p. 167; CAB 32/2; Busch, *Britain, India and the Arabs*, 459; CHAR 17/27. Also see Beloff, *Britain's Liberal Empire*, 255–256; Kedourie, *Chatham House*, 239–241; Wasserstein, *British in Palestine*, 12–14; Gilbert, *Companion*, 4/2: 1372; CAB 24/126, 172–173; CO 732/4, pp. 170, 228; Gilbert, *Companion*, 4/3: 1428–1430, 1432; CO 732/5, p. 542; CO 733/13, p. 415; Morris, *Righteous Victims*, 79.
39. Amery, whose mother apparently was a Hungarian Jew, concealed his Jewish ancestry. Weizmann quoted in Klieman, *Foundation of British Policy*, 197n63. Yale quoted in Kedourie, *England*, 154. Palestinian Arab slogan quoted by Samuel found in CO 733/26, p. 112. Also see Gilbert, *Companion*, 4/3: 1483; Meinertzhagen, *Middle East Diary*, 108, 118; Andrew Alderson and Simon Trump, "Britain's Secret Jew Who Paved the Road to Israel," *Sunday Telegraph*, January 10, 1999, 10; Barnes and Nicholson, *Leo Amery Diaries*, 1: 170–171; Kedourie, *Chatham House*, 74; Kedourie, "Arab-Israeli Conflict," 559–560, 564; Morris, *Righteous Victims*, 79.
40. Jewish immigration in the 1930s and 1940s helped counter the influx of one hundred thousand Arab immigrants during 1922–1946 who were attracted to Palestine's relative economic prosperity. Churchill quoted in Rhodes James, *Speeches*, 3: 3107. Also see Gilbert, *Winston S. Churchill: 1922–1939*, 1072n1; Howard Sachar, *History of Israel*, 167–168; CAB 32/2.
41. Churchill quoted in CO 733/3, p. 387; Gilbert, *Companion*, 4/3: 1617. Also see Meinertzhagen, *Middle East Diary*, 104–106; Lewis, "Pro-Islamic Jews"; CAB 24/126, pp. 194–196; Howard Sachar, *History of Israel*, 167–168, 172; Morris, *Righteous Victims*, 21, 104.
42. Churchill quoted in Gilbert, *Companion*, 4/3: 1601; CAB 32/2; Meinertzhagen, *Middle East Diary*, 104; Gilbert, *Companion*, 4/3: 1937. Weizmann quoted in Feith, "Palestine and Zionism," 227. Also see Gilbert, *Companion*, 4/3: 1599–1600; CO 733/16, p. 259; CZA Z4/3823; CAB 32/2; Rhodes James, *Speeches*, 3: 3107–3108.
43. Churchill quoted in CO 733/11, p. 695; Gilbert, *Winston S. Churchill: The Stricken World*, 632. Churchill White Paper quoted in CO 733/34, pp. 326–328,

330. Also see Klieman, *Foundation of British Policy*, 185–186, 197; CO 733/19; CO 733/11, pp. 691; CO 733/34, pp. 297, 317, 323–332; Sykes, *Israel*, 71–72; Gilbert, *Winston S. Churchill: The Stricken World*, 646.
44. Weizmann quoted in Gilbert, *Winston S. Churchill: The Stricken World*, 660. Also see Sykes, *Israel*, 82–83, 93; "The Churchill Renunciation" (editorial), *Jewish Chronicle*, July 7, 1922, 7–9; "The Churchill Memorandum," *Jewish Chronicle*, August 19, 1927, 22; Michael Cohen, *Churchill*, 143; Gilbert, *Winston S. Churchill: The Stricken World*, 643; Kedourie, *Chatham House*, 73; *Documents Relating to the Palestine Problem*, 8; Gilbert, *Winston S. Churchill: The Stricken World*, 660.
45. CO 733/26, 110.
46. Churchill quoted in Paterson, *Seat for Life*, 262. Also see Rhodes James, *Revolution*, 145–146, 166, 192–195; Jenkins, *Churchill*, 370–376, 381, 387; K. Young, *Churchill and Beaverbrook*, 83; A. Clark, *Tories*, 45–46; Beaverbrook, *Politicians and the War*, 28; Blake, *Unknown Prime Minister*, 233–235; Carlton, *Churchill and the Soviet Union*, 31; Gilbert, *Companion*, 4/3: 1808; Soames, *Winston and Clementine*, 278, 286; Addison, *Home Front*, 234.
47. Churchill quoted in K. Young, *Churchill and Beaverbrook*, 83. Also see Gilbert, *Companion*, 5/1: 533–534, 1006; A. Clark, *Tories*, 45–46; Kedourie, "Arab-Israeli Conflict," 560.
48. Churchill quoted in Gilbert, *Companion*, 5/1: 544, 995. Also see Addison, *Home Front*, 238; CHAR 18/2, p. 18; Gilbert, *Companion*, 5/1: 545–546, 1214; Safran, *Israel*, 27; Wasserstein, *British in Palestine*, 164; Michael Cohen, *Churchill*, 150–154, 158–168; Barnes and Nicholson, *Leo Amery Diaries*, 1: 538, 546.
49. Churchill quoted in Churchill, *World Crisis: 1916–1918*, 2: 336; Churchill, *World Crisis: The Aftermath*, 464. Also see Churchill, *World Crisis: The Aftermath*, 461–466.
50. Gilbert, *Companion*, 5/1: 1334.
51. "Jewish Religious Education Board: Festival Dinner," *Jewish Chronicle*, January 22, 1926, 18, 21.
52. "Mr. Churchill's Challenge," *Jewish Chronicle*, April 8, 1921, 21.

CHAPTER 5. TOGETHER IN THE WILDERNESS
1. Jenkins, *Churchill*, 443–444; Soames, *Winston and Clementine*, 341.
2. Cowles, *Winston Churchill*, 308–9.
3. Graham Stewart contends that Churchill did not exclude himself from the government in 1931 but was excluded. Gilbert, *Winston S. Churchill: 1922–1939*, 414, 809–831; Soames, *Winston and Clementine*, 333, 419; Rhodes James, "Politician," 113; Rhodes James, *Revolution*, 218–233, 239–242, 295–303; Stewart, *Burying Caesar*, 98; Jenkins, *Churchill*, 498–504; Gilbert, *Companion*, 5/3: 521, 820n1.
4. Churchill quoted in Gilbert, *Winston S. Churchill: 1922–1939*, 337; Rhodes James, *Speeches*, 5: 4676; Churchill, *India*, 30, 34. Also see Gilbert, *Winston*

S. Churchill: 1922–1939, 338; Soames, *Winston and Clementine*, 350; Churchill, *India*, 29; Collins and Lapierre, *Freedom at Midnight*, 9.
5. Howard Sachar, *History of Israel*, 173–174.
6. Howard Sachar, *History of Israel*, 175–178; Michael Cohen, *Churchill*, 170–171;
7. David Ben-Gurion quoted in Howard Sachar, *History of Israel*, 182. Also see Howard Sachar, *History of Israel*, 186, 191, 213.
8. Churchill quoted in Rhodes James, *Speeches*, 5: 4672; Churchill, "The Palestine Crisis," *Sunday Chronicle*, September 22, 1929, reprinted in Churchill, *Collected Essays*, 2: 169; Gilbert, *Companion*, 5/2: 62. Also see Churchill, "Our Task for Peace in Palestine," *Glasgow Evening News*, February 28, 1930, reprinted in Churchill, *Collected Essays*, 2: 188.
9. Churchill quoted in Churchill, "Our Task for Peace in Palestine," *Glasgow Evening News*, February 28, 1930, reprinted in Churchill, *Collected Essays*, 2: 189–190; Churchill, "The Palestine Crisis," *Sunday Chronicle*, September 22, 1929, reprinted in Churchill, *Collected Essays*, 2: 171.
10. Churchill quoted in Churchill, "The Palestine Crisis," *Sunday Chronicle*, September 22, 1929, reprinted in Churchill, *Collected Essays*, 2: 170; Rhodes James, *Speeches*, 5: 4673.
11. Churchill quoted in Churchill, "Our Task for Peace in Palestine," *Glasgow Evening News*, February 28, 1930, reprinted in Churchill, *Collected Essays*, 2: 189; Gilbert, *Companion*, 5/2: 220. Also see Gilbert, *Companion*, 5/2: 221.
12. Churchill quoted in Churchill, "The Palestine Crisis," *Sunday Chronicle*, September 22, 1929, reprinted in Churchill, *Collected Essays*, 2: 168–170. Also see Gilbert, *Companion*, 5/3: 600–601.
13. Churchill quoted in Gilbert, *Companion*, 5/3: 827, 5/2: 960–961, 969.
14. Churchill quoted in Gilbert, *Winston S. Churchill: 1922–1939*, 448. Also see Rhodes James, *Speeches*, 7: 7800; Morris, *Righteous Victims*, 128.
15. Churchill quoted in Rhodes James, *Speeches*, 5: 5263; The Truth about Hitler," *Strand*, October 30, 1935, CHAR 8/518; Gilbert, *Companion*, 5/3: 735n3. Also see Gilbert, *Winston S. Churchill: 1922–1939*, 485–486; Gilbert, *Churchill: A Life*, 520; Gilbert, *Exile and Return*, 162.
16. Churchill quoted in Gilbert, *Winston S. Churchill: 1922–1939*, 889; Gilbert, *Companion*, 5/3: 913n1; "Germany's Discipline for the Old Austria," *Daily Telegraph and Morning Post*, July 6, 1938, CHAR 8/612, p. 15.
17. Churchill quoted in Gilbert, *Winston S. Churchill: 1922–1939*, 800; Gilbert, *Companion*, 5/3: 913n1; CHAR 8/733/102; Attlee, "The Churchill I Knew," 23.
18. Churchill quoted in CHAR 2/315, p. 8; Churchill, *Step by Step*, 44–46. Also see Gilbert, *Exile and Return*, 198; CHAR 2/315, pp. 3–4; Gilbert, *Churchill War Papers*, 1: 445.
19. Churchill quoted in Rhodes James, *Speeches*, 6: 5714, 5716. Weizmann quoted in Litvinoff, *Essential Chaim Weizmann*, 223. Also see CHAR 20/258, p. 77; CHAR 1/286, p. 130.
20. Churchill quoted in Gilbert, *Companion*, 5/3: 338. Also see Morris, *Righteous Victims*, 127–128; Gilbert, *Exile and Return*, 164; Teveth, *Ben-Gurion*, 511;

Howard Sachar, *History of Israel*, 199–201; Morris, *Righteous Victims*, 138–139; Gilbert, *Companion*, 5/3: 624, 1289n1; CHAR 2/317, p. 15; Gilbert, *Winston S. Churchill: 1922–1939*, 848.
21. Churchill quoted in Gilbert, *Companion*, 5/3: 599, 602, 604.
22. Churchill quoted in Gilbert, *Companion*, 5/3: 605, 609. Also see Howard Sachar, *History of Israel*, 187, 195, 196.
23. Churchill quoted in Gilbert, *Companion*, 5/3: 599, 605, 611.
24. Churchill quoted in Gilbert, *Companion*, 5/3: 602, 604–606, 608.
25. Churchill quoted in Gilbert, *Companion*, 5/3: 608, 616.
26. Churchill quoted in Gilbert, *Companion*, 5/3: 598, 601, 607, 610. Also see Gilbert, *Exile and Return*, 161.
27. Churchill quoted in Gilbert, *Companion*, 5/3: 601–604. Also see Howard Sachar, *History of Israel*, 182–183.
28. Churchill quoted in Gilbert, *Companion*, 5/3: 606, 611,615.
29. Howard Sachar, *History of Israel*, 204–206.
30. Howard Sachar, *History of Israel*, 204–211; Gilbert, *Exile and Return*, 181; Berlin, "Weizmann," 50–51; Kedourie, *Chatham House*, 230–231.
31. Josiah Wedgwood quoted in Gilbert, *Companion*, 5/3: 596–597. Also see Rose, *Gentile Zionists*, 132–133, 148.
32. Churchill quoted in Churchill, "Why I Am against Partition," *Jewish Chronicle*, September 3, 1937, CHAR 8/563, p. 7. Also see CHAR 2/315, p. 18.
33. Churchill quoted in Churchill, "Why I Am against Partition" 7–8; Gilbert, *Companion*, 5/3: 890; CHAR 2/315, p. 44. Also see Michael Cohen, *Churchill*, 176–177.
34. Churchill quoted in Rose, *Gentile Zionists*, 132–133, 148; Teveth, *Ben-Gurion*, 597. Also see CHAR 2/315, p. 14; Rose, *Baffy*, 45.
35. Churchill quoted in Gilbert, *Winston S. Churchill: 1922–1939*, 848–849; Gilbert, *Companion*, 5/3: 764.
36. Churchill quoted in Rhodes James, *Speeches*, 6: 5887; Gilbert, *Companion*, 5/3: 735–736n3. Also see CHAR 2/315, pp. 9–12.
37. Churchill quoted in Rhodes James, *Speeches*, 6: 6047. Also see Gilbert, *Exile and Return*, 211.
38. Howard Sachar, *History of Israel*, 211–222; Gilbert, *Companion*, 5/3: 1289n1; Kedourie, "Arab-Israel Conflict," 561, 565–566.
39. Churchill quoted in Rhodes James, *Speeches*, 6: 6033, 6036–6039; Barnes and Nicholson, *Leo Amery Diaries*, 1: 535.
40. Ben-Gurion quoted in Howard Sachar, *History of Israel*, 224. See also: Safran, *Israel*, 30; Gilbert, *Winston S. Churchill: 1922–1939*, 1069; Gilbert, *Exile and Return*, 239; Roberts, *Holy Fox*, 128–129; Michael Cohen, *Churchill*, 178–181; Howard Sachar, *History of Israel*, 223; Zweig, *Britain and Palestine*, 4–5.
41. Churchill quoted in Rhodes James, *Speeches*, 6: 6134–6136. Also see Weizmann, *Trial and Error*, 411.
42. Churchill quoted in Rhodes James, *Speeches*, 6: 6132 Also see Berlin, "Weizmann," 56.
43. Churchill quoted in Gilbert, *Companion*, 5/3: 654n2, 820; Rhodes James,

Speeches, 6: 6035. Roosevelt quoted in Grose, "President versus the Diplomats," 35. Also see Hull, *Memoirs*, 2: 1530–1531.
44. Churchill quoted in Rhodes James, *Speeches*, 6: 6129, 6132–6134.
45. Churchill quoted in Rhodes James, *Speeches*, 6: 6036, 6135–6137. Also see Gilbert, *Winston S. Churchill: 1922–1939*, 1072.
46. Churchill quoted in Rhodes James, *Speeches*, 6: 5886, 6034, 6129, 6131.
47. Rhodes James, *Speeches*, 6: 6134, 6137; Bethell, *Palestine Triangle*, 44. Also see CHAR 2/359; Gilbert, *Companion*, 5/3: 1505.
48. Berlin, "Life and Opinions," 232; Churchill, "Moses," 209.

CHAPTER 6. CHAMPION IN WAR

1. Bolchover, *British Jewry*.
2. Wasserstein, *Britain and the Jews*, 30–31, 45, 303, 316; Gilbert, *Companion*, 4/2: 1028–1029; Dilks, *Sir Alexander Cadogan*, 597; PREM 4/51/8, pp. 716–717; PREM 4/52/3, pp. 525–531; *FRUS 1943: The British Commonwealth, Eastern Europe, the Far East*, 38; Howard Sachar, *History of Israel*, 238; Wyman, *Abandonment of the Jews*, 97–98, 105, 159; Zweig, *Britain and Palestine*, 93, 96–97; Harvey, *War Diaries*, 247; G. Cohen, *Churchill and Palestine*, 94.
3. Churchill quoted in PREM 4/52/5, p. 1291; CO 967/98.
4. Weizmann quoted in Gilbert, *Churchill and Zionism*, 24; Berlin, "Chaim Weizmann's Leadership," 193.
5. Draft War Cabinet instructions in Gilbert, *Churchill War Papers*, 1: 564n3; Churchill quoted in CHAR 19/4; Churchill, *Second World War: Their Finest Hour*, 154; PREM 4/51/9, p. 938. Also see Gilbert, *Churchill War Papers*, 2: 419; CO 967/98; PREM 4/52/5, p. 929.
6. Wyman, *Abandonment of the Jews*, 4, 19–58, 72–75; Beschloss, *Conquerors*, 39, 59; Feingold, *Politics of Rescue*, 305; Zweig, *Britain and Palestine*, 135, 137; U.S. Holocaust Memorial Museum Web site, http://www.ushmm.org/; Gilbert, *Exile and Return*, 257–258.
7. On September 12, 1941, Churchill received a report from Bletchley Park: "The fact that the Police are killing all Jews that fall into their hands should by now be sufficiently appreciated. It is not therefore proposed to continue reporting these butcheries specially, unless so requested." Churchill quoted in Rhodes James, *Speeches*, 6: 6474. Also see M. Smith, "Bletchley Park," 264–269; Hinsley, *British Intelligence*, vol. 2, app. 5, 670–671; Breitman, *Official Secrets*, 92–97; Richard Breitman, "Holocaust Secrecy Now Abets More Genocide" (letter to the editor), *New York Times*, November 29, 1996, A: 36; John Keegan, "What the Allies Knew" (op-ed), *New York Times*, November 25, 1996; Stafford, *Churchill and Secret Service*, 297–299; Gilbert, *Churchill War Papers*, 3: 1175nn1–2; Gilbert, *Winston S. Churchill: Finest Hour*, 1174.
8. Churchill quoted in "From the Prime Minister," *Jewish Chronicle*, November 14, 1941, p. 24; Wyman, *Abandonment of the Jews*, 24. Roosevelt quoted in Beschloss, *Conquerors*, 39. Also see "100th Birthday," *Jewish Chronicle*, November 14, 1941, p. 16; Beschloss, *Conquerors*, 38.

9. Churchill quoted in PREM 4/51/7; Rhodes James, *Speeches*, 6: 6675.
10. Statement quoted in Wasserstein, *Britain and the Jews*, 155. Also see CAB 195/2, p. 21; FO 371/30924, pp. 105–107; Brecher, *Reluctant Ally*, 110–111; Wasserstein, *Britain and the Jews*, 107, 117–118, 146–156, 164, 183; Wyman, *Abandonment of the Jews*, 75; Breitman, *Official Secrets*, 150–153; Rhodes James, *Chips*, 347; Laquer, *Terrible Secret*, 92.
11. Churchill quoted in Churchill, *Second World War: Triumph and Tragedy*, 597; Rhodes James, *Speeches*, 7: 7113–7114. Also see Ulam, *Stalin*, 596–598; Soames, *Winston and Clementine*, 503.
12. Churchill quoted in Rhodes James, *Speeches*, 7: 7145; Soames, *Winston and Clementine*, 527–528. Also see Gilbert, *Holocaust*, 790; Wyman, *Abandonment of the Jews*, 325.
13. PREM 8/627/40477.
14. Churchill quoted in PREM 4/51/9, p. 826. Also see Gilbert, "'The Most Horrible Crime,'" 5; Wasserstein, *Britain and the Jews*, 256–257; Michael Cohen, *Churchill*, 213, 225–226; CAB 65/43, WM (44)104, p. 82; Kimball, *Churchill and Roosevelt*, 3: 287; Howard Sachar, *History of Israel*, 242; CHAR 20/38A; CHAR 20/234, p. 143.
15. Churchill quoted in PREM 4/52/5, p. 1127; FO 371/42809, p. 164; CZA Z4/14696 II. Also see PREM 4/51/8, pp. 433, 436, 443, 465, 468, 472–480, 541–544, 547–548, 576–581, 601–602; Rhodes James, *Speeches*, 7: 6798; Wasserstein, *Britain and the Jews*, 199; PREM 4/52/5, p. 1129; Wyman, *Abandonment of the Jews*, 78, 176, 244–245.
16. The Bottomley letter was brought to my attention by Dr. Goldman of the Department of Defense. CAB 121/001.
17. Churchill quoted in PREM 4/51/10, p. 1370; FO 371/42809, p. 164, 169. Eden quoted in FO 371/42809, p. 164; Wasserstein, *Britain and the Jews*, 282. Bottomley quoted in Spaatz Papers, Library of Congress. Also see PREM 4/51/10, pp. 1343, 1368–1369; FO 371/42809, pp. 161–170; Wasserstein, *Britain and the Jews*, 277, 280–289; Neufeld and Berendbaum, *Bombing of Auschwitz*, xi, 266–267; Gilbert, "Contemporary Case," 73; Feingold, "Bombing Auschwitz," 202; Stafford, *Churchill and Secret Service*, 300; Breitman, *Official Secrets*, 211; Breitman, "Failure to Provide," 137; London, *Whitehall and the Jews*.
18. Howard Sachar, *History of Israel*, 244; Wyman, *Abandonment of the Jews*, x, 158, 172, 316; Wasserstein, *Britain and the Jews*, 38–41, 43–49, 71, 74, 118, 306–307; Gilbert, *Exile and Return*, 260–261, 264, 267; CAB 65/10; Zweig, *Britain and Palestine*, 119–122, 144–146, 174–175; CAB 65/25, WM(42)29, p. 119; CAB 65/26, WM(42)64, pp. 82–83; Michael Cohen, *Churchill*, 275; PREM 4/52/5, pp. 1098–1099.
19. Churchill quoted in G. Cohen, *Churchill and Palestine*, 89; PREM 4/52/3, p. 506; PREM 4/52/5, p. 1029; CZA Z4/14.696 I; Addison, *Road to 1945*, 253. Also see Gilbert, *Churchill War Papers*, 1: 518; PREM 4/52/3, p. 511; CHAR 20/179; Woodward, *Documents on British Foreign Policy*, 4: 361–362; PREM 4/52/5, pp. 1092, 1247–1249.

20. Laski quoted in PREM 4/51/8, p. 478. Churchill quoted in PREM 4/52/3, p. 506; PREM 4/52/5, p. 1247; CAB 65/39, p. 4. Also see Howard Sachar, *History of Israel*, 236–237; PREM 4/51/8, pp. 541–547; Rhodes James, *Speeches*, 7: 6769; PREM 4/52/5, pp. 1097, 1162; PREM 4/52/3, pp. 499–503, 507–509, 541–547.
21. Churchill quoted in PREM 4/52/5, pp. 1025, 1029. Also see Gilbert, *Churchill War Papers*, 1: 518, 564n3; CHAR 19/4; Barnes and Nicholson, *Leo Amery Diaries*, 1: 580; G. Cohen, *Churchill and Palestine*, 89; PREM 4/52/5, pp. 984, 987–989, 977, 1019, 1025–1031, 1097, 1247; Zweig, *Britain and Palestine*, 151–153, 155; Gilbert, *Exile and Return*, 260; Howard Sachar, *History of Israel*, 254; PREM 4/52/1, p. 214; Wyman, *Abandonment of the Jews*, 160–175; CZA Z4/302/28; Hull, *Memoirs*, 2: 1535–1536; *FRUS 1944*, 615–616, 617n21; Roberts, *Holy Fox*, 3, 128.
22. Churchill quoted in PREM 4/51/2, pp. 110–111; PREM 4/51/1, p. 87; Gilbert, "'The Most Horrible Crime,'" 3; Rose, "Churchill and Zionism," 151. Also see PREM 4/51/2, p. 116; PREM 4/51/8, pp. 745–746; Wasserstein, *Britain and the Jews*, 63, 320; Zweig, *Britain and Palestine*, 31n46, 126n45; CHAR 17/2, p. 52–53.
23. Churchill quoted in Gilbert, *Churchill War Papers*, 1: 609; Churchill, *Second World War: Their Finest Hour*, 614. Also see Gilbert, *Churchill War Papers*, 1: 603–609; PREM 4/51/1, p. 87; CAB 65/10, WM (40)299; Dilks, *Sir Alexander Cadogan*, 338; Wasserstein, *Britain and the Jews*, 59–68.
24. Churchill quoted in PREM 4/51/1, p. 37; CO 733/446/7, pp. 10, 14. Also see PREM 4/51/1, pp. 38–39; CO 733/446/8, p. 63; CO 733/446/7, pp. 11–15; Wasserstein, *Britain and the Jews*, 70, 128–135.
25. Churchill quoted in Churchill, *Second World War: Hinge of Fate*, 81. Also see Churchill, *Second World War: Grand Alliance*, 555–629; FO 371/32661; Barnes and Nicholson, *Leo Amery Diaries*, 1: 774–775; Zweig, *Britain and Palestine*, 118–127; Wyman, *Abandonment of the Jews*, 158–159.
26. Churchill quoted in PREM 4/51/2, p. 123. Also see PREM 4/51/2, pp. 121–124; FO 371/32661; Wasserstein, *Britain and the Jews*, 161; Zweig, *Britain and Palestine*, 140–143; CAB 195/2, p. 22; Barnes and Nicholson, *Leo Amery Diaries*, 1: 897.
27. Churchill quoted in PREM 4/51/4, pp. 208, 215, 219. Also see Wyman, *Abandonment of the Jews*, 98, 109, 115–119, 123; Wasserstein, *Britain and the Jews*, 183–184, 186, 188; *FRUS 1943: The Conferences at Washington and Quebec*, 96, 197, 342–346; Dallek, *Franklin D. Roosevelt*, 446; Feingold, "Bombing Auschwitz," 297; PREM 4/51/4, pp. 211–213; CAB 195/2, p. 235.
28. Churchill quoted in Gilbert, *Churchill and Zionism*, 24; Gilbert, *Churchill War Papers*, 1: 749, 3: 643. Also see Gilbert, *Churchill War Papers*, 1: 127–128, 265, 748, 750, 2: 121, 189, 191, 419; Churchill, *Second World War: Their Finest Hour*, 154; PREM 4/52/5, pp. 1386–1387; Zweig, *Britain and Palestine*, 22n14; Churchill, *Second World War: Grand Alliance*, 140, 152, 658; Michael Cohen, *Churchill*, 207, 217, 223–224; CAB 65/19, WM (41)102; PREM 4/51/9, p. 938; Morris, *Righteous Victims*, 166.

29. Churchill quoted in Howard Sachar, *History of Israel*, 241; PREM 4/52/3, p. 506A; PREM 4/51/4, p. 219; PREM 4/51/1, p. 37; Barnes and Nicholson, *Leo Amery Diaries*, 1: 994.
30. Smuts quoted in CZA Z4/302/27. Weizmann quoted in PREM 4/52/3, p. 514. Also see Gilbert, *Churchill War Papers*, 1: 748–749.
31. Churchill quoted in CHAR 19/4; G. Cohen, *Churchill and Palestine*, 89. Also see Gilbert, *Churchill War Papers*, 1: 518, 530, 651, 748, 2: 334–335; G. Cohen, *Churchill and Palestine*, 89; Michael Cohen, *Churchill*, 211; PREM 4/52/5, pp. 1386–1387, 1422–1424; PREM 4/52/3, p. 496; Wasserstein, *Britain and the Jews*, 32.
32. Churchill quoted in Wallace, *Price of Vision*, 211. Hull quoted in Hull, *Memoirs*, 2: 1535–1536. Also see Brecher, *Reluctant Ally*, 91; Beschloss, *Conquerors*, 41; Wyman, *Abandonment*, 14–15; Campbell and Herring, *Edward R. Stettinius, Jr.*, 170; Bohlen, *Witness to History*, 203.
33. Amery quoted in Barnes and Nicholson, *Leo Amery Diaries*, 1: 897. Also see PREM 4/52/5, pp. 1092–1093, 1096–1099; Gilbert, *Exile and Return*, 259, 268–269; Howard Sachar, *History of Israel*, 228–229.
34. Churchill quoted in Churchill, *Second World War: Grand Alliance*, 658; PREM 4/52/5, p. 1248; Wallace, *Price of Vision*, 211. Also see Gilbert, *Churchill War Papers*, 2: 334–335; Churchill, *Second World War: Their Finest Hour*, 2: 154; Churchill, *Second World War: Grand Alliance*, 140, 152, 224–237; Michael Cohen, *Churchill*, 217; Kedourie, *Chatham House*, 226, 237–239, 272; Zweig, *Britain and Palestine*, 174n107; CHAR 20/179; Ignatieff, *Isaiah Berlin*, 118–119; CZA Z4/14792.
35. PREM 4/52/5, pp. 992–993; PREM 4/52/1, pp. 88–89, 100, 107–109.
36. Kedourie quoted in Kedourie, "Arab-Israeli Conflict," 571. Also see Gilbert, *Churchill War Papers*, 1: 530; Zweig, *Britain and Palestine*, 89–91; Bethell, *Palestine Triangle*, 144; PREM 4/52/5, pp. 1328, 1331–1334; PREM 4/51/11, pp. 1486; CO733/443/18.
37. Churchill, *Second World War: Grand Alliance*, 224–234, 287–288.
38. Churchill quoted in Litvinoff, *Letters and Papers*, 20: 125–126; Gilbert, *Churchill and Zionism*, 23. Also see Michael Cohen, *Churchill*, 219; Weizmann, *Trial and Error*, 427–428.
39. Churchill quoted in Churchill, *Second World War: Grand Alliance*, 715; G. Cohen, *Churchill and Palestine*, 83. Subcommittee quoted in CAB 91/1, ME(o)(42)4; colonial official William Battershill quoted in CO 733/443/18. Also see Churchill, *Second World War: Grand Alliance*, 294, 714; Kedourie, *Chatham House*, 222–225; Kedourie, *Islam*, 68; Gilbert, *Churchill War Papers*, 3: 682–683, 686–687; Zweig, *Britain and Palestine*, 101.
40. Churchill quoted in Gilbert, *Churchill War Papers*, 3: 1258; Zweig, *Britain and Palestine*, 107; PREM 4/52/5, pp. 1327. Also see CAB 95/1, ME(o)(42)4; Zweig, *Britain and Palestine*, 101–112; PREM 4/52/5, pp. 1385, 1389–1390; CAB 65/19, WM(41)87, p. 242.
41. Churchill quoted in PREM 4/52/5, p. 1366; CZA Z4/14.696 I.
42. War Cabinet report in CAB 95/1, ME(o)(42)4. Also see Zweig, *Britain and*

Palestine, 148–149; Churchill, *Second World War: Hinge of Fate*, 53–94, 336–367.
43. Weizmann quoted in Litvinoff, *Letters and Papers*, 20: 301, 313. Churchill quoted in Churchill, *Second World War: Hinge of Fate*, 786; PREM 4/52/5, p. 1327. Also see PREM 4/52/5, pp. 1291–1292; PREM 4/52/3, p. 531, 546.
44. Churchill quoted in PREM 4/52/3, p. 432. Also see PREM 4/52/3, pp. 433–434.
45. At the March meeting, Moshe Shertok, a Palestinian Jewish leader, expressed more skepticism about a federation scheme headed by Ibn Saud. Weizmann quoted in PREM 4/52/3, p. 515. Berlin and colonial official William Battershill quoted in CO 733/443/18. Also see PREM 4/52/3, pp. 511–517; *FRUS 1943: The Near East and Africa*, 760–761.
46. Churchill quoted in PREM 4/52/3, p. 511. Also see PREM 4/52/3, pp. 512A, 513.
47. Churchill quoted in Zweig, *Britain and Palestine*, 174n107; Wallace, *Price of Vision*, 211. Also see PREM 4/52/3, p. 506A; PREM 4/51/4, p. 219; Litvinoff, *Letters and Papers*, 21: 90n2; Gilbert, *Winston S. Churchill: The Stricken World*, 561; *FRUS 1943: The Near East and Africa*, 792–793; PREM 4/52/3, pp. 483–484.
48. Ibn Saud quoted in *FRUS 1943: The Near East and Africa*, 773–775. Winant quoted in PREM 4/52/5, p. 1117. Roosevelt quoted in *FRUS 1943: The Near East and Africa*, 790.
49. Weizmann's paraphrase in PREM 4/52/3, p. 483. Ibn Saud quoted in FO 371/35164. Churchill quoted in CO 733/443/19, p. 82. Also see CAB 195/2, p. 257–258; CO 733/443/18; Brecher, *Reluctant Ally*, 86–87, 143; *FRUS 1943: The Near East and Africa*, 776–780, 784–785, 812–813; Feingold, *Politics of Rescue*, 216.
50. Churchill-Roosevelt meeting minutes quoted in *FRUS 1943: The Conferences at Washington and Quebec*, 932. Roosevelt quoted in Dallek, *Franklin D. Roosevelt*, 447. Also see *FRUS 1943: The Conferences at Washington and Quebec*, 678, 930; *FRUS 1945: The Near East and Africa*, 699; Hull, *Memoirs*, 2: 1533.
51. PREM 4/52/5, pp. 1093.
52. Stanley quoted in CAB 195/2, p. 234. Churchill quoted in CAB 65/39, p. 5; PREM 4/52/5, p. 1092. Amery quoted in Barnes and Nicholson, *Leo Amery Diaries*, 1: 897. Also see PREM 4/52/5, 1093.
53. Amery quoted in Barnes and Nicholson, *Leo Amery Diaries*, 1: 897. Also see PREM 4/52/5, 1096–1099; CAB 65/39, pp. 3–7; CAB 195/2, pp. 233–237.
54. Churchill quoted in PREM 4/51/8, p. 475. Also see PREM 4/52/3, p. 509; PREM 4/52/5, pp. 1069, 1073; CAB 66/44, p. 102.
55. Churchill quoted in PREM 4/52/1, p. 202. Also see Donoughue and Jones, *Herbert Morrison*, 255–257; Kelemen, "Labour Ideals"; Weizmann, *Trial and Error*, 411–412; PREM 4/52/1, pp. 203–205; FO 371/35038, pp. 131–132A; CAB 195/2, pp. 93, 186, 235; Zweig, *Britain and Palestine*, 175.
56. Churchill quoted in Gilbert, *Churchill and Zionism*, 24; Ignatieff, *Isaiah Berlin*, 118–119; Penkower, *Decision on Palestine Deferred*, 362.

57. CAB 66/44, pp. 102–110.
58. CAB 66/44, pp. 102–110; Michael Cohen, *Retreat from the Mandate*, 165–171.
59. Churchill quoted in PREM 4/52/5, p. 1029. Also see PREM 4/52/1, pp. 190–191; CZA Z4/14792.
60. Churchill and other War Cabinet minutes quoted in CAB 65/45, pp. 24–27. Also see Barnes and Nicholson, *Leo Amery Diaries*, 1: 966; PREM 4/52/5, p. 1098.
61. Churchill quoted in PREM 4/52/1, p. 168.
62. Churchill quoted in CZA Z4/302/28. Also see Zweig, *Britain and Palestine*, 175; Wasserstein, *Britain and the Jews*, 300; PREM 4/52/1, p. 51; Michael Cohen, *Churchill*, 258.
63. CAB 127/270; PREM 4/52/1, pp. 51–75.
64. There were a few generally compatible accounts of the meeting, including a couple by Weizmann and one by Churchill's aide Martin. Churchill quoted in Litvinoff, *Letters and Papers*, 21: 244; CZA Z4/14792. Also see PREM 4/52/3, pp. 410–411, 414–420, 424; CHAR 2/315, p. 18; Litvinoff, *Letters and Papers*, 21: 246; Michael Cohen, *Churchill*, 307.
65. Weizmann quoted in CZA Z4/14792. Churchill quoted in *FRUS 1945: The Conferences of Malta and Yalta*, 14. Also see Wasserstein, *Britain and the Jews*, 302; FO 371/45376, p. 48; *FRUS 1945: The Conferences of Malta and Yalta*, 10–14.
66. Churchill quoted in Rhodes James, *Speeches*, 7: 7034–7035. *Jewish Chronicle* quote from "The Prime Minister's Statement" (editorial), *Jewish Chronicle*, November 24, 1944, 8. Also see Wasserstein, *Britain and the Jews*, 304; CZA Z4/14792; PREM 4/52/5, pp. 882–886; PREM 4/51/11, pp. 1486–1489, 1495–1499, 1508–1513; Litvinoff, *Letters and Papers*, 21: 252n2; Bethell, *Palestine Triangle*, 184–186; Zweig, *Britain and Palestine*, 176.
67. Churchill quoted in PREM 3/296/9, p. 203–204. Also see PREM 3/296/9, pp. 205–207; Churchill, *Second World War: Triumph and Tragedy*, 247–283.
68. Churchill quoted in PREM 4/52/3, pp. 360, 397. Eden quoted in PREM 4/52/3, p. 360. Also see PREM 4/52/3, pp. 358–376, 395–401.
69. Churchill quoted in Litvinoff, 21: 305n1. Roosevelt quoted in *FRUS 1945: The Near East and Africa*, 690–691. Stalin quoted in *FRUS 1945: The Conferences of Malta and Yalta*, 924. Also see PREM 4/52/3, pp. 310, 341–343.
70. Eddy's contemporary official account is used here, instead of a slightly different version published in 1954 through a pro-Arab organization. Churchill quoted in CAB 65/51, p. 79. Ibn Saud quoted in *FRUS 1945: The Near East and Africa*, 689–690. Also see Brecher, *Reluctant Ally*, 143; Eddy, *F.D.R. Meets Ibn Saud*, 30, 34–36; *FRUS 1945: The Near East and Africa*, 694–695; Churchill, *Second World War: Triumph and Tragedy*, 348–349.
71. Ibn Saud quoted in *FRUS 1945: The Near East and Africa*, 689. Churchill quoted in Rhodes James, *Speeches*, 7: 7120. Also see Safran, *Saudi Arabia*, 57–63; Kedourie, *Chatham House*, 228–230; Sykes, *Israel*, 239.
72. Ibn Saud quoted in *FRUS 1945: The Near East and Africa*, 687. Roosevelt

quoted in *FRUS, 1945: The Near East and Africa*, 2–3. Also see Yergin, *The Prize*, 395, 397, 399–403; Eddy, *F.D.R. Meets Ibn Saud*, 30; Bohlen, *Witness to History*, 203–204; Campbell and Herring, *Edward R. Stettinius, Jr.*, 211; *FRUS 1945: The Near East and Africa*, 7–9, 679–682.

73. Roosevelt quoted in Grose, "President versus the Diplomats," 38. Also see Litvinoff, *Letters and Papers*, 21: 305n1; PREM 4/52/3, pp. 341–343; *FRUS 1945: The Near East and Africa*, 690–691.
74. Childs, *Britain since 1945*, 47–48; Bullock, *Life and Times*, 47, 164; CZA Z4/302/27; Michael Cohen, *Churchill*, 252; Ignatieff, *Isaiah Berlin*, 118–119; Howard Sachar, *History of Israel*, 241; CHAR 20/234, pp. 20–22; PREM 4/52/1; PREM 4/52/5, p. 774; CO 733/461/6, p. 45.
75. Weizmann quoted in CHAR 20/234, p. 42. Churchill quoted in CHAR 20/194. Also see PREM 4/52/3, pp. 323–327; 335–336, 338; CHAR 20/234, pp. 13–14, 18–19, 21, 23, 31, 34, 37–41; *FRUS 1945 The Conference of Berlin*, 2: 244–260; CHAR 2/560, p. 153.
76. Churchill quoted in CHAR 20/234, pp. 8, 50. Also see Litvinoff, *Letters and Papers*, 21: 244, 246; Edmonds, *Setting the Mould*, 117; CHAR 20/234, p. 21.

CHAPTER 7. ZIONIST AT THE END

1. Safran, *Israel*, 28, 31.
2. Labour resolution quoted in Alderman, *British Politics*, 125. Also see Grose, "President versus the Diplomats," ix, 32–44 Alderman, *British Politics*, 124; Gilbert, *Exile and Return*, 272–296; Howard Sachar, *History of Israel*, 249–274; Bullock, *Life and Times*, 167; *FRUS 1945: The Near East and Africa*, 772–773; *FRUS 1946*, 7: 652–667.
3. Gilbert, *Exile and Return*, 297–309; Howard Sachar, *History of Israel*, 277–314.
4. Weizmann quoted in Litvinoff, *Letters and Papers*, 22: 67. Churchill quoted in Litvinoff, *Letters and Papers*, 22: 120n9. Also see Gilbert, *Churchill and Zionism*, 26; Litvinoff, *Letters and Papers*, 22: 70n2, 74n2, 120n9.
5. Churchill quoted in CZA, Z5/1133; Gilbert, *Winston S. Churchill: "Never Despair,"* 253. Also see Gilbert, *Winston S. Churchill: "Never Despair,"* 210–211.
6. Churchill quoted in Soames, *Winston and Clementine*, 535. Also see Jenkins, *Churchill*, 279–280.
7. Channon quoted in Rhodes James, *Chips*, 426. Meinertzhagen quoted in Meinertzhagen, *Middle East Diary*, 211. Also see Gilbert, *Churchill and Zionism*, 26; Gilbert, *Winston S. Churchill: "Never Despair,"* 155, 417; Churchill, *Second World War: Gathering Storm*; Rhodes James, *Speeches*, 7: 7404; A. Clark, *Tories*, 265; Cesarani, *Jewish Chronicle*, 193–195.
8. Churchill quoted in Rhodes James, *Speeches*, 7: 7329, 7373, 7376, 7375; Gilbert, *Winston S. Churchill: "Never Despair,"* 230.
9. Churchill quoted in Rhodes James, *Speeches*, 7: 7378. Also see Kyle, *Suez*, 20–21; Devereux, *Formulation of British Defence Policy*, 6–7.

10. Churchill quoted in Rhodes James, *Speeches*, 7: 7329, 7378–7379; Gilbert, *Winston S. Churchill: "Never Despair,"* 237.
11. Churchill quoted in Rhodes James, *Speeches*, 7: 7377. Also see CZA, Z5/1133.
12. Churchill quoted in Rhodes James, *Speeches*, 7: 7330, 7372, 7376.
13. Churchill quoted in Rhodes James, *Speeches*, 7: 7375–7376, 7379, 7487.
14. Churchill quoted in Rhodes James, *Speeches*, 7: 7374–7376, 7404; Gilbert, *Winston S. Churchill: "Never Despair,"* 244.
15. Churchill quoted in Rhodes James, *Speeches*, 7: 7374, 7376.
16. Churchill quoted in Rhodes James, *Speeches*, 7: 7404, 7457, 7476, 7549. Also see Bethell, *Palestine Triangle*, 358; V. Smith, *Oxford History of India*, 829–833; Gaddis, *The United States*, 351; Rhodes James, *Speeches*, 7: 7404, 7421–7425, 7445–7446, 7457, 7476, 7504, 7549; Gilbert, *Winston S. Churchill: "Never Despair,"* 359–360.
17. Churchill quoted in Rhodes James, *Speeches*, 7: 7422, 7425, 7476. Conservative MP Cuthbert Headlam diary quoted in Ball, *Parliament and Politics*, 490.
18. Churchill quoted in Gilbert, *Winston S. Churchill: "Never Despair,"* 371. Also see "Anti-Jewish Riots in Britain," *Jewish Chronicle*, August 8, 1947, 1, 5.
19. Howard Sachar, *History of Israel*, 327, 331; Ignatieff, *Isaiah Berlin*, 180.
20. Churchill quoted in Gilbert, *Winston S. Churchill: "Never Despair,"* 411. Also see Howard Sachar, *History of Israel*, 336–338.
21. Churchill quoted in Rhodes James, *Speeches*, 7: 7654; "Conservatives and Palestine," *Jewish Chronicle*, October 22, 1948, 8. Also see Boothby, *My Yesterday, Your Tomorrow*, 212; Gilbert, *Winston S. Churchill: "Never Despair,"* 404, 421–422, 432–433; Gaddis, *We Now Know*, 89; Rhodes James, *Speeches*, 7: 7671, 7710.
22. Litvinoff, *Letters and Papers*, 23: 196n1; Boothby, *My Yesterday, Your Tomorrow*, 211; Gilbert, *Churchill and Zionism*, 23–24.
23. Berlin quoted in Berlin, "Weizmann," 57. Also see Berlin, "Weizmann," 57–59.
24. Churchill quoted in Rhodes James, *Speeches*, 7: 7766–7767. Also see Rhodes James, *Speeches*, 7: 7768–7769. Some historians, such as William Roger Louis and Bevin's sympathetic biographer Alan Bullock, claim that Bevin was not anti-Semitic. For their defense of Bevin see Louis, "British Imperialism," 1; Bullock, *Foreign Secretary*, 165–166, 169, 182–183.
25. Howard Sachar, *History of Israel*, 347–353; Morris, *Righteous Victims*, 259; Safran, *Israel*, 225.
26. Bevin quoted in PREM 8, 627/40477. Also see Howard Sachar, *History of Israel*, 353; Louis, *British Empire*, 17; Safran, *Israel*, 341.
27. Bevin quoted in Louis, *British Empire*, 43. Also see Louis, *British Empire*, 570; Ovendale, *End of the Palestine Mandate*, 16.
28. Rhodes James, *Speeches*, 7: 7774, 7777, 7778, 7780. Also see Howard Sachar, *History of Israel*, 346; Gilbert, *Winston S. Churchill: "Never Despair,"* 453.
29. Rhodes James, *Speeches*, 7: 7777.
30. Rhodes James, *Speeches*, 7: 7777.
31. Rhodes James, *Speeches*, 7: 7779; Churchill, *Second World War: Closing the Ring*, 471.

32. Rhodes James, *Speeches*, 7: 7779, 7782.
33. Rhodes James, *Speeches*, 7: 7782.
34. Churchill quoted in Rhodes James, *Speeches*, 7: 7782. Also see Kedourie, *Chatham House*, 231–233; Morris, *Righteous Victims*, 221–222; Louis, "British Imperialism," 24; Bullock, *Foreign Secretary*, 594; Safran, *United States and Israel*, 223–224.
35. Chiefs of Staff quoted in PREM 11/489. Churchill quoted in Shuckburgh, *Descent to Suez*, 250; PREM 11/465, p. 16.
36. Churchill quoted in Gilbert, *Winston S. Churchill: "Never Despair,"* 1093.
37. Churchill quoted in Rhodes James, *Speeches*, 8: 8060; Shuckburgh, *Descent to Suez*, 29. Also see Kyle, *Suez*, 9, 40.
38. Churchill quoted in PREM 11/465, pp. 8, 16; CAB 131/13; Gilbert, *Winston S. Churchill: "Never Despair,"* 1093.
39. Churchill quoted in Rhodes James, *Speeches*, 8: 8229. Also see Gilbert, *Winston S. Churchill: "Never Despair,"* 557–558; Kedourie, Chatham House, 230–231; Morris, *Righteous Victims*, 221–222, 260.
40. Churchill quoted in Moran, *Churchill*, 540; PREM 11/208; PREM 11/186, p. 10; PREM 11/941, p. 111. Lloyd quoted in PREM 11/490, p. 3. Also see PREM 11/186, pp. 2–14; PREM 11/490, pp. 2–10.
41. Churchill quoted in PREM 11/465, p. 24; PREM 11/941, p. 67; Moran, *Churchill*, 67; Ovendale, *Transfer of Power*, 97–98; PREM 11/481, 4.
42. Churchill quoted in Rhodes James, *Speeches*, 8: 8327, 8432; Gilbert, *Winston S. Churchill: "Never Despair,"* 1008; Colville, *Fringes of Power*, 663; Gilbert, *Churchill and Zionism*, 27. Also see Rhodes James, *Speeches*, 8: 8432; Colville, *Fringes of Power*, 664.
43. Churchill quoted in Gilbert, *Churchill and Zionism*, 27; Gilbert, *Winston S. Churchill: "Never Despair,"* 1096.
44. Churchill quoted in Gilbert, *Winston S. Churchill: "Never Despair,"* 557; Rhodes James, *Speeches*, 8: 8431; Shuckburgh, *Descent to Suez*, 250; PREM 11/941, 55. Also see Gilbert, *Winston S. Churchill: "Never Despair,"* 1096.
45. Churchill quoted in Gilbert, *Winston S. Churchill: "Never Despair,"* 557, 1008; Howard Sachar, *History of Israel*, 395–403; Gilbert, *Winston S. Churchill: "Never Despair,"* 1096–1097; Rhodes James, *Speeches*, 8: 8327.
46. Churchill quoted in Rhodes James, *Speeches*, 7: 7779, 8: 8327; PREM 11/207, 2–5; Gilbert, *Winston S. Churchill: "Never Despair,"* 558, 1008. Also see Gilbert, *Winston S. Churchill: "Never Despair,"* 558, 1008, 1096; Shuckburgh, *Descent to Suez*, 250.
47. Gilbert, *Winston S. Churchill: "Never Despair,"* 1097.

CONCLUSION

1. Soames, *Winston and Clementine*, 179; Gilbert, *Companion*, 4/2: 871–872; Rhodes James, *Speeches*, 6: 6248.
2. Rhodes James, *Speeches*, 6: 6248.

BIBLIOGRAPHY

Addison, Paul. *Churchill: The Unexpected Hero*. Oxford: Oxford University Press, 2005.
———. *Churchill on the Home Front, 1900–1955*. London: Pimlico, 1995.
———. *The Road to 1945: British Politics and the Second World War*. London: Pimlico, 1994.
Ahrari, Mohammed E. *The Dynamics of Oil Diplomacy: Conflict and Consensus*. New York: Arno Press, 1980.
Alderman, Geoffrey. *The Jewish Community in British Politics*. Oxford, U.K.: Clarendon Press, 1983.
———. *Modern British Jewry*. Oxford, U.K.: Clarendon Press, 1992.
Allfrey, Anthony. *Edward VII and His Jewish Court*. London: Weidenfeld and Nicolson, 1991.
Alteras, Isaac. *Eisenhower and Israel: U.S.-Israeli Relations, 1953–1960*. Gainesville: University Press of Florida, 1993.
Ambrose, Stephen E. *Eisenhower: The President*, vol. 2. New York: Simon and Schuster, 1984.
Anderson, Stuart. *Race and Rapprochement: Anglo-Saxonism and Anglo-American Relations, 1895–1904*. Rutherford, N.J.: Fairleigh Dickinson University, 1981.
Anisimov, Oleg. *The Ultimate Weapon*. Chicago: Regnery, 1953.
Annan, Baron Noel Gilroy. *Our Age: Portrait of a Generation*. London: Weidenfeld and Nicolson, 1990.
———. "Three Generations in England." *Daedalus* 107, no. 4 (Fall 1978), 81–110.
Arnot, Robert Page. *The Impact of the Russian Revolution in Britain*. London: Lawrence and Wishart, 1967.
Ashley, Maurice. *Churchill as Historian*. London: Secker and Warburg, 1968.

Asquith, H. H. *Letters to Venetia Stanley*. Oxford: Oxford University Press, 1982.

———. *Memories and Reflections, 1852–1927*, vol. 2. Boston: Little, Brown, 1928.

Athanassopoulou, Ekavi. *Turkey: Anglo-American Security Interests, 1945–1952: The First Enlargement of NATO*. London: Frank Cass, 1999.

Attlee, Clement Richard. "The Churchill I Knew." In *Churchill by His Contemporaries*. London: Hodder and Stoughton, 1965.

———. *Purpose and Policy: Selected Speeches, May 1945–Nov. 1946*. Edited by Roy Jenkins. London: Hutchinson, 1947.

———. *War Comes to Britain: Speeches of the Rt. Hon. C. R. Attlee, M.P.* Edited by John Dugdale. London: V. Gollancz, 1940.

Avineri, Shlomo. *The Making of Modern Zionism: The Intellectual Origins of the Jewish State*. New York: Basic Books, 1981.

Baker, Ray Stannard. *What Wilson Did at Paris*. Garden City, N.Y.: Doubleday, Page, 1922.

Ball, Stuart, ed. *Parliament and Politics in the Age of Churchill and Attlee: The Headlam Diaries, 1935–1941*. Cambridge: Cambridge University Press, 1999.

Barnes, John, and David Nicholson, eds. *The Empire at Bay: The Leo Amery Diaries*, vol. 2, 1929–1945. London: Hutchinson, 1988.

———. *The Leo Amery Diaries*, vol. 1. London: Hutchinson, 1980.

Barnett, Correlli. *The Collapse of British Power*. New York: William Morrow, 1972.

Baylis, John, and Alan Macmillan. "The British Global Strategy Paper of 1952." *Journal of Strategic Studies* 16, no. 2 (June 1993), 200–226.

Bayme, Steven. "Jewry and Judaism." In Mitchell, *Victorian Britain*, 411–413.

Beaconsfield, Earl of. *Coningsby, or The New Generation*. London: Longmans, Green, 1900.

———. *Lord George Bentinck*. London: Longmans, Green, 1881.

———. *Tancred, or The New Crusade*. London: Longmans, Green, 1900.

Beaverbrook, Lord. *Politicians and the War, 1914–1916*. London: Collins, 1960.

Bein, Alex. *Theodore Herzl: A Biography*. Translated by Maurice Samuel. Philadelphia: The Jewish Publication Society of America, 1940.

Bell, Coral. *Negotiation from Strength*. London: Chatto and Windus, 1962.

Beloff, Lord. *Britain's Liberal Empire, 1897–1921*. London: Methuen, 1969.

———. "The End of the British Empire and the Assumption of World-Wide Commitments by the United States." In Louis and Bull, *Special Relationship*, 249–260.

Ben-Moshe, Tuvia. *Churchill, Strategy and History*. Boulder, Colo.: Lynne Rienner, 1992.

Ben-Sasson, H. H., ed. *A History of the Jewish People*. Cambridge, Mass.: Harvard University Press, 1976.

Berlin, Isaiah. "Benjamin Disraeli, Karl Marx and the Search for Identity." In *Against the Current*, 252–286. New York: Viking Press, 1980.

———. "Chaim Weizmann." In Berlin, *Personal Impressions*, 32–62.

———. "Chaim Weizmann's Leadership." In Berlin, *The Power of Ideas*, 186–194.

———. "Einstein and Israel." In Berlin, *Personal Impressions*, 144–155.

———. "Jewish Slavery and Emancipation." In Berlin, *The Power of Ideas*, 163–185.
———. "The Life and Opinions of Moses Hess," In *Against the Current*, 213–251. London: Pimlico, 1997.
———. "The Origins of Israel." In Berlin, *The Power of Ideas*, 143–161.
———. *Personal Impressions*. London: Hogarth Press, 1980.
———. *The Power of Ideas*. London: Chatto and Windus, 2000.
———. "Winston Churchill in 1940." In Berlin, *Personal Impressions*, 1–22.
Bethell, Nicholas. *The Palestine Triangle: The Struggle for the Holy Land, 1935–48*. New York: G. P. Putnam's Sons, 1979.
Bermant, Chaim. *The Cousinhood: The Anglo-Jewish Gentry*. London: Eyre and Spottiswoode, 1971.
Beschloss, Michael. *The Conquerors*. New York: Simon and Schuster, 2002.
Black, Eugene C. *The Social Politics of Anglo-Jewry, 1880–1920*. Oxford, U.K.: Basil Blackwell, 1988.
Blake, Robert. *Disraeli*. London: Eyre and Spottiswoode, 1966.
———. *Disraeli's Grand Tour: Benjamin Disraeli and the Holy Land, 1830–1831*. New York: Oxford University Press, 1982.
———. *The Unknown Prime Minister: The Life and Times of Andrew Bonar Law, 1858–1923*. London: Eyre and Spottiswoode, 1955.
Blake, Robert, and William Roger Louis, eds. *Churchill*. New York: W. W. Norton, 1993.
Bolchover, Richard. *British Jewry and the Holocaust*. Cambridge: Cambridge University Press, 1993.
Bohlen, Charles E. *Witness to History, 1929–1969*. New York: W. W. Norton, 1973.
Bonham Carter, Violet. *Winston Churchill as I Knew Him*. London: Weidenfeld and Nicolson, 1995.
Boothby, Robert John Graham, Baron. *My Yesterday, Your Tomorrow*: London: Hutchinson, 1962.
Bowle, John. *Viscount Samuel: A Biography*. London: V. Gollancz, 1957.
Bowler, Peter J. *The Invention of Progress: The Victorians and the Past*. Oxford, U.K.: Basil Blackwell, 1989.
Boyle, Peter G., ed. *The Churchill-Eisenhower Correspondence, 1953–1955*. Chapel Hill: University of North Carolina Press, 1990.
Brecher, Frank W. *Reluctant Ally: United States Foreign Policy toward the Jews from Wilson to Roosevelt*. New York: Greenwood Press, 1991.
Breitman, Richard. "The Failure to Provide a Safe Haven for European Jewry." In *FDR and the Holocaust*, edited by Verne W. Newton, 129–143. New York: St. Martin's Press, 1996.
———. *Official Secrets: What the Nazis Planned, What the British and Americans Knew*. New York: Hill and Wang, 1998.
Briggs, Asa. *Victorian People: A Reassessment of Persons and Themes, 1851–67*. Chicago: University of Chicago Press, 1970.
Broad, Lewis. *Winston Churchill*. London: Hutchinson, 1952.
Brodie, Bernard, ed. *The Absolute Weapon: Atomic Power and World Order*. New York: Harcourt, 1946.

———. *War and Politics.* New York: Macmillan, 1973.
Broglie, Duc de, ed. *Memoirs of the Prince de Talleyrand,* vol. 2. Translated by Raphael Ledos de Beufort. London: Griffith Farran Okeden and Welsh, 1891.
Bryant, Arthur. *Triumph in the West.* New York: Doubleday, 1959.
Bryson, Thomas A. *American Diplomatic Relations with the Middle East, 1784–1975.* Metuchen, N.J.: Scarecrow Press, 1977.
———. *Seeds of Mideast Crisis: The United States Diplomatic Role in the Middle East During World War II.* Jefferson, N.C.: McFarland, 1981.
Buber, Martin. *A Land of Two Peoples: Martin Buber on Jews and Arabs.* Edited by Paul R. Mendes-Flohr. New York: Oxford University Press, 1983.
Bullen, Roger, ed. *Documents on British Policy Overseas, 1945,* vol. 2. London: H.M.S.O., 1985.
Bullock, Alan. *Ernest Bevin: Foreign Secretary, 1945–1951.* New York: W. W. Norton, 1983.
Burbidge, William Frank. *Field-Marshal Smuts, Soldier and World Statesman.* London: W. S. Cowell, 1943.
Busch, Briton Cooper. *Britain, India and the Arabs.* Berkeley: University of California, 1971.
Butler, Rohan, and M. E. Pelly, eds. *Documents on British Policy Overseas, 1945,* vol. 1. London: H.M.S.O., 1985.
Campbell, Thomas M., and George C. Herring. *The Diaries of Edward R. Stettinius, Jr., 1943–1946.* New York: New Viewpoints, 1975.
Campbell-Johnson, Alan. *Mission with Mountbatten.* London: R. Hale, 1953.
Capstick, Peter Hathaway. *Warrior: The Legend of Colonel Richard Meinertzhagen.* New York: St. Martin's Press, 1998.
Carlton, David. *Anthony Eden: A Biography.* London: Allen and Unwin, 1981.
———. *Churchill and the Soviet Union.* New York: St. Martin's Press, 2000.
Casillas, Rex J. *Oil and Diplomacy: The Evolution of American Foreign Policy in Saudi Arabia, 1933–1945.* New York: Garland, 1987.
Charmley, John. *Churchill: The End of Glory.* London: Hodder and Stoughton, 1993.
———. *Churchill's Grand Alliance: The Anglo-American Special Relationship, 1940–57.* London: Hodder and Stoughton, 1995.
———. *Lord Lloyd and the Decline of the British Empire.* New York: St. Martin's Press, 1987.
Carr, Edward Hallett. *Conditions of Peace.* New York: Macmillan Company, 1943.
Cesarani, David. *The Jewish Chronicle and Anglo-Jewry, 1841–1991.* Cambridge: Cambridge University Press, 1994.
Chester, Edward W. *United States Oil Policy and Diplomacy: A Twentieth Century Overview.* Westport, Conn.: Greenwood Press, 1983.
Childs, David. *Britain since 1945: A Political History.* London: Methuen, 1986.
Churchill, Randolph S. *Winston S. Churchill,* vol. 1, *Youth, 1874–1900.* Boston: Houghton Mifflin, 1966.
———. *Winston S. Churchill,* vol. 2, *Young Statesman, 1901–1914.* London: Heinemann, 1967.

———. *Winston S. Churchill: Companion*, vol. 1, part 1, *1874–1896*. London: Heinemann, 1967.
———. *Winston S. Churchill: Companion*, vol. 1, part 2, *1896–1900*. London: Heinemann, 1967.
———. *Winston S. Churchill: Companion*, vol. 2, part 1, *1901–1907*. London: Heinemann, 1969.
———. *Winston S. Churchill: Companion*, vol. 2, part 2, *1907–1911*. London: Heinemann, 1969.
———. *Winston S. Churchill: Companion*, vol. 2, part 3, *1911–1914*. London: Heinemann, 1969.
Churchill, Winston S. *The Age of Revolution*. Vol. 3 of *A History of the English-Speaking Peoples*. London: Cassell, 1957.
———. "The Battle of Sidney Street." In *Thoughts and Adventures*, 41–47. Oxford, U.K.: Library of Imperial History, 1974.
———. *The Collected Essays of Sir Winston Churchill*. 4 vols. Edited by Michael Wolff. [London]: Library of Imperial History, 1976.
———. *Great Contemporaries*. London: Leo Cooper, 1990.
———. *The Great Democracies*. Vol. 4 of *A History of the English-Speaking Peoples*. New York: Dodd, Mead, 1958.
———. *India*. London: Thornton Butterworth, 1931.
———. *Lord Randolph Churchill*. 2 vols. New York: Macmillan, 1906.
———. *Marlborough: His Life and Times*. 2 vols. London: George G. Harrap, 1966. First published in 1933.
———. "Moses: The Leader of a People." In *Thoughts and Adventures*, 209–213. Oxford, U.K.: Library of Imperial History, 1974.
———. *My African Journey*. New York: W. W. Norton, 1990. First published in 1908.
———. *The River War*. 2 vols. London: Longmans, Green, 1899.
———. *Savrola*. London: Leo Cooper, 1990. First published in 1899.
———. *The Second World War*, vol. 1, *The Gathering Storm*. Boston: Houghton Mifflin, 1985.
———. *The Second World War*, vol. 2, *Their Finest Hour*. Boston: Houghton Mifflin, 1985.
———. *The Second World War*, vol. 3, *The Grand Alliance*. Boston: Houghton Mifflin, 1985.
———. *The Second World War*, vol. 4, *The Hinge of Fate*. Boston: Houghton Mifflin, 1985.
———. *The Second World War*, vol. 5, *Closing the Ring*. Boston: Houghton Mifflin, 1985.
———. *The Second World War*, vol. 6, *Triumph and Tragedy*. Boston: Houghton Mifflin, 1985.
———. *Step by Step, 1936–1939*. New York: G. P. Putnam's Sons, 1939.
———. *The Story of My Early Life: A Roving Commission*. New York: Charles Scribner's Sons, 1958. First published in 1930.

———. *The Story of the Malakand Field Force.* London: Longmans, Green, 1901.
———. *Winston Churchill on America and Britain: A Selection of His Thoughts on Anglo-American Relations.* Edited by Kay Halle. New York: Walker, 1970.
———. *The World Crisis: 1911–1914.* New York: Charles Scribner's Sons, 1924.
———. *The World Crisis: 1915.* London: Thornton Butterworth, 1923.
———. *The World Crisis: 1916–1918.* 2 vols. London: Thornton Butterworth, 1927.
———. *The World Crisis: The Aftermath, 1918–1928.* London: Thornton Butterworth, 1929.
Churchill, Winston S. [Churchill's grandson]. *His Father's Son: The Life of Randolph Churchill.* London: Weidenfeld and Nicolson, 1996.
Clark, Alan. *The Tories: Conservatives and the Nation State, 1922–1997.* London: Weidenfeld and Nicolson, 1997.
Clark, Ian, and Nicholas J. Wheeler. *The British Origins of Nuclear Strategy, 1945–1955.* Oxford, U.K.: Clarendon Press, 1989.
Cohen, Gavriel. *Churchill and Palestine, 1939–1942.* Jerusalem: Yad Izhak Ben-Zvi Publications, 1976.
Cohen, Michael J. "American Influence on British Policy in the Middle East during World War Two: First Attempts at Coordinating Allied Policy on Palestine." *American Jewish History Quarterly* 67 (September 1977), 50–70.
———. *Churchill and the Jews.* London: Frank Cass, 1985.
———. "Direction of Policy in Palestine, 1936–1945." *Middle Eastern Studies* 11, no. 3 (October 1975), 237–261.
———. *Fighting World War Three from the Middle East: Allied Contingency Plans, 1945–1954.* London: Frank Cass, 1997.
———. *Palestine, Retreat from the Mandate: The Making of British Policy, 1936–45.* New York: Holmes and Meier, 1978.
———. *Palestine and the Great Powers, 1945–1948.* Princeton: Princeton University Press, 1982.
———. *The Rise of Israel: The Anglo-American Committee on Palestine, 1945–1946.* New York: Garland, 1987.
———. *Truman and Israel.* Berkeley: University of California Press, 1990.
Cohen, Michael J., and Martin Kolinsky, eds. *Britain and the Middle East in the 1930s.* London: Macmillan, 1992.
Cohen, Mitchell. *Zion and State: Nation, Class, and the Shaping of Modern Israel.* New York: Columbia University Press, 1992.
Cohen, Stuart. *English Zionists and British Jews: The Communal Politics of Anglo-Jewry, 1895–1920.* Princeton: Princeton University Press, 1982.
Collins, Larry, and Dominique Lapierre. *Freedom at Midnight.* New York: Simon and Schuster, 1975.
Colville, Sir John Rupert. *Footprints in Time.* London: Collins, 1976.
———. *The Fringes of Power: 10 Downing Street Diaries, 1939–1955.* New York: W. W. Norton, 1985.
Commission of the Churches on International Affairs. *Christian Responsibility in World Affairs.* New York: The Commission, 1949.

Coote, Colin Reith, ed. *A Churchill Reader: The Wit and Wisdom of Sir Winston Churchill*. Boston: Houghton Mifflin, 1954.

Cowles, Virginia. *Winston Churchill: The Era and the Man*. New York: Harper and Brothers, 1953.

Crook, D. P. *Darwinism, War, and History: The Debate over the Biology of War from the "Origin of Species" to the First World War*. Cambridge: Cambridge University Press, 1994.

Dallek, Robert. *Franklin D. Roosevelt and American Foreign Policy, 1932–1945*. Oxford: Oxford University Press, 1981.

Darwin, John. *Britain, Egypt and the Middle East Imperial Policy in the Aftermath of War, 1918–1922*. Hong Kong: Macmillan, 1981.

Davenport, Ernest Harold, and Sidney Russell Cooke. *The Oil Trusts and Anglo-American Relations: The History and Politics of Oil*. Westport, Conn.: Hyperion Press, 1976.

Davis, Eli, and David A. Frenkel. *Ha-Kamea ha-Ivri: Mikrai, refui, kelali: Im tatslumim ve-iyurim rabim*. Jerusalem: Makhon le-madae ha-Yahadut, 1995.

Defries, Harry. *Conservative Party Attitudes to Jews, 1900–1950*. London: Frank Cass, 2001.

Dehio, Ludwig. *The Precarious Balance: Four Centuries of the European Power Struggle*. New York: Knopf, 1962.

De Santis, Hugh. *The Diplomacy of Silence: The American Foreign Service, the Soviet Union, and the Cold War, 1933–1947*. Chicago: University of Chicago Press, 1983.

Devereux, David R. *The Formulation of British Defence Policy towards the Middle East, 1948–56*. London: Macmillan, 1990.

Diggins, John P. *Mussolini and Fascism: The View from America*. Princeton: Princeton University Press, 1972.

Dilks, David, ed. *The Diaries of Sir Alexander Cadogan, 1938–1945*. London: Cassell, 1971.

———. *Neville Chamberlain*. Cambridge: Cambridge University Press, 1984.

Disraeli, Benjamin. *Lord George Bentinck: A Political Biography*. London: Longmans, Green, 1872. First published in 1851.

———. *See also* Beaconsfield, Earl of.

Divine, Robert A. *Eisenhower and the Cold War*. Oxford: Oxford University Press, 1981.

Documents Relating to the Palestine Problem. London: Jewish Agency for Palestine, 1945.

Donoughue, Bernard, and G. W. Jones. *Herbert Morrison: Portrait of a Politician*. London: Weidenfeld and Nicolson, 1973.

Dunbabin, J. P. D. *International Relations since 1945: A History in Two Volumes*. 2 vols. London: Longman, 1994.

Eade, Charles, ed. *Churchill, by His Contemporaries*. London: Hutchinson, 1953.

Eddy, William A. *F.D.R. Meets Ibn Saud*. New York: American Friends of the Middle East, 1954.

Eden, Anthony. *Full Circle*. Cassel: London, 1960.
Edmonds, Robin. "Churchill and Stalin." In Blake and Louis, *Churchill*, 309–326.
———. *Setting the Mould: The United States and Britain, 1945–1950*. Oxford, U.K.: Clarendon Press, 1986.
Edwardes, Michael. *The Last Years of British India*. London: Cassell, 1963.
Eisenhower, Dwight D. *The White House Years: Mandate for Change, 1953–1956*. Garden City: Doubleday, 1963.
Eliot, George. *Daniel Deronda*. Edited by Graham Handley. Oxford, U.K.: Clarendon Press, 1984.
Emmert, Kirk R. *Winston S. Churchill on Empire*. Durham, N.C.: Carolina Academic Press and the Claremont Institute for the Study of Statesmanship and Political Philosophy, 1989.
Endelman, Todd M. " 'A Hebrew to the End': The Emergence of Disraeli's Jewishness." In *The Self-Fashioning of Disraeli: 1818–1851*, edited by Charles Richmond and Paul Smith. Cambridge: Cambridge University Press, 1998.
Feingold, Henry L. "Bombing Auschwitz and the Politics of the Jewish Question during World War II." In Neufeld and Berenbaum, *The Bombing of Auschwitz*.
———. *The Politics of Rescue: The Roosevelt Administration and the Holocaust, 1938–1945*. New Brunswick, N.J.: Rutgers University Press, 1970.
Feis, Herbert. *Churchill, Roosevelt, Stalin: The War They Waged and the Peace They Sought*, 2nd ed. Princeton: Princeton University Press, 1967.
———. "Petroleum and American Foreign Policy." Food Research Institute, Stanford University, Stanford, Calif., 1944.
Feith, Douglas J. "Palestine and Zionism, 1904–1922." In Muller, *Churchill as Peacemaker*, 210–262.
Feldman, David. *Englishmen and Jews: Social Relations and Political Culture, 1840–1914*. New Haven: Yale University Press, 1994.
Ferguson, Niall. *The World's Banker: The History of the House of Rothschild*. London: Weidenfeld and Nicolson, 1998.
Finestein, Israel. *A Short History of Anglo-Jewry*. London: Lincolns-Prager, 1957.
Fish, M. Steven. "After Stalin's Death: The Anglo-American Debate over a New Cold War." *Diplomatic History* 10, no.4 (1986), 333–355.
Folliot, Denise, ed. *Documents on International Affairs, 1953*. London: Oxford University Press, 1956.
Foster, R. F. *Lord Randolph Churchill: A Political Life*. Oxford, U.K.: Clarendon Press, 1981.
Freedman, Lawrence. *The Evolution of Nuclear Strategy*. New York: St. Martin's Press, 1983.
Frey, Linda, and Marsha Frey, ed. *The Treaties of the War of the Spanish Succession*. Westport, Conn.: Greenwood Press, 1995.
Friedberg, Aaron L. *The Weary Titan: Britain and the Experience of Relative Decline, 1895–1905*. Princeton: Princeton University Press, 1988.
Fromkin, David. *A Peace to End All Peace: Creating the Modern Middle East, 1914–1922*. London: A. Deutsch, 1989.

Gaddis, John Lewis. Conclusion to Gaddis, Gordon, and May, *Cold War Statesmen Confront the Bomb*.
———. *Strategies of Containment*. Oxford: Oxford University Press, 1982.
———. *The United States and the Origins of the Cold War, 1941–1947*. New York: Columbia University Press, 1972.
———. *We Now Know*. New York: Oxford University Press, 1997.
Gaddis, John Lewis, Philip H. Gordon, and Ernest R. May, eds. *Cold War Statesmen Confront the Bomb*. Oxford: Oxford University Press, 1999.
Ganin, Zvi. *Truman, American Jewry, and Israel, 1945–1948*. New York: Holmes and Meier, 1979.
Gardiner, A. G. "Mr. Churchill." In *Pillars of Society*, 55–63. London: James Nisbet, 1913.
———. *Portraits and Portents*. New York: Harper and Brothers, 1926.
Garrard, John A. *The English and Immigration, 1880–1910*. London: Oxford University Press, 1971.
Gelb, Leslie H. *Anglo-American Relations, 1945–1949: Toward a Theory of Alliances*. Harvard Dissertations in American History and Political Science. New York: Garland, 1988.
Gerard, James W. *Peace of Utrecht*. New York: G. P. Putnam's Sons, 1885.
Gilbert, Martin. *Auschwitz and the Allies*. New York: Holt, Rinehart and Winston, 1981.
———. *Churchill: A Life*. New York: Henry Holt, 1991.
———. *Churchill and Zionism*. London: World Jewish Congress, 1974.
———. *Churchill's Political Philosophy*. Oxford: Oxford University Press for the British Academy, 1981.
———. *The Churchill War Papers*, vol. 1, *At the Admiralty, September 1939–May 1940*. New York: W. W. Norton, 1993.
———. *The Churchill War Papers*, vol. 2, *Never Surrender, May 1940–December 1940*. New York: W. W. Norton, 1995.
———. *The Churchill War Papers*, vol. 3, *The Ever-Widening War, 1941*. New York: W. W. Norton, 2001.
———. "The Contemporary Case for the Feasibility of Bombing Auschwitz." In Neufeld and Berenbaum, *The Bombing of Auschwitz*.
———. *Exile and Return: The Struggle for a Jewish Homeland*. Philadelphia: Lippincott, 1978.
———. "From Yalta to Bermuda and Beyond." In Muller, *Churchill as Peacemaker*, 304–332.
———. *The Holocaust*. New York: Holt, Rinehart and Winston, 1985.
———. "'The Most Horrible Crime.'" *Times Literary Supplement*, June 7, 1996, 3–5.
———. *Winston S. Churchill*, vol. 3, *1914–1916*. London: Heinemann, 1971.
———. *Winston S. Churchill*, vol. 4, *The Stricken World, 1916–1922*. Boston: Houghton Mifflin, 1975.
———. *Winston S. Churchill*, vol. 5, *1922–1939*. London: Heinemann, 1976.

———. *Winston S. Churchill*, vol. 6, *Finest Hour, 1939–1941*. London: Heinemann, 1983.

———. *Winston S. Churchill*, vol. 7, *Road to Victory, 1941–1945*. London: Heinemann, 1986.

———. *Winston S. Churchill*, vol. 8, *"Never Despair," 1945–1965*. Boston: Houghton Mifflin, 1988.

———. *Winston S. Churchill: Companion Documents*, vol. 3, part 1, *July 1914–April 1915*. London: Heinemann, 1972.

———. *Winston S. Churchill: Companion Documents*, vol. 3, part 2, *May 1915–December 1916*. London: Heinemann, 1972.

———. *Winston S. Churchill: Companion Documents*, vol. 4, part 1, *January 1917–June 1919*. London: Heinemann, 1977.

———. *Winston S. Churchill: Companion Documents*, vol. 4, part 2, *July 1919–March 1921*. London: Heinemann, 1977.

———. *Winston S. Churchill: Companion Documents*, vol. 4, part 3, *April 1921–November 1922*. London: Heinemann, 1977.

———. *Winston S. Churchill: Companion Documents*, vol. 5, part 1, *The Exchequer Years, 1922–1929*. Boston: Houghton Mifflin, 1981.

———. *Winston S. Churchill: Companion Documents*, vol. 5, part 2, *The Wilderness Years, 1929–1935*. Boston: Houghton Mifflin, 1981.

———. *Winston S. Churchill: Companion Documents*, vol. 5, part 3, *The Coming of War, 1936–1939*. Boston: Houghton Mifflin, 1981.

Gilmour, David. "The Unregarded Prophet: Lord Curzon and the Palestine Question." *Journal of Palestine Studies* 25, no. 3 (Spring 1996), 60–68.

Goldsworthy, David, ed. *The Conservative Government and the End of Empire, 1951–1957*, vol. 1. London: Crown, 1994.

Goodwin, Frederick K., and Kay R. Jamison. *Manic-Depressive Illness*. New York: Oxford University Press, 1990.

Gowing, Margaret. *Independence and Deterrence: Britain and Atomic Energy, 1945–1952*. London: Macmillan (for the United Kingdom Atomic Energy Authority), 1974.

Gravier, Charles. "Memoir of M. de Vergennes at the Beginning of the Reign of Louis XVI, in 1774." In *Theory and Practice of the Balance of Power, 1486–1914*, edited by Moorhead Wright. London: Rowman and Littlefield, 1975.

Grayson, Richard. "The Cabinet Minister's Traitor Son." *History Today* 55, no. 9 (September 2005), 6–7.

Grigg, John. "Churchill and Lloyd George." In Blake and Louis, *Churchill*, 97–111.

Grose, Peter. *Israel in the Mind of America*. New York: Schocken Books, 1984.

———. "The President versus the Diplomats." In Louis and Stookey, *The End of the Palestine Mandate*, 32–60.

Hahn, Peter L. *The United States, Great Britain, and Egypt, 1945–1956: Strategy and Diplomacy in the Early Cold War*. Chapel Hill: University of North Carolina Press, 1991.

Halévy, Elie. *A History of the English People in the Nineteenth Century*. Translated by E. I. Watkin. New York: Barnes and Noble, 1961.

———. *Victorian Years, 1841–1895: Incorporating "The Age of Peel and Cobden"*. London: Benn, 1951.

———. *The World Crisis of 1914–1918: An Interpretation*. Oxford, U.K.: Clarendon Press, 1930.

Handley, Graham, ed. *Daniel Deronda*, by George Eliot. Oxford, U.K.: Clarendon Press, 1984.

Harbutt, Fraser J. *The Iron Curtain: Churchill, America, and the Origins of the Cold War*. New York: Oxford University Press, 1986.

Haron, Miriam Joyce. *Palestine and the Anglo-American Connection, 1945–1950*. New York: Peter Lang, 1986.

Harper, John Lamberton. *American Visions of Europe: Franklin D. Roosevelt, George F. Kennan, and Dean G. Acheson*. New York: Cambridge University Press, 1994.

Harriman, W. Averell, and Elie Abel. *Special Envoy to Churchill and Stalin, 1941–1946*. New York: Random House, 1975.

Harvey, John, ed. *The War Diaries of Oliver Harvey*. London: Collins, 1978.

Hathaway, Robert M. *Ambiguous Partnership: Britain and America, 1944–1947*. Contemporary American History Series. New York: Columbia University Press, 1981.

Heath, F. W. *Great Destiny*. New York: G. P. Putnam's Sons, 1965.

Henriques, Robert. *Marcus Samuel*. London: Barrie and Rockliff, 1960.

Hertslet, Edward. *Map of Europe by Treaty*, vol. 1. London: Butterworths, 1875.

Hertzberg, Arthur, ed. *The Zionist Idea*. New York: Meridian Books, 1960.

Herzl, Theodor. *The Jewish State: An Attempt at a Modern Solution of the Jewish Question*. New York: Scopus, 1943.

Hess, Moses. *Rome and Jerusalem*. New York: Jewish Radical Education Project, 1996.

Hinsley, F. H., ed. *British Intelligence in the Second World War*, vol. 2. London: H.M.S.O., 1981.

Hoff, Joan. *Ideology and Economics: U.S. Relations with the Soviet Union, 1918–1933*. Columbia: University of Missouri Press, 1974.

Hogan, Michael J. *America in the World: The Historiography of American Foreign Relations since 1941*. New York: Cambridge University Press, 1995.

Holland, Robert. "The British Empire and the Great War, 1914–1918." In Louis and Brown, *Oxford History of the British Empire*, 114–137.

Holmes, Colin. *Anti-Semitism in British Society, 1876–1939*. London: E. Arnold, 1979.

Hughes, Emmet J. *The Ordeal of Power: A Political Memoir of the Eisenhower Years*. New York: Atheneum, 1963.

Hull, Cordell. *The Memoirs of Cordell Hull*, vol. 2. New York: Macmillan, 1948.

Hurwitz, David Lyon. "Churchill and Palestine." *Judaism* 44, no. 1 (Winter 1995), 3–33.

Hyam, Ronald. "Churchill and the British Empire." In Blake and Louis, *Churchill*, 167–185.

———. *Elgin and Churchill at the Colonial Office, 1905–1908*. London: Macmillan, 1968.

Ignatieff, Michael. *Isaiah Berlin.* New York: Metropolitan Books, 1998.
Iriye, Akira. *Across the Pacific: An Inner History of American-East Asian Relations.* Chicago: Imprint Publications, 1992.
Ismay, Baron Hastings Lionel. *Memoirs.* New York: Viking Press, 1960.
Jack, Marian. "The Purchase of the British Government's Shares in the British Petroleum Company, 1912–1914." *Past and Present* 39 (April 1968), 139–150.
Jäckel, Eberhard. *Hitler's World View.* Translated by Herbert Arnold. Cambridge, Mass.: Harvard University Press, 1981.
Jackson, Lesley Jackson. *The New Look: Design in the Fifties.* New York: Thames and Hudson, 1991.
Jackson, Michael. *A Scottish Life: Sir John Martin, Churchill and Empire.* Edited by Janet Jackson. New York: Radcliffe Press, 1999.
Jamison, Kay R. *Touched with Fire: Manic-Depressive Illness and the Artistic Temperament.* New York: Free Press Paperbacks, 1994.
Jenkins, Roy. *Baldwin.* London: Collins, 1987.
———. *Churchill: A Biography.* New York: Farrar, Straus and Giroux, 2001.
———. *Gladstone: A Biography.* New York: Random House, 1997.
Jennings, Louis J. *Speeches of the Right Honourable Lord Randolph Churchill, 1880–1888.* 2 vols. London: Longmans, Green, 1889.
Jones, A. Philip, ed. *Britain and Palestine, 1914–1948: Archival Sources for the History of the British Mandate.* Oxford: Oxford University Press for the British Academy, 1979.
Jones, G. Gareth. "The British Government and the Oil Companies, 1912–1924: The Search for an Oil Policy," *Historical Journal* 20, no. 3 (1977), 647–650.
Jones, Martin. *Failure in Palestine: British and United States Policy after the Second World War.* London: Mansell, 1986.
Jones, R. V. "Churchill and Science." In Blake and Louis, *Churchill,* 427–441.
Kadish, Sharman. *Bolsheviks and British Jews: The Anglo-Jewish Community, Britain and the Russian Revolution.* London: Frank Cass, 1992.
Kahler, Miles. *Decolonization in Britain and France: The Domestic Consequences of International Relations.* Princeton: Princeton University Press, 1984.
Kaiser, David E. *Politics and War: European Conflict from Philip II to Hitler.* Cambridge, Mass.: Harvard University Press, 1990.
Katz, Shmuel. *A Biography of Vladimir (Ze'ev) Jabotinsky.* 2 vols. New York: Barricade Books, 1996.
Keay, J. Seymour. *Spoiling the Egyptians: A Tale of Shame.* G. P. Putnam's Sons, 1882.
Kedourie, Elie. "The Arab-Israeli Conflict." In Laquer and Rubin, *The Israel-Arab Reader,* 559–572.
———. *The Chatham House Version and Other Middle-Eastern Studies.* Hanover, New Hampshire: University Press of New England, 1984.
———. *England and the Middle East: The Destruction of the Ottoman Empire, 1914–1921.* London: Bowes and Bowes, 1956.
———. *In the Anglo-Arab Labyrinth: The McMahon-Husayn Correspondence and Its Interpretations, 1914–1939.* London: Cambridge University Press, 1976.

---. *Islam in the Modern World*. New York: Holt, Rinehart and Winston, 1980.
Keegan, John. *The Battle for History: Re-fighting World War Two*. Toronto: Vintage, 1995.
---. *Churchill's Generals*. New York: G. Weidenfeld, 1991.
---. *The Second World War*. London: Pimlico, 1997.
Kelemen, Paul. "Labour Ideals and Colonial Pioneers: Wedgwood, Morrison and Zionism." *Labour History Review* 61, no. 1 (Spring 1996), 30–48.
Kennedy, Paul. *The Rise and Fall of the Great Powers*. New York: First Vintage Books, 1989.
Kersaudy, Francois. *Churchill and De Gaulle*. New York: Atheneum, 1982.
Keynes, John Maynard. *The Economic Consequences of Mr. Churchill*. London: L. and V. Woolf, 1925.
Kimball, Warren. *Churchill and Roosevelt: The Complete Correspondence*. 3 vols. Princeton: Princeton University Press, 1984.
Kissinger, Henry. *Diplomacy*. New York: Simon and Schuster, 1994.
---. *A World Restored: Europe after Napoleon*. New York: Grosset and Dunlap, 1964.
Kitchen, Martin. *British Policy towards the Soviet Union during the Second World War*. Basingstoke, U.K.: Macmillan, 1986.
Kitson Clark, G. S. R. *An Expanding Society: Britain, 1830–1900*. New York: Cambridge University Press, 1967.
---. *The Making of Victorian England*. London: Routledge, 1991.
Klieman, Aaron S. *Foundation of British Policy in the Arab World: The Cairo Conference of 1921*. Baltimore: Johns Hopkins Press, 1970.
---. *Palestine in Postwar United States and World Affairs*. Vol. 11 of *American Zionism*. New York: Garland, 1991.
---. *Recognition of Israel: An End and a New Beginning*. Vol. 13 of *American Zionism*. New York: Garland, 1991.
Knight, Amy. *Beria: Stalin's First Lieutenant*. Princeton: Princeton University Press, 1993.
Knock, Thomas J. *To End All Wars: Woodrow Wilson and the Quest for a New World Order*. New York: Oxford University Press, 1992.
Kobler, Franz. *The Vision Was There: A History of the British Movement for the Restoration of the Jews to Palestine*. London: Lincolns-Prager, 1956.
Kraus, Rene. *Winston Churchill*. Philadelphia: Lippincott, 1940.
Kuklick, Bruce. *American Policy and the Division of Germany: The Clash with Russia over Reparations*. Ithaca, N.Y.: Cornell University Press, 1972.
Kuniholm, Bruce Robellet. *The Origins of the Cold War in the Near East: Great Power Conflict and Diplomacy in Iran, Turkey, and Greece*. Princeton: Princeton University Press, 1994.
Kyle, Keith. *Suez*. London: Weidenfeld and Nicolson, 1991.
LaFeber, Walter. *America, Russia, and the Cold War, 1945–1992*. New York: McGraw Hill, 1993.
Lammers, Donald. " 'Who Will Do the Work?' The Loss of Empire in British

Popular Fiction after the Second World War." *Centennial Review* 22, no. 3 (1978), 255–280.

Laquer, Walter. *The Terrible Secret: Suppression of the Truth about Hitler's "Final Solution."* Boston: Little, Brown, 1980.

Laquer, Walter, and Barry Rubin, eds. *The Israel-Arab Reader.* New York: Facts on File Publications, 1985.

Lawrence, T. E. *Seven Pillars of Wisdom.* Middlesex, U.K.: Penguin Books, 1983.

Lee, Martha F. "Nesta Webster: The Voice of Conspiracy." *Journal of Women's History* 17, no. 3 (Fall 2005), 81–104.

Leffler, Melvyn P. *A Preponderance of Power: National Security, the Truman Administration, and the Cold War.* Stanford, Calif.: Stanford University Press, 1992.

Lewis, Bernard. *The Emergence of Modern Turkey.* London: Oxford University Press, 1961.

———. "The Pro-Islamic Jews." *Judaism* 17, no. 4 (Fall 1968), 391–404.

———. "The Question of Orientalism." *New York Review of Books,* June 24, 1982, 49–56.

Litvinoff, Barnet. *The Essential Chaim Weizmann.* London: Weidenfeld and Nicolson, 1982.

———, ed. *The Letters and Papers of Chaim Weizmann,* vols. 20–23. New Brunswick, N.J.: Transaction Books, 1979–1980.

Lloyd George, David. *Memoirs of the Peace Conference,* vol. 2. New York: Yale University Press, 1939.

———. *War Memoirs,* vol. 2, *1915–1916.* Boston: Little, Brown, 1933.

———. *War Memoirs,* vol. 4, *1917.* Boston: Little, Brown, 1934.

Lockman, J. N. *Meinertzhagen's Diary Ruse: False Entries on T. E. Lawrence.* Grand Rapids, Mich.: Cornerstone Publications, 1995.

London, Louise. *Whitehall and the Jews, 1933–1948.* Cambridge: Cambridge University Press, 2000.

Louis, William Roger. "American Anti-Colonialism and the Dissolution of the British Empire." In Louis and Bull, *Special Relationship,* 261–283.

———. *The British Empire in the Middle East, 1945–1951: Arab Nationalism, the United States, and Postwar Imperialism.* New York: Oxford University Press, 1985.

———. "British Imperialism and the End of the Palestine Mandate." In Louis and Stookey, *The End of the Palestine Mandate,* 1–31.

———. "Churchill and Egypt, 1946–1956." In Blake and Louis, *Churchill,* 473–490.

———. *Imperialism at Bay: The United States and the Decolonization of the British Empire, 1941–1945.* New York: Oxford University Press, 1978.

———. *In the Name of God, Go!: Leo Amery and the British Empire in the Age of Churchill.* New York: W. W. Norton, 1992.

———. Introduction to Louis and Brown, *The Oxford History of the British Empire,* 1–45.

Louis, William Roger, and Judith M. Brown. *The Oxford History of the British Empire: The Twentieth Century.* Oxford: Oxford University Press, 1999.

Louis, William Roger, and Hedley Bull. *The "Special Relationship": Anglo-American Relations since 1945.* New York: Oxford University Press, 1986.

Louis, William Roger, and Roger Owen. *Suez 1956.* New York: Oxford University Press, 1989.

Louis, William Roger, and Robert W. Stookey. *The End of the Palestine Mandate.* Modern Middle East Series. Austin: University of Texas Press, 1986.

Lowenthal, Marvin, ed. *The Diaries of Theodor Herzl.* New York: Dial Press, 1956.

Lucas, W. Scott. *Divided We Stand: Britain, the U.S., and the Suez Crisis.* London: Hodder and Stoughton, 1991.

Mack, John E. *A Prince of Our Disorder: The Life of T. E. Lawrence.* Cambridge, Mass.: Harvard University Press, 1998.

Macmillan, Harold. *Tides of Fortune, 1945–1955.* New York: Harper and Row, 1969.

Maier, Charles S. *The Cold War in Europe: Era of a Divided Continent.* Princeton: M. Wiener, 1996.

Marsden, Victor E., trans. *The Protocols of the Meetings of the Learned Elders of Zion.* 1934.

Marsh, Edward. *A Number of People.* New York: Harper and Brothers, 1939.

May, Ernest, and Gregory F. Treverton. "Defence Relationships: American Perspectives." In Louis and Bull, *Special Relationship,* 161–182.

Mayer, Arno J. "The Power Politician and Counterrevolutionary." In Stansky, *Churchill: A Profile.*

McGowan, Norman. *My Years with Churchill.* New York: British Book Centre, 1958.

McKay, Derek, and H. M. Scott. *The Rise of the Great Powers, 1648–1815.* London: Longman, 1983.

Meinertzhagen, Richard. *Middle East Diary, 1917–1956.* London: Cresset Press, 1959.

Miller, Aaron David. *Search for Security: Saudi Arabian Oil and American Foreign Policy, 1939–1949.* Chapel Hill: University of North Carolina Press, 1980.

Millis, Walter, ed. *The Forrestal Diaries.* New York: Viking Press, 1951.

Mitchell, Sally, ed. *Victorian Britain: An Encyclopedia.* New York: Garland, 1988.

Modder, Montagu Frank. *The Jew in the Literature of England: To the End of the 19th Century.* Philadelphia: Jewish Publication Society of America, 1939.

Monroe, Elizabeth. *Britain's Moment in the Middle East, 1914–1971,* 2nd ed. Baltimore: Johns Hopkins University Press, 1981.

Montague Browne, Anthony. *Long Sunset: Memoirs of Winston Churchill's Last Private Secretary.* London: Cassell, 1995.

Monypenny, William Flavelle, and George Earle Buckle. *The Life of Benjamin Disraeli, Earl of Beaconfield,* vol. 3. New York: Macmillan, 1914.

Moran, Baron Charles McMoran Wilson. *Churchill: Taken from the Diaries of Lord Moran; The Struggle for Survival, 1940–1965.* Boston: Houghton Mifflin, 1966.

Morgenthau, Hans Joachim. *In Defense of the National Interest: A Critical Examination of American Foreign Policy.* New York: Knopf, 1951.

Morris, Benny. *Righteous Victims: A History of the Zionist-Arab Conflict, 1881–2001.* New York: Vintage Books, 2001.
Morton, Daniel Oliver, and Levi Parsons. *Memoir of Rev. Levi Parsons: First Missionary to Palestine from the United States,* 2nd ed. Burlington, Vt.: Chauncey Goodrich, 1830.
Muller, James W., ed. *Churchill as Peacemaker.* Cambridge: Cambridge University Press, 1997.
Nachmani, Amikam. *Great Power Discord in Palestine: The Anglo-American Committee of Inquiry into the Problems of European Jewry and Palestine, 1945–1946.* Totowa, N.J.: Frank Cass, 1987.
Neufeld, Michael J., and Michael Berenbaum. *The Bombing of Auschwitz: Should the Allies Have Attempted It?* New York: St. Martin's Press, 2000.
Nicholas, H. G. *The United States and Britain.* Chicago: University of Chicago Press, 1975.
Nicolson, Harold. *The Congress of Vienna.* New York: Harcourt, Brace: 1946.
Northcliffe, Alfred Viscount. *My Journey round the World.* Philadelphia: Lippincott, 1923.
Odell, Peter R. *Oil and World Power,* 8th ed. New York: Viking Penguin, 1986.
Ovendale, Ritchie. *Britain, the United States, and the End of the Palestine Mandate, 1942–1948.* London: Royal Historical Society, 1989.
———. *Britain, the United States, and the Transfer of Power in the Middle East, 1945–1962.* London: Leicester University Press, 1996.
———, ed. *British Defence Policy since 1945.* New York: St. Martin's Press, 1994.
———. "Egypt and the Suez Base Agreement." In J. Young, *Foreign Policy of Churchill's Peacetime Administration,* 135–153.
Owen, Roger. *Conflicts in the Contemporary Middle East.* Oxford, U.K.: Oxford Project for Peace Studies, 1990.
Owen, Roger, and Robert Sutcliffe. *Studies in the Theory of Imperialism.* London: Longman, 1972.
Painter, David S. *Oil and the American Century: The Political Economy of U.S. Foreign Oil Policy, 1941–1954.* Baltimore: Johns Hopkins University Press, 1986.
Palmer, R. R. *A History of the Modern World.* New York: Alfred Knopf, 1978.
Pappe, Ilan. *Britain and the Arab-Israel Conflict, 1948–51.* New York: St. Martin's Press, 1988.
Parker, Robert Alexander Clarke. *Chamberlain and Appeasement.* New York: St. Martin's Press, 1993.
———. *Churchill and Appeasement.* London: Macmillan, 2000.
Parker, Robert Alexander Clarke, and Correlli Barnett. *Winston Churchill: Studies in Statesmanship.* London: Brassey's, 1995.
Parry, J. P. *The Rise and Fall of Liberal Government in Victorian Britain.* New Haven: Yale University Press, 1993.
Parsons, Anthony. *They Say the Lion: Britain's Legacy to the Arabs: A Personal Memoir.* London: J. Cape, 1986.
Paterson, Tony. *A Seat for Life.* Dundee: David Winter and Son, 1980.

Pearce, Edward. "Eminent Edwardian Editors." *History Today* 50, no. 4 (April 2000), 28–33.
Pelling, Henry. *Churchill's Peacetime Ministry, 1951–55*. Basingstoke, U.K.: Macmillan, 1996.
———. *Winston Churchill*. London: Macmillan, 1989.
Penkower, Monty Noam. *Decision on Palestine Deferred: America, Britain and Wartime Diplomacy, 1939–1945*. Portland, Ore.: Frank Cass, 2002.
Peretz, Marty. "The God That Did Not Fail." *New Republic,* September 8, 1997. Online edition.
Podet, Allen Howard. "Anti-Zionism in a Key U.S. Diplomat: Loy Henderson at the End of World War II." *American Jewish Archives* 30 (November 1978).
———. *The Success and Failure of the Anglo-American Committee of Inquiry, 1945–1946: Last Chance in Palestine*. Lewiston, N.Y.: E. Mellen Press, 1986.
Poliakov, Léon. *From Voltaire to Wagner*. Vol. 3 of *The History of Anti-Semitism*. Translated by Miriam Kochan. New York: Vanguard Press, 1975.
———. *Suicidal Europe, 1870–1933*. Vol. 4 of *The History of Anti-Semitism*. Translated by George Klin. Philadelphia: University of Pennsylvania Press, 1985.
Ponting, Clive. *Churchill*. London: Sinclair-Stevenson, 1994.
Porter, Andrew. *The Oxford History of the British Empire: The Nineteenth Century*. Oxford: Oxford University Press, 1999.
Public Papers of the Presidents of the United States: Dwight D. Eisenhower, 1953. Washington, D.C.: Government Printing Office, 1960.
Pugh, Martin. *State and Society: British Political and Social History, 1870–1992*. New York: Routledge, 1994.
Rabinowicz, Oskar K. *Winston Churchill on Jewish Problems*. London: Lincolns-Prager, 1956.
Ragussis, Michael. *Figures of Conversion: "The Jewish Question" and English National Identity*. Durham, N.C.: Duke University Press, 1995.
———. "The 'Secret' of English Anti-Semitism: Anglo-Jewish Studies and Victorian Studies." *Victorian Studies* 40, no. 2 (Winter 1997), 295–307.
Ramsden, John. *Man of the Century: Winston Churchill and His Legend since 1945*. New York: Columbia University Press, 2002.
Reguer, Sara. "Rutenberg and the Jordan River: A Revolution in Hydro-Electricity." *Middle Eastern Studies* 31, no. 4 (October 1995), 691–729.
Reinharz, Yehuda. *Chaim Weizmann: The Making of a Zionist Leader*. New York: Oxford University Press, 1985.
Reynolds, David. *Britannia Overruled: British Policy and World Power in the Twentieth Century*. London: Longman, 1991.
———. "A 'Special Relationship'? America, Britain and the International Order since 1945." *International Affairs* 62 (1985–1986), 1–20.
Rhodes James, Robert. *Anthony Eden*. London: Weidenfeld and Nicolson, 1986.
———. *The British Revolution: British Politics, 1880–1939*, vol. 2. London: Hamish Hamilton, 1977.

―――, ed. *Chips: The Diaries of Sir Henry Channon*. London: Weidenfeld and Nicolson, 1967.
―――. *Churchill: A Study in Failure, 1900–1939*. New York: Penguin Books, 1981.
―――. "The Enigma." In Muller, *Churchill as Peacemaker*, 6–23.
―――. "The Politician." In *Churchill Revised: A Critical Assessment*, 63–129. New York: Dial Press, 1969.
―――, ed. *Winston S. Churchill: His Complete Speeches, 1897–1963*. 8 vols. New York: Chelsea House, 1974.
Riasanovsky, Nicholas V. *A History of Russia*. New York: Oxford University Press, 1984.
Rich, Paul. "British Imperial Decline and the Forging of English Patriotic Memory, c. 1918–1968." *History of European Ideas* 9, no. 6 (1978), 659–680.
Roberts, Andrew. *Eminent Churchillians*. New York: Simon and Schuster, 1994.
―――. *The Holy Fox: A Biography of Lord Halifax*. London: Weidenfeld and Nicolson, 1991.
―――. "Salisbury: The Empire Builder Who Never Was." *History Today*, October 1999, 45–51.
Robinson, Ronald. "Imperial Theory and the Question of Imperialism after Empire." *Journal of Imperial and Commonwealth History* 12, no. 2 (1984), 42–54.
Robinson, Ronald Edward, and John Gallagher. *Africa and the Victorians: The Official Mind of Imperialism*. London: Macmillan, 1981.
Rose, Norman, ed. *Baffy: The Diaries of Blanche Dugdale, 1936–1947*. London: Vallentine, Mitchell, 1973.
―――. *Churchill: An Unruly Life*. London: Simon and Schuster, 1994.
―――. "Churchill and Zionism." In Blake and Louis, *Churchill*, 147–166.
―――. *The Gentile Zionists: A Study in Anglo-Zionist Diplomacy, 1929–1939*. London: Cass, 1973.
Rosen, Robert. *Saving the Jews: Franklin D. Roosevelt and the Holocaust*. New York: Thunder's Mouth Press, 2006.
Rosenberg, Jonathan. "Before the Bomb and After: Winston Churchill and the Use of Force." In Gaddis, Gordon, and May, *Cold War Statesmen Confront the Bomb*, 171–193.
Rostow, W. W. *Europe after Stalin*. Austin: University of Texas Press, 1982.
Roth, Cecil. *Benjamin Disraeli: Earl of Beaconsfield*. New York: Philosophical Library, 1952.
―――. *Essays and Portraits in Anglo Jewish History*. Philadelphia: Jewish Publication Society of America, 1962.
―――. *A History of the Jews in England*. Oxford, U.K.: Clarendon Press, 1941.
Rothschild, Miriam. *Dear Lord Rothschild*. Philadelphia: Balaban, 1983.
Rothwell, V. H. *British War Aims and Peace Diplomacy, 1914–1918*. Oxford, U.K.: Clarendon Press, 1971.
Rubenstein, Amnon. *From Herzl to Rabin*. New York: Holmes and Meier, 2000.
Rubin, Barry. "Anglo-American Relations in Saudi Arabia, 1941–45." *Journal of Contemporary History* 14, no. 2 (April 1979), 253–267.

———. *The Great Powers in the Middle East, 1941–1947: The Road to the Cold War.* London: Frank Cass, 1980.

Rubinstein, W. D. *A History of the Jews in the English-Speaking World: Great Britain.* New York: St. Martin's Press, 1996.

Sachar, David B. "David K. Niles and United States Policy toward Palestine: A Case Study in America Foreign Policy." B.A. dissertation, Harvard University, 1959.

Sachar, Harry. "Dr. Moses Gaster." *New Judea* 20, no. 8 (May 1944), 125–126.

Sachar, Howard Morley. *The Course of Modern Jewish History.* New York: Delta, 1977.

———. *Europe Leaves the Middle East, 1936–1954.* New York: Knopf, 1972.

———. *A History of Israel: From the Rise of Zionism to Our Time.* New York: Alfred A. Knopf, 1996.

Safran, Nadav. *Israel: The Embattled Ally.* Cambridge, Mass.: Belknap Press of Harvard University Press, 1981.

———. *Saudi Arabia: The Ceaseless Quest for Security.* Ithaca, N.Y.: Cornell University, 1988.

———. *The United States and Israel.* Cambridge, Mass.: Harvard University Press, 1963.

Said, Edward W. *The Palestine Question and the American Context.* IPS Papers 1. Beirut: Institute for Palestine Studies, 1979.

Samuel, Viscount. *Memoirs.* London: Cresset, 1945.

Sayigh, Yazid, and Avi Shlaim. *The Cold War and the Middle East.* Oxford, U.K.: Clarendon Press, 1997.

Schechtman, Joseph B. *The United States and the Jewish State Movement: The Crucial Decade, 1939–1949.* New York: Herzl Press, 1966.

Schroeder, Paul W. "Did the Vienna Settlement Rest on a Balance of Power?" *American Historical Review* 97, no. 3 (1992), 683–706.

———. *The Transformation of European Politics, 1763–1848.* Oxford, U.K.: Clarendon Press, 1994.

Schwartz, Thomas A. *America's Germany: John J. McCloy and the Federal Republic of Germany.* Cambridge, Mass.: Harvard University Press, 1991.

Scott, A. MacCallum. *Winston Spencer Churchill.* London: Methuen, 1905.

Seeley, John Robert. *The Expansion of England.* Edited by John Gross. Chicago: University of Chicago Press, 1971.

Segev, Tom. *The Seventh Million: The Israeli and the Holocaust.* Translated by Haim Watzman. New York: Hill and Wang, 1993.

Seldon, Anthony. *Churchill's Indian Summer: The Conservative Government, 1951–55.* London: Hodder and Stoughton, 1981.

Shepherd, Naomi. *The Zealous Intruders: The Western Rediscovery of Palestine.* San Francisco: Harper and Row, 1987.

Shlaim, Avi. *War and Peace in the Middle East: A Critique of American Policy.* New York: Whittle Books in association with Viking, 1994.

Shuckburgh, Evelyn. *Descent to Suez: Diaries 1951–56.* New York: W. W. Norton, 1987.

Shwadran, Benjamin. *The Middle East, Oil, and the Great Powers*. New York: Wiley, 1974.

Silverberg, Robert. *If I Forget Thee, O Jerusalem: American Jews and the State of Israel*. New York: Morrow, 1970.

Smith, Justin Davis. *The Attlee and Churchill Administrations and Industrial Unrest, 1945–55: A Study in Consensus*. London: Pinter Publishers, 1990.

Smith, Michael. "Bletchley Park and the Holocaust." *Intelligence and National Security* 19, no. 2 (Summer 2004), 262–274.

Smith, Vincent Arthur. *The Oxford History of India*, 3rd ed. Edited by Percival Spear. Oxford, U.K.: Clarendon Press, 1967.

Snetsinger, John. *Truman, the Jewish Vote, and the Creation of Israel*. Stanford, Calif.: Hoover Institution Press, 1974.

Soames, Mary. *Winston and Clementine: The Personal Letters of the Churchills*. Boston: Houghton Mifflin, 1999.

Spiegel, Steven L. *The Other Arab-Israeli Conflict: Making America's Middle East Policy, from Truman to Reagan*. Middle Eastern Studies 1. Chicago: University of Chicago Press, 1985.

Stafford, David. *Churchill and Secret Service*. Woodstock, N.Y.: Overlook Press, 1998.

Stansky, Peter. *Churchill: A Profile*. New York: Hill and Wang, 1973.

Stein, Leonard. *The Balfour Declaration*. Jerusalem: Magnes Press, 1983.

Steiner, Zara S. *The Foreign Office and Foreign Policy, 1898–1914*. London: Cambridge University Press, 1969.

Steininger, Rolf. *The German Question: The Stalin Note of 1952 and the Problem of Reunification*. New York: Columbia University Press, 1990.

———. "John Foster Dulles, the European Defense Community, and the German Question." In *John Foster Dulles and the Diplomacy of the Cold War*, edited by Richard H. Immerman. Princeton: Princeton University, 1990.

Stewart, Graham. *Burying Caesar: Churchill, Chamberlain and the Battle for the Tory Party*. London: Weidenfeld and Nicolson, 1999.

Stoff, Michael B. *Oil, War, and American Security: The Search for a National Policy on Foreign Oil, 1941–1947*. Yale Historical Publications: Miscellany, 125. New Haven: Yale University Press, 1980.

Storr, Anthony. "The Man." In *Churchill Revised: A Critical Assessment*, 229–274. New York: Dial Press, 1969.

Strachey, Lytton. *Eminent Victorians*. New York: G. P. Putnam's Sons, 1918.

Strom, Arne. *Uncle Give Us Bread*. London: Allen and Unwin, 1936. First published in Danish in 1934.

Suleiman, Michael W., ed. *U.S. Policy on Palestine: From Wilson to Clinton*. Normal, Ill.: Association of Arab-American University Graduates, 1995.

Sulzberger, C. L. *A Long Row of Candles: Memoirs and Diaries, 1934–1954*. New York: Macmillan, 1969.

Sykes, Christopher. *Cross Roads to Israel*. London: St. James Place, 1965.

Taylor, A. J. P. *The Struggle for Mastery in Europe, 1848–1918*. Oxford History of Modern Europe. Oxford, U.K.: Clarendon Press, 1954.

Teveth, Shabtai. *Ben-Gurion: The Burning Ground, 1886–1948*. Boston: Houghton Mifflin, 1987.

Thompson, John. *Russia, Bolshevism, and the Versailles Peace*. Princeton: Princeton University Press, 1966.

Thompson, Kenneth. *Winston Churchill's World View: Statesmanship and Power*. Baton Rouge: Louisiana State University, 1983.

Thompson, Reginald William. *The Yankee Marlborough*. London: Allen and Unwin, 1963.

Thompson, Reginald William, and Sir Desmond Morton. *Churchill and Morton: The Quest for Insight in the Correspondence of Major Sir Desmond Morton and the Author*. London: Hodder and Stoughton, 1976.

Thompson, W. H. *Sixty Minutes with Winston Churchill*. London: Christopher Johnson, 1953.

Thomson, Malcolm. *The Life and Times of Winston Churchill*. London: Odhams Press, 1946.

Thorne, Christopher G. *Allies of a Kind: The United States, Britain, and the War against Japan, 1941–1945*. New York: Oxford University Press, 1978.

Tidrick, Kathryn. *Heart-Beguiling Araby*. Cambridge: Cambridge University Press, 1981.

Tierney, James. "Britain and the Commonwealth: Attitudes in Parliament and Press in the United Kingdom since 1951." *Political Studies* 6, no. 3 (1958), 220–233.

Truman, Harry S., and Robert H. Ferrell. *Off the Record: The Private Papers of Harry S. Truman*. Give 'Em Hell Harry Series. Columbia: University of Missouri Press, 1997.

Ulam, Adam Bruno. *The Bolsheviks: The Intellectual and Political History of the Triumph of Communism in Russia*. Cambridge, Mass.: Harvard University Press, 1998.

———. *Expansion and Coexistence: Soviet Foreign Policy, 1917–73*. New York: Praeger / Holt, Rinehart and Winston, 1974.

———. *The Rivals: America and Russia since World War II*. New York: Viking Press, 1971.

———. *Stalin: The Man and His Era*. Boston: Beacon Press, 1989.

U.S. State Department. *Foreign Relations of the United States, 1942: The Near East and Africa*. Washington, D.C.: Government Printing Office, 1963.

———. *Foreign Relations of the United States, 1943: The British Commonwealth, Eastern Europe, the Far East*. Washington, D.C.: Government Printing Office, 1963.

———. *Foreign Relations of the United States, 1943: The Conferences at Washington and Quebec*. Washington, D.C.: Government Printing Office, 1970.

———. *Foreign Relations of the United States, 1943: The Near East and Africa*. Washington, D.C.: Government Printing Office, 1964.

———. *Foreign Relations of the United States, 1944: The Near East, South Asia, and Africa, the Far East*. Washington, D.C.: Government Printing Office, 1965.

———. *Foreign Relations of the United States, 1945: The Conference of Berlin (The

Potsdam Conference). 2 vols. Washington, D.C.: Government Printing Office, 1960.

———. *Foreign Relations of the United States, 1945: The Conferences of Malta and Yalta.* Washington, D.C.: Government Printing Office, 1955.

———. *Foreign Relations of the United States, 1945: The Near East and Africa.* Washington, D.C.: Government Printing Office, 1969.

———. *Foreign Relations of the United States, 1946,* vol. 7. Washington, D.C.: Government Printing Office, 1969.

———. *Foreign Relations of the United States, 1947,* vol. 5. Washington, D.C.: Government Printing Office, 1969.

———. *Foreign Relations of the United States, 1952–54,* vol. 5. Washington, D.C.: Government Printing Office, 1983.

Venn, Fiona. *Oil Diplomacy in the Twentieth Century.* Basingstoke, U.K.: Macmillan, 1986.

Vital, David. *The Origins of Zionism.* Oxford, U.K.: Clarendon Press, 1975.

Wallace, Henry Agard. *The Price of Vision: The Diary of Henry A. Wallace, 1942–1946.* Edited by John Morton Blum. Boston: Houghton Mifflin, 1973.

Walters, E. P. *A History of the League of Nations.* London: Oxford University Press, 1960.

Ward, Adolphus William, and G. P. Gooch, eds. *The Cambridge History of British Foreign Policy,* vol. 1. Cambridge: Cambridge University Press, 1922.

———. "The Peace of Utrecht and the Supplementary Pacifications." In Ward, Prothero, and Leathes, *The Cambridge Modern History,* 437–459.

Ward, A. W., G. W. Prothero, and Stanley Leathes. *The Cambridge Modern History.* Cambridge: Cambridge University Press, 1934.

Warwick, Paul. "Did Britain Change? An Inquiry into the Causes of National Decline." *Journal of Contemporary History* 20, no. 1 (January 1985), 99–133.

Wasserstein, Bernard. *Britain and the Jews of Europe, 1939–1945.* London: Leicester University Press, 1999.

———. *The British in Palestine: The Mandatory Government and the Arab-Jewish Conflict, 1917–1929.* London: Basil Blackwell, 1991.

———. *Herbert Samuel: A Political Life.* New York: Oxford University Press, 1991.

Watt, Donald Cameron. *Succeeding John Bull: America in Britain's Place, 1900–1975.* New York: Cambridge University Press, 1984.

Weber, Max. *The Protestant Ethic and the Spirit of Capitalism.* New York: Charles Scribner's Sons, 1976.

Webster, Charles K., ed. *British Diplomacy, 1813–1815: Select Documents Dealing with the Reconstruction of Europe.* London: G. Bell and Sons, 1921.

———. *The Congress of Vienna, 1814–1815.* London: Oxford University Press, 1919.

———. *The Foreign Policy of Palmerston, 1830–1841: Britain, the Liberal Movement, and the Eastern Question.* 2 vols. London: G. Bell, 1951.

———. "The Pacification of Europe, 1813–1815." In Ward and Gooch, *The Cambridge History of British Foreign Policy.*

Webster, Nesta H. *The French Revolution: A Study in Democracy.* London: Constable, 1919.

Wedgwood, Josiah C. *The Seventh Dominion*. London: Labour, 1928.
Weidhorn, Manfred. *A Harmony of Interests: Explorations in the Mind of Sir Winston Churchill*. Rutherford, N.J.: Fairleigh Dickinson University Press, 1992.
Weizmann, Chaim. *Trial and Error*. New York: Harper and Brothers, 1949.
Wells, H. G. "Russia in the Shadow." *New York Times*, November 21, 1920.
Wheeler-Bennett, John, ed. *Action This Day: Working with Churchill*. London: Macmillan, 1968.
Wilson, Jeremy. *Lawrence of Arabia: The Authorized Biography of T. E. Lawrence*. New York: Atheneum, 1990.
Wingfield-Stratford, Esme Cecil. *Churchill: The Making of a Hero*. London: V. Gollancz, 1942.
Wolfson, Jonathan. "Winston Churchill and Zionism, 1921–1950." Ph.D. dissertation, Selwyn College, University of Cambridge, 1993.
Woodward, Sir E. L., ed. *Documents on British Foreign Policy, 1919–1939*. 65 vols. London: H.M.S.O., 1946.
Wyman, David S. *The Abandonment of the Jews: America and the Holocaust, 1941–1945*. New York: Pantheon Books, 1984.
Yergin, Daniel. *The Prize*. New York: Simon and Schuster, 1991.
Young, Major Sir Hubert. *The Independent Arab*. London: John Murray, 1933.
Young, John W. "Churchill, the Russians and the Western Alliance: The Three-Power Conference at Bermuda, December 1953." *English Historical Review* 101, no. 401 (October 1986), 889–912.
———. "Cold War and Detente with Moscow." In J. Young, *Foreign Policy of Churchill's Peacetime Administration*.
———, ed. *The Foreign Policy of Churchill's Peacetime Administration, 1951–1955*. Leicester: Leicester University Press, 1988.
———. *Winston Churchill's Last Campaign*. Oxford, U.K.: Clarendon Press, 1996.
Young, Kenneth. *Churchill and Beaverbrook*. London: Eyre and Spottiswoode, 1967.
Zubok, Vladislav M. "Soviet Intelligence and the Cold War: The Small Committee of Information, 1952–53." Cold War International History Project. Washington, D.C.: Woodrow Wilson Center, 1992.
Zweig, Ronald W. *Britain and Palestine during the Second World War*. Suffolk, U.K.: Boydell Press, 1986.

INDEX

Aaronsohn, Aaron, 75
Abadan refineries, 197
Abd al-Aziz al-Saud. *See* Ibn Saud
Abdullah, king of Jordan: Arab federation proposal and, 106, 108, 110, 111, 112; assassination of, 252; Churchill's perception of, 128–129, 193, 194, 249–250, 252; Greater Syria proposal and, 213; Ibn Saud rivalry with, 193, 198, 204; Palestine and, 103, 225
Adler, Hermann, Chief Rabbi, 45, 60
Admiralty, 14, 17, 18, 66–67, 69, 171, 175, 184, 186, 190; Churchill's forced resignation from, 74
Africa, 12, 17, 101–102; Churchill's racial views and, 13; proposed Jewish settlements in, 56–59, 62, 208, 219, 223. *See also* North Africa; *specific countries*
Agadir crisis (1911), 17
agriculture. *See* land development
air power, 14
Aleppo, 185
Alexander II, tsar of Russia, 83
Aliens Act of 1905, 49–50, 51, 58, 60, 63, 64, 65, 82
Allenby, Edmund, 77, 79, 91, 105–106, 112; anti-Zionism of, 126–127
Amery, Leo, 129, 134–135, 160, 163, 191, 193, 200; as Committee on Palestine member, 208, 209; as pro-Zionist, 129, 164, 207
Amritsar massacre (1919), 81
anarchists, 18, 66
Anglicanism, 42
Anglo-American Commission of Inquiry (1946), 229, 234, 235, 246
Anglo-Egyptian Treaty (1936), 251
Anglo-Persian Oil Company, 66–67
Anschluss (1938), 141, 149, 162
Anti-Nazi League, 150
anti-Semitism, 6, 38, 39–40, 47–48, 53, 54; Bolshevik Revolution as trigger for, 80, 84, 88; Britain and, 6, 40, 43, 50, 56, 64, 66, 68, 70–71, 80–82, 84, 86, 87, 88, 100–101, 164, 171–174, 179, 180, 185, 191, 208, 232, 240, 243–244; British anti-Zionism as result of, 174, 176; canards of, 6, 40, 81; Christian accusations and, 39–40, 42; Churchill's reactions to, 3, 44, 48–51, 67, 81–84, 87, 88–89, 149, 150; coining of term, 42; Jewish homeland as answer to (*see* Zionism); "Jewish problem" and, 2–3; Nazi ideology and, 142, 148–150, 162, 180 (*see also* Holocaust); Poland and, 150, 162, 228; *Protocols of the Elders of*

323

324　INDEX

anti-Semitism (*continued*)
Zion and, 80–81, 82; Randolph Churchill's countering of, 45; Russian history of, 44, 47, 49, 51, 54, 56, 57, 58, 59, 68, 80, 83–84, 85, 136, 150, 151; United States and, 193
appeasement policies, 162, 164, 165, 166, 171, 174, 192, 197, 229, 231–232
Aqsa Mosque, al-, 143
Arabia. *See* Ibn Saud; Saudi Arabia; sherifians
Arabi Pasha, 44
Arab-Israeli War (1948), 218, 230, 240–241, 243, 244, 246, 251, 252; Palestinian Arab refugees and, 249
Arab League, 220
Arab Legion, 240, 250
Arab revolt (1936–1939), 152, 162–163
Arabs: anti-Zionism of, 70, 91, 112, 126, 130–131, 204–205, 206, 219–220, 221, 226; Balfour Declaration and, 93, 156; British appeasement/favoring of, 74, 75, 92, 106, 113, 128–130, 132, 162–166, 174–176, 191–194, 200–201, 204, 220–221, 225, 227, 229, 236, 240, 243, 244, 250, 264; British Cabinet Committee proposal and, 210–211; British diminished influence with, 221; British romanticization of, 128, 237, 264; Churchill's relations with, 92–93, 106, 128–129, 195, 219–220; Churchill's view of, 2, 3, 4, 13, 90, 114, 128–129, 145, 155, 185–186, 194, 195, 207, 237–238, 248–249, 264, 265; conquest of Palestine by, 39; as Fascist/Nazi supporters, 154, 160, 169, 193, 197; federation proposals for, 106–108, 163, 172, 194, 196, 197–205, 211, 219, 220, 225, 226, 235; First World War and, 75–76, 126, 127, 129, 146, 154, 168; Israeli war with (*see* Arab-Israeli war); Jerusalem's grand mufti and, 112; London conference (1939) and, 163; nationalist movement of, 105, 226 (*see also* pan-Arabism); Palestine partition rejection by, 230, 243, 244; Palestinian Arabs differentiated from, 249–250; revolts by, 94, 110, 152, 162–163, 192, 194, 197, 238; Roosevelt's statements and, 193,

221–222. *See also* Palestinian Arabs; sherifians; *specific countries*
Aramco, 220
Argentina, 58
Ashkenazi Jews, 117
Ashley, Edward (Earl of Shaftesbury), 52
Asia, 13–14, 26, 32, 53, 55
Asquith, Herbert, 63, 65, 72, 74, 79; anti-Semitism of, 70–71
Association of Levant States (proposed), 209, 213
Assyrians, 39
Ataturk (Mustafa Kemal), 91
Atlantic Charter (1941), 177, 202
atomic bomb, 14, 35
Attlee, Clement, 150, 210, 244; anti-Zionism of, 174, 223, 227, 228–229, 231, 232, 235, 238; Churchill's outlook vs., 31–32, 34, 35, 228, 239, 240, 243; election (1945) win of, 30; Palestine policy and, 233, 237, 241, 251, 252; Potsdam conference and, 224
Auschwitz-Birkenau, 31, 178, 179, 180; liberation of, 183; proposed bombing of, 172, 181, 182
Austria, 15, 140, 141, 150, 162
Austro-Hungarian Empire, 18

Babylonians, 39
balance of power, 15, 16, 18, 23, 25–34, 89
Baldwin, Stanley, 133, 134, 140, 142, 161
Balfour, Alfred, 50, 56, 76–77, 101, 102, 104, 126, 130, 131, 134, 208
Balfour Declaration (1917), 2, 6–7, 69, 87, 104, 114, 129, 131, 146; Arabs and, 93, 118, 125, 127, 156; British policy move from, 141, 166, 167, 168, 225; British reversals in favoring, 101; Churchill as implementer of, 99, 102, 137; Churchill's criteria for fulfillment of, 157–158; Churchill's defense of, 118, 133, 137, 153, 157, 207, 249, 254, 260; Churchill's inconsistency on, 78, 90–91, 96, 97, 103–104, 135, 254; Churchill's message on twenty-fifth anniversary of, 202–203; contradictions in, 126; dilution of, 137, 166; issuance of, 76–77, 78; Jewish national home meaning and, 77, 86, 116; Lloyd George

on, 79; Palestine Mandate and, 78, 133, 158, 195; Transjordan's exclusion from, 111; United States and, 77, 166
Baltic states, 20
banking, 44, 56
Baring family, 44
Baruch, Bernard, 215–216, 222, 320
Beaverbrook, Max, 105, 134
Bedouin, 198
Beirut provinces, 74
Belgium, 72, 171
Bell, Gertrude, 111
Bendern, Count de, 48
Benes, Edvard, 162
Ben-Gurion, David, 144, 158, 160–161, 217; as Israeli prime minister, 244, 256; on Jewish state, 164
Berlin, Isaiah, 39, 42–43, 88, 123–124, 169, 203, 240; on British abandonment of Weizmann, 242–243
Berlin bombing raids (1943), 181
Berlin crisis (1948–1949), 33, 241, 264
Bermuda conference (1943), 189, 193
Bernadotte plan (1948), 241
Bevin, Ernest, 227, 228–229, 234, 235, 238, 241; anti-Semitism of, 243–244, 246–247, 251; Arab relations with, 250, 252, 254; Churchill's attack on, 246–247; Holocaust reaction of, 180; snubbing of Weizmann by, 243
Big Three meetings, 27–28, 29, 30, 32–34, 179, 193, 206, 215, 216, 219, 223
Bir Yaakov, 120–121
Bischoffsheim family, 43
Black Sea, 187
Bletchley Park, 177, 178, 200
blood libel, 53, 54
Board of Trade (Britain), 17, 63, 106
Boer War, 48, 66
Bolshevik Revolution (1917), 21, 77, 80, 81, 82, 84, 88, 264
Bolshevism/Communism, 6, 18, 19–25, 35, 90; antagonism to Jewish nationalism by, 56, 77, 86; Churchill's view of, 3, 20–23, 36, 70, 82–85, 86, 87, 88–97, 116, 137, 139, 259, 260, 262, 264, 265; Greece and, 218, 238; Hess and, 53, 88; Hungary (1919) and, 82; international revolution ideology and, 20; Jewish immigrants and, 116–117; Jews' reputed link with, 3, 77, 80, 82–89, 96, 100, 116–117, 120, 125, 128, 136, 150–151, 244, 246; Russian Civil War and, 19, 21, 23, 80, 135, 136; Russian-German separate peace and, 78, 80; self-determination and, 90; Zionism as refutation of, 87–88, 117, 139. *See also* Cold War; Russia
Bonar Law, Andrew. *See* Law, Andrew Bonar
Boothby, Robert, 231, 242
Bottomley, Norm, 182
Bracken, Brendan, 184, 197, 241
Bridges, Edward, 200, 206, 213
Britain. *See* Great Britain
Britain, Battle of (1940), 28, 197, 262
British Empire: Arabs and, 164; breakup of, 238, 251; as Churchill concern, 12, 25, 26, 31, 34, 68, 90, 95, 119, 128, 142–145, 147, 163, 169, 202, 233, 238–239, 251, 260, 262; as civilizing agent, 7, 12–13, 70, 123, 144–145, 147; Fascist countries' threat to, 152–154; financial commitments to, 101–102; Jewish potential state in, 160; Jews and, 48, 70, 145; Muslim population of, 90; threats to, 25, 90, 141, 152–153, 228; Zionism and, 5, 57–58, 62, 63, 68, 86, 123, 145, 154, 169, 228. *See also* Egypt; Great Britain; India; Palestine
British Petroleum, 66
Brook, Norman, 206, 207
Brooke, Alan, 234
Bruce, Victor Alexander (Lord Elgin), 59, 60
Bulgaria, 188
Burke, Edmund, 21
Burma, 200, 238
Butler, Rab, 253
Byzantine Empire, 39

Cabinet Committee on Palestine, 207–213, 214, 216, 225; map of plan, 214
Cadogan, Alexander, 240
Cairo Conference (1921), 111, 135, 147
Calinescu, Armand, 150
Campbell-Bannerman, Henry, 51, 60, 63, 65

Canada, 58
capitalism, Jews and, 44, 48, 50, 52, 55, 66, 67
Carlsbad Declaration (1921), 128
Cassel, Ernest, 46, 67
Castlereagh, Lord (Robert Stewart Castlereagh), 15, 16, 28
Catholics, 39, 42, 80, 82
Cecil, Hugh, 22
central Europe. *See* eastern and central Europe
Chamberlain, Austen, 81, 105
Chamberlain, Joseph, 56
Chamberlain, Neville, 22, 140, 142; appeasement and, 162, 165, 171, 231; Baldwin rivalry with, 134; Palestine policy of, 164–165, 166, 167, 168, 172, 184, 227, 247; resignation of, 171. *See also* White Paper (1939)
Channon, Henry, 231–232
Chelmno, 172
Cherwell, Lord, 253
Chiefs of Staff (Britain), 250
China, 34
Christianity, 30, 36, 90; demonization of Jews and, 39–40; evangelicals and, 4, 6, 52, 262; Jewish conversions to, 40, 41, 52, 54; Judaism's links with, 42, 45, 47, 85, 87, 124; millennial vision of, 52, 262; Palestine and, 72, 78, 79, 192
Churchill, Charles Henry (cousin), 52
Churchill, Clementine (wife), 27, 65, 121; Churchill's letters to, 19, 25, 29, 32, 145, 152, 231, 259
Churchill, Jenny Jerome (mother), 28, 43, 46, 47; American birth of, 10, 17, 27; Churchill's letters to, 16, 17, 41, 48; death of, 11, 127; on Jews, 48, 81
Churchill, Marigold (daughter), 127
Churchill, Randolph (father), 10, 12, 14–15, 16, 22, 28, 36–37, 49, 51, 52, 58, 141, 239; devotion to Disraeli of, 2, 41, 44, 46, 47; as exchequer chancellor, 134; Jewish friendships of, 38, 43–45, 46, 260–261
Churchill, Randolph (son), 150, 187
Churchill, Winston: abdication crisis and, 142, 161; Admiralty and, 14, 17, 18, 66–67, 69, 74, 171, 175, 184, 186, 190; as

amateur painter, 112, 136; anti-Bolshevism of, 3, 20–23, 82–85, 86, 87, 88–97, 116, 137, 139, 259, 260, 262, 264; anti-Nazism of, 3, 19–20, 22, 141, 148–153, 173, 259, 262, 264; anti-Semitism and, 3, 48, 49, 81–82, 83–84, 87, 88, 149; background of, 10, 265; birth of, 38, 40; as Board of Trade president, 17, 63, 106; career crash of, 3, 18–19, 69, 74, 169–170; career resuscitation of, 134; Cold War and, 17, 30–37, 195, 228, 233, 236, 241, 246, 260, 264, 265; as colonial secretary, 2, 3, 4, 82, 97, 98–122, 133–139, 147, 153, 168, 184, 235, 263; as colonial under-secretary, 13, 16, 101; contradictory aspects of, 9–10, 137–138, 264–265; Dardanelles disaster and, 18, 23, 28, 71, 72, 74, 75; depressive bouts of, 28, 30, 32, 223, 231, 242, 264, 265; Disraeli as influence on, 2, 12, 41, 63–64, 85, 89, 211, 225, 237, 248, 258, 261, 265; drinking by, 160, 220; Dundee constituency of, 64, 65, 80; early career of, 10, 11–18, 38–64; election losses of, 28, 30, 31, 133, 223, 224; enthusiasm of, 14; Epping seat of, 133–134; establishment's exclusion of, 175; as European union advocate, 236; as exchequer chancellor, 2, 134, 137, 140; father's influence on, 2, 14–15, 16, 36–37, 44, 45–46, 47, 134, 260–261; fatigue of, 227–228, 253; financial losses of, 140; first major Middle East speech by, 101, 104; first statement on Jewish homeland by, 57, 61–62; First World War and, 17, 18–19, 23, 69–75, 78–80, 259, 264; forebodings of, 264; foreign policy perspective of, 22, 26, 32–34, 140–142; historical consciousness of, 2, 35–36, 47, 84, 248, 256, 258, 259, 260, 263, 264, 265; Holocaust response of, 172, 176–182, 196, 208, 226, 236, 239–240, 248; Home Office and, 17, 66; Ibn Saud's dislike of, 220; impressionability of, 4, 105; inconsistency of, 9–10, 137–138, 264–265; "iron curtain" phrase of, 30, 260; Israeli independence statement of, 240–241; Jerusalem's capture and, 78–79; Jewish constituents of, 1, 39, 48–50, 51, 57–65, 67, 70, 74, 95, 97, 115, 117, 122, 124, 255, 260, 261; Jewish friendships of, 43–44, 46, 60, 67, 81, 96–97, 261; Jewish sympathies of, 2, 3, 7, 38, 40–41, 45–48, 65–68, 81–82, 85–86, 142, 148–152, 167, 173, 189, 265; Lawrence's influence on, 105, 106, 107; lionization of, 28; maiden public speech of, 12; on mass democracy, 22–23; as munitions minister, 78, 79–80; optimism of, 36, 265; Palestine partition views of, 159–160, 161, 212, 215, 243, 263; as Peel Commission witness, 152–159; policy vindications of, 173; political expediency/pragmatism of, 4, 8, 9, 22, 34, 36, 43, 63, 67, 98–99, 104–105, 131, 134, 265; political isolation of, 3, 7, 21, 25, 133–134, 139, 140–170, 175; post-First World War foreign policy priorities of, 26–27, 98; post-Second World War despair of, 28–32; prescient predictions of, 5–6, 262; as prime minister, 1, 3, 10, 15, 26, 27–36, 171–199, 228, 250–258, 262; prioritization of goals by, x, 7, 260; racial views of, 13–14, 31, 46–47, 138; resignation (1954) from political life by, 36; rhetorical feats of, 103–104; romanticism of, 4, 12, 17–18, 68, 265; Second World War and, 1, 3, 15, 17, 19, 21–22, 26, 27–36, 141, 160, 161, 171–199, 231, 262; short attention span of, 137; special-interest politics and, 64; speech (1921) at Hebrew University site of, 117, 137–138; speech (1921) defending Balfour Declaration of, 103–104; speech (1922) defending Balfour Declaration and Palestine Mandate of, 105, 117, 137; speech (1938) on Zionist improvement of Palestine of, 167–168; speech (1939) attacking Chamberlain White Paper of, 165, 185; speech (1949) endorsing Israel by, 246; as state secretary for war and air, 80, 82, 89–91, 94–95, 96, 98, 101, 108; Territorialism and, 57–59, 61, 68; unpopular causes of, 21, 140–142, 259–260; Victorian ideals of, 4, 5, 11–18, 89, 100, 139, 225, 261, 264, 265; as war secretary, 98; Weizmann's values and, 4, 123–134, 165; White Paper (1922) of, 118–119, 132–133, 137, 235; "wilderness years" of (*see subhead* political isolation of); worldview of, 4, 7, 8, 9–37, 51, 103, 113, 119–120, 121, 165, 190–191, 225, 236, 259–265; writing projects of, 112, 135, 140, 150, 231; Yalta agreement defense by, 179; Zionism and (*see under* Zionism); "Zionism versus Bolshevism" article by, 85–87, 88, 96, 116, 124

civilization: Britain as guardian of, 26, 28, 142–143; Churchill's belief in progress of, 3, 4, 7, 11, 12, 14, 17, 18, 31, 32, 36, 37, 71–72, 100, 119–120, 123, 125, 138, 146, 155–156, 215, 225, 236, 259, 260, 262, 264; Churchill's perceived threats to, 19–20, 22, 142–143, 167; Churchill's view of Arabs in context of, 155; Jewish Palestinian homeland as protector of, 4, 5, 8, 53, 55, 70, 100, 103, 113, 119–123, 125, 136, 138, 139, 141–142, 145–146, 154–156, 167, 169, 190–191, 195, 225, 237, 248–249, 255, 256, 261–262

Cohen family, 43

Cold War, 17, 30–37, 195, 228, 233, 236, 241, 246, 264, 265; Churchill's "iron curtain" concept and, 30, 260. *See also* Russia

Collins, Michael, 127

Colombia, 205

Colonial Office (Britain), 2, 3, 4, 13, 16–17, 82, 97, 98–122, 137–139, 164, 168, 190; anti-Semitism and, 174; anti-Zionism and, 176, 184, 222; Churchill's reliance on staff of, 99, 105–106, 107, 108, 111, 112–113, 135, 137, 175; Jewish immigration and, 183, 186–187, 188; Jewish state plan and, 199; snubbing of Weizmann by, 243

Colville, Jock, 255

Comintern, 20

Committee of Imperial Defence, 164

Communism. *See* Bolshevism/Communism; Cold War

Communist International (Comintern), 20

Como, Lake, 231

concentration camps, 162. *See also* extermination camps
Congress of Vienna (1814–1815), 11, 15–16, 23
Congreve, Walter, 108, 112
Conservative Party (Britain): Aliens Act and, 49, 50, 51; anti-Semitism and, 1, 81, 82, 100–101; Churchill's move from, 10, 11, 14, 18, 48, 50–51; Churchill's position in, 10, 21, 22, 25, 79–80, 104–105, 134, 135, 230, 231, 241; Churchill's unpopularity with, 99, 133, 140–141, 142, 143, 160–161, 231, 239; coalition governments and, 80, 100, 133, 142; Disraeli and, 42–43, 44, 64; election loss (1929) of, 142; election loss (1945) of, 30, 223, 224; government cost cutting and, 100; Jewish members of, 44, 46, 50–51; Middle East policy and, 95, 103; nineteenth-century imperialism and, 12; return to power of (1951–1955), 32, 33, 228, 250–258; Second World War Palestine policy and, 176; U.S. relations and, 27; Zionism and, 1, 80, 99, 100, 102, 104–105, 142, 144, 173, 185, 215, 228, 231, 232, 247, 250. *See also* White Paper (1939)
Constantinople, 71, 74, 89
Convention of *1899*, 251
Council of Europe, 15, 26
Cox, Percy, 129
Cranborne, Viscount (Robert Arthur James Gascoyne-Cecil), 176, 191, 208
Cromwell, Oliver, 150
Crusades, 39, 79
Cuba, 16
cultural Zionism, 3, 255
Curzon, George Nathaniel, 76, 83, 91, 98; wariness of Arabs of, 106, 107
Curzon Line, 179
Cyrenaica, 233
Czechoslovakia, 22, 162

Daily Mail, 104–105
Daily Mirror, 65
Daladier, Edouard, 162
Damascus, 74, 75, 94, 106. *See also* Syria
Damascus blood libel (1840), 53, 54

Daniel Deronda (Eliot), 52, 61
Dardanelles disaster (1915), 18, 23, 28, 71, 72, 74, 75
Darien II (refugee ship), 187, 191
democracy, 18, 27, 191, 265; Churchill's view of, 22–23; Israel as, 244
depression (economic), 134
détente, 33
Deterding, Henri, 66
Dill, John, 202
displaced-persons camps, 228–229, 249
Disraeli, Benjamin, 12, 14, 56, 89, 130; as Churchill influence, 41, 44, 45, 61, 63–64, 225, 261; Jewish background of, 41–43, 46–47, 81, 85; on Jews' divine favor, 2, 38, 40, 45, 46, 47, 52, 61, 68, 70, 85, 87, 89, 124, 136, 171, 192, 195, 209, 211, 237, 248, 258, 261, 265
Dizengoff, Meir, 120, 121
Dresden bombing, 31
Dreyfus, Alfred, 47–48, 54, 151
Dulberg, Joseph, 51, 57, 58, 60, 63, 64, 65, 67
Dulles, John Foster, 253
Dundee (Scotland), 64, 65, 80, 102, 133
Dunkirk evacuation (1940), 192
Dvorkovitz, Dr., 67
Dyer, Reginald, 81

East Africa: Churchill's imperial interest in, 12, 13, 95; Jewish homeland suggested in, 56–59, 62
eastern and central Europe: Churchill's Russian containment plan for, 16, 29; Jewish immigrants in England from, 49, 56, 67; Jewish immigrants in Palestine from, 53; Jewish refugees from, 182–183, 244, 246; massacres of Jews in, 40, 196, 200; Soviet control over, 223
Easter riots (Jerusalem, 1920), 126–127
Eddy, William, 219–220
Eden, Anthony, 34, 189; anti-Zionism of, 174, 203, 222; Holocaust reports and, 179, 181–182; Middle East policy and, 197, 199, 200, 203–204, 205, 209, 210, 213, 215, 218–219, 250, 251, 253, 254
Edward VII, king of Great Britain, 40–41

Edward VIII, king of Great Britain (later Duke of Windsor), 142, 161, 166
Egypt, 32, 44, 90, 108, 219; British conflict with, 228, 232, 233, 238, 251–252; British troop withdrawal from, 143, 144; Churchill's strategic view of, 25, 95, 99, 104, 123, 141, 144, 145, 147, 153, 163, 197, 228, 233–234; Israel attacked by, 230, 246; Israeli armistice with, 244; Israel's strategic importance and, 254, 255; Nazi threat to, 197, 202
Egyptian Expeditionary Force, 108
Einsatzgruppen, SS, 176, 177
Eisenhower, Dwight D., 32, 179
Elath, Eliahu, 255, 256, 257, 261
electrification concession, 101, 103, 105, 117, 125, 137, 146, 167, 168
Elgin, Lord (Victor Alexander Bruce), 59, 60
"Elijah's Mantle" (R. Churchill), 44
Eliot, George, 40, 52, 61, 68
Elliot, Walter, 241
Engels, Friedrich, 53
England. See Great Britain
English Zionist Federation, 61, 69, 76. See also Zionist Review
Epping (Wanstead, Woodford), 133–134
Eritrea, 189
eugenics, 13
European unification, 236
evangelical Christians, 4, 6, 52, 262
extermination camps, 176, 178, 179, 181, 182. See also Auschwitz-Birkenau

Faisal ibn Hussein, 92, 93, 106, 108, 110, 194, 199, 221; Churchill's characterization of, 128; view of Palestinian Arabs of, 129
Fascism, 18, 19, 20, 21, 22, 36, 168; Arab supporters of, 154, 160, 169, 193; as British imperial threat, 152–154, 160, 161, 169. See also Italy; Nazi Germany
"final solution." See Holocaust
First World War, 11, 14, 17, 64, 69–80, 83, 244; Arab allegiances in, 75–76, 126, 127, 129, 146, 154, 168; breakup of Ottoman Empire and, 68, 70–75, 77–78, 90–92, 135, 197, 199; British mandates and, 25, 77–78, 158; changed world order following, 18–21, 24–25; Churchill's memoirs of, 112, 135; Churchill's view of, 23, 259, 264; Jewish allegiances and, 75, 86, 124, 136, 165–166, 192; Palestinian Arabs and, 126; pan-Arab concept and, 197, 199; Paris conference following, 19, 23–27, 93, 103, 131, 159; Russia's withdrawal from, 78–79, 80; Zionist movement and, 68, 69, 70, 195 (see also Balfour Declaration)
First Zionist Congress (1897), 4, 38, 55–56, 262
Foreign Office (Britain), 23, 107, 180–183, 206, 222, 250–251, 253; Anglo-Egyptian conflict and, 252; anti-Semitism and, 174; Arabism of, 243; Jewish Palestinian immigration barriers of, 183, 188; Jewish state plan and, 99, 208, 210; Negev settlement and, 257; outdated policies of, 244; snubbing of Weizmann by, 243; Zionist extremism and, 217
Forest, Maurice de, 46
France, 15, 19, 40, 45; Churchill's view of, 13, 21, 26, 92; Dreyfus case and, 47–48, 54; Holocaust and, 178; Nazi invasion of, 171, 192; Palestine claims of, 39, 71, 72, 92, 93, 103, 108, 131; Syria claims of, 71, 72, 74, 75, 111, 200; Syrian mandate of, 77, 91, 92, 93, 106, 194, 197, 199, 200, 209, 218; Zionism and, 92, 93
Free French, 199, 200
free trade, 16, 17, 142
French Congo, 17
French Revolution, 45, 86

Gailani, Al-. See Rashid ali al-Gailani
Galilee, 158, 210, 213
Gallipoli. See Dardanelles disaster
Gardiner, A. G., 9
gas chambers, 172
Gascoyne-Cecil, Robert Arthur James. See Cranborne, Viscount
Gaster, Moses, 60–61, 62, 64, 65, 67, 68, 70, 97, 116
Gaza protests (1921), 126

genocide. *See* Holocaust
Gentile Zionists, 1, 3, 4–5, 7, 55, 111, 113; British War Cabinet and, 207, 208; Chamberlain White Paper and, 164; Palestine partition opposition by, 159; in United States, 192; view of Arabs of, 129
Germany: anti-Semitism in, 53; Balfour Declaration's reception in, 77; Churchill's view of, 13, 16, 24–25, 26, 33, 35, 99; First World War and, 18, 19, 69, 75, 79, 83; Hess's Communism and, 53; Jewish Bolshevik leaders in, 80, 83; Jewish ethnicity and, 75, 77; Jewish Reform movement in, 53; oil interests and, 66; post-Second World War and, 29, 33, 35, 36; Russian ties with, 19–20, 25, 79, 80; Versailles Treaty and, 19, 90; Zionism and, 56. *See also* Nazi Germany
Gladstone, William, 14, 41, 44, 47, 90
Great Britain: abdication crisis in, 142, 161, 166; anti-Semitism and, 6, 40, 43, 50, 56, 64, 66, 68, 70–71, 80–82, 84, 86, 87, 88, 100–101, 164, 171–174, 179, 180, 185, 191, 208, 232, 240, 243–244; Arab policies of (*see under* Arabs; Palestinian Arabs); decline in power of, 31–32, 36; economic problems of, 94, 101, 134–135; golden age of, 11–18; Holocaust response in, 176–177, 178–183; Jewish historical expulsion from, 6, 40; Jewish historical restoration to, 150; Jewish immigration barriers and, 49–50, 51, 60, 65, 66, 183, 208; Jewish refugees and, 188–189; Jewish statesmen in, 70, 71, 76, 78, 81, 100; Jews' status in, 1, 3, 6–8, 38, 40–47, 66, 75–76, 85–86, 136; labor strikes in, 94; League of Nations and, 26; Middle East and, 68, 69–76, 94–95, 101, 103, 106–112, 134, 144–145, 221 (*see also* Balfour Declaration; Mesopotamia; Palestine); Munich agreement and, 162, 165, 231, 232; political scene (1930s) in, 142–143; strategic interests of, 141–142, 152–153, 161, 163–164, 191 (*see also* British Empire); U.S. relations with, 17, 26–27, 29, 34, 165, 166, 175, 196, 233, 234, 238; war debt and, 27, 32; Weizmann's belief in values of, 123–124, 243; withdrawal from Palestine by, 230; Zionism and (*see under* Zionism); Zionist extremist attacks and, 216–217, 232. *See also* First World War; Second World War; *specific government offices, political parties, and political leaders*
Greater Syria proposal, 93, 106, 209, 210, 213, 225
great leaders theory, 14, 22–23, 27
Great Powers, 11, 15, 16, 17, 23, 26, 28, 262; Middle East division by, 71–72, 96; Middle East involvement of, 52; post-Second World War and, 30, 32; Zionist appeal to, 56. *See also* Big Three meetings
Greece, 90, 103, 193, 197; civil war in, 218, 238
Grey, Edward, 70, 71
Grigg, P. J., 180
Guatemala, 34
Guinness, Walter. *See* Moyne, Lord
gunrunning, Zionist, 131, 137, 219

Ha'am, Achad, 255
Haifa, 135, 190, 209, 251, 252
Haj Amin al-Husseini, 112, 162, 250, 252
Halifax, Lord (Edward Frederick Lindley Wood), 22, 172, 185, 203, 227, 247
Harrison report, 229
Hashemite clan, 74, 198, 199, 210
Hatikvah (Zionist anthem), 118
Hebrew University (Jerusalem), 117, 124, 137, 162
Hebron, 143
Hegelian Communism, 53
Hejaz, 106, 107, 198
Herzl, Theodor, 3, 4, 54–56, 70, 75, 121, 130; Dreyfus case and, 151; Zionist argument of, 87–88, 255
Hess, Moses, 53–54, 55, 70, 88, 169
Hinduism, 228, 237
Hiroshima bombing (1945), 31, 35
Hirsch, Lionel, 41, 46
History of the English-Speaking Peoples (Churchill), 150

Hitler, Adolf, 27, 29, 148, 162, 166; Arabs and, 154, 193; Jewish extermination and, 152, 176, 177, 180, 208, 256; rise to power of, 19, 25–26; U.S. entrance into war and, 188. *See also* Nazi Germany

Hoare, Samuel, 134

Holocaust, 3, 6, 152, 171, 172, 176–183, 196, 200, 207, 226, 227, 236, 239–240, 248; British intelligence about, 176–177, 200; Jewish state as redemption of, 185, 208, 256; world's awareness of, 179, 188; Zionist intensified response to, 203. *See also* refugees, Jewish

Home Office (Britain), 17, 66, 207

Hoskins, Harold, 205, 206, 219, 220, 222

Huleh salient, 210

Hull, Cordell, 166, 193

Hungary, 82; Jewish deportations from, 179, 180, 181, 182; Jewish refugees from, 191

Hurley, Patrick, 205

Husseini. *See* Haj Amin al-Husseini

Hussein ibn Ali, 74, 75, 92, 93, 106, 107, 108, 110, 198, 199

hydraulic power, 101

Ibn Saud, 74, 107, 128, 193, 194, 195, 252; anti-Zionist/anti-Jewish stance of, 204–205, 206, 220, 221, 225; Arab federation proposal and, 196–204, 225, 226; Churchill's meeting with, 219–221, 223, 227, 243; Churchill's tribute to, 237–238, 265; Greater Syria proposal and, 210, 213; Roosevelt's relations and, 204–205, 221–222

immigrants. *See* Jewish immigration and immigrants

independence movements. *See* nationalism; self-determination

India, 89, 200; Amritar massacre and, 81; importance to Churchill of, 13, 16, 25, 31, 139, 141, 142, 143, 144, 147, 153, 163, 197, 202, 233, 260; independence of, 228, 238; Jewish governing officials in, 100; Muslims in, 76, 90, 92, 237; partition of, 238

Indonesia, 247, 248

Inquisition, 41

internationalism, 18, 26

"international Jews" concept, 86, 87–88, 96

Iran (formerly Persia), 94, 95, 197

Iraq (formerly Mesopotamia), 90, 91, 154, 221; Arab uprising (1920) in, 110; Arab uprising (1941) in, 192, 194, 197, 238; British high commissioner of, 129; as British mandate, 10, 25, 77, 93, 94, 95, 102, 105, 107; Churchill's policy toward, 134; ethnic/religious differences in, 110; Israel attacked by, 230; oil production in, 135; proposed Arab rulers of, 106, 110, 112, 128, 129; Shiite majority in, 110; Turkish threat to, 103

Iraqi National Assembly, 129

Ireland, 99, 105, 112, 117, 127, 130, 153

Irgun, 213, 232, 242

"iron curtain" concept, 30, 260

Isaacs, Rufus Daniel (Lord Reading), 100

Islam, 72, 74, 75, 154; Churchill's imperial policy and, 90, 92, 237; Churchill's view of, 4, 13, 125, 128, 155, 200; India and, 76, 90, 92, 237; Jerusalem violence and, 143; Jews and, 41, 96, 129–130, 205, 219, 221; Sunni/Shia division in, 110; Wahhabis and, 128, 225, 265. *See also* Arabs; sherifians

Ismay, Hastings, 211, 212, 218

isolationism, 27

Israel, State of, 93; ancient history of, 39; Arab defeat by (1948–1949), 218, 230, 240, 241, 243, 244; Britain's role in founding, 6–7; Churchill's defense of, 243–244, 246–250; Churchill's groundwork in founding, 137; Churchill's prescience about, 5–6, 262; Churchill's view of, 1, 63, 228, 240–241, 251–258, 260–261; Cold War and, 250; as democracy, 244; diplomatic recognition of, 218, 244; founding of, 56, 230, 240; as haven, 256; land gains by, 244; map (1949) of, 245; military power of, 252, 253; Palestinian Arabs and, 249; population doubling in, 256; Transjordan and, 250; U.S. backing of, 228, 244. *See also* Arab-Israeli War; Palestine

Italy: bombing of Palestine by, 190; Churchill's view of, 19, 20, 21; Jews' historical expulsion from, 40, 42; as strategic threat to Britain, 27, 141, 150, 152–154, 160, 161, 165

Jabotinsky, Vladimir, 75, 91, 145, 158
Jaffa violence (1921), 113, 116, 120, 126–127
Japan, 26, 28, 30, 35, 153, 188, 201, 223
Jedda, 75
Jerome, Jenny. *See* Churchill, Jenny Jerome
Jerusalem: Arab-Israeli war and, 240, 241, 242, 250; Arab riots (1920) in, 91, 126–127; British conquest of, 78–79, 135; British continued mandate in, 158; British high commissioners in, 108; Disraeli's trip to, 52; division of, 244, 255, 256; Jewish ancient sovereignty in, 39; Jewish-Arab violence in (1929), 143; Jewish sacred sites in, 143, 255; Ottoman Empire and, 74; as proposed Big Three meeting site, 216; as proposed British-controlled state, 209, 210, 213; sherifian activity in, 126; Zionist terrorism in, 232
Jerusalem, mufti of, 112, 143, 154, 193, 194
Jerusalem conference (1921), 111–112
Jewish Agency (Palestine), 144, 145, 187, 188, 217
Jewish Chronicle, 49, 50, 62, 64–65, 87, 88; Churchill's Holocaust-recognition message to, 177–178; on Churchill's inconsistency, 138; Churchill's opposition to partition plan and, 159; on Churchill White Paper, 133; editorial praise for Churchill in, 66, 217
Jewish immigration and immigrants (Britain), 48–50, 51, 58, 63, 66, 67, 68, 208
Jewish immigration and immigrants (Palestine), 1, 52–54, 68, 93, 111, 114–115; Anglo-American Committee and, 229, 234; Arab objection to, 151, 166, 221; barriers to, 183–184, 228–229; Bolshevist ties attributed to, 116–117, 120, 244; British curtailments of, 162, 163, 164, 166, 175, 224, 230; Churchill's reversal on, 235–236; Churchill's views on, 114–116, 118, 137, 138, 153–157, 163, 166–167, 172, 173, 185–188, 191, 219, 232, 242, 249; Churchill White Paper on, 132; disasters and, 186, 187–188; "economic absorptive capacity" phrase and, 235; expected annual numbers of, 130, 131; harsh treatment of, 186–188; humanitarian basis of, 167, 185, 186, 188; illegal, 131, 183, 186, 187–188; Israeli population increase from, 256, 257; MacDonald government's backing of, 144; from Nazi persecution, 152, 166, 185–186; Palestine partition plan and, 215; Passfield White Paper's suspension of, 143; Peel Commission proposed limit to, 158; pioneer settlements of, 120–121; Roosevelt's appeal for, 221; Russian border closure and, 134; Samuel's suspension of (1921), 114, 127, 132, 137; U.N. recommendation for, 229; War Cabinet policy and, 208; Zionist extremists and, 217; Zionist projections for, 131. *See also* refugees, Jewish

Jewish immigration and immigrants (United States), 54, 68, 183, 246
Jewish national homeland: as asylum from persecution, 38, 167, 196; Balfour Declaration on, 76, 78, 116; as British long-term objective, 115–116; British officials' opposition to, 174; British support for, 62, 69, 71; British understanding of, 77, 132; Churchill's avowed commitment to, 207, 254; Churchill's definition (1922) of, 132–133; Churchill's time frame for, 131, 194; Churchill's view of, 1, 3, 39, 61–62, 68, 113, 115–117, 132–133, 139, 145, 190–191, 196, 232, 236–237, 247, 262; English historical interest in, 51–57, 68; Herzl and, 54–55; Hess and, 53–54; as Holocaust response, 196; Jewish center vs., 115–116; Jewish opponents of, 71; Jewish state vs., 56, 70, 76–77, 86, 131, 157, 204; Palestinian Arab rights and, 146; Peel state proposal and, 158–160; as political Zionist goal, 2–3; Territorialist proposal for, 56–59, 68; Victorian ro-

manticization of, 38–39, 40, 52, 68; and White Paper (1939) proposal of Arab state, 164. *See also* Israel, State of; Zionism
"Jewish problem," 2–3, 6, 40
Jewish state: in Arab federation proposal, 196–205, 219, 220, 226; biblical heritage of, 255; British Cabinet Committee proposal for, 207–213, 225; Churchill's changed position on, 170, 172, 196, 197–199, 200–201, 202, 204, 208, 210; Churchill's detachment toward, 223, 227, 240; as Churchill's distant goal, 194; Churchill's prediction of, 262; Churchill's promotion of, 219–220; as Holocaust redemption, 185, 208, 227; Ibn Saud's opposition to, 204–205; national home vs., 56, 70, 76–77, 86, 131, 157, 204; Peel proposal for, 158–160; proposed population of, 201, 207; Weizmann's call for, 223; White Paper (1939) vs., 164, 183–184; Woodhead proposal for, 162–163. *See also* Israel, State of
Jewish State, The (Herzl), 54–55
Jewish Territorial Organization, 57
Jews: anti-Zionists among, 67, 71, 75, 76, 215–216; Arab hostility to, 142, 204–205, 221; assimilation of, 40, 55; in Baghdad, 110; biblical heritage of, 255; Bolshevik/Communist reputed ties of, 3, 77, 80, 82–89, 96, 100, 116–117, 120, 125, 128, 136, 150–151, 244, 246; British alien legislation and, 49–50, 51, 58, 60, 63, 64, 65, 82; British government posts of, 70, 71, 76, 78, 81, 100; British historical treatment of, 6–7, 38, 40–41; as British troops, 75, 86, 180, 190; businesses open on Sunday and, 63; Christian conversions of, 40, 41, 52, 54; as Churchill's constituents, 23, 39, 48–50, 57–60, 61, 63–65, 67; Churchill's view of, 2, 3, 4, 5, 7, 13, 38, 40–41, 43–48, 60, 65–68, 80–82, 85–86, 96–97, 124–125, 135–136, 138, 142, 148–152, 156, 167, 173, 189, 248, 261, 265; as civilizing agents, 4, 5, 8, 70, 136, 138, 261; demonization of, 39; Disraeli's dictum about, 2, 38, 40, 45, 46, 47, 52, 61, 68; 70, 85, 87, 89, 124, 136, 171, 192, 195, 209, 211, 237, 248, 258, 261, 265; historical displacement of, 38, 39–40, 119; historical suspicions about, 125; internal divisions among, 61; "international" vs. "national," 86, 87; mass murders of, 39–40, 152, 162, 176–183 (*see also* Holocaust; pogroms); Muslims and, 41, 96, 129–130, 205, 219, 221; Nazi scapegoating of, 142, 148–150, 151, 152, 153, 162, 169, 207; perceived as revolutionaries, 86, 87–88; perceived power of, 75–76, 77, 80, 81, 82, 85, 89, 145, 153, 191–192; political emancipation of, 38, 40, 42, 44–45, 75–76; racialized view of, 41, 42, 46–47, 53, 70, 81, 85, 138, 156; United States and, 145, 149, 153, 166, 185, 189, 191–193, 229, 255. *See also* anti-Semitism; Zionism
Jews' Free School, 45
jingoism, 25
Jordan (formerly Transjordan), 93, 103, 131, 134, 158, 207, 210, 221; Abdullah's rule of, 111, 112, 198, 204, 249–250, 252; Arab federation proposal and, 108, 196, 204; Churchill's policy toward, 252–253; Greater Syria proposal and, 209, 211, 213; Israel attacked by, 230, 240, 249–250, 256; Israeli skirmishes with, 254; Jerusalem control and, 244, 255; Muslims in, 90; Palestinian Arabs and, 243, 249; separation from Palestine of, 108, 111–112, 135; Sunni majority in, 110
Jordan River, 101, 108, 125–126
Joynson-Hicks, William, 64, 78
Judenstaat, Der (Herzl), 54–55

Kedourie, Elie, 40, 107, 111–112, 196
Kemal, Mustafa (Ataturk), 91
Kerensky, Alexander, 84, 103
Kerr, Philip (Lord Lothian), 175
Khedive Tewfik Pasha, 44
King David Hotel bombing, 232
Kitchener, Horatio Herbert, 71, 74
Kook, Avraham Yitzchak, 117
Koran, 219, 221
Kristallnacht (1938), 162
Kun, Bela, 82

Kurds, 110
Kuwait, 107

Labor Zionists, 130–131
Labour Party (Britain): Churchill's defeat by, 30, 223, 224; Middle East and, 200–201, 215, 244; policy problems of, 244, 246; White Paper (1939) on Palestine and, 164; Zionism and, 173–174, 185, 227, 228–229, 232, 238, 239, 240, 241, 243. *See also* Attlee, Clement; Bevin, Ernest
land development: British anti-Zionist curbs on, 143, 164, 191; Churchill's belief in, 5, 121, 147–148, 191, 248–249, 265; Israeli success with, 256–257; Palestinian Arabs and, 125–126, 146, 155, 248–249, 261; proposed Jewish state and, 209, 210; Zionist success with, 4, 6, 115, 120–123, 136, 138, 155–156, 161, 191
Laski, Harold, 184, 208
Laski, Nathan, 49–50, 60, 63, 64, 65, 67, 169, 208
Latin America, 183
Law, Andrew Bonar, 21, 79–80, 101, 102, 133, 208
Law, Richard, 208, 210
Lawrence, T. E. (Lawrence of Arabia), 93, 108, 126, 129, 199, 237; as Churchill influence, 105–106, 107; myth of Arab Revolt and, 75
League of Nations, 21, 135, 159; Churchill's view of, 26, 27; Middle East mandates and, 78, 104, 109, 126, 173, 195, 209, 232, 234; Palestine Mandate ratification by, 133; Permanent Mandates Commission of, 164
Lebanon, 93, 174, 197, 200, 209, 213, 220, 253; attack on Israel by, 230
Lenin, Vladimir, 20, 77, 83, 88
Leviticus, 5
Liberal Association (Dundee), 102
liberalism, nineteenth-century, 4, 6, 17, 30, 36, 37, 82
Liberal Party (Britain): Balfour Declaration and, 99; Churchill's disfavor with, 133; Churchill's move to, 10, 14, 18, 21, 48, 50–51, 57, 78, 80; coalition government and, 80, 100, 133; Jews and, 44, 48, 51, 56–57, 59, 60, 63–65, 81, 100; Middle East policy and, 95, 200–201; Ottoman breakup and, 70, 71, 89; White Paper (1939) and, 164; Zionism and, 80, 185, 215, 247
Libya, 219
Litvinov, Maxim, 82
Lloyd, George, 175, 186
Lloyd, Selwyn, 252, 253
Lloyd George, David, 18; Arabs and, 128–129; Churchill and, 16, 21, 80, 105, 106, 107, 130, 142, 144, 224, 259; Jews and, 56–57, 81, 82; Ottoman policy of, 89, 104; Palestine and, 71, 72, 76, 79, 94–95, 99, 104, 114, 131, 247; Transjordan and, 111, 135
Lod airstrip, 209, 241
London conference (1939), 163
Longfellow, Henry Wadsworth, 178
Lord George Bentinck (Disraeli), 45, 87
Lothian, Lord (Philip Kerr), 175
Lyttelton, Oliver, 187

Macaulay, Thomas Babington, 264
MacDonald, Malcolm, 167, 169
MacDonald, Ramsay, 142–143, 144, 147
MacMichael, Harold, 216
Madison Square Garden rally (1942), 178
Malenkov, Georgi, 33
Manchester. *See* North-West Manchester
Manchester Guardian, 49, 122
Marlborough, Duke of, 10, 22, 43, 148
Marsh, Edward, 62
Martin, John, 196, 202, 215, 217
Marx, Karl, 53
mass democracy, 22–23
Mauritius, 183, 186, 187
Mazzini, Giuseppe, 53
McMahon, Henry, 74, 108
Mecca, 74, 75
Mediterranean area, 152, 153–154, 197
Meinertzhagen, Richard, 91, 105–106, 112, 129, 232
Meir, Yaakov, 117
Melchett, Henry, 160, 181, 213

"Memorandum upon the Pacification of the Middle East" (Churchill), 135
Mesopotamia. *See* Iraq
Middle East: British costs in, 94–95, 101, 103, 107, 134; British diminished influence in, 221; British mandates in (*see* Iraq; Palestine); British regional approach to, 106–112; Churchill's anti-Bolshevist policy in, 89–97; Churchill's detachment from, 112, 218; Churchill's lack of expertise on, 99–100; Churchill's strategic approach to, 4–5, 107–108, 134, 144–145, 160–161, 172, 191, 195–199, 233, 250–251; First World War and, 68, 71–72, 74–75, 77–78, 90–92, 135, 197, 199; Great Power involvement in, 52; Israel's strategic importance in, 228, 246, 250; Second World War and, 165, 195–201; Soviet Union and, 218; Sunni-Shia division and, 90, 110; United States and, 104, 222, 223, 224, 229, 237, 243. *See also* Zionism; *specific countries and regions*
millenarianism. *See* Second Coming
Molotov, Vyacheslav, 182
Mongols, 30
monotheism, 45, 47
Montagu, Edwin, 71, 76, 81, 100
Montefiore family, 56
Moors, 155
Moran, Lord, 253, 254
Morgenthau, Henry, 101
Morocco, 17
Morrison, Herbert, 174; Palestine partition plan and, 208–215, 216, 217, 219, 225, 229, 232, 234, 235; pro-Zionism and, 207
Morrison-Grady plan (1946), 229, 232, 234
Moses, 169–170
Mount of Olives, 52
Mount Scopus, 117
Mount Zion, 38
Moyne, Lord (Walter Guinness), 174, 187, 191, 194, 200, 202, 208; assassination of, 216–217, 222, 225
Muhammad, prophet, 154

Munich Agreement (1938), 162, 165, 231, 232
Muslims. *See* Islam
Mussolini, Benito, 20, 152, 153–154, 161, 162, 193

Nahas Pasha, 251
Najd (Arabia), 74
Napoleon I, emperor of the French, 14, 22–23, 29
Napoleon III, emperor of the French, 81
nationalism, 3, 24, 53, 54, 150–151; Arabs and, 105, 226 (*see also* pan-Arabism); India and, 237. *See also* Jewish national homeland; Zionism
Nazi Germany, 3, 6, 27, 29, 35; Anschluss and, 141, 149, 162; appeasement of, 162, 165, 231, 232; Arab supporters of, 154, 192, 193, 194, 197; bombings of Britain by, 28, 197, 262; Britain as sole opponent of, 192; British politicians' early view of, 22, 25–26; Churchill's strategic view of, 152–153, 160, 165, 199; Churchill's warnings about, 141, 142, 148–153, 161, 166, 168, 173, 259, 262, 264, 265; invasion of Poland by, 171; Jewish extermination policy of, 176–183; Jewish persecution in, 142, 148–150, 151, 152, 153, 162, 169, 207; Soviet Union and, 19–20, 22, 28, 176, 177, 195. *See also* Second World War
Negev desert, 158, 159, 198, 208, 210, 213, 215, 241, 248; Israeli development of, 256–257
Neguib, Mohammed, 251–252
New Zionist Organization, 144
Nili spy ring, 75
Noon, Firaz Khan, 200
North Africa, 190, 193, 197, 202; proposed Jewish settlements in, 189, 208, 219, 223; refugee camps in, 189
Northern Arab Army, 75
North-West Manchester: anti-pogrom protest in, 47, 58; Churchill as MP from, 1, 2, 39, 48, 49–50, 51, 57–65, 67, 70, 74, 95, 97, 115, 117, 122, 124, 255, 260, 261; Territorialism and, 57–58
Norway, 26, 171

nuclear weapons, 14, 35
Nuremberg Laws (1935), 148, 154

Office of Strategic Services (U.S.), 205
oil supply, 197, 198, 219, 220, 221, 222, 226; Egyptian tanker blockade and, 251, 252; Iraq production of, 135; prices of, 66–67, 82
orange groves, 120, 122
Ordnungspolizei, 177
Ormsby-Gore, William, 100
Ottoman Empire, 39, 41, 52, 55, 56, 68, 69; Arab supporters of, 75, 126, 127, 129, 146, 154, 168; Balfour Declaration's reception in, 77; breakup of, 68, 70–75, 77–78, 90–92, 135, 197, 199; Churchill's strategic interest in, 89–96, 99; Liberal Party's view of, 89; as Sunni, 110. *See also* Turkey

Pakistan, 238
Pale of Settlement, 54
Palestine: Arab federation proposal and, 196–199, 226; Arabian sherifians and, 93, 107–108, 110, 111, 137; Arab-Jewish radicalization and, 144; Arab population of (*see* Palestinian Arabs); British commitment to Jewish homeland in (*see* Balfour Declaration); British financial concerns and, 101, 134–135, 229; British high commissioner in, 113–116, 127, 129–130, 133, 174, 176, 187; British high commissioner's departure from, 230; as British mandate, 25, 77–78, 126, 133, 135, 145, 152, 156–158, 161, 163, 168, 173, 184, 195; British strategic interests in, 86, 141–142, 144, 152–153, 159, 160, 161, 163–166, 169, 191, 229, 233–234, 262; chief rabbis of, 117; Churchill as colonial secretary in, 2, 3, 5, 98–100, 137, 147, 194–195, 235, 263; Churchill's fascination with, 147–148; Churchill's hopes for Arab-Jewish relations in, 15, 130, 137, 161; Churchill's limited knowledge of, 263; Churchill's memoirs on, 135; Churchill's pro-Ottoman policy and, 90–91, 95–96; Churchill's proposed arming of Jews in, 172, 175–176, 189–190, 207, 208; Churchill's proposed relinquishment of, 224, 232–233, 234, 237; Churchill's self-defined role in, 194; Churchill's visits to, 119–125, 126, 136, 161, 248, 261; Churchill's vs. British policy on, 142, 163, 195; demographic balance in, 70, 76, 115, 130, 132, 151, 152, 157, 163, 164, 166, 167, 194; Disraeli's romanticization of, 40, 52, 68; eastern border of, 108; economic crisis in (1926–1928), 134; electrification concession in, 101, 103, 105, 117, 125, 137, 146, 161, 167, 168; evangelical Christians and, 4, 6, 52; French claims to, 39, 71, 72, 92, 93, 103, 108, 131; Ibn Saud's claim to, 204–205; Iraqi oil pipeline to, 135; Jewish-British armed clashes in, 228, 229, 231, 232, 236, 237, 238, 239, 240; Jewish development of, 5, 6, 115, 120–123, 125, 136, 138, 146, 155–156, 161–162, 167–168, 191, 248, 261, 265; Jewish historical claim to, 38–40, 52–56, 59–62, 113, 118, 145, 154; Jewish military strength in, 190; Jewish population (1917) in, 76; Jewish population (1922) in, 130; Jewish population (1932–1935) in, 152, 157; as Jewish sacred place, 119, 255–256; Muslim population in, 90; Mussolini's bids for, 154; Ottoman control of, 39, 68; pan-Arabism and, 107–108, 163, 210; partition plans for (*see* Palestine partition); as Roman province, 155; Second World War and, 172, 175–176, 189–190, 199–207, 227; self-government and, 108, 127, 151, 156; Transjordan's separation from, 111–112; violence in, 91, 113–114, 116, 120, 126–127, 137, 143, 144, 147, 152, 162, 163, 218, 229, 231, 232, 236, 237, 238, 240. *See also* Jerusalem; Jewish immigration and immigrants; Jewish national homeland; Jewish state; Zionism
Palestine partition: British Cabinet Committee plan for, 209–211; Churchill's views on, 161, 193, 196, 237, 243, 263; Morrison plan for, 207–215, 216, 217, 219, 225, 235; Peel Commission on, 152–162, 168, 196, 207, 209, 210; Soviet support for, 246; U.N. plan for,

229–230, 240, 249; Woodhead Commission on, 162–163
Palestinian Arabs: as anti-British, 126, 141, 145, 146, 154, 160, 168–169, 194; as anti-Zionist, 70, 92, 93, 126, 137, 176, 205, 223, 226; Arab federation plan and, 196, 199, 225, 226; British Balfour Declaration commitment and, 99, 127, 156; British Cabinet Committee partition proposal for, 210–212; Chamberlain's White Paper and, 164; Churchill's encounters with, 118–119, 122, 130, 131, 132; Churchill's imperial outlook and, 103, 144, 260; Churchill's Jewish state proposal and, 198; Churchill's moderated view of, 237; Churchill's negativity toward, 4, 100, 103, 114, 115, 122, 125–128, 139, 141, 142, 145, 146–147, 154, 155–156, 159, 167, 168–169, 172, 185–186, 190, 191, 193, 194, 195, 207, 212, 239, 243, 245, 248–249, 261, 264, 265; Churchill White Paper (1922) and, 132, 133; as differentiated from other Arabs, 249–250; election boycott by, 133; Faisal's view of, 129; Fascist leanings of, 154, 160, 169, 194; Ibn Saud and, 225; Jewish antipathies of, 129–130, 154; London conference (1939) and, 163; as majority, 70, 76, 115, 130, 132, 151, 152, 157, 163, 164, 166, 167; as minority in potential Jewish state, 157, 194; Ottoman government and, 75, 126, 127, 129, 168; partition plans and, 158–160, 210–212, 230, 243; Passfield White Paper (1930) and, 143; proposed Palestinian governments and, 106, 115, 127, 156; radicalization of, 144; as refugees, 249; revolt (1936–1939) of, 152, 162, 163, 194; Roosevelt's proposal for, 185; Transjordan's land takeover from, 243, 249; violence and, 91, 113, 116, 120, 126–127, 137, 143, 144, 145, 147; Zionist land development and, 3, 120, 122–123, 125–126, 146, 155–156, 191, 248–249, 261
Palmerston, Lord (Henry John Temple), 52, 56
pan-Arabism, 107–108, 163, 194, 196, 197–199, 200–203, 210, 220–221, 226, 264

Pan-European Union, 236
Paris Peace Conference (1919), 19, 23–27, 93, 103, 131, 159
Passfield, Lord, 143; White Paper (1930), 143–144
Patria (refugee ship), 186, 187, 194
Pearl Harbor attack (1941), 28, 188, 201
Peel, Robert, 152, 156, 157
Peel Commission (1937), 152–160, 161, 168, 196; partition proposal, 158–160, 162, 207, 209, 210
Persia. *See* Iran
petrodollars, 220
Philby, Hugh St. John, 196, 205
pogroms: Polish post-Second World War, 228; Russian, 44, 47, 49, 51, 54, 56, 57, 58, 59, 68, 80, 83, 84, 85
Poland, 15, 19, 20, 223; extermination camps in, 31, 172, 176, 178, 179, 181; Nazi invasion of, 171; plight of Jews in, 150, 162, 228
Polish Air Force, 181
political Zionism, 2–3, 4, 54–56
Portal, Charles, 181
Portugal, 42
Potsdam conference (1945), 30, 223, 224, 235
Primrose League, 12, 14, 44
progress, belief in. *See* civilization
Protestants, 39, 70
Protocols of the Elders of Zion, The (forged text), 80–81, 82, 87
Prussia, 15
Punjab massacre (1948), 31
Puritans, 150

Quebec Conference (1943), 206

racial hierarchy, 13–14; Anglo-Saxons' place in, 13, 31; Churchill's view of Arabs and, 264; Jewish identity and, 41, 42, 46–47, 53, 70, 81, 85, 138, 156
Radek, Karl, 88
Rashid Ali al-Gailani, 194, 197, 238
Reading, Lord (Rufus Daniel Isaacs), 100
refugees, Jewish, 182–183, 186–189, 190–191, 192; Churchill and, 215; in displaced-persons camps, 228–229; feared Communist ideology of, 244,

refugees, Jewish (*continued*)
246; Roosevelt and, 205–206; Zionist concerns about, 203. *See also* Jewish immigration and immigrants
refugees, Palestinian Arab, 249
religious Zionism, 3
"Retribution" (Longfellow), 177
Revisionists, 143, 144, 158
revolutions of 1848, 87
right-wing Zionists. *See* Revisionists
Rishon Lezion (Zionist settlement), 4, 120, 121–122, 123, 124, 136, 138, 261
ritual murder charges, 6, 40
Roman Empire, 11, 39, 155
Romania, 150, 187
romanticism, 4, 12, 17–18, 52, 53, 68, 265
Rome and Jerusalem (Hess), 53
Roosevelt, Franklin: Churchill's relations with, 27, 29, 177, 188, 204, 206, 216, 219; Ibn Saud and, 204–205, 221–222; Jewish political power and, 192–193; Palestine policy and, 166, 185, 193, 195, 197, 204, 205, 206, 211, 213, 215, 216, 226; plight of European Jews and, 172, 178, 189, 205–206
Rothschild, Alfred, 43
Rothschild, Edmond de, 121
Rothschild, James de, 117, 178–179
Rothschild, Lionel de (Lord Rothschild), 46
Rothschild, Lionel Walter de (Lord Rothschild), 76
Rothschild, Nathaniel de (Natty) (Lord Rothschild), 43, 44, 46, 50, 51, 56, 58, 67
Rothschild family, 43, 44, 52, 56
Royal Air Force, 246
Royal Dutch Shell, 66
Royal Navy, 66, 67
Russia (later Soviet Union), 41, 63; balance of power and, 15, 16, 25, 27, 29–34, 63, 90; Balfour Declaration's reception in, 77; Bolshevik Revolution and, 21, 77, 80, 81, 82, 84, 88, 264; border closing by, 134; Churchill's view of, 13, 19–22, 25, 26, 29–33, 89–90, 98, 103, 153, 165, 179, 181, 182, 195, 223, 224, 228, 233, 241, 253, 263, 264, 265; First World War and, 18, 20, 24, 27, 69, 75; First World War withdrawal by, 78–79, 80; Jewish immigration and, 54, 120–121, 138, 183, 244, 246; Jews and, 44, 47, 49, 51, 54, 56, 57, 58, 59, 68, 80, 83–84, 85, 86, 87, 100, 136, 150–151, 151, 244, 246; Nazi Germany and, 19–20, 22, 28, 176, 177, 195; nuclear weapons and, 35; *Protocols of the Elders of Zion* forgery and, 81; Turkey and, 71, 72, 103; U.N. Palestine partition plan and, 229, 246; Zionism and, 56, 218, 244. *See also* Bolshevism/Communism; Cold War; Stalin, Joseph
Russian Civil War, 19, 21, 23, 80, 135, 136
Rutenberg, Pinchas, 101, 103, 120, 146, 167, 168; Churchill's defense of, 105, 117, 125, 137
Rutherford, Watson, 67

Samuel, Harry, 50
Samuel, Herbert, 70, 71, 77, 78, 86, 106, 107, 111, 117; Arab federation/Jewish government plan of, 196, 199; Churchill's partition opposition and, 160; Churchill White Paper drafted by, 118, 132, 133; Jewish immigration limits and, 114, 127, 163, 235; Jewish national home meaning and, 132; as Palestinian high commissioner, 113–116, 127, 129–130, 133, 176
Samuel, Marcus (Lord Bearsted), 66, 67
Samuel, Samuel, 67
San Remo agreement (1920), 77–78, 90, 102
Sassoon, Reuben, 41
Saudi Arabia (formerly Arabia), 173, 198, 230; British relations with, 92–93, 94, 104, 106–107, 112, 203–204, 219–221, 225, 265; founding of, 128; independence of, 77; Nazi support by, 193, 194; oil reserves of, 198, 220, 221, 226; Ottoman Empire and, 72, 74, 75; Palestine's exclusion from, 108. *See also* Arabs; Ibn Saud; sherifians
scientific advancement, 5, 11, 14, 35, 36
Second Coming, 4, 52, 262
Second World War, 27–36, 171–226; appeasement and, 162, 164, 165, 166, 171,

231, 232; Arabs and, 193, 194, 197, 198, 237–238, 264; atomic bomb and, 14, 35; Battle of Britain and, 28, 197, 262; Big Three and, 27–34, 179, 193, 206, 215, 216, 219, 223; British anti-Semitism during, 171–172, 173, 174, 179, 180; British bombing proposals and, 172, 181, 182; British Jewish brigade and, 180; Churchill on lead-up to, 17, 19, 21–22, 141, 160, 161, 164; Churchill's envisioned peace conference for, 32, 223; Churchill's leadership during, 1, 3, 15, 27–36, 171–199, 262; Churchill's memoirs of, 231; Churchill's pessimism following, 29, 31–32; Churchill's Zionist identification and, 170, 195–196, 260, 263, 264; displaced persons and, 228–229; Jewish refugees and, 182–183, 186–189, 190–191, 192, 203, 205–206, 215, 244, 246; Middle East and, 165, 195–201, 218; Nazi expansion and, 28, 162, 195; North Africa and, 197, 202; Palestinian Arabs and, 154; Palestinian Jews and, 165–166, 172, 176; United States and, 28, 188, 192, 201; White Paper (1939) policy continuance during, 184–185; Zionism and, 2, 172–175, 195, 224–225, 240. See also Holocaust; Nazi Germany
secret diplomacy, 24
self-determination, 18, 20, 24, 25, 27; Churchill's view of, 90, 128, 159, 202, 228, 260
Sephardic Jews, 60, 117
Seventh Zionist Congress (1905), 57
Sèvres, Treaty of (1920), 90
Shaftesbury, Earl of (Edward Ashley), 52
Sharett, Moshe, 256
Shaw, George Bernard, 10
Shell Oil, 66, 67, 82
sherifians, 92–93, 94, 103, 105, 198, 221; British Palestinian administration and, 126, 137; Churchill's view of, 128–129; First World War and, 154; proposed Arab federation and, 106–112, 199
Shia Muslims, 110
Shuckburgh, Evelyn, 250
Shuckburgh, John, 132, 164, 201
Sidebotham, Herbert, 111, 114, 122, 131

Sidney Street saga, 66
Sikorski, Wladyslaw, 181
Silverman, Sidney, 236
Simpson, Wallis, 142
Sinclair, Archibald, 160, 182, 207
Skoda military factories, 162
Smith, F. E., 83
Smuts, Jan Christian, 76, 166, 191, 208
Soames, Christopher, 242
Socialist Party (Britain), 11, 25, 26–27, 142, 144, 147, 173; ebbing of Zionist support by, 222–223
socialist Zionism, 3, 144, 244
Social Revolutionary Party (Russia), 54
South Africa, 16, 43, 76, 166, 191
Soviet Union. See Cold War; Russia
Spaatz, Carl, 182
Spain, 40, 41, 42, 155, 189
Spears, Edward, 174, 202, 204
Stalin, Joseph, 27, 29, 30, 31, 33, 162, 193, 195, 206; Churchill policies and, 179, 181, 182, 223; purges of Jews and, 150, 151; Zionism and, 218, 246
Stanley, Oliver, 174, 188, 206–207, 208, 224
Stanley, Venetia (later Montagu), 71
State Department (U.S.), 191, 203, 222, 229
Steevens, G. W., 10
sterilization, forced, 13
Stern Gang, 216–217, 222
stock market crash (1929), 134, 140
Strang, William, 252
Strategic Air Forces (U.S.), 182
Struma (refugee ship), 187–188
St. Stephen's Club, 44
Sudan, 13, 16, 123, 125, 251
Sudetenland, 162
Suez Canal, 44, 103, 197, 221, 233, 234; Egyptian blockade of, 251, 252
Suez War (1956), 253
suffrage, universal, 22, 23
summit conferences, 32–34, 195. See also Big Three meetings
Sunday commerce, 63, 65
Sunni Muslims, 110
Supreme Moslem Council, 112
Sverdlov, Jacob, 83
Sykes-Picot agreement (1916), 75, 93

Syria, 74, 75, 154, 174; Arab federation proposal and, 196, 199; Arab independence movement and, 93; British Cabinet Committee proposal for, 209, 210, 213; Churchill's independence proposal for, 197, 200; as French mandate, 77, 91, 92, 93, 106, 194, 197, 199, 200, 209, 218; Greater Syria proposal, 93, 106, 209, 210, 213, 225; Israel attacked by, 230; Palestinian Arabs and, 185; sherifians and, 106, 111
Syria Palaestina, 39, 71, 72, 106

Tancred (Disraeli), 70
tank warfare, 14
Tartars, 39
Tchitcherin, George, 82
Tehran conference (1943), 206
Tel Aviv, 120, 190, 209
Temple, Henry John (Lord Palmerston), 52, 56
Ten Commandments, 45
Territorialism, 56–59, 60, 61, 62, 68
terrorism, 216–217, 222, 231, 232, 242
Times (London), 81, 110, 111, 114, 178, 242
Transjordan. *See* Jordan
tree planting, 120, 136, 155
Tripolitania, 189
Trotsky, Leon, 83, 86, 87, 88
Truman, Harry, 30, 223, 229, 255
"Truth about Hitler, The" (Churchill), 148–149
Turkey (post-1919), 197, 238; British troops in, 94; Churchill's strategy and, 104, 126; Greek conflict with, 103; Jewish immigration barriers in, 183, 187–188

Ukraine, 80
Uncle Give Us Bread (book), 21
United Nations, 32, 35, 233; Palestine partition plan of, 229–230, 240, 243, 244, 249
United States: anti-Semitism and, 193; Arab-Jewish policies and, 205, 221–222, 246; Balfour Declaration's reception in, 77; British Labour government and, 241, 246; British Palestine policy and, 234–235; British strategic interests and, 165, 166, 175, 196, 233, 234, 238; Churchill's pro-Zionism and, 173, 196, 256, 257; Churchill's view of, 9, 10, 11, 13, 17, 22, 26, 27, 30, 32, 33–34, 36, 145, 153, 165, 166, 180, 188, 191–192, 196, 197, 228, 235, 254–255, 256; Fascist Italy and, 20; First World War and, 18, 26, 27, 69, 75; Holocaust reaction by, 171, 181, 185; Israel's relations with, 228, 230, 244; Jewish immigration and, 54, 68, 183, 246; Jewish refugees and, 189, 229; Jews' perceived influence in, 145, 149, 153, 166, 185, 191–193, 255; League of Nations and, 26; Middle East and, 104, 222, 223, 224, 229, 237, 243; neutrality of, 27, 28; nuclear weapons and, 35; Second World War and, 28, 188, 192, 201, 206; U.N. Palestine partition plan and, 229, 243; Zionism and, 70, 91, 145, 185, 196, 197, 201–205, 215–216, 226, 251. *See also* Roosevelt, Franklin
universal suffrage, 22, 23

V-E (Victory in Europe) Day, 29, 30
Versailles, Treaty of (1919), 19, 90, 102, 146
Vichy France, 194, 197
Victoria, queen of Great Britain, 11, 12, 40
Victoria Jewish Hospital, 65
Victorian era, 4, 5, 11–18, 20, 22, 25, 32, 36, 89; characteristics and beliefs of, 11–12, 130, 264, 265; Jewish identity and, 38–39, 40, 41–44, 45, 46–47, 52, 68, 85; Zionists as sharing values of, 100, 119, 121, 138, 139, 141–142, 225, 261
Vienna, 162
V-J (Victory over Japan) Day, 30
V-2 rockets, 28

Wahhabis, 128, 225, 265
Wailing Wall (Jerusalem), 143, 255
Wales, 66, 240
Wallace, Henry, 192, 194, 204
Wannsee conference (1942), 176
War Cabinet (Britain): anti-Zionism and, 172–173, 175, 190, 191, 201, 208; Arab relations and, 198, 219–220; Balfour Declaration and, 76–77, 79; Churchill's

appointment to, 171, 172, 184; Churchill's pro-Zionist plea to, 193, 195, 199, 207; Committee on Palestine, 207–213, 217–218, 225; First World War and, 69, 72, 79, 80; Jewish extermination reports and, 178; Jewish Palestinian immigration and, 183, 187, 188; Middle East and, 200, 201, 206; White Paper's enforcement and, 184–185; Zionist extremists and, 217
War Council (Britain), 71, 72, 95
War Department (U.S.), 206
Warsaw uprising (1944), 179
Washington Press Club, 254, 257
Wauchope, Arthur, 147
Wavell, Archibald, 186, 193–194
Webb, Beatrice, 143
Webster, Nesta, 86
Wedgwood, Josiah, 158, 160, 164
Weizmann, Chaim, 70; American Jews and, 191, 192; background of, 60; on Balfour Declaration's weakening, 132; British rejection of, 242–243; British response to Palestinian Arab violence and, 143, 144; British values of, 4, 123–124, 129, 138, 175, 191, 223; Churchill and, 4, 60, 74, 96–97, 108, 123, 124, 130, 133, 160, 163, 165, 169, 174, 175, 176, 180, 181, 190, 191, 192, 196, 198, 201–204, 209, 213, 215–216, 222, 232, 240, 257, 261; Churchill's avowed commitment to Zionism and, 171, 184, 202–203; Churchill's distancing from, 218–219, 223, 230, 242; Churchill's eulogy for, 255–256; on Churchill's impressionable temperament, 105; on Churchill's "soundness," 152; Churchill White Paper (1922) and, 132, 133; Holocaust response and, 180, 181, 182, 208; Jewish immigration and, 114, 131, 186; Jewish state and, 76, 196, 199, 200, 202–203, 208, 209, 211; militant Zionists vs., 144; Palestine partition proposal and, 158, 160, 213, 215; Palestinian Arabs and, 93, 122; Palestinian loan and, 135; as president of Israel, 240, 255; United States and, 196, 197, 201, 202, 203–204, 205, 216; Zionist extremists vs., 217

Weizmann, Jack, 215
Weizmann, Vera, 203
Welles, Sumner, 203
Wertheimer family, 43
West Bank, 158, 243, 250
Western Wall (Jerusalem), 143, 255
West Germany, 35
White Paper (1922), 118–119, 132–133, 137, 235
White Paper (1930), 143–144
White Paper (1939), 164–165, 166–167, 175, 188, 219, 242; as barrier to Palestinian Jewish state, 183–184; Churchill's moderation on, 235; Churchill's opposition to, 166–169, 172–173, 183–184, 185, 192, 195, 207, 230; continuance under Churchill of, 184, 189, 194; extension discussions on, 193; Morrison plan as repudiation of, 208, 212; postwar continuance of, 224; Weizmann's plea against, 223
White Russians, 21, 80, 83, 84, 89
Wilhelm II, kaiser of Germany, 16, 18
Wilson, Woodrow, 18, 23, 24, 90
Winant, John, 205
Windsor, Duke of. *See* Edward VIII
Wise, Stephen, 202, 219, 222
women's suffrage, 23
Wondrous Tale of Alroy, The (Disraeli), 52
Wood, Edward Frederick Lindley. *See* Halifax, Lord
Wood, Kingsley, 207
Woodhead Commission, 162–163
World Crisis, The (Churchill), 112
World War I. *See* First World War
World War II. *See* Second World War

xenophobia, 49, 50, 68, 174

Yalta conference (1945), 29, 30, 179, 193, 216, 219, 231
Yemen, 163, 230
York massacre (1190), 6, 40
Young, Hubert, 105
Younger, George, 100

Zaid (sherifian prince), 106
Zangwill, Israel, 6, 57, 58, 59, 61, 67
Zionism: Arab opposition to, 70, 91, 112,

Zionism (*continued*)
126, 130–131, 204–205, 206, 219–220, 221, 226; Arab sherifians and, 93, 106, 107, 108, 111; background of, 2–3, 4, 38, 51–56, 262; as Bolshevism antidote, 87–88, 117, 139; Bolshevist attacks on, 77, 86; British policies and, 6–7, 8, 50–59, 68, 75–76, 80, 99, 100, 104, 106, 112, 113, 126, 131–132, 141, 143–144, 152–154, 160–161, 163–164, 172–174, 175, 183–184, 185, 191, 195, 206–207, 212–213, 215, 222–225, 228–229, 231, 235, 242–243; Churchill's anti-Bolshevism and, 84–89, 91, 92, 98–99, 136; Churchill's defense of, 133, 136, 152–161, 167–168, 171–182, 184, 190–216, 207, 219, 224, 226, 228, 246–249, 250, 254–255; Churchill's detachment from, 69–70, 72, 74, 78, 79, 80, 95–96, 97, 100, 102–103, 108, 112, 113, 132–135, 137, 175, 218–219, 222–223, 227, 230, 231, 232, 235, 241, 257, 260; Churchill's evolved belief in, 1–8, 9, 11, 36–37, 39, 40, 47, 54, 57, 58–63, 67–68, 113, 115–122, 125, 130, 138–139, 141–142, 169–170, 195, 225, 231–232, 254, 255, 260–265; Churchill's inconsistency on, 95, 97, 113, 137–138, 195, 230–231, 234, 235, 236, 241–242, 243–244, 254–255, 257, 265; Churchill's prescience (1908) about, 262; Churchill's rejection of violent acts of, 213, 216–217, 232, 236, 239, 242; Churchill's strategic interests and, 93, 144, 145–146, 160, 239; civilizational value of, 4, 5, 6, 70, 100, 103, 113, 119–123, 125, 136, 138, 139, 141–142, 145–146, 154–156, 167, 169, 190, 191, 195, 225, 237, 248–249, 255–258, 261–262, 264; extremist violence and, 186, 196, 212–213, 216–217, 222, 232, 236, 238, 239, 240, 242; first permanent agricultural settlement and, 4, 120, 121; First World War and, 68, 69, 70, 195; gunrunning and, 131, 137, 219; Herzl's concept of, 4, 54–56, 190–191; historical basis of, 100, 118–119, 136, 138, 145, 155, 169, 191, 195, 248, 256, 257, 260, 262, 264; Holocaust and, 176, 178, 181, 182–183, 196, 200, 203, 208, 248; humanitarian basis of, 54, 68, 100, 113, 118–119, 138, 142, 151–152, 167, 169, 186, 189, 195, 196, 200, 225, 235–236, 256, 257; international sympathy for, 227; Jewish opponents of, 67, 71, 75, 76, 190–191; key arguments for, 138; London conference (1939) and, 163; mid-1920s foundering of, 134; Passfield White Paper and, 143–144; as political dynamite, 231, 235; political goals of, 2–3, 4, 54–56; Protocols of the Elders of Zion forgery and, 80–81; right-wing (Revisionist) faction and, 143, 144, 158; Roosevelt and, 205–206, 222, 226; satellite settlement proposals and, 189, 208, 219, 223; Second World War and, 2, 172–175, 182–183, 186–189, 190–193, 195, 196, 212, 224–225, 240; Territorialists and, 56–59, 62; U.N. partition acceptance by, 230; U.S. opponents of, 205–206, 215–216, 222, 226; U.S. supporters of, 145, 203; Weizmann's values and, 123–124, 223. *See also* Jewish national homeland; Jewish state; Palestine

"Zionism versus Bolshevism" (Churchill), 85–87, 88, 96, 116, 124

Zionist Association, 146, 207

Zionist Congress (1939), 164

Zionist Executive (Palestine), 144

Zionist Federation. *See* English Zionist Federation

Zionist Organization, 114, 115, 133, 134

Zionist Review, 78, 87, 97, 125

Zion Mule Corps, 75

Zola, Emile, 48